LA MATTANZA
The Sicilian Madness

LA MATTANZA

The Sicilian Madness

by Charles Carmello

FREUNDLICH BOOKS
New York

Published by Freundlich Books
(A division of Lawrence Freundlich Publications, Inc.)
212 Fifth Avenue
New York, N.Y. 10010

Distributed to the trade by Kampmann & Company
9 East 40th Street
New York, N.Y. 10016

Library of Congress Cataloging-in-Publication Data

Carmello, Charles, 1921–1985.
　La mattanza.

　I. Title.　II. Title: Sicilian madness.
PS3553.A745M3　1986　　813'.54　　86-22965
ISBN 0-88191-040-6

10　9　8　7　6　5　4　3　2　1

Italy was Italy,
when Sicily was a pup.
And Sicily will be Sicily,
when Italy is gobbled up.
Come on you heathen bastards,
who never went to mass.
Get on your Italian knees,
and kiss my Sicilian ass.

An old Sicilian song

BOOK ONE

T HE sky was filled with dark clouds and he thought it was going to rain, that is, until he spotted the spewing steel mills.

As he drove through Pittsburgh, he was depressed by the dirty streets and the cheap bars.

He knew he should have gone directly to Miami, but there was no time. The cops were closing in. He was definitely exhausted and he needed to hole up.

He checked into the William Pitt Hotel. Money wasn't a problem and he wanted the best the town had to offer. But after examining several suites, he settled for the least dirty one.

He showered, shaved, changed his shirt, and looked out at Pittsburgh. Safe for awhile, he thought; the New York cops would think he'd headed south. He thought of Freddie Tatado lying in a hospital bed with a bullet in his stomach. Tatado was a Brooklyn thug who had wanted to muscle

3

in on Tiger's operations. He wished Freddie would die so he could get back to his business in New York.

With time on his hands, Tiger visited three sleazy bars, surprised at the heavy action. The music was loud, the booze flowed, and the women were there for business. He spent the rest of the week watching T.V. and waiting for word that Tatado had died. It was eleven days before he received the news. Less than ten minutes later, he left the hotel and headed north. As he drove, an idea hit him and he laughed. He knew how he was going to get his revenge on Pittsburgh.

In New York he tried to interest his father in bankrolling a row of bars and porno stores, but his father wasn't interested. So he took his idea to his father's friends and they liked what he had to say—and they also liked the idea of slipping one over on Tiger's father.

It took Tiger two weeks to raise the money and return to Pittsburgh. He quietly leased two dozen buildings and set about construction. When the work was close to completion, he imported an army of hookers from Miami and turned them loose on the streets.

Within two months, all operations were making a profit. Then Tiger's father stuck out his paws, called in the investors, ominously returned Tiger his money, and took over the operations for himself.

When Tiger protested, he was told to keep his mouth shut. And he did.

T IGER thought of his father. After forty years, Tiger still found him unknowable.

His father was a physically powerful man with a violent, quick temper. Rarely had he seen his father laugh, and even then, his laugh was a threat. His eyes were hooded, watchful, and filled with suspicion. He was a stranger even to his family.

4

Tiger grew up in a big stucco house in Brooklyn. Twenty-four hours a day, indifferent, hardfaced men would arrive to see his father, spend a few moments in half-grunted conversation, then slide back into their cars.

Tiger brought coffee and sandwiches, ran errands. He stayed in the background.

Korea gave Tiger his chance to escape and he enlisted in the Marines. When he told his father, Tiger was surprised that he hadn't tried to interfere.

In the Marines, Tiger liked the violence of boot camp—rapt with everything the hand-to-hand instructors had to teach. He loved stretching his stamina, working until all his muscles vibrated with fatigue; every night falling dead asleep.

It was during basic training that he met Pete again. In Brooklyn he had seen him many times at his father's house. But he had never never been allowed to speak directly to him, since Pete's father was one of the mysterious callers who came in the middle of the night.

Now Pete and Tiger became friends, at last free of their fathers. Sex and whiskey became the nectar of their lives, and later in Korea they discovered that bloody combat was intoxicating. While others in their outfit dreaded combat, Tiger and Pete reveled in the bloody firefights. Even the company commander referred to them as a couple of butchering bastards.

During the Inchon landings, Tiger found himself in an ambush. He charged into the middle of the enemy before he was hit. Pete, seeing his friend on the ground in a pool of blood, screamed and something within him snapped. With his M1 he charged into the enemy troops, driving them away or killing them.

Tiger, shipped stateside, recuperated in Brooklyn Veterans Hospital, and when the war ended, Pete returned home. They picked up their friendship again. Tiger's father had offered him a job as a street banker, but Tiger had other ideas of what he wanted to do with his life. Still turned on from the war, he knew he needed combat to sustain him. He decided to go into business for himself and form his own mob rather than live as one of his father's flunkies.

He started out by recruiting Big Che, a hulking strong-arm who ran a book on the Brooklyn docks. Second, he brought in Ralphie Canzanna, a local tough who was looking to spread his wings. In a week he welded together another dozen crazies—most just back from the war. In a month there was nothing left to steal, so he decided it was time to move against the families' profitable operations. Wearing ski masks, they hit a dozen Harlem horse parlors the first month and that put everyone in a good mood. But someone snitched and soon they started to feel the heat from the families. A friendly detective tipped him that the families are going to use the police to do their dirty work. Tiger called his gang together, split the money, and ordered them to scatter. Pete headed out West, Big Che went to Florida, and Ralphie found a hole somewhere and disappeared.

As for Tiger, he was about to leave for Chicago when he received a message from his father to meet him at his Uncle Lulu's restaurant. When he arrived he found his father in a back room with an untouched glass of wine before him.

"You really did it this time, didn't you?" said his father.

But Tiger wasn't in the mood for a lecture and snapped, "Don't worry about me, I can take care of myself."

"So I notice."

"Why did you send for me?" snapped Tiger.

Silently his father studied him before extending a slip of paper to his son. "This is the address of my cousin who will hide you until this blows over."

Tiger shredded the slip of paper, dropped it into the glass of untouched wine, and walked out the door.

T IGER drove to a deserted corner and found a pay phone, and waited. Fifteen minutes later the detective called him back—with the name of the gang member who'd snitched. Tiger hung up, phoned the man, and set up a meeting for later that night.

The cab let him out. Tiger waited until the taxi's taillights disappeared. He retraced his steps more than two blocks, turned left, and was lost in the shadows of a deserted warehouse. The door he'd chosen gave when pushed, and he was inside, surrounded by mildew and decay.

It took him only a moment to work his way through the vacant warehouse to the fire escape overlooking the alley. He waited patiently, silent and unmoving. Over an hour went by and still he waited.

Then a man entered the alley and Tiger was tense, waiting for the man to cross the pool of light, to make sure it was the snitch who fingered him. Calling the man's name softly, the man was quickly alert, looking for the source of the voice. Then he found Tiger. He froze, his hand beginning to make a movement never completed as Tiger pulled the trigger.

A week later they nailed Tiger just outside Chicago and brought him back to New York in shackles. On the flight back he decided he could beat the murder, since there were no witnesses. As for robbing the horse parlors, the old man could square that fast enough. But in court a strange thing happened. His father hired a nickel-plated lawyer to represent him. Tiger couldn't believe it. With all the heavy mouthpieces on his father's payroll, why did he pick a shyster to represent him?

A week later the judge threw out the murder charge and most of the robberies, but the jury found him guilty on the remaining horse parlor robbery charge. Upon receiving a one-to-four sentence, he caught a glimmer of his father's cunning. By the time the bailiff led him back to his cell, he knew his father had set him up; and Tiger, putting two and two together, realized the bookie parlors his boys had robbed belonged to his father.

7

THE Sicilian waiter had seen Tiger many times. Although he didn't know who Tiger was, he knew a heavy when he saw one. Tiger sipped his third cup of coffee as he looked through the window, studying the street of porno stores and strip joints. He sat watching men move from store to store in pursuit of their needs.

It had been years since he had created the porno operations, still he never forgot the sting of his father's greed. He found little satisfaction in knowing he had been right all along about Pittsburgh's potential. It became a gold mine. But it wasn't his.

The seat across from him creaked to the weight of a three-hundred-pound gorilla who was having difficulty squeezing into the booth. Big Che.

Big Che had wide nostrils and deep shadowed eyes. To Tiger, the face was a death mask, never hinting at the emotions, feelings, or thoughts passing through it. If there were any.

"How's it going?" asked Tiger.

The big man grunted, letting out his breath. "If this fucking town didn't have porno, they'd have no reason to keep it open."

Tiger smiled without comment, knowing the big man was a chronic complainer, but he also sensed something hidden behind the death mask. He sat back and sipped his coffee, knowing the huge man would speak when the time came.

"I hear Philly the Jew ended up in the trunk of a car," the gorilla said. "Was he yours?"

Tiger knew his face had registered surprise. "What makes you say that?"

"I thought you were having some trouble with him."

"So what? He owed me a few bucks and he squared it up."

The big man changed the direction of the conversation. "How's the old man?" he asked.

"Pissing and moaning as usual," said Tiger, still sensing a fencing match in progress. "I have to close a couple horse parlors."

"How come?"

"A couple cops got themselves hung from a roof, and everyone's getting a little of the heat."

The giant nodded his understanding and slid an envelope across the table to Tiger. "There's a hundred grand in there."

"Where's the operations receipts?"

"I sent them up to your old man," said Big Che.

Tiger slid the envelope into his briefcase and settled back. "How are the new films going?"

"They're almost sold out," said the big man, still trying to get comfortable in the booth.

Tiger smiled, holding out a ring of keys. "You know where the package is. I had Coco drop it off last night."

Big Che's head shot up. "How come the bastard didn't give a hello?"

For a brief second, Tiger's eyes narrowed. "Because I told him not to."

A few shipments had been interrupted, so Tiger had decided to change his schedules, not wanting to fall into any patterns.

The big man fidgeted and Tiger could almost hear the wheels grinding.

"What's your problem?" asked Tiger.

"I've been meaning to ask you something. It's okay if you did it, but I just wanted to check with you."

Tiger remained silent, waiting.

"Joe the Arab dumped a load of films on the street last week, and they put one hell of a dent in our pocketbook. They weren't the J. B. line," continued Big Che. "But they were the same talent."

Instantly Tiger knew something was wrong but decided not to jump to any conclusions. "What were the color of the boxes?" he asked softly.

"Red, white, and blue stripes."

Now Tiger knew he had a problem. The J. B. films were a popular porno line, with the talent under contract to his father. If the line of films had been compromised, then

9

someone was going to get hurt. From Tiger's tight expression Big Che smelled trouble. "We got knocked off, didn't we?"

"I don't know for sure, but check the new shipment against what the Arab's selling. If they match up, bring him to me. But I don't want him damaged. I need to know what's going on."

"If the films match up, where do you want me to bring the Arab?"

"Bring him to the warehouse on Bridgeport Street."

TIGER sat in the small dingy office listening to the silence. His father's porno operations were sizable, he thought, but a knock off could put a dent in the operations for at least six weeks. It would take that long to shoot new films, process them, and set up the secret distribution schedules. Such a setback would put the old man in a bad mood.

Twenty minutes later, looking through a small window, he saw the overhead door open, lights flash over the walls of the warehouse, as the big car came to an abrupt stop just short of the office door. Big Che was not alone. One of Che's men pushed the nattily dressed Arab into the office. The little man was smiling, but Tiger could smell fear.

"Hey, Tiger," he smiled in a supplicating gesture. "What's this all about?"

Getting to his feet, Tiger stepped softly up to the little man. "Joe, you better listen good to me," he said, pausing for effect. "If you lie or play any games, I'm going to hurt you bad. You understand that?" he ended and allowed the silence to descend.

Then the Arab's smile broadened, his hand arched in a movement of humble honesty. "Whatever you want to know, Tiger, I'll give you straight answers."

"You dumped a load of my new films and I want to know

where you got them," he said, recording the instant look of desperation.

"Hey, Tiger, honest, I didn't know they belonged to you."

"So where did you get them?" snapped Tiger, knowing the Arab was going to lie to him.

"Some guy came in and offered me ten cases cheap. So I bought them," he said imploringly.

A kick to the shins and a punch in the stomach sent the screaming Arab across the room. Big Che grabbed him, dragging him before Tiger again, who grabbed the Arab's fingers and snapped two of them. The sound of the broken bones could be heard above the man's screams.

Tiger grabbed the Arab's other hand as the little man begged for mercy.

"Please, Tiger, please," he screamed. "I'll tell you the truth."

Tiger released the pressure on the fingers but held on to the arm.

"The Feds gave me the stuff. They threatened to put me away on a porno rap."

That threw a shock wave through Tiger. "Did they say why?"

"They said they wanted to put you and your father out of business," he spit out between sobs.

On the drive back to New York, Tiger wondered how his old man was going to take the information.

T IGER'S Brooklyn office was in a three-story building hidden in the shadows of the elevated train. Both sides of the street were lined with Italian food shops, filled with delicacies—anchovies to zeppolies. Tiger liked the busy, bustling street, filled with the aromas of Pecorino Romano, pepperoni, proscuitto, mozzarella, and a thousand other Italian glories.

He parked the car and crossed the street, remembering

11

the police raid of a few weeks ago. They roped off the street, searched the building from top to bottom, but by some fluke, failed to find the contraband he had hidden in the cellar. Out of revenge, the cops wrecked the place and confiscated all the records and documents they could find.

After that incident, Tiger moved his center of operations to another location, with the Lippo family in charge. He kept the raided building as a front.

As usual, the reception area was filled with people looking to make a deal. He brushed past them, headed for his private office with Pete, his top lieutenant, trailing.

Once inside, the door closed, Pete asked about the Pittsburgh trip. Tiger shrugged, deciding not to mention the Federal situation until he had more information.

He sat at the desk and busied himself unbagging and opening a container of coffee from the deli down the street.

"What have you heard from Ralphie?" asked Tiger.

"He landed an hour ago, he said he wanted a cup of coffee with you."

Tiger looked up sharply, not liking the sound of that. "Cup of coffee" meant "Alone and private." So either Ralphie found a hot lead in Los Angeles or he had found trouble. "Where's the meet?" asked Tiger.

He read the paper Pete handed him and thought of sending someone ahead to check out the location, which could be a restaurant, a shoe shine parlor, or an empty lot. But he knew his paranoia was getting the best of him if he started suspecting Ralphie. He put the address in his pocket as Pete placed a pile of envelopes on the desk before him.

"This is the money from the stores and the three horse parlors we closed," said Pete.

"What's the tally?"

"Two hundred thousand, less payoffs and expenses," said Pete.

Tiger was quick to pick up Pete's hesitation. "What's the problem, Pete?"

"Sonny's stores have dropped again."

At the mention of his brother's name, Tiger found it difficult to control his anger and keep his face blank.

"How bad?"

"Almost five grand," answered Pete.

Tiger let out a long sigh. He knew Sonny was skimming from the stores. He had hoped his brother would keep his stealing down to a few hundred dollars a week, but lately, he was getting greedy. And five thousand dollars wasn't something Tiger could hide from his father.

"I'll have a talk with him. Have him here in the morning," said Tiger.

Pete let the answer slide. "Your father also wants you to bring the envelopes out to him."

"He say what else he wants?" asked a surprised Tiger.

Pete shook his head, "Nope, but we also have another problem."

Tiger guessed it was going to be one of those days. "What now?"

"Florida refuses the new J. B.'s."

That twisted Tiger's head around. "They say why?"

"Barko says the Feds threatened to close his operations if he handled our stuff again," said Pete.

Tiger turned livid. "Get Barko on the phone. Who does he think he's hustling?"

But Pete stood his ground. "Boston, Cleveland, and Chicago said the same."

That took the wind out of Tiger's sails. "Did they say why?"

Pete shrugged. "They say something seems to be bugging the Feds about you."

Tiger was concerned. So why the heat?

"Call Rizzo, the lawyer, have him back them off."

Pete's expression remained blank. "I already did."

T IGER found Ralphie sitting in a coffee shop, feeling a twinge of envy at his nice suntan. Tiger said, "What happened in L.A.?"

13

"The Feds were waiting in L.A. when I landed," said the wiry man.

"What did they want?"

"They asked a lot of questions, nothing they couldn't have asked in New York. They wanted to know about Cinex."

Tiger let that sink in. Cinex was a private carting business he'd started a few years earlier. As soon as the company began to show a profit, the old man moved in and grabbed it for himself. His father's excuse was always the same: He had more mouths to feed than Tiger.

"I told them," Ralphie continued, "that I owned all the outstanding stock, and I could prove it."

"What did they say to that?"

Ralphie grunted. "I don't think they gave a shit. I got the feeling the whole thing was just a fishing trip."

"Why? What were they looking for?"

The wiry man rubbed his chin as he thought about it. "I don't know. Just a feeling I got that they were sending you some kind of message."

Tiger's brows shot up. "What kind of message?"

"Who knows?" shrugged the man. "Why else would they bother? But if they knew enough to have agents at the airport, then they knew I was coming."

Tiger didn't like it. "It sounds like we have a snitch in the Coast operations." Tiger sighed. "I think I better tell my father to check the Coast for a snitch."

TIGER's father spent most of his days in what Tiger called his office in the Gravesend section of Brooklyn. The office was in a private, two-story house, set back from the street, half-hidden by thorn bushes and the branches of an ailanthus tree.

A large sign nailed to the porch post read:

MEMBERS ONLY

Tiger always found the sign a joke. No one ever referred to the office as a club. The members called it "the office," and the local cops dubbed it "the zoo," and the members they called "the animals."

Tiger parked in front of the house and scanned the street before nodding at the hardfaces stationed outside, and walked up the path to the house.

Inside, the outer office was a study in cheap Celotex and imitation wall paneling. It contained a depressing collection of old and mismatched furniture, to which the smell of old perspiration and stale smoke clung like another coat of paint.

Three card games were going on, and two groups of men held quiet conversations at opposite ends of the room, but the whole effect was suspenseful rather than noisy. Along the wall sat the strange ones, gazing off into space, their minds engaged in some unknowable inner processes. These were the spooky ones, the ones Tiger was most afraid of. Their cloudy world could be penetrated only by his father, when and if their special talents were needed.

Tiger made his way through the crowded room, nodding at one or two men he knew. He had little in common with most of the flunkies who spent eighteen hours a day hanging around the office, chained by his father, each afraid that if he walked out of the room, the old man would choose that moment to ask for a favor. And everyone in that room wanted to be chosen, for they all knew that the fastest way to recognition was to do the old man a favor.

The hardface at the door passed Tiger into his father's private office. The room was lit by a bare bulb in a ceiling fixture. The desk itself was covered with neat piles of money. His father sat behind the oversized desk, looking like a miniature Mussolini, with a big black cigar stuck in his mouth. He was piling bills onto one of the stacks.

15

Sitting in the shadows directly behind the old man was Toto, a tall, cadaverous deaf-mute, with an eagle's nose, thin, cruel mouth and wild eyes, hooded like the eyes of a hawk. Toto's left hand lay in his lap, a gnarled and twisted mass of uselessness. Tiger had many times heard the whispered tale of how Toto used a large rock to smash his own hand and how he had squeezed the pulp through the handcuff to escape a rival mob. Looking at the hand and at Toto's expressionless eyes, he could believe anything said about this strange creature who was his father's butcher.

Like everyone else, Tiger was afraid of Toto. In whispers, the oldtimers called him *La Angelu de Mort*—The Angel of Death—and whenever Toto was seen on the streets, mothers snatched their children from his path and ran to protect them from Toto, who had *Il Mal Occhio*—The Evil Eye. Others on the street clutched their sacred amulets and quickly turned their backs. The old people blamed every sudden illness, accident, or death on The Angel of Death.

The Sicilians avoided Toto for another reason: It was widely believed that The Angel of Death had a gift of probing other people's minds. Tiger admitted to not knowing whether this was true or not of Toto. But to be on the safe side, he always kept a tight rein on his thoughts whenever he was around his father's bodyguard.

Coming into the room, he closed the door quietly behind him and waited for his father to acknowledge his presence, but his father ignored him, continuing to count his money, now turning one of the large piles into a series of small piles.

"Payday?" asked Tiger, in a way of conversation.

"I have to take care of my boys outside. They deserve it."

Shit, thought Tiger, he knew if his father didn't throw some scraps to the animals outside, they would soon think about picking his bones clean. He thought he saw Toto stir and quickly suppressed his thoughts.

His father put down the pile of bills from which he had been counting. "You have been over to see your mother?"

16

"I just came from there."

"And how is she?"

Tiger knew his father had his own lines into the hospital and could never figure why he always asked the same question. He answered, as he always did, "She keeps asking for you."

His father let out a soft sigh, as he always did. "I'll see her tomorrow," he said softly.

Tiger wanted to scream, "Hey, Papa, it's been a year of tomorrows." But instead he said, "She'll like that."

"What does the doctor say?"

Tiger shrugged. "What he always says. She's getting better."

"That's good, no?"

"What's good about having Momma in a nut house?" said Tiger, noticing his father's eyes tighten.

"What would you have me do?" asked his father softly.

"I could take her home with me and Jeanne."

The old man shook his head, grunted, and went back to his piles of money, saying nothing. Tiger's thoughts wandered back to the week his mother had broken down. One day she was fine, the next . . .

It started at breakfast, he recalled. She was sitting quietly, as usual, picking at her food, when suddenly she looked across the table at him and without a word of warning started screaming, calling his father Satan. She jumped to her feet, scattering silverware and china, racing from room to room, screaming all the while, returning while they sat there still in shock, unable to move as she held a crucifix in Don Corso's face and screamed, "Go from me, Satan, go from me!" Then suddenly, before he could even move toward her, she sat down at the table and placed the crucifix carefully alongside a plate. She picked up a piece of cheese and nibbled at it as if nothing had happened.

Hope against hope that it was a passing hysteria, Don Corso had gone off to the office. But later the same day someone called to tell him she'd opened all the windows and screamed obscenities at the neighbors, all the time, hurling every small breakable object out the window. When he arrived home he found her crouched in a closet, singing an old Sicilian lullabye to herself.

The next morning, before leaving for the office, he locked her in her room. But the moment she was alone, she dismantled the bed, smashed down the heavy door and, once free, used a hatchet to destroy all the furniture. A neighbor called and he raced home to find her sitting amid the rubble, repeating over and over the name of her dead sister.

He found it painful remembering that last day, the day he had to have her committed. He stopped counting his payout and said flatly: "I didn't call you here to talk about your mother."

Tiger realized the subject was closed. "Then what?"

Coldly, his father looked up at him. "I got someone coming over and I want you here."

Tiger glanced at Toto, but again the subject was closed. He put the briefcase on the floor next to the desk, took out a folder, and put it in front of his father. "The cash from Pittsburgh and New York," said Tiger.

"Any problems in Pittsburgh?"

Tiger ran the question through his mind; the tone was a little too casual. He thought fast and answered. "I'm keeping my eyes on a few things," he said softly. "I'll let you know what develops."

After a long silence, his father nodded and slipped the cash into a lower desk drawer. Tiger settled back, confident he had won for the moment, but still wary of thinking in Toto's presence. Instead, he allowed the problem of Sonny to crowd into his thoughts. "Sonny's heading into trouble."

For a moment he thought his father might not have heard, but Tiger knew better, so he added, "He's playing with Iggy's people."

Still no answer, so he knew the old man was going to continue to ignore him. He searched his mind for some hook to catch his father with, then tried a third attack. "If Sonny gets too close to them, they will put him on ice."

18

His father picked up another pile of bills and resumed his counting. "What makes you think so?"

"Because Iggy is a degenerate who knows you don't care about your own son, and that's all the excuse Iggy needs," said Tiger, trying to suppress his vehemence.

His father ignored the outburst, picked up another pile of bills and resumed his counting.

Tiger shrugged softly. "I just thought you'd want to know what your son is up to," said Tiger between clenched teeth.

His father's hand stopped, poised over one of the piles. There was a long stillness, then the counting continued. "Damn it, Pa, you can't let it happen," said Tiger. In the darkness behind his father, he felt rather than saw Toto stiffen, and Tiger knew he was walking on thin ice. His father's continued silence sent him over the edge of caution.

"If you put the word out on the streets, Iggy's boys will back off," he said. Still silence, broken only by the soft paper noise, as the counting continued.

"Pa, he's your son."

The words were hardly out of his mouth when his father slapped the bills down on the desk, ripped the cigar out of his mouth, and pointed it at Tiger like a stiletto. He began to speak low and furiously.

"I want you to listen good to me because I'll say this only once. I have only one son and his name is Joey Corso. You understand that? One son, so don't talk to me about anybody else."

Tiger trembled before his father's rage, but some dim family feeling compelled him forward. "You're wrong, Pa, you're wrong. You have no right to shut out Carmine and Sonny. It's not right."

His father's expression was frozen. From across the desk, he could feel Toto's eyes on him. His father's mouth opened a fraction as he snapped.

"Drop it."

But Tiger leaped to his feet, leaned across the desk and for the first time in his life shouted at his father.

19

"I can't let it go, Pa. It's killing Momma!"

Behind his father, Toto was suddenly on his feet, his mouth twisted into a grotesque threat. Stunned, Tiger saw precisely the same expression on his father's face. As he looked, the mask that was his father's face relaxed, and at the same instant, Toto's expression returned to normal. As if seeing it through a fog, Tiger knew he was witnessing duplicated emotions, which could only mean that Toto and his father communicated silently, beyond comprehension.

He sat down again, realizing for the first time in his life that his father had the capacity to love. Maybe not much, he told himself, maybe it was only a drop, but that drop was for his mother. Tiger was overwhelmed by the knowledge. Never had Tiger seen the slightest sign of affection pass between his parents.

He thought of his mother, painfully thin, always dressed in the traditional black. Black shoes, black stockings, black veil, black on black, black, black, black, until he wondered if her soul was also black.

She always moved around the huge house silent and watchful. An unsmiling, bitter woman, displaying no warmth or love or indeed any emotions at all, not even anger.

He remembered one day as a child, he was crying for some long forgotten reason, and his mother entered the room. He went to her to be comforted, but instead she grabbed him by the hair and banged his head against the wall, screaming. "A man never cries! A man never cries! A man never cries!"

And to this day, whenever he felt the need to cry, he saw her cold bleak eyes, her tonelessly shrill voice and her threatening posture, and grew silent and afraid.

His father continued counting his money but stopped to look at Tiger with a strange intensity. The look in his eyes also told him there would be no more talk of Momma. His father puffed his cigar, put down the stack of bills, leaned forward for a better look at Tiger.

"Let me tell you a few things about your brothers Carmine and Sonny. When Carmine was a boy, I could tell he

20

wasn't going to turn out the way I wanted, so instead, I sent him to college, hoping he would become a doctor, or even a lawyer. You know, the family could always use another lawyer. Maybe I could have made him a judge. I had the connections. So why did he do what he did?"

Tiger felt the suffering behind the question. His father's shoulders tightened, and suddenly he slammed his fist on the desk, sending money in all directions.

"He had no right to put that damn collar around his neck and sell his ass to God. What the hell did God ever do for him? I paid for everything."

Tiger sat silently as his father struggled to regain his composure. He looked away, not quite ready to take in the picture of his father in the grip of emotion. When the old man spoke again, it was after a long sigh, and his words seemed directed at no one.

"I suppose your brother needed something to hide behind—to mask his girlish ways." A tightness choked off the words and threatened to silence him again, but he struggled through it. "Now he sits in Saint Rocco's Church, telling other people how to live their lives." His father's laugh was caustic. "Your brother is a degenerate, a fag.

"As for Sonny, he's a waste. Anyone who needs a needle in his arm is already dead. I wish he'd die and spare us the shame."

Out of the corner of his eye, Tiger noted Toto looking at the old man as if feeling his pain.

"You disobeyed me and put him in charge of three of my stores," he said, pointing his cigar at Tiger. "I said nothing because I wanted you to see what your brother was really like. But what did you do—you covered up his stealing and prolonged his cancerous ways." Tiger thought it best to remain silent.

"Your brother used you to get back at me for something his sick mind made up."

Don Corso reached into a side drawer, took out a packet of papers, and dropped them on the desk. "His betting losses for the past month." Tiger picked up the packet.

21

Tiger was duly shocked. "Ten grand!" he exclaimed, feeling sick. He knew Sonny had a heavy drug habit, figuring it best to have his brother steal a little than have him on the streets begging for a fix. But this?

"I just thought his habit was a little out of hand, I didn't know."

"I know what you thought, but you never notice your brother destroys everything he touches."

Tiger let out a tired sigh. "He's still my brother, Pa."

"Sonny is no one's brother. He's like all junkies."

Before Tiger could answer, his father continued: "And now we have another problem with your brother."

Tiger held his breath, wondering what surprise his old man was about to spring on him.

"My bookies tell me Sonny paid those tabs just this morning, and he has been blowing money all over town. I know the money didn't come from the stores; he wasn't skimming enough. So find out where it comes from."

Tiger had been expecting that and wondered what was to become of Sonny. The buzzer sounded, interrupting his thought. His father picked up the phone.

"Yeah," he said, listening a moment, then covered the mouthpiece and looked at his son. "You can go now. I'll call you later."

So Tiger left.

T HE Lippo brothers had for years lived up to their names: King Kong, Godzilla, The Bear, and Cobra. The leader was Cobra, a tall, slinky, and casually vicious professional. The four animals filled the tiny office, while Tiger sat alone by the window as Cobra made his report.

"When we got your call, we started to put bits and pieces together and it all comes up Marvin's lab."

Tiger's expression turned sour. "That don't make sense. Why should he jeopardize a good thing for a few lousy bucks? Not to mention the beating he would get."

22

Cobra shook his head. "We don't think it was Marvin, but his lab man."

"Izzy Kaplan?"

Cobra nodded. "We know the negatives were in the laboratory and it fits the timetable," said Kong.

"Why do you say that?" asked Tiger.

"Because with luck, they would need five days to make a duplicate negative, run off a print, print and make boxes, and get it distributed in Pittsburgh."

"Where were the boxes stored?" asked Tiger softly.

"Marvin's," said Cobra.

Tiger looked from face to face. Studying each in turn.

"Then one of you fucked up."

It was Godzilla who jumped in. "It was me, Tiger. I didn't know Marvin had a new system in."

Tiger looked at Cobra. "What's he talking about?"

"Marvin installed a new system of high-speed processing."

"So?"

"So Godzilla dropped them off in the morning. But when he comes back at lunch, Kaplan's made two instead of one."

Godzilla shouted defensively. "Whoever heard of not processing film in the dark?"

"Since Godzilla had always processed film in the dark, he wouldn't realize Marvin's new system was designed to allow processing in full daylight. That's why we're sure it was Kaplan who knocked us off," Tiger said to no one in particular. "Nice, Mister Kaplan, very nice," Tiger said, looking back at the brothers. "It was Mister Kaplan who sold the print to the people who knocked us off."

Kong jumped to his feet, a madness in his eyes. "I'll eat the bastard's heart out."

But Tiger waved him to silence. "Kaplan was working for the Feds."

Tiger studied the four brothers. "I don't want our friend Kaplan hurt—by anyone," Tiger said. "Do you all understand that?"

The Bear lunged to his feet. "But we can't let the bastard

23

get away with this, Tiger. The creep will think he has a license," said the Bear.

In frustration Kong chimed in. "He's right, Tiger. We have to break both his legs."

Again Tiger waved them to silence. "Kaplan will be taken care of, but at the right time, not now. I don't want anyone pissing off the Feds right now. So starting tomorrow, we'll shift our film work to Archie's laboratory and leave all the old shit at Marvin's."

As he drove across town he thought of his brother, realizing he felt little pain at Sonny's betrayal: betrayal implied a violation of trust and he'd never trusted his brother. As for the game Sonny was playing with Iggy, he knew Helen was behind it. But still he found it difficult to believe Sonny was willing to get himself killed over a pig broad.

He studied the rearview mirror, studying the car trailing him. He observed only one occupant in the car, so he figured it wasn't a professional tail. Whoever it was had picked him up after leaving the Lippo warehouse, and perhaps, wondered Tiger, the tail wanted him to know the place had been blown. Well, in either case, Tiger didn't give a damn, so long as the driver maintained his distance.

He sat quietly in his uncle's restaurant surrounded by Grecian statuary and Sicilian landscapes. To Tiger, the place was a comfortable sanctuary for a man with a tail on his ass. As he sipped his wine, a tall, sharp-featured man entered, waited for his eyes to adjust to the dim light, then headed straight for Tiger.

"I got to talk to you," the man said without preamble.

Tiger recognized him and waved him to the seat opposite. "Want something to eat?"

"Just coffee."

As the waiter scurried away, Tiger studied the man. Turk was one of his father's street bankers, a man whose job it was to keep the street lenders supplied with money. Of all the men on his father's payroll, Turk was about the only one Tiger really liked.

"Is that tail outside yours?" asked Turk seriously.

Tiger nodded. "He's keeping me honest."

"You want I dump the bastard in a garbage can?"

Tiger shook his head. "He might be Federal."

Turk nodded his understanding, knowing of the new law —an automatic five years for assaulting a Federal officer. "Then I'll make sure there are no witnesses," he said coldly.

Tiger smiled softly. "Thanks, but I can handle him. Now what can I do for you?"

Turk studied the room, protecting against eavesdroppers. "I'm getting rumbles that a load of horse is going to be dumped on my turf."

Tiger settled back as he studied the man again. "How did you come by this information?"

"My South Jamaicans," said Turk, taking another check of the room. "They say it's cheap, pure, and by the kilo."

Tiger gave that some thought. "It could just be some outlaws looking to spread their wings?"

But Turk shook his head. "The Jamaicans were told to get ready, that it's here but their bosses don't want it distributed yet," said a nervous Turk. "You know young bucks are greedy, they want their fast bucks now."

To Tiger, if the information was correct, it sounded like a well-organized operation. Except for the family, such organizations didn't exist. The day of big-time, top-to-bottom dealers was gone. The independents had taken over, selling and reselling. When the dealer at the bottom worked for the importer at the top. But that wasn't profitable anymore for the families—too much exposure—too easy for the law to bust the bottom and work their way up the ladder. They never got far before they hit a stand-up guy who wouldn't rat—but it was too disruptive a way to do

25

business. Tiger knew it was possible for some outlaws to dry up the streets, raise the street value, and make one hell of a killing, but even then, it would require considerable organization to pull it off. And if you're talking big money and organization, you're talking family.

"Can you get some kind of fix on the suppliers?" asked Tiger.

"I already have my feelers out," answered Turk.

"Then you better be careful."

"I intend to," said Turk as he rose to his feet, leaving the untouched coffee on the table. "Are you going to tell your old man?"

Tiger knew his father wouldn't appreciate Turk's having come to him first. "I'll need more information before I bother him."

Turk smiled his relief. "Thanks, Tiger."

He watched Turk leave the restaurant. Tiger was sure his father wasn't involved in drugs.

Tiger was always intimidated by the hustle and bustle of Big Tony's auto scrapyard. The many noises and activities were everywhere, saturating the mind with uncertainty. Slowly he maneuvered the big car along the gutted roadway, past towering mountains of derelict vehicles, pounding steel cutters, and armies of swooping cranes. Once past the madness, he drove to the little building marked "Office," and pulled alongside a huge man yelling at the workers.

"Hey, fat bastard," screamed Tiger, as he emerged from the car.

The big man smiled as he grabbed Tiger in a bear hug. "Hey, Tiger, you out slumming today?" he said with great affection.

"How you been, fat boy?"

"Great, Tiger," he said joyfully. "Yourself?"

"Fine, how's that raunchy brother of yours?"

Tony laughed. "I saw him last week in Florida. I told him since you been a big shot, you don't come visit friends anymore."

Tiger grinned. He always liked the easy-going Tony and his brother Bobo.

"How's he doing?" asked Tiger gently.

"I spent the week listening to his bitching. He misses you, he misses Brooklyn, and he wants to come back."

In awe Tiger shook his head. "After three heart attacks?"

"That's what I keep telling him, but you know he don't listen, he says he needs to get back in action." Tiger laughed. "I'll send him a couple of good-looking broads, that'll give him action. Tell him to enjoy his retirement and give him my love."

"I will, Tiger," said Tony, taking a pause as his smile faded. "What can I do for you?"

"Have Bobby meet me in an hour," he said softly.

"Same place?"

"Same place," answered Tiger.

"Anything else?"

"I got a tail on my ass."

Tony didn't bother to raise his head. "Take a turn around the block and when you pass again I'll block the road with a crane. And don't be a stranger."

TIGER parked under the bridge near the water. The putrid smells of the swamp stung his nostrils. He often used this place for special meetings because it was open and observable for a mile around.

A nondescript sedan pulled up alongside Tiger's waiting vehicle. The man walking toward him wore a trench coat that masked a police uniform. He wore no hat. The two men shook hands.

27

"How's it going, Tiger?"

"Fine, Bobby, fine."

"What can I do for you, Tiger?"

Tiger took no offense at Bobby's abruptness. He knew the policeman couldn't afford to be seen with him.

"I got a rumor a load of heroin is coming in, probably through South Jamaica."

Bobby knew better than to ask where the information came from. Instead he asked, "When's it coming in?"

"That's the problem, I don't know. I hear they're holding back for a big splash."

"Damn it," said Bobby as he paced away from Tiger. He turned back shaking his head. "The last thing I need is to have the city strung out—no dope, lots of dope—it'll be a fucking zoo."

"That's why I'm here."

"I appreciate that, Tiger," said Bobby, pacing back and forth in thought. "Do you know if any of the families are involved?"

"I can't be sure."

"Shit."

"I'll feed you what information I get," said Tiger, "but you better be careful where you step."

Bobby's smile was tight. "I'll be damned careful."

Tiger nodded and opened his car door. Bobby yelled, "Hey!"

Tiger turned, questioning. "Tell your old man I'm an inspector now."

Tiger grinned, stepped back to him and shook Bobby's hand. "Congratulations. At this rate you'll wind up commissioner."

"Shit," smiled Bobby. "I'll be lucky to get the chance to sweep his office."

Tiger could see the tightness behind the smile.

T IGER lived in a modest ranch house in a predominantly Italian community. It gave him a sense of security having his family surrounded by relatives and friends, neighbors who were quick to notice strangers and quick to doubt their motives.

Like himself, his neighbors were dog people, with an Italian bulldog, German shepherd, or Doberman in every backyard.

It was early evening, and the craziness of the day was over until morning. Now all he wanted was to spend the evening with his family.

Jeanne, his wife of fifteen years, was a pretty woman, quiet and easy-going. The marriage had been an arrangement, with the chief purpose of uniting the Corso and Ippolito families. The union was sought by Don Corso because the Ippolito connection meant security. But whatever the satisfactions of the fathers, it had worked out for the principals. In most arranged marriages, the principals spend a lifetime as acquaintances. Tiger knew all this when he accepted the agreement. Aware he was purchasing a companion for the good of both families.

He also recognized his obligations to protect and provide for her. With ample funds to maintain her in reasonable comfort and style.

Before their marriage, the Ippolito and Corso families gathered often in Don Corso's country home. Jeanne often observed the taciturn Joey Corso, quiet, alone, and aloof, always sitting or standing at attention. A soft-spoken man, polite, but with the politeness of the indifferent. He appeared always to need to be alone, distant, and hoping not to be noticed.

Jeanne had the impression he was neither shy nor outwardly warm, just dead. When she learned Joey Corso was to be her future husband, she recoiled. She protested to her father, but he would listen to none of it.

Over the next two years, she studied him from a distance, constantly filled with dread. She studied his body movements, his careful catlike grace, his neatness and courtly manners, which always seemed to be clouded by the wall he placed between himself and others.

He carried himself well, a true Sicilian, a confident man.

Yet Jeanne sensed a deep pain within him, well hidden. Why, she wondered, was his face so etched with bitterness? Who was this unsmiling, well-mannered man?

However, since he was essentially a private man, Tiger felt no obligation to share with her his private thoughts. At first he found marriage a ritual, a monotonous routine he tolerated. Like having a sleep-in housekeeper he occasionally had sex with. So he resigned himself to his existence at home.

But Jeanne was a woman who was infected with a desire to live. She had had years of being submerged, first by her doom-and-gloom family and now by her husband.

Jeanne was no longer satisfied to remain in the background, living each day as the day before, sitting home waiting for an indifferent husband to meet his manly obligations.

She had always taken pride in her beautiful home. She took pride in her little garden and she took pride in herself. Now she wanted a man, her man. She wanted him to be a friend, someone to talk to, to chide, to be ridiculous with, and to be part of.

She understood her husband was trained in the hard life; so was she. All her family had, including a brother who died for it. She had lived with it, where a smile is a threat rather than a promise—or an expression of pleasure.

After two months of marriage, Jeanne knew she couldn't continue living with a stranger. She knew she had to do something to break through his quiet reserve, to crack the shell surrounding him or she would find herself old before thirty.

For the next few months, she knocked herself out devising ways to make him laugh. Jokes, handstands, and funny faces didn't work. She tried a drop of menstrual blood in his coffee as a love potion. Nothing.

Then one night during her nightly ritual of entertainment, she was rewarded. She spotted a minute crack, a slight smirk. Then came a grin and finally laughter, a long,

30

delightful laugh. Jeanne was ecstatic. His laughter was strong and vibrant and filled her with strange emotions.

Slowly their private world ripened, and together they found a sharing neither ever had expected. Tiger surrendered to Jeanne all the love he had bottled up since childhood.

J EANNE was sitting at the kitchen table when he got home. She was slicing peppers and watching the end of a T.V. movie. He saw the tears in her eyes and smiled.

"That looks like a two-toweler at least," he chuckled.

She waved him to silence as the music rose to the final moment, the young doctor disappearing into the sunset as the heroine watched him go.

Tiger poured himself a cup of coffee, then came and sat opposite her as the credits crawled across the screen. He reached over and turned off the set. She sniffled and smiled at him.

"I guess I don't have to ask if you liked the show," said Tiger.

She laughed briefly and wiped away a tear. "I wish you could have seen it, Joey." She sniffled again.

Her passion for sad movies amused and touched him. She seemed to identify with every downtrodden or beaten character, the more miserable the better, always rooting for the underdog.

She launched into her story, slicing peppers as she talked. Only part of him listened. The rest of him noted the details of the room, the swift movement of the hands, the stillness of the house. He interrupted her in mid-sentence.

"Where are the kids?"

"At Aunt Rose's." She took a breath and continued. "So the girl tells her love she should've . . . "

"What's for supper?"

31

She looked up at him. "Peas and macaroni, the way you like them."

He nodded his approval as she went on with her story, unoffended by the interruption. "So the girl stays with him up on the mountain until he gets well. And then one day he gets the call to go back. . . . "

Tiger's mind wandered as Jeanne retold the tragic story. The sound of her voice soothed him and helped him sort out the events of the day. It was part of their routine, therapeutic for them both.

"I wish you could have seen it, it was beautiful."

"Sorry I missed it."

She rinsed the peppers, refilled the pot, and put it on the stove. She turned, looking closely at him. "You look tired."

"It's been that kind of day."

"You want to eat early or wait for the kids?"

"I'd like to go to bed early tonight."

She grinned impishly. "That's a good idea," she said, almost under her breath.

He laughed and swatted her affectionately on the rear. After fifteen years, the excitement was still there.

T HAT night Jeanne felt the intensity of her husband's body and knew it had been a difficult day for him. Usually their lovemaking was gentle, warm, and exciting; but tonight it was savage and magical.

The call came from his father at one in the morning, and Tiger was dressed and out of the house in minutes. She lay back in the comfortable bed, feeling a touch of annoyance at having lost her warm teddy bear.

Damn Don Corso with his middle of the night meetings. Why couldn't her husband have been a shoe salesman?

Wrapping the comforter around her shoulders, she recalled the intensity of his body and tried to imagine the world he lived in.

32

At HIS father's office the usual hardfaces were still on duty. And the usual assortment of flunkies milled around the outer office. Many eyes followed Tiger as he walked into the back room, where his father sat alone with Toto.

"Sit over against the wall," said his father, indicating a chair in the corner. "And speak only if I tell you to."

Tiger sat for more than twenty minutes. Occasionally he looked over at Toto, who sat with his eyes closed, still as death, the crushed hand in his lap, the other hand in his pocket.

Don Corso worked methodically on his books. Just as Tiger was about to speak, the buzzer sounded. "Yeah," said his father. "Send him in."

An elderly man came slowly into the room. He was dressed quietly, and his manner suggested breeding. He stood straight but respectfully before Don Corso. Tiger found himself staring at the profile. It was a face he knew, but from where?

"How are you, Patsy?" asked his father, rising to shake hands with the newcomer.

"Fine, Don Corso, fine." As he released his host's hand, the man called Patsy looked quickly around the room, his eyes flickering over Toto, the book on the desk, Tiger, everything in the room.

Tiger observed that the man was really older than he looked, frail, his movements slow and deliberate, but with total dignity.

"It saddened us to hear of Angelina's operation," said his father. "I hope all is well."

Patsy shrugged his narrow shoulders. "It's women's troubles. The doctor took something out, now all she does is cry that she is only half a woman. As if it mattered at our age."

Don Corso put on an expression of sadness and concern. "I am sorry to have added to your burdens by summoning you here."

The old man shrugged again. "Such is life. There are no guarantees."

33

"How true, how true," answered Don Corso as he abruptly sat, while the older man remained standing.

"I have a most unpleasant order for you," said Don Corso. All reflection of sympathy gone from his voice. "I want you to understand these orders come from others, not from me."

Bullshit, thought Tiger. Then with sudden panic he glanced at Toto, who still sat motionless with his eyes closed.

"My friends want you to go to the police and confess to the killing of those two policemen."

It took Tiger a moment to realize his father was referring to the two cops found hanging from the edge of a roof. Tiger wanted to laugh out loud. He figured the cops would chase this skinny old man out of the station house. He wondered what kind of game his father was playing. He didn't believe his old man could be serious, sending Patsy to take the rap for those killings.

"How long will I have to remain in prison?" asked Patsy in dead earnest. It was obvious that the question made Don Corso uncomfortable. He squirmed, and Tiger was surprised because he had never seen his father squirm before.

"Maybe ten, fifteen years," said Don Corso softly.

Tiger looked at the sad old man, wondering what kind of man he was. He had heard of people who lived to die for their dons. Assholes, losers, like those lining the walls of the outer office. Misfits, each and all, but this old man was no misfit.

His father's pretense was still flowing: "I know they are asking a heavy sacrifice from you, Patsy, but these killings have made bad trouble for our friends in City Hall."

Tiger heard the silence build as he looked at Patsy. He had never seen such eyes. They were pale blue, almost frosty, but slightly out of focus, so that they projected a limpid gentleness. That gaze jogged his memory. He saw a small house and himself as a small boy being handed a large cookie. This man was his uncle, his Uncle Patsy.

"Your son has grown into a fine looking man," said Patsy.

Don Corso beamed. "Thank you, my old friend."

Patsy continued his probe of Tiger. "The eyes are a little soft."

"They will harden with experience," said Don Corso.

Tiger began to feel like a horse on the auction block. Patsy smiled at him but continued to speak to his father. "He has the look of the hungry tiger," he said, coming closer to examine Tiger's features. To Tiger he said softly, "You have your mother's eyes." Then he abruptly turned to Don Corso. "May I smoke?"

"Of course," said his father with an expansive gesture.

Slowly, the frail old man lit a long DiNobili. He faced Tiger again. "Don Corso brought me to America and shared his good fortune with me. For this I have been grateful and loyal. I am a soldier in your father's army. As a soldier I was ordered to kill two policemen, and I asked no questions."

Tiger had been listening intently, hanging on every word.

"Even though I had heard that the two policemen were dealing in drugs. I even heard that the same policemen were about to tell a grand jury the name of the family they were involved with."

Tiger looked hard at his father, wondering if the story was true? He couldn't believe any of the families would be insane enough to invite such reprisals.

"So I killed them, and after I killed them I hung them from the roof for all to see."

"They certainly saw them," said Don Corso caustically. Tiger was too fascinated to speak.

Patsy continued to study Tiger. "Now Don Corso's friends want to correct a mistake, a mistake they made."

Tiger looked up at the gentle face, listening for some hidden message. Patsy's lips moved again, but it took two attempts before the words came out: "With my life."

Tiger felt sorry for the man, he had long ago learned that this kind of loyalty earned nothing but a kick in the ass. He also had few if any illusions about his father or his friends. He knew their loyalties were always first and foremost to themselves. He also knew that though he was *born* a member of the family—with certain rights of blood—he was still nothing until he was *made*—formally admitted as a member. If his father should die before he was made, he'd end up like the animals in the outer office, begging to do favors for people like his father.

Patsy was still talking, now pacing slowly around the space between Tiger and the desk. From the look on the man's face, Tiger knew Patsy had made a decision.

"Now I am to be rewarded for fifty years' loyalty. Rewarded with the privilege of dying in a cage like a sewer rat."

He turned swiftly to Don Corso, a slight edge to his voice. "I have lived my life like a man. I have earned the right to die like a man."

Silence closed in on the room before Don Corso finally spoke. "Is there no way to work this out?"

"I mean no disrespect, my Don, but I must remain firm," said Patsy softly.

Don Corso was motionless for almost a minute as he looked at the frail, slender soldier. He stood up and stuck out his hand. Patsy took it. "Go in peace, my friend," said Don Corso.

"Thank you, my Don," said the gentle old man.

Patsy turned and Tiger saw a flicker of sadness in the old eyes. He felt a momentary urge to put his arm around the frail shoulders, but he stayed where he was.

Patsy left the room, followed a moment later by a silent Toto. When the door closed on The Angel of Death, Tiger said, "Who was that man?"

His father's surprise was evident. "You don't remember him?"

"I remember him being around when I was a kid, I also remember his name, Patsy, but nothing else."

"His name is Pasquale Colombo."

Suddenly Tiger let out a low whistle. "The Eagle?"

His father looked away. "Some have called him that."

Tiger was in shock. That frail old man was a legend. The

Eagle was known in mob circles as the killer of killers. Police on three continents had wanted him at one time or another. Tiger found it difficult to match the man with the reputation.

"Unbelievable," said Tiger. "What happens to him now?"

His father started in on his books again. After a moment he looked up. "A note will be pinned on his body and it will be dropped at a police station. That should cool the heat."

Tiger shivered at his father's cold dismissal of the subject, the discarding of an old friend. "It seems like one hell of a way to reward fifty years of loyalty," said Tiger, studying his father's face. "It might make some people wonder."

Don Corso looked up sharply. "It is never healthy to wonder."

Tiger got the message. He hesitated before asking the next question. "What family do you think is into drugs?"

"Drugs are hard to hide, hard to keep secret," his father said. "I think my friends just made a mistake, and I think they decided to take the easy way out."

Tiger wasn't buying that. The family never admitted to a mistake. The family had enough people in their pockets to convict the pope of a sex crime. So leaving Patsy's body with a note wasn't going to do a damn thing to cool the heat. It was only going to create more, and his father had to know that, so what the hell was all this about? Why this game? And come to think of it, why had his father brought him to witness it? Was it a warning?

The thoughts whirled and he was glad Toto wasn't around to read his mind. He was sure Patsy was being silenced for some reason deeply hidden under what his father told him. He knew his father wasn't into drugs; at least he hoped he wasn't, because if he was, a lot of people were going to get killed. And Tiger intended to make sure he wasn't one of them.

Sonny sat on the other side of Tiger's desk, dressed like a faggot, wearing an Apache headband, leather pants, and a buckskin jacket. Tiger guessed the outfit was a matter of status among his friends. It annoyed him. His brother stole enough to dress better.

"Let's get to the point," said Tiger. "You've been ripping off the stores."

"Says who?" shot back Sonny.

"Says the books, and if that weren't enough," he threw a packet of papers on the desk, "these are your markers."

Sonny tried to remain cool. "Those markers are my business, and what happens between me and the old man is of no concern to you."

Tiger fought against the surge of anger. "You used me to get back at your father because you're a degenerate," he lashed out. "If you have a hardon for the old man, why didn't you go after him like a man, with a gun?"

Sonny jumped to his feet and stalked to the door. "Tell me what I owe you, big brother, and save the bullshit."

"Sit down," commanded Tiger.

But Sonny wasn't in the mood to listen as he zipped up his jacket. Taking his time he reached for the doorknob.

Tiger lowered his voice and said, "Do yourself a favor and don't make me forget you're my brother, Sonny."

Sonny hesitated, fighting some deep inner emotion before retracing his steps and sitting down. "Let's get something straight, Tiger. The old man owes me. He owes me for all the extras he gave you and Carmine."

Tiger felt his gorge rise, remembering the years spent flunkying in his father's house. Plus a three-year stretch in the can. More years as a street banker for peanuts and Don Corso taking away everything he ever built for himself. The old man gave him nothing. It was Sonny and Carmine who got the new cars, went to the best schools, while his mother pampered the hell out of both of them. And to what purpose? Carmine was a fag in clerical drag, while Sonny became a pincushion.

All this flashed through his mind in the time it took to

gather up the markers. "You've been spending money all over town. Where did you get it?"

Sonny sneered, "Like you said, I ripped off the stores."

"Well, I hope you stole enough to keep you a while, because you're out of a job."

Something like panic flickered in Sonny's eyes, but he recovered quickly. "Papa's idea?"

"Mine also."

Slowly Sonny rose to his feet. "I guess there's nothing left to talk about."

Tiger looked up. "I still would like to know why you were stealing."

The sneer disappeared from Sonny's face as he walked to the window. "You and Papa could've checked with the hospital. But I guess it was easier to believe I was still back on the needle."

"Why did you need so much money?"

Sonny turned, pain etched in his features, the muscles around his mouth tightened. "I'm trying to buy Helen back."

The statement lay between them like vomit, one man ashamed and the other contemptuous.

Since Sonny was nineteen, every blind alley in his life was mapped out by Helen—sad-faced, elfin, flat-chested Helen with the big green eyes, long mousy hair, and total, blind dedication to Sonny. Having no will of her own, she reflected his, and by the time she was twenty, she'd acquired a hundred-dollar-a-day habit. Together they were a sorry pair, spending their days hustling fixes and their nights sleeping in cellars. Soon Helen was tricking for any price, and Sonny was out stealing. It ended with Sonny doing three years in the Kentucky cure farm, and Helen becoming the playmate of a two-bit dealer named Iggy Friedman.

Now Sonny wanted Helen back, but Iggy had a wall around her. And Tiger knew Iggy would sooner turn Helen over to his street pimps than let Sonny have her back.

"Have you seen her since you came home?" asked Tiger.

39

Sonny shook his head, the tension in his face settling into bitterness. "Iggy has her holed up somewhere," he said.

Tiger remembered seeing her about six months back. She wasn't pretty anymore. She looked forty, and the elfin quality was gone.

"Helen's not the girl you left behind, Sonny," said Tiger. "She's a full-blown junkie with a steady supply, so what can you offer her?"

Sonny's shoulders slumped. "I know that, but I just want to talk to her, Tiger."

"What's to talk about? You said yourself you were trying to buy her back. With what? There's not enough money in the world to make Iggy give her back. Besides, what makes you think she would want to give up all she has?"

"She could take the cure like I did."

Tiger tried to be as gentle as he could. "And if Helen doesn't want to take the cure?"

"Then I'll buy her all the junk she wants."

"And what happens when you run out of money?" asked Tiger.

"I made a score, I can keep her a long time."

Tiger laughed. "About all you're going to do, Sonny, is get yourself killed."

Sonny's laugh was grim and painful. "Without her, what the hell have I got to live for anyway."

Tiger leaned across the desk and studied the seriousness on his brother's face. "You got your whole damn life ahead of you, that's what."

"Some life," he shouted. "Without her I'm nothing."

Tiger had heard it all before and said, "Why don't you find a decent girl to squander your goodies on?"

Sonny got to his feet and rushed for the door, turning to glare back at his brother, tears running down his cheeks. "You prick," he snarled. "What the fuck do you know about it?"

Tiger took a step forward, to say something, anything.

"Fuck off," shouted Sonny as he opened the door and went through it like a shot, slamming the door behind him.

40

LATER in the morning, Tiger was reading a story in the *Daily News* about a body found lying in an alley behind a police station with a note pinned to it. He sat back trying to recall Uncle Patsy as he had looked when he gave him the big cookie.

Pete stuck his head in the door. "Bobby's on o-nine, and I got an old lady out here who says she wants to talk to you."

"She say what she wants?"

"Just that she says she wants to talk to the Tiger."

Tiger frowned as he unlocked the left top drawer. "Tell her I'm out of town."

"She saw you come in."

"What does she look like?"

Pete shrugged. "Like an old lady."

"You're not making it easy for me, Pete," said Tiger, annoyed. "What's her fucking name?"

"She won't say."

Tiger waved him off. "Have her wait until I finish with Bobby," he said, taking the phone out of the drawer.

"Yeah, Bobby. What have you got?"

"You're right, Tiger. The smell is all over the place, but I can't seem to get a handle on it yet."

"Where have you checked?"

"Everywhere, halfway around the globe, not a rumble."

"Damn, the stuff has to be coming from someplace."

"Maybe your informant was smoking his own stuff."

Tiger didn't find that amusing. "I can vouch for him."

"Okay. Have you found out anything?"

Tiger shook his head. "Nothing. But the moment I do I'll call you right away."

"Same here."

Tiger returned the phone to his desk, but it rang again. "Yeah?"

"It's me, Turk."

Excitement gripped Tiger. "What do you have?"

"Plenty, but we're going to have to meet."

"Same place?" asked Tiger.

41

"Same place, at seven-thirty."

Tiger put the phone away, walked across the room, opened the door a crack to peek at the old woman. Sitting bolt upright, she was dressed in black, the uniform of the Italian widow, with the veil pulled back to reveal weather-beaten features. There was something vaguely familiar about her.

"Bring her in, Pete."

The old woman brushed off Pete's offer of help and walked proudly into the office, her defiant expression not masking obvious fear.

"Can we get you some coffee?" asked Tiger.

Her deep black eyes were set in a mesh of crows' feet and laugh lines, but it was obvious to Tiger that this crone hadn't laughed in years. The chiseled mask of bitterness was deeply ingrained. Clearly petrified, she looked from Pete to Tiger, then asked, "Are you Tiger?"

"Yes, I am known as Tiger," he said softly. "Please sit down."

She glanced uncomfortably at Pete. "I have to talk to you alone."

Tiger knew Pete hadn't searched her for weapons, but he felt comfortable with her and signaled Pete to leave. As the door closed, he indicated the chair. She lowered herself to the edge of it without taking her eyes off Tiger. He sat across from her, noting the appearance and signs of extreme old age, observing the thin, dry skin of her hands, the folds of skin at her neck.

"What can I do for you?"

She looked over her shoulder, satisfying herself Pete was gone. "Do they call you Joey Corso?"

"Yes."

"How did you come by the name Tiger?"

The question threw him, partly because he wasn't used to being interrogated, partly because he had had the name so long he almost couldn't remember. "I think one of my uncles called me that after a fight in a schoolyard."

"Do you remember the uncle's name?"

42

He shook his head as he thought. "I think it was Uncle Patsy, but I'm not sure."

The answer seemed to satisfy the old woman. From under her coat, she removed a manila envelope and handed it to him, her face relaxing in the shadow of a smile.

"You have a long memory," she said.

He studied the envelope, turning it over in his hands, then made as if to open it. She reached across to put her withered hand on his. He discovered that he didn't find her touch offensive.

"Read it when you are alone," she said.

"What is it?"

She shrugged her narrow shoulders. "I do not know." To his puzzled look she offered another suggestion of a smile. "Pasquale made me promise to give it to you when he is dead."

The morning paper was on his desk, and he folded his hands over the headline. "I read about Patsy's death in the papers."

"Such is life," she said, echoing Patsy's words to Don Corso. "There are no guarantees." She looked at him and he found it difficult meeting her steady gaze.

"Who are you?" asked Tiger.

Her gaze wavered. "I am sister to your mother."

Now Tiger recognized the slight resemblance, but his confusion deepened. He knew his mother had a twin sister who had died or returned to the old country, but he knew of no other sister. And this woman sitting across from him looked at least forty years older than his mother.

The thought passed through Tiger's mind last night, Patsy had looked years older than he should have.

"I am wife to Pasquale Colombo," the old woman said softly. Then, not as if correcting herself, but rather as if amplifying the thought: "His widow."

Remembering Patsy's words, he asked, "You are Angelina?"

The old woman's eyes narrowed briefly, then in a single

43

movement, which almost belied her years, she got to her feet. "I go now," she said, pulling down her veil.

"Why haven't I ever seen you before?"

She looked at him, her gaze direct and unfearing. "I did not want to be seen," she said simply.

Something was wrong. Tiger could feel it. "Why haven't you been to see your sister?"

Her eyes remained steady. "Because it was forbidden."

"Forbidden? By who?" exclaimed Tiger.

"By Don Corso," she said simply.

"But why would he do that?" asked Tiger, not liking this gray conversation.

Her expression was indecipherable: "Because Don Corso is a God unto himself."

She turned and started for the door. Tiger moved quickly around the desk to intercept her. "I'll drive you home. Where do you live?"

She turned and looked up at him, "If your mother wants you to know she will tell you." With that, and without another word, she made her way through the door, past the others in the outer room toward the vestibule. He paced behind her, moving quickly to open the outer door for her. She looked again, and said, "Now that Patsy is no more, I will go to see my sister."

Tiger smiled. "She will like that."

The old woman nodded, secured her veil, and went out into the sunlight. Tiger closed the door behind her, deep in thought, and paced back into his office.

"She certainly makes an impression," said Pete.

He spent the next hour alone, reading and rereading Patsy's letter, carefully examining the key that fell out of the envelope. He wondered what madness awaited him when he turned the key.

The old woman's identity puzzled him. Despite the fleeting family resemblance, he would've taken bets that she wasn't his aunt. He was positive she wasn't Patsy's wife, since he knew Angelina tipped the scales at over two hundred pounds. Besides, she had had an operation for "women's problems" and the lady who just left was well beyond the years of women's problems. So who the hell was she? Tiger told himself, something was screwy.

He put the puzzle aside and pressed the button under the lip of the desk. Pete stuck his head in the door. "Yeah, Tiger?"

"I'm leaving for the day, but before you go home, pick up a couple of flashlights and a crowbar. Meet me at my house around eleven."

Pete's face broke into a mischievous grin. "We going to do a little stealing?"

Tiger shook his head, "Nope, we're going to pay our respects to the dead."

IT occurred to Tiger that a visit to Carmine might help shed some light on the mystery woman. He drove across town and parked up the street from Saint Rocco's. His mind was preoccupied with the puzzles of the day. As he locked his car, he walked to the rectory, failing to see the two men blocking the sidewalk, until he found himself looking into the scowling face of Chief of Detectives Lieutenant Joseph F. X. Malone.

"I see someone left your cage unlocked, chief," said Tiger, recovering some of his poise.

Malone laughed mirthlessly. "Did you think your old man could keep me out of circulation forever?" Malone and his partner had once busted Tiger, breaking a couple of ribs in the process. Don Corso's lawyers forced the department to punish him, and he'd spent six years on Staten Island—cop purgatory, especially for cops who lived at the other end of the city. Malone had been transferred a month after he had bought a house in the northernmost neighborhood of the Bronx.

Tiger decided to ignore the question and stared at the chief's paunch. "Looks like the pickings in Staten Island were pretty good."

45

Hatred flashed in Malone's eyes. "Maybe this time I'll break the rest of your ribs."

Tiger laughed, "I see you haven't lost any of your charm."

Malone pointed his finger in Tiger's face in a gesture of contempt. "You open your mouth again and I'll close it permanently," he said, the hatred oozing.

Tiger's eyes frosted over as he glanced at the short detective with Malone. "Do your boss a favor and put him back in his cage before he bites himself."

Malone's eyes twisted with hate. He opened his jacket to expose his .38. Tiger cursed his stupidity for letting the burly detective box him in without a witness. The other detective surprisingly stepped between them.

"What's this all about, chief?" he asked.

Malone stood firm, his hand poised above the revolver. Without taking his eyes off Tiger, he said out of the side of his mouth, "I go back a long way with this bastard's family. Every time they did damage, I had to clean up the bodies. Now I hear they're gonna dump a ton of heroin on the streets."

The anger hit Tiger like a fist, filling him with a hate he knew he wouldn't be able to suppress. The remark showed Tiger the depth of Malone's biased ignorance.

Tiger knew the Council had long ago outlawed drugs with a death sentence if caught. It was true, in the old days, when the Italians controlled the families, drugs were a large part of their income. That is, until the Sicilian War Lords gained control and wantonly killed what they considered to be *disonorante degenere animale*—dishonorable degenerate animals. But people like Malone always used their hate to lump people into desired categories. "Don't push your luck, you fat bastard."

Suddenly Malone's gun was out and cocked. The other detective whisked himself aside, unholstered his pistol as he moved.

The voice came from the shadows. "Is this a private party?" asked Carmine, seemingly oblivious to the guns.

46

Malone's eyes narrowed as the priest took a position between Tiger and the weapons. "How are you, Tiger? Did you want to see me about something special?" he asked smoothly.

Malone returned his gun to the holster and looked past the priest to Tiger. "You owe your brother for this one."

T IGER settled into the big wing chair in the rectory office. Carmine sat at his desk. A picture of Pope John XXIII looked benevolently down from the wall behind him. The pope's picture, the statue of the Immaculate Virgin with a votive candle glowing, another statue, this one of Saint Rocco, against the opposite wall, and a gallery of other pictures and paintings, reflecting all kinds of taste and talent. These were Carmine's army. In their presence, as well Carmine knew, Tiger was nervous.

"What brings big bad brother to this quiet part of town?"

They had been talking around the subject for five minutes, filling in the gaps talking about Jeanne and the kids. Carmine knew better than to believe his older brother came to visit him out of brotherly love.

Tiger could never get used to having a brother who looked and dressed like Saint Anthony. He swallowed his annoyance and decided to get right to the point.

"What do you know about Angelina Colombo?"

Carmine's eyebrows shot up. "Boy, that's really out of left field. I read about the killing this morning and now you start talking about Zi Angelina. What's going on?"

Tiger maintained a disinterested expression. "Nothing. Now that's she's a widow, I figured she might need some help."

Carmine laughed, a laugh like granite cracking. "Since when did you ever give a damn about her or anyone else?" To Carmine, Joey was a thug, hard and unemotional. A duplicate of his father. Neither had the qualities of gentleness and compassion needed to raise them above the level of animals. The truth of the matter was that he feared both of them.

Tiger shrugged it off. He owed his brother one. "It's not a family affection trip, but she is family," said Tiger, knowing Carmine lived in a world of his own.

Carmine accepted that—more or less. "Okay, what do you want to know?"

"Tell me what you know about her."

Carmine looked at his brother, trying to fathom the extent of his brother's seriousness. "I don't know anything about her. I can't even remember what she looked like. Patsy always came around alone and it's been years since I last saw him."

"What did she look like?"

Carmine took a moment to think back. "I remember she was a big woman, friendly in a Sicilian way," he said, picking up the *Daily News.* "Is it true the things they say he did?"

Tiger shrugged. "You know how reporters are. They like to sell papers."

Carmine threw the paper down. Tiger eyed him narrowly and asked, "How many sisters did Momma have?"

Again, Carmine showed his surprise. "One, an identical twin. Why?"

"You sure?"

"How could I know for sure? She faded out before I was born. Anyway, I only know of one. Why? What's going on in that feverish head of yours?"

Tiger shook his head as if to brush away his brother's flippancy. "Do you remember," he persisted, "anything at all about Momma's sister or Uncle Patsy?"

Carmine shook his head doubtfully. "No-o-o," he said, "only that Angelina was his second wife."

Tiger sat up. "What happened to Patsy's first wife?"

"I understand she went back to Sicily."

"Do you know why she went back?"

Carmine shrugged. "Only that she didn't like America."

"When was that, do you know?" asked Tiger.

Carmine laughed. "You're kidding. That was before I was born."

"Do you remember what his first wife's name was?"

Carmine pondered for a moment. "I think it was Camille."

Tiger was silent for almost a minute, while Carmine's curiosity built to fever pitch. Then Tiger quietly said, "A woman came to my office today. She said she was Patsy's wife and Momma was her sister, but she sure as hell wasn't Zi Angelina."

"How can you be sure?"

"I remember once seeing Angelina, she was two hundred pounds if she was an ounce. This old woman was ninety pounds soaking wet."

Carmine's confusion deepened. "Is it possible the first wife returned from Sicily?"

"Anything's possible, I guess. But don't you think it strange she shows up in my office the morning after Patsy's death?"

Quite abruptly, Tiger knew he had no intention of following the instructions in Patsy's letter until he knew the rules of the game better.

T HE woman was under sixty. She sat looking out the window. Her eyes were focused on something in the remote distance that only she could see.

Tiger came into the room. He observed her absorption in the distance, the lax hang of her hands, the lack of expression in her face. The tiny spark of hope that always flew up in him as he approached the door to her room glowed and died.

"Hello, Momma."

He had a cake box tied with a ribbon in his hands. He put it in her lap. "I brought your favorite cookies, Momma."

He didn't expect her to answer, and he knew the nurses

49

and orderlies would eat the cookies. He brought them because there had been a time when she liked them. There
had been a time when she could make sense of the fact that
Jeanne made them and that Joey, her son, brought them.
Every visit offered a hope that she might again remember.

"How do you feel, Momma?"

Her gaze came back halfway. Her mouth moved slowly as
she forced a single word, with great difficulty, "P-P-Papa?"

It was always the same. Tiger was never sure if his mother
was asking for her husband or thought Tiger was Papa.

"He'll come soon, Momma," he lied. Knowing she knew
he wouldn't come, and drew behind her curtain.

"Did you have any visitors today, Momma?"

She studied her fingers, looking at the bone of one
knuckle under the transparent skin.

"Was Carmine here?" he asked, but she continued to
retreat into her interior world.

"Was Jeanne here, Momma?" he asked. Her fascination
with her knuckle was almost total.

"Was your sister here, Momma?" But she continued to
examine her hands. Her interest shifted to the tip of her
fingernail, but suddenly a tiny tear formed in the corner of
her eyes.

"Was your sister here, Momma?" He saw the muscle in
the hands tighten, the fingers now almost becoming a claw.
"Was your sister here, Momma?" Was he getting through
to her? "Was she here?"

The tears ran down her cheek. "My sister is dead," she
said, then shook her head as if to correct herself. "My sister
went back to Sicily."

"Which was it, Momma? Did she go back to Sicily or did
she die?"

Her head slumped, but her expression jelled into a
strong determination. "She is dead . . . in Sicily."

Tiger wondered how faulty her memory actually was and
how far she was from reality.

"An old woman," he said, slowly and carefully to his
mother, "came to see me today. She said she was your sister
and wife to Patsy Colombo."

The hands dropped motionless into her lap. Her eyes were cast down, her face a study in vagrant emotion.

"She said she was coming here, Momma. To see you. Did she? Did she come to see you, Momma?"

Her hands began to tremble, at first slightly, and then uncontrollably. The tremor moved up her body. Her eyes filled with terror. Her whole body was suddenly shaking. He took her hand and gently stroked it.

"It's all right, Momma. It's all right."

His voice soothed her somewhat, and the terror sank back into the depths of her eyes. The tremor passed. She looked at him, the first time she had looked into his eyes since his arrival, the first time in weeks. Softly, she asked, "Pasquale . . . he is dead?"

He was shocked. Unable to lie to her, he said, "Yes, Momma, he is dead."

She took a moment to confirm what he had said. "How did he die?"

Tiger searched for the right words. "He was shot."

Her eyes began to dart about the room, the terror returning.

"What is it, Momma? What are you afraid of?"

"You must stop my sister," she snapped. "She must not come."

"Why can't she come here, Momma?" he asked, sensing his father's presence in the background.

"She's in danger. She'll . . . she'll be hurt."

"Who is going to hurt her, Momma?" Tiger asked.

But she shook her head violently. "Don't ask, just stop Camille."

Camille, he thought. "How can I help her if I don't know who's after her?"

She grabbed his sleeve and pulled him down. Her grip was strong, tenacious, and her voice commanding. "You must do what I say. Stop her."

According to Momma's law, the subject was closed.

"Where will I find her, Momma?"

She pulled him down again and whispered into his ear an address in another part of Brooklyn. "But don't tell Papa."

"Why is Camille in danger from Papa?"

The old woman lowered her head, becoming fascinated with the fingers of her left hand again. Her voice lowered as she whispered, "If Papa knows she is alive, he will kill her."

Damn, thought Tiger, wondering what kind of Pandora's box he had opened. "Why, Momma?"

She held her hand up for a moment, studying it. Then her gaze shifted to the cityscape outside her window, and her eyes seemed to go out of focus. Her voice seemed to come from far away. "Ask me no more."

He knelt by her, covering her hands with his, looking up into her face. In her eyes he saw again the shadow of terror.

"Don't be afraid, Momma. I'll take care of your sister."

Tears filled the corners of her eyes as she pulled him close, and he felt the hot tears gently burn his cheeks. He wanted to cry for joy, never having seen his mother shed a tear before. He felt the pain of not being able to take this delicate creature in his arms and hug her.

"I will go now, Momma," he said, kissing her on the forehead. He wanted to throw his arms around her neck. But the hand clutching his sleeve forestalled that desire.

"I promise you," he said, "that no harm will come to your sister."

She reluctantly released his sleeve.

TIGER arrived early at Lulu's restaurant and was anxious to hear what information Turk had acquired. Since it was a slow night, his uncle Lulu himself waited on Tiger. The meal was delicious and the conversation with Lulu stimulating. After dinner Tiger realized Turk was an hour late. Nervously he wondered what had delayed him, fully aware of the man's usual punctuality.

He waited another half hour, then left a message for Turk with Lulu.

Thirty minutes later Tiger stood in the funeral parlor where Patsy was laid out in a rude wooden coffin. The plainness of the coffin was the first sign something was wrong. The second was the lack of flowers, and the third was the absence of mourners. He guessed the word was out that Patsy had died in dishonor. Tiger wondered why. He vividly remembered the scene from the night before, and he could recall nothing dishonorable in his actions. In Tiger's eyes, Uncle Patsy's decision to die like a man was right.

An old man sat in the back of the room as if separating himself from the whole affair. Near the coffin, two women sat in silent prayer, their heavy veils hiding their features. Tiger was certain neither was Angelina or Camille.

The weeping widows lined the walls, like a row of vultures, dread creatures who spent their lives searching out death. Their chant was a death cry, a screech to the heavens to witness their homage to the dead. But Tiger suspected their act was an effort to bring themselves to the attention of the Lord.

Since childhood Tiger had been imbued with the Sicilian's fatalistic sense of the tragic. Despising their pagan circus qualities and pious ritual orations, Tiger never claimed to understand all the nuances of Sicilian tradition —of which there were many, all leading to unforgivable sin. But looking down at his Uncle Patsy's forever silent features, he felt empty. No man, thought Tiger, should ever have the power to make a man die alone.

HE SENSED the tail the moment he left the funeral home, but he was unable to spot anything. He made a quick left, jumped three red lights, made another turn, pulled over to the side, cut the lights, and waited. Nothing. But he knew they were still down there. Damn, thought Tiger, he had no time for a cat-and-mouse game with a professional team.

A block further, he pulled over to a pay phone and dialed. The voice that answered was rough in tone, noncommittal in attitude.

"You recognize the voice?" asked Tiger.

"Yeah."

"I need a favor."

"How long?"

Tiger looked at his wrist watch. "About twelve minutes."

There was a long silence. "Come ahead."

Tiger drove through many streets. After a mile he headed along a deserted stretch, turned into a dirt road and headed into the Canarsie swamps. He knew every foot of the twenty square miles of the Brooklyn marshlands. In the middle of the swamp, the city maintained a garbage incinerator. His cousin Frankie held the contract.

Tiger drove slowly, his headlights allowing him to avoid the many obstacles in the gutted road. Suddenly two men stood in the road. Tiger recognized his cousin Frankie. Tiger hit the brakes, opened the car door, and vacated the driver's seat as Frankie's companion jumped into the car and sped away. Frankie led Tiger to an incline, motioning him to lie quietly on the ground. They waited, and a moment later a large sedan picked its way along the gutted road in pursuit of Tiger's car.

Frankie let out his breath. "You were right, Tiger," he said. "Who were they?"

Tiger shrugged. "Who the hell knows? What now?"

"Tommy will run them around until daylight and maybe then we'll get a make on them," he said, holding out a set of keys to Tiger. "My car's down in the gully. Take it, it's clean."

T IGER passed the house twice before he found it. Then memories came in a flood. The little house, half buried by trees and bushes, had changed little since he'd last seen it as a boy.

He parked the car around the corner, glad it was a moonless night. No dogs barked at strangers. Everything about this episode was odd.

Tiger knocked softly at the door and then waited in the eerie silence for an answer. Straining his ears, he heard nothing. He knocked again, then called softly, "It's me, Tiger." He knocked a third time. "I have a message from my mother."

He held his breath and waited. A deadbolt was thrown and the door opened a crack. All he could see in the darkened doorway was a pair of eyes.

"I just came from the hospital. Momma wants me to talk to you."

The door opened suddenly and Tiger was pulled through the blackness to the rear of the house. Still in the darkness, he was led down a flight of stairs and through a room that smelled of stale human occupancy. The door closed behind him and a light came on. He was in a small, sparsely furnished room with a narrow bed in the corner, a table with two chairs, a small battered club chair, and an old floor lamp. His guide turned to him.

"We talk here."

In the dim light, Tiger studied her features, realizing that she was much frailer than he'd thought from seeing her earlier in his office.

"Momma says you can't come to the hospital. She says you will be in danger."

With an effort she lowered herself into one of the chairs, eyeing Tiger carefully. "My life is almost over and I must do what I must."

Tiger let out a sigh. "My mother is afraid. This is not good for her," he said, hoping to get through to her.

She let the silence drag, then nodded. "I will wait," she said simply.

Tiger smiled his relief and sat down opposite her. He wished he had a cup of coffee. "Why does Momma think my father will hurt you?"

Her eyes narrowed. "You must not know."

"I have to know. I gave Momma my word to help you."

She looked closely at him, skepticism showing in the set of her mouth. "Can you protect me from the long arm of Don Corso?"

Tiger thought carefully before answering. "If I have to."

The silence was heavy as she weighed his words. After a moment, he felt she had accepted him. "Don Corso believes I am dead," she said with a shrug. "If he knows I am still alive, others will die."

The simple remark startled Tiger. Why such hate from his father? "Now that you are back in America, how long do you think you can hide from him?"

She spoke slowly and deliberately, as the little bells in Tiger's head rang. Her cold eyes held him, measured him.

"He will never find me."

"How can you be sure?"

Again she measured him. He sensed she was fighting to arrive at some decision. "I have been in this cellar for thirty years."

It took a moment for the full meaning of her words to hit him. "My God!" He was dumbfounded. He asked himself how could this be. He looked around the airless apartment. Tiger found it impossible to imagine what madness had taken hold of his family thirty-five years ago.

"You are really Zi Camille, aren't you?" he asked, not knowing what else to say.

"Si. I am your mother's sister."

Tiger smiled. "And Angelina?"

Camille seemed suddenly tired. "Angelina is sister to Pasquale. He bring her to America to tell everyone she is his new wife."

Tiger could figure the rest. "To protect you?"

"To protect Pasquale," she said simply.

"And where is Angelina now?" he asked, knowing she wasn't one of the women under the heavy veils.

It was a soft voice that spoke from the shadows. "I am here, signore."

He didn't bother to turn around. He knew a gun was pointed at him. He laughed, keeping his eyes on Camille, thinking, these broads are something else. "Who's sitting in the funeral parlor?"

"Friends."

Tiger slowly turned and smiled at the heavyset woman half hidden in the shadows. "I am happy to meet you, Angelina."

She smiled tentatively, lowering the pistol. Tiger looked over his shoulder at Camille. "Does my mother know all this?"

"Yes," said Camille.

And now Tiger could see why his mother was in the hospital. Years of this stress had wrenched her sanity loose from its moorings. This was the secret, thought Tiger, that wore out the delicate works of her mind. He felt a surge of anger at his father for allowing such a secret to corrode her soul.

"Will you let me take both of you to a safe place?"

Camille shook her head. "We are safe here."

"What about food, clothes? What about getting out to see other people?"

"Everything we need is here. The house is mine. Pasquale built it. It is strong."

Tiger nodded. It seemed the ladies had it all together. He had a sudden pang of guilt, knowing he had to have some answers. "Do either of you know why Pasquale was killed?"

Both women remained silent. Then Camille snapped bitterly, "Ask Don Corso."

"Why? What reason would he have?" he asked.

Camille shrugged. "Don Corso doesn't need a reason. But perhaps he found out about me," she said suspiciously.

Tiger couldn't buy that. "I don't think so. If what you say is true, how he felt about you, then he would have been here already."

Angelina stepped in closer. "For the past two weeks Pasquale was acting very nervous."

Tiger looked sharply at her. "He say why?"

"Just that Don Corso was closing in on him."

57

"What could he have meant by that?"

"I don't know," she said, seeing the terror in Camille's eyes. "I think he had offended Don Corso."

Offending his father wasn't difficult, thought Tiger.

"When it is safe I will take you to see your sister. She needs you."

Tiger was an hour out of New York City when the newsflash came over WCBS. He looked at Pete, half asleep in the passenger seat.

"Did you hear that?" asked Tiger.

"Hear what?"

"Some spade shot Joe the Boss."

Pete turned and looked at Tiger with slumber-filled eyes.

"Fuck him," said Pete with a soft sigh. "I was dreaming of humping Raquel Welch."

Tiger smiled. "Was she any good?"

Pete half shrugged. "I've had better."

Tiger laughed. "Even you don't believe that."

Pete measured Tiger. "Big Tit Rosie, she was some kind of a dog."

Tiger burst into randy laughter. "Yeah, you're right. She was something special. How come you never married her?"

"They say marriage is a sea of joy. I don't swim too good."

"You'll have to settle down sometime. I did with Jeanne," said Tiger seriously.

Pete broke into a bright smile. "Then maybe I should have married Jeanne," said Pete, feeling good at Tiger's smile.

Tiger turned off the parkway and headed along Route 17, wondering what the hit on Joe the Boss was all about. The news report gave no details, saying merely that a black man, posing as a photographer at a political rally had shot Joe the Boss while he posed for pictures with the candidate. Tiger didn't like the smell of it. Blacks don't go around

58

shooting Italian bosses—at least not if they cared about their health. The thing stinks, mused Tiger. It doesn't make sense.

He circled Swan Lake and took the high road through the mountains. Twenty minutes later he turned off onto a dirt road, which he followed to its end. There he stopped and cut the engine. Pete woke up and looked out the window at the blackness. "We still in America?"

"Get the flashlights," Tiger said, turning on the map light to study Patsy's letter. "It's off to the left," he said.

Pete followed him along a dark trail, hardly more than a deer track, which brought them out alongside a high picket fence. Pete looked up sourly. "I hope you don't think I'm climbing this damn thing?"

Tiger laughed. "There's a gate."

"What the hell is this place?"

"An old graveyard," said Tiger, as they moved along the fence.

"Shit!" said Pete, a doubtful tone to his voice.

Halfway down the fence they found the gate and went in. The graveyard had long been abandoned and was overgrown with weeds and brambles.

"What are we looking for?" asked Pete.

"A mausoleum with the name Scapaci."

"Who's Scapaci?"

"I guess the guy who's buried there," said Tiger.

"No shit, Tiger. I mean, why are we looking for the mausoleum?"

"I got a couple of broads meeting us there."

"Terrific," said Pete sourly.

Tiger stopped before a large structure, almost a small house. The name SCAPACI was carved boldly above the door in Gothic capitals.

"This is it," said Tiger.

Pete played the light over the carved name. Deep shadows advanced and retreated as the flashlight beam moved.

"Hey, Tiger, I got a great idea," he said as he studied the eeriness of the place.

"What?"

"Let's get the fuck out of here."

"You'll change your mind when you see the two broads."

"Shit, Tiger, you're knocking me out with your one-liners."

"Then stop getting spooked about nothing."

"Cemeteries make me nervous. I keep thinking the people we hit are waiting for us."

Tiger ignored him and tested the grillwork on the mausoleum door and put the key into the lock. To his surprise, it turned silently. The door opened smoothly, as if the hinges had been recently oiled.

Playing the light over the interior, he saw four crypts. Aiming the light at the lower crypt, he stepped into the vault.

"Hand me the crowbar," commanded Tiger.

With Pete's help, he wedged the crowbar under the lid of the heavy sarcophagus, and with much effort they lifted the heavy stone.

Pete looked into the recess first, taking a second to absorb what he was seeing. Then he said, intensely, almost under his breath: "Bingo!"

Tiger was too shaken to answer as his light played over the rows of clear plastic bags filled with money.

Pete laughed gleefully. "We found King Solomon's mines."

Tiger was still too stunned to answer. After a moment, Pete stopped laughing. "You weren't ready for this, were you?"

Tiger shook his head. Now he understood the line in Patsy's letter: "This can make you free."

"Christ, Tiger, I never saw so much money," said Pete in awe. "How much do you think is here?"

Tiger's answer was slow in coming. "At least forty dollars."

"Shit," said Pete, pulling out a single bag and examining its contents, making a rough count. "A hundred grand a bag," he calculated, "and there are about forty, fifty bags. That's four, five million? I don't believe this."

They piled the plastic bags on the floor. Pete found a letter addressed to Tiger. "This is for you."

Tiger studied the scrawly writing, recognizing it as Patsy's. It was addressed to JOEY TIGER CORSO. Tiger was tempted to open it but decided to put it in his pocket instead.

In the corner of the sarcophagus, Pete found two Berettas fitted with silencers.

Tiger took the guns and examined them, hefting each in turn and handing one back to Pete. "Let's get the money into the car and think of a safe place to hide it."

"I got a piggy bank."

"I think we need something stronger."

"Ever tried to open one?" asked Pete evenly.

They were acting silly, Tiger realized, but the whole experience, even the moonless night and the eerie setting in the abandoned cemetery was weird, unsettling. Not to mention the money.

They carried the bags of money outside. "My country place isn't far from here, " said Tiger. "We'll take it there."

Within minutes the trunk was filled and the few bags that wouldn't fit there were stashed on the rear seat.

"You know me a lot of years, Tiger," said Pete. "I don't ask questions, but what the hell is this all about?"

Tiger looked at him. "Let's get out of here and I'll fill you in."

They retraced their way down the deserted dirt road and circled Swan Lake. On one hand Tiger was exhausted; but on the other, he was keyed up by the experience.

"How are you going to keep your old man from grabbing the money?"

It was about all Tiger had thought about since leaving the cemetery, and still the answer eluded him. "I guess I'm not going to tell him."

"You forgetting Toto?" Pete asked.

"I ain't forgetting nothing," Tiger said, a great anger filling him as he blurted out: "Not that degenerate Toto, not my father, not nobody, is taking another damn thing away from us again!"

Pete was startled by the vehemence of Tiger's answer.

He smiled inwardly at Tiger's use of the word "us." It was like Korea again.

As Pete sat there watching Tiger drive, he glanced occasionally at him. Tiger was the brother he never had. Even though they were not *sangue du sangue*—blood of blood, they were the closest thing to it. They were sacred *compari* to each other. Pete knew he would die for Tiger.

Pete also liked the people Tiger surrounded himself with. Not misfits and crazies like his father's flunkies, but brainy guys with brass balls. Tiger never expected anyone around him to be honest—just honorable.

He angled into a daydream about what he would do with the money if it was his. Then Tiger turned into a rutted road that led to the rear of Tiger's country place.

It was a large house that Tiger had bought years before from his father, who had originally built it as a hideaway in the event of trouble. The house was built into the side of a hill overlooking a lake. It was constructed of steel plate masked over with fieldstone and brick, with a slate roof. The windows were bulletproof and shatterproof plastic. It was a private fortress in which Tiger always felt completely comfortable. Tiger thought it was the logical place to hide Patsy's money.

Tiger got out of the car. "Let's make some coffee and sort all this out."

TIGER unlocked the front door and they stepped into the house. Even before the lights came on, both men knew something was wrong. The living room was a shambles. Every piece of furniture was smashed. Great gaping holes had been chopped into the walls. The fireplace had been attacked by what must have been a huge mallet; it was reduced to a pile of broken bricks and plaster.

Pete had his piece out, every muscle tense, all his nerves alert. Tiger was almost stunned to silence. The damage was without rhyme or reason, totally disorganized and vicious. It was like Korea all over again: destruction for destruction's sake.

Tiger moved slowly through the rubble, followed by Pete. Both men picked up bits and pieces of debris and put them back down, almost aimlessly, knowing nothing would ever fit together again.

Tiger climbed over the pile of bricks and plaster and examined the inner surface of the chimney, where a small lined compartment had been built into the side of the vent. The money he had hidden there was gone.

He looked around the room and couldn't believe anyone would do so much damage just for money. Could it have been the Feds? No, he didn't think so. This was the work of a sick mind, distorted and uncontrollable. He could feel the hate in every blow that had been struck.

He worked his way back to the door, snapped open a window panel, and examined the alarm system. He found nothing wrong with it. Yet the house was wrecked. Well, thought Tiger, it looked like someone didn't like him.

Pete returned from looking over the house. "It's clean."

Tiger hadn't expected it to be otherwise. He looked at Pete. "Forty grand is missing, so this could just be a ripoff, or it could be something bigger."

"What do we do now?"

Tiger thought about it. "As soon as we get to my house, I want you to take off for another state. I don't care what state you pick, but find one with a large tract of land. Something with plenty of wide open spaces. If you have to build a house on it, make it strong like this one. Stock up with supplies, enough for a year. Spend whatever you need, then bury the rest of the money."

Pete took it all in. "And then?"

Tiger proceeded to lay out a complicated sequence of moves.

"Why so elaborate?"

"If I don't know where you are or what you did with the money, then Toto can go fuck himself."

Pete burst into laughter. "I love it. It may get me killed, but I love it."

"Just be careful. We can't afford to make a mistake. So make sure you don't contact anyone until the job is completed. And you'll have to do the job alone. Oh, and take your old lady with you. I don't want her becoming a target if it gets out that you disappeared."

Pete's smile was tight. "I intend to. I still like her. Besides, I know how sharp your father's claws are."

Despite his frivolous manner, Tiger knew from long experience that when things got hairy, Pete was as cunning as a wolverine.

"On your way to wherever you're going, have the money checked in case it's from a bank job, a kidnap, or funny money."

"Bite your tongue."

Tiger looked over the carnage again. "Let's get out of here."

They returned to New York City.

Tiger let himself into the house. His two Dobermans sniffed him out, greeted him, and went about their business.

In the kitchen he made himself a pot of coffee, intercepting the first cup as it dripped from the machine. He sat at the table with the coffee, looking at the letter on the table. A tiny noise startled him, and he turned quickly to find Jeanne, sleepy-eyed, standing in the doorway.

"You hungry?" she asked.

He shook his head. "I'm just having coffee."

She pecked him on the cheek. "Don't stay up too late."

"Goodnight," said Tiger.

"Goodnight, dear."

He quickly drank the first cup and poured another as he thought of who it might have been that demolished his house. He knew Sonny had made a score, but he couldn't attribute such insane damage to his brother. The letter on the table was crowding other thoughts from his mind. After a brief hesitation he started to open the letter. But little bells began to jingle in the back of his head, and he felt a

64

strange sensation, almost a premonition. He hesitated, shook off the feeling, and opened the envelope. Inside he found a single slip of paper and a small toy frog clicker, similar to the kind the military sometime use for night signaling. One click means where are you and two clicks means here I am. Tiger tried the toy, but nothing happened. He assumed it was broken and put it aside as he picked up the letter and read:

Tiger Joey Corso:
If you are reading this letter, then you have all the money. I have left it to you for two reasons. One because I love you and two because I want you free from Don Corso. He is a bad man and soon he will try to use you badly.

For many years I have done him many favors, then I did special favors for his friends, that is where the money comes from. It is clean so do not be afraid to spend it.

Sooner or later Don Corso will want to use you like he has used me for over fifty years. Don't let him. Take the money, and take Camille, Angelina, and your family and go away before it is too late.

The toy frog is a trick I learned to confuse Toto. It is quiet, but for some reason it affects his thinking.
Your Uncle,
Pasquale Colombo

Tiger thought of the letter, disappointed at not receiving sufficient answers. He wanted to know about the animosity between Camille and his father. He also wanted to know why the money was given to him. Was it to put him under obligation to Camille and Angelina? Well, it had been a crazy day, and he finally sat exhausted on the sofa in the living room and fell asleep.

Two hours later, Ralphie called from the office to tell him Pete had to run out of town to a funeral, and he would cover the office for him.

"Your brother Sonny was looking for you," said Ralphie.

"He say what he wanted?"

"Just that it was important."

Tiger felt the knot in his stomach. "He's off the payroll, and I don't want to see him around the office anymore."

"Maybe," said Ralphie, "that's what has him nervous."

"Anything else?" asked Tiger.

"O-nine called, said it was important."

Tiger wondered if it had been Bobby or Turk on the line. He quickly changed his clothes, rushed down the stairs, and decided to call Bobby first. He heard Jeanne on the phone and shouted, "So long, honey," as he dashed out the door.

She yelled after him, "Frankie left your car in the driveway. He said to tell you it was Snow White who borrowed your car."

"Fucking Feds!" thought Tiger.

TIGER drove to the nearest roadside phone and dialed the emergency number Bobby had given him. There was no answer, so he thought it best to call Tony at the yard.

"Yeah?" came Tony's rough voice.

"It's me," said Tiger.

"My friend has been trying to get in touch with you. Give me your number."

Tiger read the number on the pay phone in reverse to Tony.

It was ten minutes before Bobby called back, and Tiger immediately sensed the excitement in his voice.

"I think I found the source. We have to meet right away."

"Same place?"

"Same place," answered Bobby.

"Give me two hours."

BOBBY was waiting under the Canarsie Bridge. He started talking at once, without handshake or greeting.

66

"Listen, Tiger. This thing is getting hairy. I had to do a heavy favor for this information, but it might be worth it. What I got is only rumor, but it scares the hell out of me."

Tiger remained silent, but excited.

"My snitch says it's a group of rogue cops working out of the property clerk's office. He says they have been switching heroin for milk sugar."

"Shit!" exclaimed Tiger.

"Yeah, shit," Bobby repeated, bitterly.

Tiger was more than disturbed by the news. The property clerk's office was like Fort Knox. "Where do we go from here?"

"Nowhere. It's a dead end. All I have is a rumor, not enough to start a serious investigation and not without tipping our hand."

"So where are we?"

"I'm sending in a man. Unofficial, of course."

Tiger nodded. "Did your boy have any idea how much heroin had been switched?"

"He couldn't be sure," said Bobby, scratching the back of his head. "But he thought about sixty million dollars' worth."

Tiger was aghast. "I don't believe you. Your snitch is bullshitting you."

But Bobby slowly shook his head. "I checked with the D.A.'s office. Johnny Holzer said at last estimate he thought there was about two hundred million dollars' worth of narcotics in the clerk's office."

Tiger was flabbergasted. "What the hell are they doing with so damn much laying around for?" he asked in annoyance.

"It's all evidence in criminal cases, some go back as far as five years," said Bobby soberly.

Tiger shook his head in amazement. "Can I talk to your snitch?" he asked, measuring the inspector.

"Hell, no!" snapped Bobby. "He's scared to death, and there's another thing that's getting through to me: The two cops found hanging from that roof last week worked for the clerk's office. And just two days ago we found a stiff in the gutter behind the six-two, with a note attached saying he was the hitter."

Tiger knew he was talking about Uncle Patsy. "And you don't buy it?"

"Are you serious?" answered a caustic Bobby. "Either the family is becoming senile, or it's some kind of smoke-screen."

Tiger knew Bobby was right. None of the pieces fit.

Bobby was studying him. "You learn anything?"

Tiger shook his head, "Nothing yet."

"Tiger . . . you know if the families are involved, I got to stop them."

Tiger was slow to answer. "If someone in the family is involved, they're not going to let you."

Bobby looked soberly at Tiger. "I know, but I have to try."

Tiger felt sorry for Bobby. Don Corso had financed his education to pay off a favor he owed Bobby's old man. To Tiger's knowledge, Bobby had never rented out his badge to anyone. And Bobby hated drugs, in any shape. His kid brother had bought it from an overdose. Bobby played by the rules in a game that had no rules. Tiger knew the poor bastard couldn't see that everything pointed to Don Corso.

"Bobby?"

"Yeah, Tiger?"

"My old man has a street banker named Turk. You know him?"

Bobby opened his car door and looked over his shoulder at Tiger. "Yeah, I know him. Why?"

"He was my tip, and I'm worried about him. He hasn't checked in with me since yesterday."

"Is he a friend of yours?"

"Kind of."

Bobby was slow to speak. "I'm sorry, but he was fished out of the river this morning."

As Tiger drove home, he started to get things into focus. He knew Turk as a street banker had to make enemies, but his father's cloak of protection damn near made Turk bulletproof on the streets. So Tiger looked elsewhere for the cause of Turk's murder. And he had little doubt it was related to something he had learned about the narcotics.

As he drove, he tried to make sense out of it all. But he didn't really care. Turk was his old man's problem. And sixty million dollars in junk was Bobby's problem. Tiger's problem was to figure a way to get his family the hell out of town.

Toward the end of the week things began to happen. Tiger still hadn't heard from Pete. He hoped his friend didn't decide to abscond with his five million. Joe the Boss still clung to life, and the newspapers hung on every medical report. The longer he lingered, the more the reporters speculated in wild rumors.

On Friday morning Tiger arrived at the office to find a totally annoyed Ralphie.

"What's up?" asked Tiger.

"Your father's creep was here, waiting, when I opened up this morning."

"Toto?" asked a wide-eyed Tiger. "What the hell did he want?"

Ralphie held out a small manila envelope. "The lousy bastard stood there staring at me for ten minutes before he let me have the damn letter."

Tiger laughed. "That's why my father keeps him around, to make people nervous."

"Well, I hope to hell he does read minds, because I kept thinking, 'SUCK MY PRICK. SUCK MY PRICK.' "

Tiger couldn't contain his laughter. Ralphie found it contagious and joined in.

Leuci, the accountant, emerged from his office wearing

69

a somber expression. "It just came over the radio. Joe the Boss is dead."

Ralphie stopped laughing and let out a low whistle. "Shit. It looks like there's gonna be a gala funeral. You going?"

Tiger shrugged. "Not unless I have to." Joe the Boss wasn't one of Tiger's favorite people. Lately, against the Council's instructions, the Boss began publicly moving into politics. Associating with politicians was an ego trip, and he stupidly allowed a nigger photographer to bullshit him into stepping away from his bodyguard for a picture, winding up with three slugs in him. Even so, he managed to live for a week.

In his private office, Tiger read the note: "Pick me up at eight."

It was unsigned, but he recognized his father's bold handwriting and wondered, what now? Could his old man have got some whiff? About what? Camille? The money? He backtracked his movements, recalling nothing that could have tripped him up. He felt whatever his father wanted, it had nothing to do with Camille or the money.

He pulled out the toy frog clicker, wondering if it would really work when he met up with Toto. He hoped so. Otherwise, there was going to be a bloody killing, and he hoped it wasn't going to be his.

T HE door to his office suddenly burst open. Sonny, dirty, disheveled, his eyes webbed with red, was thrown up against the wall. Ralphie held him, looking at Tiger.

"He shot past me, Tiger."

"What do you want here, Sonny?" asked Tiger coldly.

His brother tried to break loose, but Ralphie's grip was like iron.

"You got to help me, Tiger. You got to."

Tiger turned his back. "Get him the hell out of here."

"They needled me, Tiger! They needled me!" screamed Sonny, struggling furiously against Ralphie. Tiger turned back and for the first time noticed the signs of withdrawal. Damn, he thought.

He signaled Ralphie to loosen up. "God, Sonny, why do you do this to yourself?"

Now he knew why he hadn't heard from nor seen his brother in over a week, and he now knew it was Sonny who had wrecked his home. Forty grand buys a lot of junk, he said to himself. Together they helped Sonny into the comfortable armchair. From the smell of him, Tiger guessed Sonny had not taken a bath in a week.

"Why, Sonny? Why?"

"They kept me a week, Tiger," he sobbed. "They kept giving me needle after needle, laughing at me all the time."

Sonny quickly pulled up his sleeve, exposing the scabbed needle tracks. At the sight of the punctures, anger surged up in Tiger. He remembered the destruction of his home. He turned his back on his brother and looked out the window.

"Get him out of here, Ralphie," Tiger spat out. "I don't know what you can do with him, but get him the hell away from me."

Ralphie reached under Sonny's arm and roughly hauled him to his feet. Sonny broke away, ran around the desk, and threw himself on his knees, his arms around Tiger's legs.

"Please, Tiger, please!"

Tiger kicked free and walked away. Over his shoulder he spat at Ralphie. "Get him the hell away from me. Do it before I kill the bastard."

Sonny crawled to his brother. "Don't do this to me, Tiger. Please don't."

Suddenly Tiger grabbed his brother by the lapels, stood him up, and slammed him against the wall. "Tell me what I owe you, little brother," he said, his voice purring with hate. "Tell me what I owe you for what you did to my home?"

"I didn't do it, Tiger," he protested. "I just let them in,

71

and . . . and they went crazy. They even took the money. I didn't do it."

Tiger's eyes narrowed. "You let someone into my home?"

"You don't understand, they promised me Helen. They promised me . . . "

Tiger was close to tears, even though he was choking with rage. "You destroyed my home for that fucking cunt?" asked Tiger, shaking his brother like a rag doll. Sonny tried to wiggle loose, but Tiger's grip sent him limp. In disgust, Tiger let his brother fall to the floor.

Sonny lay on the floor, tears falling down his cheeks as he sobbed, "I remembered it was Papa's house, that's why I did it. I wanted to hurt him," he sobbed. "I needed the bastard and he pissed on me."

He buried his face in the rug and rocked back and forth in sobs. Tiger tried to hold on to the level of his anger, but watching his brother in tears drained him. He turned to Ralphie, who was still standing by like an alert Doberman.

"It's okay, Ralphie. I'll take care of him."

Ralphie nodded and walked to the door. Tiger called after him. "I need you to do me a favor."

"Name it."

"Look in Pete's black book. You'll find the number for Doctor Epstein. Call him and tell him I need to get Sonny into a cure center right away."

An hour after Dr. Epstein took Sonny away in an ambulance, Tiger still sat there, tasting the bittersweet tang of his stupid love for his brother.

Ralphie stuck his head in the door. "O-nine."

Tiger removed the phone from the drawer. "Yeah?"

"I got a lead," said an excited Bobby. "Iggy's people might be involved."

Tiger's brows shot up. "Are you sure?"

"Your old friend *uno occhio il donnola* told the Jamaicans to get their money ready."

Damn, thought Tiger, slowly letting his breath out. "Shit, Bobby. You really can pick the winners."

One Eye the Weasel was a two-bit dealer, real name Luigi Zaccone. To Tiger, he was a pimp and a degenerate. A product of the streets of Genoa, in northern Italy. To Tiger, all Italians living outside Sicily were Germans, Nazis, men of little honor, Teutonic whores who spent their history raping Sicily. The Weasel was no different and Tiger hated him.

Now Weasel was obviously looking to move into the big time. Tiger's laugh was caustic. "I guess the Irish steal it, the Italians sell it, and the Sicilians get the blame for it."

"That's about the size of it," agreed Bobby.

MOMMA greeted him with a wide smile and a cheery hello. This time she opened the box of cookies and ate two of them. He made a mental note to bring a larger box next time. For the past week, her condition had improved markedly and her vitality delighted him. They bantered back and forth for a few minutes before she abruptly changed the subject. "How is Sonny?"

Tiger wondered if his brother had been bugging her with his problems. "He's in the hospital taking the cure again."

She accepted that without comment. "And how are you?"

"I am fine, Momma," he said softly.

She studied his features a long time. "Your eyes tell me you have many troubles, but you hide them well."

He smiled gently. "I have only little ones, Momma."

Tiger knew this was going to lead somewhere. "Sonny will be all right, Momma," he said, but she ignored his statement.

"Sonny is like a little boy. He is weak because I made him

73

that way. I did not want him strong like you and Papa. I did not want him learning the ways of the hard life, but now I know it was wrong of me." She paused, then continued. "If Sonny had been born in Sicily, he would be dead. In Sicily there is no love, and where there is no love, the weak die."

Tiger had often heard stories of the hard life of the old timers, the bitter struggles, the coldness and indifference that resulted. But he wondered sometimes if what he saw as coldness was really fatalistic acceptance, asking nothing, giving nothing, living moment to moment. Or was it lethargy, laziness . . . or none of these things?

Tiger knew there was no love in Sicily. How could there be? The Greeks, Romans, Arabs, French, Italians, and the greedy Sicilian landowners had made them a displaced people in their own backyard. Three thousand years of rape and exploitation had taken their toll, leaving the Sicilians nothing, no land, no nation, and no identity. Alone, they became individuals, no longer a great culture, but instead a segmented cluster of single families with a great common bond *sangue,* or blood. The bloodline molded them together against the *stranieri,* the outsiders. Their treachery, and the cry of "*Sangue di mie sangue,*"—"Blood of my blood,"—became their banner of protection against the world. With their new-found understanding of themselves, they sat back, watched, and waited for the world to pass them by. The people of Sicily became the people time forgot.

The weakest, Tiger knew, often chose suicide to escape their plight, but the Church outlawed that, leaving them only the vendetta, believing that God would somehow hold them blameless if killed in an affair of honor. It was convoluted logic, but they could live with it. They had nothing else to believe in.

"Since," continued his mother, "Sonny could not live without love, I asked Papa to send him to the university. Sonny liked to draw gentle pictures of children. But after a year in school, they filled his head with strange, crazy ideas, bad ideas. Suddenly he was always unhappy and making everyone around him unhappy. But you must understand, he is unhappy because he is weak, and he is weak because I made him that way."

"I understand, Momma," said Tiger softly, but he didn't understand at all. The message his mother was sending didn't get through to him.

IT was late in the evening when Tiger left the hospital. He crossed the parking lot and came upon two men sitting on the hood of his car. They were lawmen, Tiger was certain of that. From their neat grooming, he figured Feds.

"Can I help you gentlemen?"

The taller one reminded Tiger of the comic strip character Smilin' Jack. He wore a devil-may-care smile as if from a computer program. Tiger could almost see the instructions: SMILE. The man's jacket was open and his .38 was exposed.

"You have a nice visit with Momma?" asked Smilin' Jack.

The blood rushed to Tiger's head, but he knew it had to be a setup. He turned swiftly at a sound to the side, where two more agents were closing in, one of them tall, black, with shoulders like a linebacker.

Tiger stood still, waiting. But Smilin' Jack didn't move.

"My friends have been dying to meet the big shot Dago they call Tiger," he said coolly.

What kind of game they were playing, Tiger didn't know; but he knew it was a game, so he decided to make a move of his own. "Now that we've met, you mind getting your ass off my car?"

Slowly Smilin' Jack slid off the hood with his computer-generated smile still in place. His sidekick just sat there.

Smilin' Jack said, "You hear that, boys? The big bad Tiger is showing his teeth."

The black agent snickered. "Yeah, I hear he's one tough greaseball."

Tiger looked at the man and could see that the black man didn't have a taste for the words.

"He looks like a fag to me," said the insolent agent with his feet on the hood.

"I bet he sucks, too," said Smilin' Jack, laughing.

Tiger restrained another surge of anger. His head pounded.

"I hear your old man is a big shot," said the smiling agent. "You a big shot too?"

A glimmer of understanding broke through the fog. Suddenly he knew the name of the game. Tiger figured that as long as he remained still, he was in no danger. Turning around, he looked deep into a camera and another cleaned-and-pressed Fed. Shit, thought Tiger, the bastards wanted a picture of him hitting a Federal agent.

"If you guys are finished jerking off," said Tiger loudly into the camera, "get to the point and tell me what the fuck you want?"

Clearly, Smilin' Jack was having trouble keeping the smile on his face.

"I'm glad you said that," answered Jack, his voice suddenly grating. "We got a message for you. We're going to get you and your greasy old man the same way we got Joe the Boss."

The two men glared at each other. Stand-off. Suddenly Tiger looked beyond Smilin' Jack to someone in the parking lot. He shouted, "Can I see you a moment, Doctor?"

The three agents turned their heads. Tiger slipped past them in a single motion, and looking back at them over the roof of the car, said, "Goodnight, gentlemen."

As Tiger parked, he thought of the incident in the parking lot. It seemed to Tiger to have been one hell of a stupid and clumsy move, and such desperation frightened him. He had always thought the Feds a class act, but not anymore.

76

From a pay phone he dialed the office and heard Ralphie's "Yeah?"

"It's me."

"The Weasel is operating out of a club in Harlem. The Kit Kat Klub," said Ralphie.

"What have his movements been like?"

"The contact says he's been running from Harlem to the Bronx, Queens, Manhattan, the Island. Oh, and one trip to Newark. He seems to be only contacting known dealers, and strictly high caliber."

"Anything else?"

"Nothing," answered Ralphie.

After hanging up the phone, Tiger guessed his friend the Weasel was setting up a network for someone.

TIGER was surprised at seeing his father standing alone at the curb. It made him comfortable to feel the Beretta under his arm and the frog clicker in his pocket. As his father settled into the passenger seat, he wondered where Toto was. He said, "Where are we going?"

"Bay Parkway Funeral Home."

Tiger wondered why his old man would visit Joe the Boss's funeral. His father had hated Joe's guts.

"How come?"

Don Corso produced an elaborate imitation of surprise. "Why shouldn't I pay my respects to a dear old friend?"

OUTSIDE the funeral parlor stood a line of limousines being eyed by a squadron of plainclothes cops and Federal agents, who were busy jotting down license numbers.

Tiger pulled to the curb in front of the undertaker's,

where a dozen hardfaces rushed to open the door for his father.

Inside the opulent lobby, the banked flowers and the raspy chattering of the crowd combined to produce a sense of camaraderie, rather than of a ceremony of death.

In the main hall, Joe the Boss's body rested in a black ebony coffin lined with white satin. A fresh lily rested beneath his palms. In this room, things were quieter. Here the floral smells were overpowering. Relatives and family friends prayed. The weeping widows wailed their death chants. Tiger went to the catafalque, stood looking down at Joe the Boss's body and smiled inwardly. He thought the fat bastard never looked better.

His father spoke a eulogy and, having heard it all before, Tiger only half listened. His father spoke of love for his fallen friend Joe Bocci, and Tiger was almost driven to laughter. Every damn Sicilian funeral he ever attended became a circus, punctuated by wild gestures of piety. Like Shakespearian actors, each in turn took center stage to express his love for the one reposing in the coffin. To Tiger's experience, the greater the display of tragic emotions, the more likely the mourner was blowing smoke.

He looked toward his eulogizing father, who smiled sadly at everyone, while black-draped women sniffled and wiped their tears away. A dozen hardfaces had tears in their eyes, and Tiger wondered which of these loyal underlings had set up Joe's hit. And the more his father talked, the more he became convinced that his old man had a finger in the pie.

As the next actor took center stage, his father eased him slowly through the crowd, across the hall, and into a private room, where a half dozen unsmiling men were sitting in silence. Tiger recognized his father-in-law, Tommy "The Lip" Ippolito, and one or two others.

His father surprised him by formally introducing him to each in turn—even to his father-in-law. Then he was quickly eased from the room.

"Wait for me in the car," murmured his father.

In the car, Tiger tried to fit some of the pieces together. His father's actions were odd. Unless? Unless his old man was moving to have him made. If so, why now? He knew he was long overdue, but why so sudden? Could this be, he wondered, the opening stroke in a plan to use him as they did Patsy? His mind turned the questions over and over, and got nowhere.

After an hour, his father emerged from the funeral parlor, followed by a half-dozen hardfaces who climbed into the car behind them. As he turned the car key, he wondered idly why his father suddenly felt the need for bodyguards.

His father smiled expansively. "Let's have a nice pleasant dinner at Lulu's."

Tiger pulled smoothly into traffic and hoped Toto wouldn't be at the restaurant. As he drove he knew he didn't want to dwell on the private meeting in the funeral home, so he said:

"Do you know about the ripoff at the property clerk's?"

He sensed a hesitation in his father. "What about it?"

"They tell me the two cops Uncle Patsy hit worked there," said Tiger, "and sixty million in junk has been taken."

Tiger kept his eyes on the road but knew his father was looking at him. "So?"

"So, I hear the Weasel and his friends have the junk and intend to dump it in our territories."

Now he knew for sure his old man was studying him. "Who are the friends?"

Tiger shrugged. "Don't know. I just know Weasel isn't smart enough to run it himself."

He drove four blocks before his father spoke again. "Who else knows of this?"

"Bobby Cassaro." And after a pause, "Turk was my tip."

He wished he had the balls to look at his father to see what the answer evoked.

"I'll look into it," his father finally said.

Tiger felt let down. He had thrown the bait at his father,

but his father wasn't biting. "Should I keep digging or drop it?" he asked.

After a long silence his father said, "Continue."

He was surprised by the answer.

TIGER's father deposited the hardfaces at a rear table, while he and Tiger passed through into a private dining room.

Inside, Tiger found the small room comfortable. He had never visited it before, and he found he liked the plush decor, the fine quality landscapes, and the leather furnishings. His Uncle Lulu was a large man who enjoyed lots of laughter, but this night he quietly took their orders and tactfully withdrew.

"Did you know who those men were I introduced you to?"

Tiger hesitated for only a second. "They were the Council."

His father raised his brows, impressed. "And do you know why I brought you here?"

Tiger was uncertain. His father never asked a question lightly. "I think you're moving to make me a *button*."

The violent reaction was instant and his father's face turned sour. "A soldier?" he said, his alarming expression deepening. "With a thousand soldiers on my payroll, I need another one?" He spat the words at Tiger. "Do you think I wasted forty years on you, to make you play soldier?"

Tiger felt the sting, like pellets of icy sleet. "I guess that didn't come out right."

It seemed forever before the frost left his father's eyes. The tension continued as Lulu came in, followed by two waiters, and began serving the food. Tiger's tension eased a bit. After the antipasto, his father looked up, using his fork for emphasis.

80

"If there is one thing I learned in the old country," he said, "it's that a bold strike at the right moment can win a war." He paused for a bite of food, letting that sink in.

"Three days ago I knew Bocci had little chance to recover."

Tiger saw the eyes looking at him, but suddenly they went vacant. "That's when it came to me, a once-in-a-lifetime opportunity to make a master stroke."

His father's face was flushed with a strange, faraway expression, alone in his own private world of plotting. "Once Bocci died I knew his family was up for grabs unless someone protected it. And . . . "

Tiger ate slowly, not tasting his food.

"I finally convinced the Council that it would be in their best interests to hold off the raiders until a suitable replacement could be found to head the new Bocci family."

Tiger was almost afraid to breathe.

"I told the Council I had such a man in mind. A man whose career they all knew, a man who's shown a careful respect for money and organization."

Don Corso paused a moment, took a sip of wine and looked intently at his son over the rim of his glass. "I have submitted your name as head of the new Bocci family."

Tiger's head spun. He had difficulty grasping his father's words. A boss? Me? He was dumbfounded. He'd sensed his old man might be leading up to a lieutenancy or even a captaincy. But to jump over consigliere and inferiore capo to capo was beyond belief. It was too much for Tiger to absorb. Through the swirl of words, he thought of the five million he spent with Pete and now saw the money in a new light. It paled in comparison to this possibility. And perhaps, he thought, Uncle Patsy's problems were personal and not family.

His father stopped talking and was narrowly looking at him. "You're not pleased?"

Tiger couldn't help but laugh giddily. "I've been hit by a train."

Don Corso sipped his wine and let the silence build.

81

Then he said, "Bocci was the smallest of families, but with the raw materials at hand, it could be the biggest. As its head you would control half the major unions, and with them you control everything that moves in this city. The Bocci family also has considerable legitimate business interests: cheese to control the pizza industry; laundries and private carting to control restaurants; license distributors to control bars; and meat packing plants, combined with trucking, to control the meat industry."

His father paused to sip his wine. "And in addition there are investments in shopping centers, department stores, fish and produce terminals, banks, hotels, loan companies, shipping, transportation, and many others."

His father continued. "Joe the Boss became lazy from too much good living. He had come a long way from the hungry streets. He treated his family badly, letting good operations stagnate. He became involved in politics, while he constantly looked around for fast-buck deals. Forgetting the family cannot survive on fast-buck deals."

Tiger was fascinated by the picture being painted. He also now knew his father was behind the Bocci killing. If not directly, he was in the background somewhere, reminding Tiger of his father's ambition to control the Bocci family for himself. With Tiger installed as capo, his father would have it all.

His father sighed. "You must understand that before the Council turns over such power to anyone, they will need the assurances that the one selected will accept the Council's judgment and support them against anyone they consider an enemy."

"And what if they decide you have become an enemy?" His father's answer was slow in coming. "I will stand by any decisions they make."

Shit, thought Tiger. That answer told him his father was very, very high in the Council. He had to be; he wouldn't leave himself open to be judged by his enemies otherwise.

He mulled over his father's words and knew any killings he had to do wouldn't bother him. Korea had stolen that virginity. But he didn't like other people picking his targets for him. Tiger didn't like living with the nightmares chosen by other people.

"Can I sleep on it?"

"I will need an answer by the end of the week. I want to move fast before the greedy ones do."

Tiger took a moment before speaking. "And if I decide against it?"

Don Corso slowly sipped his wine. "Then I have made a mistake and badly misjudged you."

T IGER was thankful for the long drive home. He needed to find some answers. He needed to balance the years of suspicion and distrust against the thought that maybe, after all, his father was finally wanting to do something for him, trying to give his life some meaning. On the other hand, there was the evidence of Patsy's letter, the money, and Camille. There was his mother's shattered mind and his aunt's fears. There were years of bitter rejection, aloneness, indifference. And yet there was this new offer, this apparent willingness to entrust him with great authority, the idea that his father might have all these years been preparing him for the terrible demands of the hard, lonely life at the top, where great power could only be attained at the cost of love and compassion.

As he drove, his muscles responded to the demands of the road. He tried to put aside his long-standing resentment, his impatience with the restraints imposed by the structure of the family. He tried to see the needs of the system. It seemed at a glance that the skilled men who made the family work smoothly had to be able to hold onto their individuality; but they had also to accept certain controls and restraints. And the family's success depended on a healthy balance—that, too, he could see.

From the Council to the street bankers, every member of

the family could maintain his individuality if they all worked toward a common goal. There was strength in unity—that had been the whole foundation of the Unione de Siciliano in the first place, back in the Middle Ages. It was unity that produced the benefits; the money that was needed so the family members could take care of their own, raise families, and live with some pride and satisfaction.

What Tiger craved at one moment became ashes the next. The money, his family, his operations, his friends, his father, the Bocci family, Camille, Sonny, and his mother became strands in a web in which he was entangled and bound. The more he was entangled, the more his brain struggled to free himself.

And threading through the whole web was the question of whether or not he could juggle the act of being boss of the Bocci family as long as Toto sat like a shadow of evil behind his father, reading his mind.

Boss, he thought and grinned, without humor. Some boss.

In the distance, out of the corner of his eye, he spotted the headlights. Whoever it was kept a discreet distance. But Tiger, fed up with being the prey, decided to bring the game to a head.

He traveled slow and steady toward the area bordering the swamp, always mindful of keeping the flickering headlights at a safe distance.

The mountains of derelict vehicles loomed up to the right, as Tiger inched along the pock-marked surface with lights out. Tiger parked in front of Tony's office, shut the engine, pulled the pistol from the seat panel, and quietly got out of the car. Further down the road, he found a derelict truck, hid behind it, and waited.

Soon the soft crunch of tires could be heard as the vehicle crawled over the rutted road. Tiger remained motionless as the large shadow passed. Tiger was surprised to see only one person in the car. Quickly he jumped into the road behind the vehicle and jogged slowly in pursuit.

The darkened car parked alongside a huge crane and cut its engine. Crouching below the line of sight, Tiger knew the man was observing the area. After a moment the car door clicked softly and the man slipped out and stood listening.

"Freeze!" shouted Tiger, moving swiftly to his right to put distance between himself and his voice. His move was none too soon. A pistol flashed, and using the flash as a bearing point, he fired a spread of four shots, two to the left, two to the right. He was rewarded by a surprised grunt and a falling body. Tiger stood immobile, waiting and listening. Then he moved to the right, keeping the vehicle between him and the target. Roughly estimating where the body had fallen, he flashed his light on and quickly off. The momentary illumination revealed a body on the ground. Rushing back to the rear, he flashed his light again from a different angle. Satisfied, he stood, taking a moment to catch his breath.

Keeping the light steady, he approached the still form. Kicking the pistol away, he used his toe to turn over the lifeless body. He had never seen the man before.

Bending down, he reached into the man's hip pocket and removed a leather case that opened to reveal a gold and blue detective's shield and identification card. Piss, piss, piss, thought Tiger, just what I needed, to kill a cop.

Searching the body, he found a set of house keys, police identification, a few dollars, and an extra clip of bullets. Picking up the man's pistol, he examined it, wondering when the New York Police Department began issuing silencers.

Ten minutes later he had the body stuffed in the trunk of the man's car. He lit a cigarette and leaned back against the car and waited.

Twenty minutes later, when Tony arrived, he explained his problem. Tony remained silent for a moment, then jumped into his fork lift, kicked off the powerful engine, and shoved the long steel tines under the car body and raised it to the edge of the empty car press. Dropping the policeman's car into the pit, he climbed the steel ladder to the tower. The walls of the huge press began to crush the vehicle.

A moment later a smoking cube of crushed steel slid down the ramp and rested with the other bales.

Leaving Tony's scrapyard, Tiger headed home. He was exhausted when he pulled into the driveway. He cut the engine and sat a moment waiting for a few barking dogs to settle down. He was glad Jeanne had left the front porch light burning. It helped brighten his gloom.

"Tiger."

It was a harsh whisper from the shadows. He froze with his hand on the doorknob, calculating distances, ready for the lunge.

"It's me. Pete."

Tiger relaxed, unlocked the door, and threw off the light switch. "Come in quick."

A shadow passed Tiger and on into the house. Tiger locked the door behind him.

"It took three hours to sneak past those damn dogs in this neighborhood," said Pete.

"I hope you do better with the two standing next to you."

"Shit," said Pete as Satan and Devil sniffed at him.

In the finished basement, Pete made himself comfortable as the two Dobermans completed their inspection.

"You hungry?" asked Tiger.

"I'm starved."

"Let's see what the dogs left."

"Thanks," said Pete.

The two men went upstairs to the kitchen. "Where did you finally settle down?"

"Florida. I picked up a twenty-four-hundred-acre tract halfway between Ocala and Daytona. It used to be a ranch, but it went broke. I picked it up for less than two million."

"What's it like?"

"The main house is on a lake in the middle of the property. It has eight bedrooms, boulder construction, oak beams a foot thick. It's a fortress."

Tiger was pouring water into the coffee machine. He grunted, "Sounds good."

"Well, I rigged the bridge leading to the island, so we can blow it from the house. I also had a contractor build a tunnel under the lake, coming out beneath the boulders, with a camouflaged Volkswagen hidden there."

"How about supplies?"

"Enough for a year and enough weapons to start a war," said Pete. He reached into his pocket and threw two folded papers on the table.

"What's this?" asked Tiger.

"The legal paper on top is your deed. It's a quit-claim deed. A Bahamian shell that you own is the owner of record."

Tiger studied the other paper. It was a map with three X's on it. "And this?"

"A map showing the spread and the road leading in and out, and the swampy part. The little dots are an escape route through the swamp. The X's are where the bodies are buried. Waterproof plastic boxes in steel-bound boxes."

"How much?" asked Tiger.

"Just over three million. That's why I put it in three places."

"That much?" said a surprised Tiger.

"And it's clean."

Tiger smiled. "You did a hell of a job."

"I know," smiled back Pete.

Tiger chewed thoughtfully on his sandwich. What a waste, he said to himself. Instead of building an empire, I may be building a mausoleum. He picked up the coffee pot.

"Bring the cups. We'll be more comfortable in the den."

Pete followed him back down the stairs to the basement and relaxed in a chair. "So when do we make the big move?"

"The picture has changed."

"Oh?" said Pete carefully.

Tiger quickly brought his friend up to date, ending with his father's offer to make him a boss.

Pete sat silently, staring, his usual bantering manner for once stilled. When he spoke, it was with an attempt to recover himself.

"Damn, I can't leave you alone for a minute."

Tiger laughed. "I guess not."

"How do you intend to handle this?" asked Pete.

Tiger shrugged. "Damned if I know."

Pete was silent for a moment, then said, "Is there any chance this is one of your old man's games?"

Tiger thought a moment, then shook his head. "I don't think so. He's greedy and he'd spit blood to get his hands on the Bocci operations."

Pete sat staring at Tiger. "You want to get rid of Toto?"

Tiger returned the cool look. "It won't be easy. He's got instincts like an animal."

"So did the Gooks," said Pete, "but we put away a lot of them, didn't we?"

Tiger studied him carefully. Toto was different, maybe not even human. "The Angel of Death sees things before they happen," said Tiger.

"That's bullshit," said Pete.

Tiger measured him. "You want to take that chance?"

Pete's lips tightened. "Hell, no, but I'll take him out with a long shot."

Tiger shook his head and again had the feeling of being tangled in a web. "If we hit Toto, my father will see it as a move against the family. Then when nothing happens, if there is no follow-up, he'll get suspicious and start digging. Then he'll find us."

A chill ran down Pete's spine. "Shit. Maybe I should hit a lot of people to make it look good."

Tiger smiled inwardly at Pete's madness. He rose to his feet, walked to a cabinet in the corner, unlocked it. "Maybe there is a better way," he said. He removed a small vial of clear liquid and held it up for Pete's inspection.

"Nitro?"

"In this house?" answered a shocked Tiger.

"Then what is it?"

"It's the base for nerve gas. It was stolen from the army six months ago. It's a penetrant chemical combined with prussic acid."

Pete reached up as Tiger put the vial in his hand. Pete stared at it as if expecting it to show its deadliness. "What do you do with it?"

"You paint a dab of it on a doorknob, a cup handle, or any surface. If someone should touch that surface, they will be dead within the hour."

"Are you serious?"

"You bet I am."

"Christ!" was all Pete could say.

"Neat, too. The heart stops. No sign of why. No messy blood or broken bones. No traces. Just a stopped heart and a dead body," said Tiger.

Pete suddenly burst into laughter. "I'll take a gallon, Tiger. I'll leave bodies all over the place," he said, his features turning sober. "Have you tested it yet?"

"On a couple of Tony's junkyard dogs," said Tiger.

Pete's eyes suddenly narrowed as enlightenment came into them.

"You sneak," he said in awe. "You were going to hit him yourself, weren't you?"

Tiger looked innocent. "I'd thought about it."

"Thought about it, hell," shot back Pete, as he jumped to his feet. "Look, Tiger, no one knows I'm back. It's perfect for me to hit him. Besides, I want to make my bones in your new family."

Tiger considered that. "On one condition."

"Name it," said Pete.

"You don't move without me. You understand?"

Pete smiled. "You got it. Now can I start clocking Toto?"

Again Tiger hoped his expression looked innocent. "I already have."

Pete grinned. "You sneaky bastard."

As he made breakfast, Tiger was glad Jeanne was out with the kids. He needed time this morning for thinking. He knew Toto was the key to everything. With him out of the picture, he could breathe easier and maneuver his way around his father.

When Tiger started his clock on Toto, he was prepared for the worst. But after two days he was shocked to find the man was a creature of habit. True, he always traveled by a circuitous route to wherever he was heading; but he always showed up at the same places at the same times. He learned Toto had a girlfriend hidden away in an apartment on 86th Street. He visited her always between two and eight in the morning after he dropped off Don Corso.

Each trip was by a different route, but no matter what direction he came from, he always ended up in the alley behind the apartment house. Once in the alley, he sneaked through the boiler room, through the long tunnel with the door at the end, which led to the apartment house hallway. What apartment the girlfriend lived in didn't matter to Tiger. He was only interested in the door at the end of the tunnel. That was his target.

The vial contained enough liquid for three dabs, each good for seven to ten minutes. After that it was harmless.

The phone rang and snapped him back to the present. For an instant, he wished someone would hit the bastard who invented the telephone.

"Yeah?"

"You read today's papers?" asked Ralphie, in an agitated state.

"No," Tiger answered, picking up the papers Jeanne had left on the table. "They're right here. What's up?"

"You better read them before you come in."

As Tiger drove past his office, he saw a small army of people milling around the front door. Rocky and Corky were blocking the entrance. Shit, thought Tiger, hoping it wasn't another raid. He drove the car into a parking lot and walked back to one of his stores. His cousin Dada was on duty this morning, so Tiger took over the office. He called Ralphie.

"What the hell's going on?" he asked.

"Reporters," said Ralphie evenly.

"Shit," said an annoyed Tiger. "I'm at Dada's."

"See you," said Ralphie, cutting the connection.

Tiger remembered the account in one of the papers: "A source close to the investigation traced the gun used in the Bocci shooting to a Cleveland pawn shop." It went on to say that the pistol was purchased by a check drawn against one of Tiger's companies. Now the newspapers were playing it up as between the Corso and Bocci families.

It was better than twenty minutes before Ralphie showed.

"What the hell took you so long?"

"I had to shake a nosy reporter," explained Ralphie.

"What did you find out?"

Ralphie sat at the desk. "The spade who shot Joe the Boss did use one of our checks."

"Says who?" snapped Tiger.

"The bank. They say it cleared today. It was one of your checks."

The thought made Tiger sick and he knew he was being set up.

"Then we have a snitch in the office."

"I don't think so," said Ralphie, shaking his head.

Tiger waited, watchful and silent.

"I looked at the check number. Do you remember Marie's saying checks were missing after the raid a couple months ago?"

"This was one of those checks?" asked Tiger.

"You got it."

Tiger sank in his chair. "Then the cops set up the Bocci hit."

"Or the Feds."

Tiger took a moment to absorb that. "What about the spook?"

"Nobody in the street knows him. I'm checking with the people in Harlem now."

"Could it be he's an import?"

"Anything's possible. That's why I have everyone out on this one," said Ralphie, who thought a moment before continuing. "Is there any chance the family did the hit?"

Tiger's eyebrows shot up. "You kidding? With ten thousand troops on the streets, they need a hambone to do their dirty work?" Besides, thought Tiger, tradition dictated that family matters be handled by family members.

"Then it was the fucking law that did the hit," said Ralphie.

Tiger nodded and took a moment to do some heavy thinking.

"I think it's time I called in some markers and try to find out what this is all about."

Ralphie nodded. "Oh, there's a roll of film being delivered to the office later. I think you'll want to see it."

"What for?"

"It's the only piece of evidence on the Bocci killing the law didn't confiscate."

Tiger showed his surprise. "Where did you get it?"

"One of our porno cameramen was free-lancing, covering the rally. He forgot about it until yesterday."

Tiger called Dada over. He was a giant of a man, some

six and a half feet tall, powerfully put together, as light as a dancer. "Go to the office with Ralphie. He's got some film. Take it over to the Lippos' and stay with it until I get there."

He turned to Ralphie. "I'll see you at Cobra's, and stay on your toes in case the Bocci boys believe that bullshit in the newspapers."

"You gonna talk to your old man about this?" asked Ralphie.

"Hell, no," he said, walking toward the rear of the store. "If you need me for anything, I'll be at the hospital."

In the hospital, he found his mother radiant and smiling. As he greeted her, the news came bursting out of her. "Papa was here, Joey." The love in her eyes and voice shocked and surprised him.

"He was here and he said he would take me home. He said he knew all about Camille, but he would forgive her."

Tiger didn't like any of this. How did his father find out? He had to know. With his mother so bubbly, he didn't have the heart to dampen her joy, but . . .

"Isn't that good, Joey, that Papa will make peace with Camille, and I can see her again?"

Tiger didn't want to put a pin in her bubble, but he had to have some answers. If not, everyone might find themselves with a noose around their necks.

"When did Papa come here, Momma, what time?"

"Early this morning, and we talked for over an hour."

"Did he say how he knew about Camille?" he asked, speaking softly so as not to alarm her.

She shook her head as she nibbled a cookie. "Papa knew. He just knew. You know, Joey, Papa always knows everything."

So someone tipped his father. He knew it wasn't Camille or Angelina. So who? Tiger chose his words carefully.

93

"Who was with Papa? Was he alone?" he asked, thinking of Toto.

"He was alone, Joey," she said, handing him a cookie.

Well, thought Tiger, that's one idea out of the way.

"But the silent one was out in the hall."

Tiger relaxed slightly, hoping it was Toto and not a hidden snitch. "Momma, what did Camille do to Papa so many years ago?"

The pain returned to her eyes. "It was so long ago. Papa said it was time to forget," she said, as she clutched his sleeve. "Do you think he lied?"

Pained by her expression, he lied. "No, Momma, no." But in the back of his mind he knew Sicilians never forgave or forgot. He had once heard someone say, "A thousand years after a Sicilian dies, he still remembers."

He looked gently down at her. "If Papa said it is time to forget, then it is time to forget."

Her face struggled toward an attempt to smile again. "But Papa did say Camille must never come to the house again, ever. But I could go see her. That's good, no?" she said, her smile returning.

It took a great effort to smile warmly at her. "You get better, Momma. Everything is going to be fine," he said, not believing it but trying to reassure her.

"Will you take me to Camille's?" she asked gently.

"Yes, Momma."

TIGER sat in the Lippos' office with Dada, Ralphie, and the four brothers. The screen was set up at the end of the darkened room. The only sound was the thuttering of the film through the projector. The screen was filled with masses of people, flags, banners, and the madness that accompanies political rallies. The only person Tiger recognized was Joe the Boss, mugging for the cameras.

"He acts like the fucking pope," said Godzilla.

"Who's the skinny guy with Bocci?" asked Tiger.

"That's Conroy," answered Ralphie.

"What's he do?"

"He's the guy Bocci was backing for Congress."

"What the hell was he giving money to that Irish bastard for?"

Ralphie shrugged, "Who knows? He was a friend of Bocci's."

"Well, he ain't no more," said Tiger caustically.

The Lippo brothers laughed as Ralphie slowed the projector.

"This is where he gets hit."

In the silence, Tiger watched as the Boss moved in slow motion among the mass of people, smiling and shaking hands. Tiger saw a tall black man with a camera walk up to the Boss, who paused to listen to the man's question.

Suddenly Kong jumped to his feet and pointed wildly at the screen. "I know that black bastard!" he yelled, looking at Tiger.

Tiger chopped his arm at Ralphie, who quickly cut the machine.

"You know him?" asked a surprised Tiger.

Kong nodded vigorously, almost too excited to talk. "He hangs out at Dreamy's place."

Dreamy's Massage Parlor in Times Square was one of the several locations Tiger's operators used for shooting porno. Still photographers and cameramen used the place for the availability of live models, and at other times to get laid.

"How do you know it's the same guy?" Tiger asked.

"I wouldn't forget that bastard," said Kong. "Me and Dreamy gave him a beating one night."

"Why?"

"He took an attitude with one of the girls. He was a nasty bastard."

"Did you ever see him after that?" asked Tiger.

"Yeah, once or twice, but without the attitude."

Tiger glanced at Ralphie. "When this is over, take Kong to Dreamy's and see what you can dig up."

Ralphie nodded and restarted the projector. The photographer and Joe the Boss moved away from Bocci's bodyguards. The photographer posed Bocci in a less crowded spot, where Bocci started mugging for the camera.

"Look," shouted the Bear. "He's reaching under his jacket."

The black man shifted the camera to his left hand, quickly raised the pistol, fired once, twice, three times. All three shots hit the Boss.

A blur blocked out the camera for a second, and the blur became a man who charged the killer and wrestled him to the ground. People were running in all directions, fleeing. Bocci was still on his feet, swaying as he fought to remain standing, but his knees buckled and he collapsed. At that moment, the only person standing was a well-dressed Italian youth, who stepped up to the struggling black and shot him in the head.

"Reverse it, Ralphie," said Tiger. "Take it back to where the boss walked away from his bodyguards."

This time he carefully watched the movement of the young Italian, looking for a setup, thinking maybe the youth didn't want the black talking. Tiger noticed the young man had a briefcase as he milled about with the other bodyguards. As the first shot rang out, the youth reached into the briefcase. But suddenly it was knocked from his hand, and a short pudgy man fell upon it, covering his head for protection. The youth, in a wild frenzy of kicks, drove the pudgy man away, reached into the briefcase, drew out a pistol, rushed to the struggling killer, and shot him in the head. Then he dropped the pistol and disappeared into the crowd.

The bodyguard did what he was supposed to do. What disturbed Tiger was the sight of Bocci's bodyguards and advisers lying on the ground covering their heads while the young man executed the killer.

"Play that part back again," said Tiger. "There was a black chick in the background, near the photographer. She's almost out of focus. I want to see if they were together."

The scene started again. The girl was dressed casually in slacks and carried a large tote bag over her shoulder. Watching her, one could see plainly that she was trying to stay close to the photographer without appearing to do so.

At the moment the photographer was wrestled to the ground, Kong leaped up. "Look, she swiped his camera case!"

The girl coolly dropped the case into her tote bag and vanished into the crowd.

Now what the hell, Tiger asked himself, was so important about that case? Too small to hold a pistol. A grenade? Money? Drugs? He knew it was important as he looked coolly at Ralphie.

"Before you go to Dreamy's," he said, "get some blow-ups of the broad and see if we can find her."

T IGER sensed something wrong the moment he turned into his street. The dogs up and down the block were in an uproar. As he pulled into his driveway, he saw two of his neighbors waiting for him. Jeanne and the kids, he thought, Christ, and leaped out of the car.

"What's the matter?" he asked alertly.

The taller man nodded at the Oldsmobile parked across the street. "Cops," he said. "They wanted to bother Jeanne, but we stopped them."

"Thanks, Richie. Where's Jeanne?"

"In the house," Richie answered.

Tiger exhaled and relaxed the muscles in his shoulders. Two detectives came warily across the street toward him, expecting momentarily to be set upon by wild dogs. The rough-featured one held a white slip of paper in his left hand as he closed in on Tiger. "Are you Joseph Corso?"

Tiger nodded, wondering who was coming at him with a subpoena.

"The Special Grand Jury orders you to appear to give testimony in its investigation into organized crime."

Tiger snapped the paper from the detective. The other one said nervously, "It's only a job with us, Mister Corso."

Aᴄᴛᴇʀ dinner Tiger relaxed with his family. Jeanne buried herself in front of the television set. His eleven-year-old daughter Cathy did her homework as Tiger played gin rummy with his son Rosario. Playing cards was a passion with each. They spent hours cheating each other, with neither exposing the other when the cheating was detected.

Tiger enjoyed teaching Rosario his bag of tricks, more as an extension of his education than as preparation for a life of crime. To keep from being cheated.

Tiger's parents, like most Sicilians, believed the only schooling necessary was that taught by the parents. Institutional education was acceptable if it coincided with the parents' thinking.

Tiger didn't subscribe to this belief. Given half an education, he might have achieved something on his own. Tiger wouldn't allow his own children to grow up in a shadow world. Education was the answer. They would get schooling to combat the handicap of being his children.

Tiger's parents treated him with indifference, so he made it a point to treat his children as friends, with respect and knowledge of the values of the old ways, but not their practice.

Long ago he explained to Rosario it was normal for a son to emulate his father. A fine form of respect, but aping was dangerous because he should be his own man, with his own identity.

Tiger explained he was born in a different era, when one had to scramble for a living because the enemies of the Sicilians, the "outsiders," had them hemmed in. They had to fight every inch. It was the rules of those hard days that had shaped him, but those rules were not applicable to him, Rosario, in this day and age. But if he were to survive he would have to make a truce with the outsiders, blend with them, but never forget for a moment that they were the enemy.

T HE wide steps of the courthouse were teeming with people. Lawyers, cops, detectives, Feds, hoods, would-be hoods, reporters, and court clerks. Without a scorecard, Tiger couldn't tell the good guys from the bad guys.

The few people he did know he ignored, cautious of hidden cameras. He stood off by himself, while his father talked with Mike Rizzo, the family lawyer.

"A lot of Dagos are gonna spill their guts today," said a rough voice in his ear. Malone, thought Tiger, and moved away without turning. The fat cop circled around, moving quickly through the crowd to plant himself in front of Tiger.

"We'll see how tough you are after this day is over."

Tiger wondered if this fat bastard was behind his subpoena. He looked Malone in the eyes and said levelly, "Take a walk, you degenerate bastard."

Malone smirked, turned, and disappeared into the crowd. Mike Rizzo came over with Don Corso. "What did he want?"

"What else? To spread his good cheer."

Rizzo noticed Tiger's expression. "I'll have the bastard back in his cage soon."

"How long do I have to hang around here?" asked Tiger.

Rizzo shrugged. "Who knows? Maybe an hour, maybe a day, maybe a week."

"Shit."

"Remember, Tiger, when you get into the jury room, you don't answer any questions except the first one. Since you're not allowed a lawyer inside, and if you answer one question other than your name, you will have to answer all related questions. So just remember the little speech we rehearsed. Also, try to recall the first five and the last five questions they ask you. That might give us some idea where their investigation is heading."

Tiger nodded. He looked around him at the hardfaces in the crowd, wondering why he saw no blacks, Jews, or Irish. Maybe only Italians committed crimes, he thought to himself wryly. Or maybe it was because they were all so well organized, that no one knows they're around.

"Joseph Corso," announced the tubby court officer.

BOOK TWO

THE grand jury had all the dignity of a traffic court. A double row of grand jurors sat stone-faced as Tiger was sworn in and seated in the witness box. A heavy-set, pin-striped man sat at the counsel table, writing with furious speed. Tiger knew the man was deliberately ignoring him, trying to make him nervous. Suddenly the man looked up. He slowly rose to his feet, looking coldly at Tiger, with eyes that reminded Tiger of the movie *Jaws.*

"Are you Joseph Corso?"

"Yes, I am."

"Speak up so the jury can hear you."

It was a grating voice, one Tiger found abrasive, but remembering where he was he raised his voice a notch. "Yes, I am."

The man picked up some papers from the table, looked at Tiger, and said it again, "Please speak up. Are you Joseph Corso?"

103

Tiger just sat there not in the mood for this idiot.

"Please speak up. Are you Joseph Corso?"

Tiger repressed an urge to get up, walk over to the man, and slap him silly. Instead, he gave him a look that dismissed him as of no account. "I'm talking as loud as I intend to."

The questioner stepped in closer to the witness box. "Of course, Mister Corso, you are a man accustomed to command, aren't you?"

Tiger sensed the trap the man had laid and remained silent.

"I asked you a question, Mister Corso."

Tiger continued to ignore him. The man turned to rake the jury with a look of triumph as he asked, "Are you the son of tough Tony Corso?"

Lawyer Rizzo had instructed him to answer only to his name, the first question, and then: "I refuse to answer that. The question violates my rights under the Fifth and Fourteenth amendments to the United States Constitution."

With a smug smile the questioner studied Tiger. He looked at some notes on a piece of paper and continued, "Is it true your father is the largest crime boss in the United States?"

"I refuse to answer on the same grounds."

"Is it not true that you are currently operating an international pornography ring for your father?" asked the questioner, throwing the revelation at the jury.

"I refuse to answer."

The questions continued, and Tiger's answers remained the same. After a while, Tiger grew bored, with no end of the questions in sight.

"When was your last conviction for narcotics violation?"

Whoa, thought Tiger, wondering where the hell that was coming from? Anyone who ever knew him knew he hated junk. Even Malone, as dumb as he was. "I refuse to answer."

"Is it true that you have or once had in your possession a copy of the report of the President's Commission on

104

Narcotics Traffic, the original of which was stolen from the desk of the president of the United States?"

Christ. Tiger wanted to burst out laughing, but he was afraid he wouldn't be able to stop. He couldn't believe anybody sane enough to be on a jury would take this nonsense seriously. He looked at the jurors. They *were* taking it seriously. "I refuse to answer."

The interrogator put his papers on the table, turned his back on Tiger, and said, "That will be all, Mister Corso."

Tiger sat stunned. That's *all?* he thought. For this I wasted a day? He looked coldly at the questioner. The word slipped out of him: "Asshole."

The man looked sharply back at Tiger. "What did you say?"

Tiger glared at the man. "I refuse to answer."

Tiger walked the two blocks to where he had parked his car, paid the attendant, and pulled out into the traffic. At the bottom of the hill, he turned left and headed along a long deserted stretch of factories and warehouses.

He saw the movement out of the corner of his eyes as something cold pressed against his neck. "Don't move, bastard," said a cold voice.

"What the hell is this?" said a startled Tiger.

"Pull over," commanded a second voice.

Tiger obeyed.

"Take it easy, friend. We just want to talk to you," said the first voice.

Tiger pulled over and put the car in park, remaining perfectly still. He recovered from his initial shock but knew he had to collect his thoughts fast. He was sure they were Bocci's friends out for revenge, and so long as he sat behind the wheel, motor running, he had a chance—a slim chance but a chance.

"What do you guys want?" he asked, turning slightly to look at them. The one pointing the gun at Tiger's head had a face like a bulldog with intelligent eyes. The other was the opposite, with cold black eyes that had looked on death before.

"We lost a friend a few days ago," the bulldog said. "What did you do with him?"

Tiger recalled a dark night, a pistol flash, a gold shield, and death. Cops, he thought. "So why are you coming to me?" said Tiger innocently.

The bulldog man leaned over the seat for a better look at Tiger. "Because our friend had a thing for you. He said you were sticking your nose where it didn't belong," said Bulldog coldly. "He was tailing you in his spare time, so we know you put him away," he said accusingly.

Tiger half turned, bringing his eyes in direct contact with the man as he used his left hand to release the door panel with the pistol. He knew the man was running a bluff because they had no proof, no witnesses, nothing to tie him to the detective. "I think you got the wrong guy, fellas," he said as he pointed his pistol at the man's face. When the man didn't shoot, Tiger knew he had taken the initiative. He didn't think they were willing to kill or be killed while they harbored doubts. "I don't know if you're ready to kill me, but I'm ready to kill you both if you don't drop your guns."

Small signs of uncertainty seeped into Bulldog's face as Tiger felt the pressure eased from his neck. The man with the bitter eyes was a different matter. The man's eyes filled with hate and Tiger knew he was going to try for it.

"Drop it or I'll blow your fucking head off," snapped Tiger loudly.

A slight hesitation crept into the black eyes as Tiger, using his right hand, snatched away Bulldog's pistol and shifted his pistol to the other man. Tiger saw the battle raging within the man as Tiger took up the slack on the trigger, ready to kill him. "Drop it now!" shouted Tiger.

The hate was still bubbling, but the man eased his grip on the pistol, letting it fall to the floor.

Tiger studied the two men, wondering if he should take their identification; but he knew these two spiders were dangerous, and he just wanted to get away. "Get out of the car, slow and easy."

106

Tiger didn't wait until they closed the car door behind them, but instead put the car in gear and hit the accelerator. At the corner he turned left, hit the Brooklyn-Queens Expressway.

Glancing down at the policeman's pistol, he knew it wasn't department issue. These guys had come ready to whack him out. Well, he thought, they'll be back. That's for sure.

Tiger hid in the dark shadows of the boiler room. The air was stale and stifling, and the heat was sweltering. He could make out Pete's outline across the room, near the entrance to the tunnel. Tiger arranged to beep Pete three times on the walkie-talkie when he spotted Toto. Pete would just have time to dab the doorknob and lose himself in the shadows of the boiler room. Tiger figured the chemical would take effect in forty minutes. He grinned in the heat. By his reckoning, Toto would be in the sack with his girlfriend in forty minutes.

At three-thirty he began to wonder what had delayed Toto. A doubt started to gnaw at him. Had Toto smelled a rat? He quickly went over his clocking. No, there shouldn't have been anything to tip him off. Something unexpected might have delayed him. He assured himself that all was well. There was no law that said a man had to get laid on schedule. He fingered the frog clicker in his pocket, which added to his assurance.

Another hour crawled by. Pete remained motionless across the room. Tiger's patience gradually frayed out completely, his annoyance growing minute by minute. He began to believe that Toto was playing tricks with his mind.

He felt a presence. He quickly looked into the alley. Nothing moved. Then, a footstep. He pressed the button on the walkie-talkie three times. For good measure, he pressed the frog clicker. The slight noise it made sounded like thunder in the stillness. His heart pounded as a shadow came through the doorway and passed within five feet of the deeper shadow in which Tiger was crouched. The shadow moved past, crossed the boiler room, headed for the tunnel. Was Pete out of the way? He could see no sign of him. Seconds crawled by. A door slammed at the end of the tunnel, and footsteps ran toward him. Tiger clicked the frog clicker again and again. Finally, Pete emerged from the shadows.

"Let's get the hell out of here," said Pete.

LAWYER Rizzo liked luxury. His office was richly furnished, and two fine paintings hung on the wall where the light showed them off at their best. Don Corso sat under the paintings as Rizzo, leaning back in his handsome leather chair, listened intently to Tiger's complete recital of the grand jury interrogation.

"That's about it," Tiger finished.

Rizzo was silent a moment longer. He glanced at Don Corso.

"I don't think they will be moving as fast as I expected," he said. "It sounds like they're on a fishing trip."

Tiger always liked Rizzo. He was comfortable with him. The lawyer had a good mind, thought fast in the clenches, and was never smug.

"Do they think I'm involved in junk?"

Rizzo smiled and continued, "All that means is that the next move is up to them. If they can prove something, they will try to put you away. But as I said, they're still on a fishing trip. If they had hard information, we wouldn't be sitting here talking."

Tiger said nothing, wondering if his father had heard nothing about Toto. Or was he, as usual, playing it cagey?

Rizzo stood up. "Let me know if they bother you again. In the meantime, forget it."

Tiger stood up and shook hands with the lawyer. He turned and looked questioningly at his father, who remained sitting underneath the paintings.

"I may call you later, after I speak to Mike," said Don Corso.

Tiger closed the office door behind him, jabbed the elevator call button, and paced impatiently up and down the hallway. He was anxious to call Pete to see if he had heard anything. It had been twelve hours since his long vigil in the boiler room. His father had not indicated anything out of the ordinary. He jabbed the call button again.

The light came on. The door opened, and Tiger's mind went out of commission for a moment. Standing in the elevator was Toto, his cold crazy eyes looking at him. Tiger felt for the clicker, found it, and for a second could hardly summon up the strength to press it. He rushed past Toto, clicking the frog as he entered the elevator. He turned following Toto with his eyes to the door of Rizzo's office as the elevator door closed. He could feel himself sweating. The elevator started down. Suddenly Tiger became aware that he was still mindlessly clicking the frog. He fought for control. He took his hand out of his pocket, looked at it, rubbed his eyes, and wiped away the beads of sweat from his forehead. When the elevator opened in the main lobby, he rushed onto the street. Forgetting all caution, he stopped in the middle of the street and looked up at Rizzo's window, half expecting to see Toto watching him.

He felt haunted. He decided that more than anything, he wanted to talk to Pete. In person. He called the number and spat out a location. A street corner across town.

TIGER raced across town. What went wrong? he kept asking himself. The chemical? No. It had certainly worked on the junkyard dogs. Then what? Did Toto sense a trap? Had he detected Tiger's thoughts? Or Pete's?

109

Tiger's mind ran around in circles like a dog in a race, but like the dog, the rabbit seemed to stay a jump ahead of him.

He parked on a shadowed corner and looked around for Pete. Apparently he hadn't arrived yet. Opening the door panel, he took out the Beretta and left it between the door and his left leg. It gave him some small comfort.

Through the rearview mirror, Tiger saw Pete slide into the parking space behind him, watched as he ambled over. Pete opened the door and slid in next to his friend.

"What did you find out?"

Pete looked at him. "Nothing. I spent half the morning wandering around the apartment house, but everything seems cool. Maybe they didn't find Toto's body yet."

"And the girl? She did us a favor and die, too?" said Tiger, an edge to his voice.

Pete shrugged. "How the hell do I know? I don't have the answers," said Pete. "I checked your father's place, no heavy activity, so I assume nobody found the body yet."

"I found it," said Tiger tightly.

Pete looked strangely at his friend. "Where?"

"At Lawyer Rizzo's."

Pete was visibly shaken. "What the fuck's it doing there?"

"He walked into Rizzo's office less than an hour ago and scared the shit out of me."

Pete was taken aback. "Then we fucked up. But what went wrong? Who was that in the boiler room?"

Tiger stared at him. "You tell me. You say the apartment house is cool, but something must have happened."

Pete thought about it. "Well, yeah, something. When I tried to speak to the super, no one was home. A neighbor said he had a heart attack during the night."

"Terrific," said Tiger bitterly.

"Coincidence?" asked Pete.

"You tell me," said Tiger.

"Well, he was the super and that would take him into the boiler room . . . " trailed off Pete.

"You got it. It had to have been him that came in last night."

"Damn."

"So where was Toto last night?"

Pete shrugged. "Who cares. I just know we better finish what we started."

Tiger nodded. He felt somewhat calmer now and knew he'd better get his thinking cap on. He thought if in that second before he got the frog clicker going, Toto smelled something, he knew his father would blanket the town, cutting off all access to Jeanne, his mother, and Camille. In that case, he and Pete would have to cut and run or stay and face down his father, Toto, and all the rest of the crazies.

Maybe Toto hadn't gone near the apartment house last night. Maybe there was a wide open shot at him. But, he thought, two heart attacks in the same building might be a little much. But if he changed locations, he would have to start a new clock. Damn, he couldn't afford the delay. He was tempted to blow the bastard away, but that would really start the old man digging. Shit, thought Tiger, the ifs and maybes were giving him a headache.

Pete waited patiently for several minutes, the silence broken only by the sound of traffic passing. Then quietly he asked, "Where do we go from here?"

Tiger let out a sigh. "We're damned if we do and damned if we don't."

"What does all that mean?" asked Pete.

"It means we better find some answers fast, and they better be the right ones."

A<small>N</small> hour later, Tiger made the last of a dozen calls and returned to Pete in the car. Twice he called Ralphie, comfortable that nothing was in the wind. He'd listened carefully to make sure Ralphie made no reference to coffee, their telephone word for trouble. He called Jeanne and listened to every intonation, every word, but he detected no hint of trouble.

Pete looked up as Tiger settled behind the wheel. Tiger looked straight ahead at the silent street.

"So far it's a go on the hit," said Tiger.

Pete let his breath out. "I'm for that."

"In three hours," said Tiger, "I'll call again. If it's still cool . . . " He let the sentence dangle.

Pete measured him, "Same place?"

Tiger nodded. "Same time, same place, but a different angle. I think I found how to hit Toto so the old man won't get suspicious."

W ITH twelve hours to kill, Pete suggested his safehouse. They could get a little shut-eye before the hit.

As a rule, Tiger distrusted high rise buildings. Nosy neighbors, bribed doormen, easy wiretaps, every stranger a potential cop or danger. Every elevator door opening could bring death. But Pete seemed to have partly solved the problem by leasing three apartments atop each other and one on both sides of the one on the middle floor. All under a different name.

Pete cooked up a batch of macaroni, after which Tiger relaxed and made his calls. He started with Ralphie.

"Yeah?"

"It's me," said Tiger.

"It's been a fucking day," he said. "I wish to hell Pete was back."

Tiger was alert. "What's up?"

"That fat bastard Malone was here."

Tiger found that surprising. "What the hell did he want?"

"That's just it, nothing, not a damn thing. He just stood there with his back against the door, his piece hanging out, and glaring at everyone like a gargoyle."

"No subpoena? No threats?"

"Nothing. When I finally told him to take a walk, he just

smiled and said he just came by to say hello to his Dago friends."

Tiger's fury boiled up. The harassment didn't make sense unless Malone had something else in mind. But what, damn it, what? "Did you call Rizzo?"

"Yeah, he said he would handle it," Ralphie said, still annoyed. "But if that Irish bastard comes back I'm gonna deck him."

Tiger swallowed his anger, brought his temper under control. Other problems were more important. "What else is happening?"

"I went to Dreamy's like you said. He remembered the broad and checked his records, but her address was a phony."

Tiger felt Ralphie's disappointment.

Ralphie continued, "Dreamy checked with some of the models. You know how those hookers are, always stealing each other's books for phone numbers. Well, bingo, one of the models had filched the black chick's book."

Tiger said nothing as he held his breath.

"Her name is Shirley Jackson, and we got the right address on her, but she has cleared out. The landlady said she left on the twenty-fourth."

Tiger's pulse raced. The twenty-fourth was the day of the Bocci hit.

Ralphie was still talking. "I've got someone checking the numbers in the book to see what comes up."

Tiger immediately sensed Ralphie's hesitation. He remained silent.

"I found Iggy and Weasel's names in the book."

That hit Tiger hard. Of course: Iggy, Weasel, the black chick, the cops and the Feds, and Bocci, all connected. It made his head swim. "Stay on it and let me know what you come up with," said Tiger.

"Also, your brother Sonny is on the loose again."

"Shit," that was all that was needed, another fucking nut running around.

On the one hand Don Corso had all the motivation and

desire to have ordered Joe the Boss killed, yet the use of a black man definitely ruled him out. On the other hand, the gun had been paid for with one of the checks the cops had seized, and that pointed to them. Yet the motivation eluded Tiger. With so many forces coming into play he became confused. Why was Turk killed? Why were the two policemen hanged? Why was Patsy hit? Where did Weasel and Iggy fit in? Or for that matter, Malone? Not to mention the detective he killed and his friends? The more he thought about it, the more confused he became. Finally, the only things he understood were his motivations for killing Toto. Greed and survival.

Iᴛ was midnight and Tiger had the nightscope trained on the door at the end of the alley. From his vantage point on the roof, he scanned the street where Toto's car was parked. Pete was hovering in the shadows, three cars away. Tiger swung the scope back, waiting for the door to open. The moment Toto stuck his head out, Pete would dab the door handle on the driver's side of Toto's car and walk away with the clicker clicking.

The door at the end of the alley opened. Tiger pressed the walkie-talkie and whispered, "Go." He saw Pete crunch down alongside the car and dab the handle, fading quickly into the shadows. Toto's pace was slow as he made his way to his car. Tiger watched as he crossed the street, silently urging him to hurry before the liquid evaporated.

Toto opened the car door on the passenger side, slid in across the seat under the wheel, and started the car.

Tiger was stunned, motionless with frustration, wishing furiously that he had brought along a rifle. He wanted to blow the bastard away. He sped down the stairs and out into the street. Toto's taillights shrank in the distance. Pete pulled up outside, his smile broad. But it quickly faded as he saw the expression on Tiger's face. Jumping into the passenger seat, Tiger screamed, "Get after that bastard!"

Pete floored the accelerator. "What happened?"

"The son of a bitch used the wrong door."

"Shit."

It took Pete three blocks to move closer to Toto's car up ahead. Then Pete slowed and waited at cruising speed.

"As soon as he hits Ditmas Avenue, move in on him."

On Ditmas a long deserted stretch of junkyards spread out before him. Tiger scanned the streets for traffic, saw none, and said, "Let's take him."

Pete hit the gas pedal, quickly overtaking Toto's car.

Tiger knew they were spotted when Toto tried to speed up. But it was too late. Pete was on him, forcing Toto's car into a steel fence. The sparks flew and the car stopped dead with steam coming from the burst radiator. Tiger was out of the car instantly. He ran to Toto's car, jerked the door open, and pulled Toto out. With his gun on the dazed Toto, Tiger dragged him to Pete's car and piled him into the rear seat. Pete backed up, turned into a side street, and sped away.

"Where to?"

Tiger held the gun pointed at Toto's head. "Hit the swamps."

They drove along Stanley and at the end turned into the marshes. Pete cut the lights, about a mile into the deserted marshlands. Pete stopped the car. Tiger looked at Pete.

"Use the chemical," he ordered.

Pete opened the vial and upended it over Toto's head. Nothing came out.

"Shit, it's empty."

The rage boiled up in Tiger. He got out of the car, reached in, pulled Toto out, and dragged him across the ground like a rag doll. Then in a single movement, he raised the gun and shot Toto behind the left ear. With the puff of the silenced pistol, bits and pieces of bone, flesh, and brain matter flew up. Toto crumbled. Tiger quickly checked his pulse, finding the sweaty skin repulsive to the touch.

"I'll get the shovels," he said.

Tiger unlocked the trunk, when suddenly a movement

swung him around. Pete was bolting down the path. Incredibly, Toto was running into the swamp, with Pete in pursuit.

Tiger jumped into the car and raced after the fleeing Toto. The running Toto filled Tiger's headlights as he crawled up Toto's tail, knocking him down with the heavy car. He slammed on the brakes and jumped out of the car as Pete was just arriving at Toto's body.

"Let's get the bastard into the ground," said Tiger. They dug a shallow grave in the hard ground, rolled the body in, and covered it over.

Tiger's hand trembled as he handed Pete his shovel and lit a cigarette. He sat on the mound of soft dirt, filled his lungs with smoke, and let his mind roam as he looked over the silent swamp.

Pete cut the car headlights, leaned back against the fender, allowing Tiger to come down from his reverie.

Thirty minutes later Tiger checked his watch.

"What are we waiting around here for?" Pete asked.

Tiger's hooded eyes studied his friend. "I want to make sure the bastard is dead."

Pete settled down on the mound of dirt beside Tiger. "Are they all like him in Sicily?"

The swamp came alive with the sound of crickets. Tiger checked his watch again. Rising to his feet he carefully examined the freshly-dug grave then looked about the swamp.

"What are you looking for?" asked Pete.

Tiger shrugged. "I was hoping to find a boulder to roll on top of the bastard."

Pete understood the fear Toto inspired in Tiger. "Fuck him, he's dead. So let's get the hell out of here."

TIGER was exhausted as he crawled into bed alongside Jeanne. He nestled against her warm body. She was half asleep but woke up enough to sense something in him that opened her eyes. She gathered him gently into her arms.

He lay there for a moment, still, smelling her fragrance. Then passion rose in him like a fountain.

Lying with her head cradled in his shoulder after both were spent, he wondered about lovemaking and death. Even in Korea, he had experienced a powerful lust after a killing.

Before a killing, all his senses were warped inward. Focused on seeing and hearing, trying to find death before it found him. There was nothing but the object, to kill. But after the blood-letting, the senses retained their sharpness without objective, and passion provided the objective. Only when those were aroused could sleep come.

Sleep came.

The telephone rang. He snatched the instrument from the cradle. It was his father's voice.

"Get down here right away."

The urgency of the tone launched him from bed. He hoped, as he dressed, that his father had enough enemies to explain Toto's death without suspecting Tiger.

He dressed casually, selecting the clothes that would give him an excuse to wear the belt with the gun buckle. The beautifully wrought silver buckle, woven with three Indian Head pennies grouped together in a triangle, with a .32 dumdum behind each penny.

From a pay phone, he called Pete and told him to be near his father's office.

Dawn was breaking as Tiger parked in front of his father's office. Hardfaces were patrolling around the house, while other groups of silent, watchful men sat in parked cars up and down the street.

Inside, the outer office was busy. The flunkies crowded and pushed, talking loudly, excitedly. Tiger pushed through them. The hardface at the rear door silently let him pass into the back room.

Don Corso was talking on the phone. Toto's absence

filled the room. Tiger sat down against the wall next to the desk, the buckle pointing unobtrusively at his father. He waited in silence. From the phone conversation, he knew Toto's car had been found, and his father's men were looking for Toto.

He felt a tightness form in his gut. His father was putting into motion the machinery that would find out which families might be making a move against him. He knew how his father's mind worked: He would gather information, then narrow it down to the Bocci family, and—if Tiger was lucky —his old man would settle for a renegade Bocci looking for revenge.

For the next two hours the calls came in hot and heavy. Between calls, Tiger had a chance to ask, "What the hell is this all about?"

But his father ignored him. Tiger decided the path of good sense was to keep his mouth shut and his ears open.

After three hours, a call came in that launched Don Corso from his chair. "Where?" he shouted into the phone. "How long ago?" Then he slammed down the phone, heading for the door.

"Come on," he said. "Toto's in the hospital."

TIGER'S mind was swirling as he sat in the back of the big car. The hardface behind the wheel drove like a lunatic. There wasn't any Toto, so what was the fucking hurry? You can't help the bastard, he's dead.

THE hospital corridors were filled with hardfaces. Tiger and his father were hurried along the hall.

A white-coated team surrounded a frosted tent atop the bed. Lights blinked off and on, wires and cables ran under the tent to instruments along the wall, plastic tubes filled with liquid penetrated the tent and ran under the bandages on the figure propped on the pillow. Only the eyes and the mouth were exposed, and they were shut.

Tiger moved in closer, feet dragging. Unable to distinguish or recognize anything about the mass of bandages. Suddenly the eyes opened, tubes were ripped free as the eyes glared at him. He froze, the hate in them overpowering. Animal sounds of rage spat at him. Toto.

He was suspended in a morass of evil, weaponless against such madness. His mind split, the room darkened, and he looked about the blackness, finding himself suddenly facing a ten-headed serpent and each serpent was Toto, grinning and snapping viciously at him with razor-sharp teeth, slashing at him, as blood matter spattered, closer and closer until the rockets exploded into a thousand particles of color, and as they slowly faded away, the darkness came again.

Little lights flickered and Tiger looked over at the twisted lifeless form on the bed. Even in death, Toto was dreadful, the eyes still open, and to Tiger they still gleamed hate from them.

His father watched in silence as Tiger came to himself. His voice said softly, "Are you ready to leave?"

Tiger nodded. His feet and legs felt as if they were made of lead, and he was wet with sweat. He wondered if Toto had said anything while he was passed out. Had he asked any questions? Mumbled something or raved? He could never ask. There was no one to ask without arousing suspicion.

He followed his father out the door.

Sitting quietly in the back of the big car, Tiger was still tense from the hospital ordeal. He was also uncertain how his father—sitting quietly beside him—would interpret his

119

erratic behavior. How could he ever explain the madness in Toto's eyes?

"I think it is time for your answer," said his father softly.

Tiger held his breath, uncertain what his father meant. Then he remembered the Council. He looked at the shadowy outline of his father, unsure whether he was serious.

"Was the gift I offered you so small that you forgot about it?" asked Don Corso in a soft tone.

Tiger felt ashamed, for many reasons, and said almost inaudibly, "I have not forgotten, and I would very much like to have it, if you are still offering."

His father was slow in answering. "We start work tomorrow."

Don Corso dropped Tiger off at home and silently continued on his way, followed by a car filled with hardfaces.

Tiger was both physically and emotionally drained, but somehow he made it to the kitchen. There his trembling fingers could barely make a pot of coffee.

The events of the past few hours crowded in on him, and he found it inconceivable that Toto survived a bullet *and* a burial.

O N the couch in the den, Tiger tried to grab a few hours' sleep, but every time he closed his eyes Toto was lurking in the darkness, waiting to snap at him with razor-sharp teeth. In panic he charged through sewers and swamps trying to escape, always managing to keep a step ahead of the flashing madness. He ran, tripping and stumbling through the dense fog of the marshland, constantly aware of the snarling, snapping jaws. Through a slight break in the fog he spied a spectral form in the distance. As he drew closer, a kindly Uncle Patsy stood there, protective arms outstretched, ready to engulf him. Suddenly Patsy disappeared, replaced by the apparition of Don Corso. In dread Tiger found himself squeezed between two hells.

120

He wondered if it had all been worth it. Yes, he answered himself. It was worth it. He was going to get it all now. He was going to have his mother, Jeanne, the kids, Camille, Che, Pete, Ralphie, the money, and the power. Oh, and how badly he wanted the power and the money.

Later in the afternoon Pete showed. Pouring two cups of coffee, Tiger brought his friend up to date on Don Corso's call in the night, his rush to the office and hospital, and Toto's subsequent death.

Pete listened attentively, his mouth half open. "I don't believe this. How many fucking lives did that bastard have?"

Tiger shrugged. "Well, whatever he had, he used them up," he said bitterly. "I think you should make an appearance at the office today."

Pete nodded. "What about those two cops who hassled you?"

Tiger shrugged. "Nothing, I can't kill them all."

Pete coolly measured him. "You know they'll be back. For what? And who the hell were they anyway?"

Tiger thought about that. He knew neither was a pro or a heavy hitter. If they were, they would have clocked him better and boxed him in good. If, as he suspected, they were really friends of the detective he had killed, they would be back. Not immediately, but soon.

What bothered Tiger most was why the detective had targeted him to begin with. He remembered the crazy one saying I was sticking my nose where it didn't belong. Where, wondered Tiger, was he sticking his nose? Weasel? The clerk's office? Then he remembered the name of the detective he had killed.

"Have this name checked. See where he worked," said Tiger, writing a name on a slip of paper.

Pete nodded. "What are you going to do today?"

"Get a couple hours sleep, then meet my old man at his house. I've decided to take his job offer."

Pete smiled from ear to ear.

Little had changed in his father's house. As usual it was neat and clean. Dimly lit and depressing as a cathedral. Heavy drapes covered the huge windows. Discolored marble statuary stood sentinel everywhere; and old Emilio Lombardo, the family retainer, seemed part of the decay.

He found his father in the kitchen relaxing over a glass of wine. "You know where the coffee is," said Don Corso softly.

Tiger took the seat opposite his father, being careful to avoid the cold blank eyes.

"Before the Council approves you," he said without preamble, "they will put you through a thorough interrogation. It is important that they be sure they are not harboring a pit viper or someone looking to play loose with their property."

Tiger looked at the inscrutable face and remained silent. It was his father's show.

"Suppose you are in a restaurant with Ralphie Canzanna and two men approach with drawn guns. What do you do?"

"Do I have a gun?"

"You have a gun," answered his father.

"And they're not cops?"

"They are not cops."

Tiger looked for hidden traps but could find none. "I guess I start shooting."

"And if you know they were sent by the Council?" asked his father, letting the question hang.

Tiger said nothing.

Don Corso explained, "The family never endangers another member needlessly. Once you see the weapons, get out of the way because Ralphie is the target."

Recognizing the flash of anger in Tiger's eyes, Don Corso said, "I understand what you are thinking, but in the eyes of the Council Ralphie is an outsider. So give me the answer the Council wants to hear."

Tiger sighed. He remembered the unsmiling faces of the Council in the funeral parlor. Their countenances told a story of hard, bitter men, tribal fanatics to whom the family meant everything. These were feudal lords. Tiger knew the Council viewed the world from only one position: Theirs.

So Tiger gave the answer everyone would want to hear: "I carry the gun for my own protection and so long as no one threatens me, I will stay out of it."

"Good," said Don Corso. "That's better."

But Tiger knew, and Tiger knew his father knew, the moment he saw a gun he was going to start shooting and fuck the Council.

As Tiger was leaving, Don Corso called him back as he scribbled a hasty note and handed it to his son. "Meet me on Monday morning."

Tiger studied the paper. It had written on it the name and address of a bank he knew well.

SINCE it was too late to visit the hospital, Tiger decided to call it an evening. He stopped at a pay phone and dialed Pete on the beeper and waited for Pete's return call.

"It's me," said Tiger.

"I'm at the office. Can you get down here?"

"What's up?"

"We got the eggplant."

"Be right there," said Tiger as he headed for his car.

Turning the key, he wondered what kind of story the black chick was going to throw at him.

Sɪɴᴄᴇ the workers had left for the day, Tiger let himself into the building. As he passed the shipping department on his way to the upper offices, Pete called, "We're in here, Tiger."

The room, an industrial loft, was piled with cartons of film, books, and video tapes. Pete came to the door, but Tiger was looking beyond him at the black chick sitting on a chair in a corner, being guarded by Ralphie. Tiger recognized her as the girl from the film.

"What did she tell you?" asked Tiger.

"Nothing. She's a Whitey hater," he said coldly, looking at her. "I would have broken her jaw, but I didn't want to damage her before you got here."

Tiger nodded and studied the girl who insolently stared back at him. She was a pretty girl, but her features were marred by hate and bitterness. Tiger pulled up a chair, reversed it, and rested his arms on its back.

"What's your name?" he asked softly.

His inquiry fell on deaf ears as the hostile eyes glared at him. "No one is going to hurt you," he said gently. "I just want to ask you some questions."

She spat on the floor, just missing Tiger's polished shoe. Turning her face away, she crossed her arms and ignored him. Tiger sat there, guessing she wasn't going to let him do this the easy way.

"You have some information I want. So you might as well understand, you're not getting out of here until I get it," he said.

He waited a decent interval, letting that sink in, before he continued. "Now we can do this the hard way or the easy way. That's up to you. If you do me good, I'll do you good. But if you do me bad, I'm going to do you very bad. Do you understand that, bitch?" he said, keenly watching her features for signs of comprehension. But she exhibited none.

"Now, I know you were with the black photographer Johnson when he shot Joe the Boss Bocci. I also know you stole his camera case and ran away," he said, noticing the slight flicker of her eyes.

124

"Now I want you to tell me what was in the camera case."

She sat there, silently rejecting anyone's presence. Tiger looked at Ralphie, nodding his head a trifle.

Ralphie stepped in close and backhanded her across the face, sending both her and the chair across the room, ending abruptly at the wall of cartons.

She quickly scrambled to her feet, screaming invectives at Tiger. Then lowering her head, she charged. But Ralphie had anticipated her move and tripped her, sending her sprawling at Tiger's feet. Both Pete and Ralphie grabbed her and yanked her to her feet.

"Now answer the man's question," said Pete coldly.

But the hate within her overwhelmed her. "You mother-fucking Mafia man, I ain't afraid of you!"

Tiger sat there, ignoring her outburst. He wondered if it was her hate talking, or was what she was hiding so important to her. He had to know.

Again he signaled Ralphie, who let loose a powerful punch to her midsection. With a loud "Oof," she doubled up and puked over Pete's pants leg. Tiger saw a touch of madness in Pete's eyes and hoped he wouldn't forget himself. He was after information, not a dead body.

Pete jerked her upward to keep her from falling. When she finished retching, Tiger let her catch her breath before continuing, "Like I said, if you do me good, I'll do you good."

She raised her glassy eyes to Tiger, who saw the welt across her face and knew she would be marked for a while. But if he didn't get what he wanted, a welt would be the least of her problems.

"What do you want to know?" she said submissively.

Pete quickly placed the chair behind her, allowing her to sit.

"What was in the camera case?" he asked softly, knowing these damn interrogations always ended the same. Spilling guts.

"Money," she said between breaths.

"How much?"

125

"Ten thousand dollars."

To Tiger that seemed a small amount for such a big hit. He guessed Johnson wasn't such a hotshot hit man after all.

"Anything else?" he asked sharply.

"I found a slip of paper with phone numbers on it. It was in Ricky's handwriting."

"Whose numbers were they?"

"I don't know. There were no names, so I never called any of them."

Tiger knew she was lying but let it pass.

"What was your connection to Johnson?"

"We were making it together, that's all."

"Did you know what he was going to do at the rally?"

She hesitated slightly. "He said he was going to make a score, get rich, and he would buy me a new car."

"With ten thousand dollars?" asked Tiger surprised.

She shook her head, but with an effort. "He said he was going to get more money when it was over."

"For shooting Bocci?"

She took a moment to shift her body while she threw careful glances at Pete and Ralphie.

"Would you like some coffee?" asked Tiger softly.

To her nod Ralphie rushed away.

"Now why did Johnson shoot Joe the Boss?"

"He wasn't supposed to shoot him. He was only being paid to scare him."

"Then why did he shoot the Boss?"

"I don't know. He said a lot of people were going to protect him. He said he was supposed to wave around a pistol, do a lot of yelling, and someone would grab him before anything happened."

"Who gave him the money?" asked Tiger.

"He said a lot of big cops were involved. Ricky said when it was over he was going to be a hero and a big shot."

Some big shot, thought Tiger. The dumb bastard was dead the moment he made the deal. Ralphie returned with the coffee. She drank it hungrily.

"Do you have the slip of paper with the phone numbers?"

She shook her head. "I threw it away."

"Why?" asked Tiger.

Her brows knit together. "Because it had no names on it I threw it away," she said, trying to appear straightforward.

She wasn't very good at it. Tiger knew she would never throw away the numbers.

"Till now you were doing well, so let's keep it that way," he said sternly. "There's no way I'm buying that. So tell me who you called."

She stared at Tiger, then shifted her gaze to Pete and Ralphie, who towered over her.

"I did call," she said sheepishly. "I thought I could shake them down for some extra bread."

"Who were they?" asked Tiger, holding his breath.

"The first one answered, 'F.B.I.' so I hung up."

"Why?"

"Because I didn't have a name, so who could I ask for?"

"And the other number?"

"I don't know where it was, but the man that answered said 'Inspector Colby's Office.' I grew afraid and hung up."

"What were you afraid of?"

Her look of astonishment was genuine. "I don't know about Johnson, but I don't have any friends in the white man's world."

Looking at her, Tiger believed her. He got to his feet wanting to ask one more question, when she said, "Aren't you going to ask me about the last number?"

"What number?" asked a surprised Tiger.

"It was to a club in Brooklyn called the Doorknob. I didn't know who to speak to so I hung up again," she said shrugging.

Tiger had never heard of the Doorknob and looked at Pete and Ralphie, but they didn't know either.

Tiger looked at the girl again. "What is your connection with Iggy?"

He saw the expression of surprise. "He's a dealer. Sometimes he gives me a decent price so I can make a fast buck."

Tiger nodded his understanding. "Do you see him often?"

"When he comes to the Kit Kat Klub."

Weasel's place, thought Tiger with surprise. "You hang out with Mister Zaccone?" asked Tiger softly, with anticipation.

"My new old man does. I don't like him," she said, hoping she didn't offend Tiger.

Tiger took a long time examining her. Then he decided to take a chance. Weasel was of the white world, so he was sure she had no love for him. He removed a roll of money from his pocket, peeled off ten hundred-dollar bills and handed them to her. As she stared at the money, the glint in her eyes told him what he wanted to know.

"I don't like Mister Zaccone either. I want you to keep an eye on him for me. Watch him quietly, keep track of his movements, but only his white friends."

"That's easy," she said with a soft smile.

"And do yourself a favor. Don't try to get close to him. You'll get yourself hurt."

She nodded.

He indicated the money. "There's more where that came from, so when you find out something, get back to me."

Ten minutes later, he had Ralphie drop her in her neighborhood. He looked at Pete. "It's been a good day, so how about I buy you a big dinner?" he said smiling.

Pete looked down at his soiled pants and said, "Thanks, friend."

SLOWING the big car, Tiger turned down the ramp to the parking garage. He parked the car and walked to the bank of elevators. He took the center elevator to the main floor of the bank, where his father waited with a portly man. Tiger was introduced to Mr. d'Elessandro, a man who smiled easily and insisted Tiger call him Mister D. Tiger liked everything about the man, including the well-tailored clothes and polished manners, which hid a hardness Tiger didn't miss. He followed his father and Mister D down several flights of stairs, through some barred doors. They stopped at a door marked PRIVATE.

They entered a small comfortable room, tastefully decorated in soft leather and fruitwood. A buffet filled the rear wall, replete with espresso machine, a bar, and trays of warm delicacies. On the left wall was a wide video screen, with built-in console beneath.

From his comfortable chair, Tiger watched his father and Mister D press a series of buttons on the console. The duet of ultrasonic tones continued for a moment before ending with Mister D's leaving the vault. Tiger found he was impressed by the performance, wondering where the hell his old man found time to become a computer engineer.

His father removed a slip of paper from his wallet, studied it before pressing another series of buttons, suddenly filling the screen with a photograph of Joe the Boss Bocci. The caption across his chest read: GIUSEPPE GUIDO BOCCILINO . . . DECEASED.

"Press the green button when you want to change the picture," said his father.

What followed was a Who's Who of the Bocci family members. The photographs were of poor quality, obviously taken on the sly without permission. Each photo was accompanied by a resume, phone number, address, special qualifications, accomplishments, and the operations they controlled for the Bocci family.

Tiger froze the video, taking a moment to study a frame. "What do all those symbols mean?"

His father studied them before answering. "The circle is for the made members who are blood of the Boccis. The circle with an X inside is a made member, and the triangle is for someone connected to a made member," his father answered, pausing a moment.

"It is important for you to understand some of the structure of the family. When a connected member is promoted to the rank of made, he is entitled to recruit one hundred trusted men who will be connected with him, answerable for their mistakes, but loyal to the Council. In a sense, the connected are the family's reserves, from which all made members are drawn," said Don Corso as he sipped his wine.

"Where the family is concerned, all rights belong to first blood, to the Council, comprised of five families. The lowest is a soldier, or a made member. Everyone else, including the connected are outsiders, with absolutely no rights. None at all. You might find the rules harsh, but they have to be if the family is to survive. Should any outsider offend a family member, regardless if the offender be the pope, the president, a policeman, or a street thief, that offended member has the right to kill the outsider, with no other member attempting to interfere."

Tiger received the message loud and clear and quickly changed the subject. "What do the stars in the upper corners mean?" he asked.

Don Corso sipped his wine before continuing. "One is for made members in good standing. Two stars are for a made member—but for reasons known to the Council—who is longer eligible for promotion. Three stars are those made members who are no longer to be trusted but will be watched until termination," said his father measuring him.

The word "termination" had a hard, cold ring to it. "Why can't they be trusted?" asked Tiger.

His father replied simply, "Because they were bloodsuckers without souls. In the 1930's the five families were controlled by the Camorra, the grafters of Naples. These were the whores who spawned the Boccis, the Maggios, and the other three families. They spit on the Sicilians as a disease, but slowly and carefully we eliminated them, until only the Boccis and the Maggios remained," said Don Corso.

"During the Vespers War in Brooklyn, while good men were dying, Bocci filled his coffers and his ranks with anyone with the price of membership. He flooded his family and friends with relatives and with those never having made their bones in the family's defense," said his father, lowering his head in shame.

Tiger was shocked and understood his father's mortification. Any man who would not kill to protect his family was a degenerate.

For over two hours he viewed the files of the associated doctors, lawyers, judges, politicians, Federal officials, policemen, and a handful of Federal agents.

Halfway through the real estate holdings, Tiger paused. He needed a cup of coffee, and his father anticipated him by extending a hot, steaming mug.

"You don't have to view anymore. I just wanted to give you some inkling of the wealth, power, and responsibility you will be facing."

Leaving the bank, Tiger recalled the varied things he had seen on the video monitor. Among the real estate holdings was a club called the Doorknob. It was operated by a made member named Salvatore "Sally Dell" Delvechicco. Now why, wondered Tiger, would Johnson have the club's telephone number in his pocket? He thought he would send someone to check out Sally Dell.

Pulling over to a pay phone, he decided to call Bobby to see what information he had on Inspector Colby.

"Yeah," answered a strange voice.

Tiger hung up, thinking he had called the wrong number.

"Yeah," said the same person.

"Let me talk to Tony," said Tiger.

"Who wants him?" asked the voice.

Tiger hoped it wasn't a cop, but he didn't care. "None of your fucking business. Now get Tony on the line," he said in anger.

The silence built as he waited, hoping Tony hadn't got himself in a jam.

"Yeah?" said Tony.

Relief flooded in on Tiger. "Who's the jerk who answered the phone?"

"A new guy. I'll straighten him out. What's up?"

"How's that mutt of yours doing?" asked Tiger.

"He's not here. He got himself infested with fleas."

"Where is he?"

"I sent him to the vet's in Staten Island."

"How long will he be there?"

"Who knows? He's pretty infested."

"Well, kick him in the ass for me and let's get together soon."

"You got it," said Tony, hanging up.

Now Tiger knew Bobby had been transferred to a Staten Island precinct and was being closely watched. Tiger wondered where that was coming from. He smelled Malone in the background, but if so, how did he get a line on Bobby? Well, with that door practically closed, he decided to slip in his own eyes and ears, to see what everyone was hiding.

A half hour later, Tiger was closeted with Tony in the office of the scrapyard.

"That's all I know, Tiger. Bobby called yesterday from a street phone and said he was blanketed, then just hung up. I rushed over to Philomena's, but she acted nervous, so I made her write me a note," he said, handing the note to Tiger.

The note read:

> Bobby's at the 104th Precinct.
> They have him doing clerk duty
> and they follow us everywhere.
> We're afraid to use the phone.

Tiger looked up at Tony, "Who we got in the 104th?"

"Everyone. The whole fucking precinct is on the take."

"Anyone who might slip a note to Bobby?"

Tony took a moment to think about that. "Maybe. One guy owes me a few favors. Mike the Cop just might do it."

Tiger scribbled a fast note, handing it to Tony. "Let's find out if Mike the Cop pays back his favors."

On his way to see his mother at the hospital, Tiger called Pete at the office.

"It's me," said Tiger.

"Can I call you back?"

Tiger gave him the number, knowing something was up. He waited ten minutes for Pete to call back.

"What's up?" asked Tiger.

"We got a glass eye," said Pete.

Shit, thought Tiger. That means the damn phones are probably tapped also. "Where's the eye?"

"On the second floor of old lady Scamadella's house. After renting it to them she tipped me."

"She say who they are?"

"Only that they weren't *Federales*."

Damn, thought Tiger. That meant they were taking pictures. And taking pictures was usually a prelude to a raid. "Have Goldberg hang around the offices for the next week or so," he said. Goldberg was a sharp criminal lawyer who liked to hang around with the hard guys. He didn't like cops, and Tiger liked him enough to have his boys throw him work. But Tiger couldn't trust him too far because he was an outsider.

"I'll see you later," he said, cutting the connection.

He dialed another number and waited.

"Yes," said a soft feminine voice.

"It's Tiger."

"Yes, Tiger. How are you?" purred the soft voice.

"Fine, Eric, fine. Is it possible to do me tonight?"

"Of course, dear. I'll do it right away."

Tiger didn't like to use outsiders, but the bugman was

133

the best electronic man in the business and had a reputation for never betraying a trust.

Tiger spent a delightful hour with his mother. He promised to bring Camille for a visit the next day.

After leaving the hospital, Tiger called Pete from a pay phone. Again he had to wait for Pete to call him back.

"We found three taps."

"Three?" said an incredulous Tiger, thankful he rarely used the office phone for important calls.

"One we traced to the peepers across the street."

"And the other two?"

"They were wireless. But he knew the receivers were in the area somewhere."

"Don't pay the phone bill this month. Let's see if they pay the phone company to keep it open."

Pete burst into laughter. "I love it. So I guess you don't want them disconnected."

"Hell, no. Let them get their rocks off. Just pass a note warning everyone."

"I already did."

T HE next morning Tiger went to meet his father at his house. A hardface let him in and told him his father had gone out and said for him to wait.

He found the living room empty, but soft footsteps were to be heard everywhere. Turning on the T.V., he tried to watch a cowboy movie but lost interest and went to the kitchen to make a pot of coffee.

He wondered who his first hit would be. He wasn't really concerned about making his bones, having lost his virginity in Korea. He just hoped it wasn't a friend. But you could never be sure; some of the Council members had twisted minds.

His father found him in the kitchen and Tiger was quick to spot the glint in the old man's eyes. He held his breath waiting. His father sat and poured a glass of wine, sipped it slowly, looking pleased with himself. Tiger felt the electricity.

"I had a meeting with the Council this morning," he said casually, "and I had some problems."

Tiger continued to hold his breath, hoping his dreams weren't about to turn to ashes.

"Because the greedy ones were moving too fast, looking to grab the best for themselves."

Tiger's heart beat against his chest.

"But I was able to sway the Council to my way of thinking," his father said, taking a sip of wine.

Tiger was ready to throw the glass of wine out the fucking window.

Don Corso let his cold enigmatic eyes fall on his son. "You are on probation for six months as head of the Bocci family, providing . . ."

Two emotions hit Tiger at the same time, relief and joy. He looked across the table at his father; and although he felt grateful for the opportunity, he still felt no love. He also knew Don Corso intended to absorb his new family, but he also knew he wasn't going to let him. He intended to make the title of boss permanent.

" . . . you meet certain obligations. The Council saw little reason for you to make your bones, having proven yourself many times in the past. You will, however, be required to attend the ritual of acceptability. If in six months you fail to measure up, your rank will be reduced to no less than captain."

Tiger sat there silently, bouyant, with no fear of failure. He did, however, wonder what the ritual of acceptability would be.

Don Corso sat back, sipped his wine, and studied his son. "How do you feel?"

"Shaken. The feeling is awesome and a little frightening. But I will try to bring you no shame," he said sincerely.

Don Corso nodded his understanding. "Take a couple of days to carefully put together your staff."

"Do I pick who I want or play politics?"

His father shrugged. "Use your discretion. If you have doubts of someone, get rid of them."

"Do I get to keep Pete, Ralphie, and Che?" he asked softly.

His father took a moment to study him. "If you vouch for them, but walk slowly with the Boss's soldiers. Your friends are still outsiders."

Tiger understood. He was not to step unnecessarily on the old guard's toes.

Suddenly, his father stood and extended his hand. "*Benvenuto mio figlio*."

Tiger grasped the hand warmly. "Thank you, my father," he answered with slight embarrassment.

Without warning, Don Corso pulled his son forward and planted a kiss on the lips of a stunned Tiger. For an instant, Tiger was sure he had received the *bacia di morte*—the kiss of death—but he quickly recovered, realizing his father had just paid him the highest compliment.

TIGER was still in a slight stupor as he arrived at the hospital with Camille and Angelina in tow. He was glad Carmine was there with his obviously nervous mother, who hadn't seen her sister in thirty-five years.

The two old women hugged, touched each other in crying disbelief, and touched some more. The "*che va*"s and "*bene*"s seemed to be all they uttered in the first emotionally charged minutes. Tiger stood off by himself as Camille introduced Angelina to Momma and Carmine. And then the endless questions began, the need to cram thirty-five years into an hour. The reunion was so animated that Tiger sat alone, feeling like an outsider.

Tiger studied Angelina. He had kindly described her as a woman of the earth. On the street outside, people would consider her a *cáfone,* a greaseball. Her clothes were drab gray and brown and of a heavy fabric. Her shoes looked orthopedic. Her hair, of which there was an abundance, was rolled back from her gentle face and into a bun, which added to her severity.

Looking at her, Tiger knew she was far from a *cáfone.* Tiger liked her. She had an impish sense of humor and a warm, motherly charm. But Tiger couldn't help but wonder what made a woman in the full bloom of youth bury herself in a mausoleum with a decaying old woman. The old woman wasn't even of her blood.

Could it be, thought Tiger, that she is a saint? He didn't think so, since the contadino, the peasant class, were not given to permitting their sons and daughters to enter religious orders. It was deemed a waste of a productive life. Had the thirty-five years with Camille been productive? Tiger found it a contradiction he didn't understand.

Aғᴛᴇʀ taking Camille and Angelina home, Tiger headed for his office, picking up a couple of containers of coffee on the way.

The moment he entered his office he felt the electricity. An invisible wall seemed to rise between him and his staff. They stood there awkwardly, almost at attention, uncertain how to act in his presence. Tiger guessed the word had already hit the streets.

"You people run out of work?" he asked, smiling.

His cousin Porky broke the ice with a sheepish handshake, followed by Marie with a big hug. One by one, the others filed by, with Ralphie and Pete adding their congratulations last.

In his private office, Tiger removed the coffee containers from the bag and handed each one. He relaxed in his chair, while Pete and Ralphie stood respectfully.

"Do me a favor and sit down, you're making me nervous," he said, taking a sip of coffee.

Pete walked to the landscape on the wall above Tiger's head and pointed to the microphone.

Tiger nodded and got to his feet. "Okay, let's take a ride."

HANDING the taxi driver a hundred dollar bill, Tiger instructed him to take a couple of turns around Prospect Park. He ordered Pete to close the partition between them and the driver. He brushed off Ralphie's attempt to explain the wall bug they had found.

"Fuck the taps. That's my old man's problem," he said, "we'll be moving out."

He told them of the meeting with his father and the six months' probation. He told them to close out the books so an orderly transition could take place. "The old staff and the Lippo brothers will remain with my father."

Not seeing any questions in their eyes, he continued, "I will be transferring some of the old guard to other families. Some of those I keep might resent the both of you, so play it cool. As for my father, you already know where you stand with him."

They sat quietly, listening with attention.

"Oh, and I might as well tell you now. As of this morning, you are both listed with the Council as being connected to me."

Tiger looked out the window, embarrassed by their misty eyes and the emotions etched on their features.

With their business finished, they took another turn around the park, relaxed, and enjoyed the scenery.

As Tiger drove home, he wondered what leeway his father was prepared to allow him in reorganizing the Bocci family.

He knew illegal operations would exist so long as man continued to walk the earth. But in the new scope of the family structure, they were passé. But like old shoes, the old guard refused to throw them away. Although experience showed the amount of income generated was very little after the lawyers, bankers, and accountants all finished laundering the money. Not enough survived to be meaningful in the financial arena.

T HE following days were hectic for Tiger. His father permitted him to purchase a small building Don Corso owned adjacent to Lulu's restaurant.

While keeping his eyes and ears open for Weasel, the two detectives who hassled him, and other snakes and spiders, he went about converting the upper floor of his new building into two emergency apartments. The rear of the main floor he turned into his offices, creating three entrances he would need for members to come and go in secrecy.

The rest of the main floor he made into a private dining room with a connecting door to Lulu's kitchen.

When work on the building was completed, he kept a constant contingency force of troops lounging in the dining room as a buffer against snoopers. The rest of the field troops he billeted in a new social club directly across the street. He filled the place with tables, chairs, a coffee machine, a bar, and video games. A home away from home.

Settling into his new offices, his first order of business was to secure pistol permits for Pete and Ralphie—not difficult since neither had criminal records.

Then he conducted interviews with all the members of his new family. One by one, he searched out the flaws in the operations, the reasons for low revenues, the greed, and the incompetence.

With the interviews over, he had a better picture of what he was up against. He felt considerable resentment of the old guard because they were piggish and greedy, constantly using their power to exploit the lower echelons. As a result, the lesser members passed up many opportunities for profit, regarding them as not worth the risks.

Handing his father a slip of paper, he said, "I would like permission for these members to be transferred or terminated."

His father's brows shot up as he studied the paper. "What do you have against them?" he asked carefully.

"Nothing. They are all friends and relatives of Joe the Boss with long records of using unnecessary muscle."

"Even scorpions have to use their stingers."

"That's true," said Tiger, "but they used their power and muscle to horn in on other members' territories rather than to expand the family's fortunes against the outsiders. They are not leaders, they are thugs who have lost the right to be even followers."

Don Corso was slow to answer, then said, "Those members I don't transfer, I'll ask the Council for permission to terminate."

Together they examined the dossiers of the connected, associated, and the other hangers-on who had flocked to the family.

Opening the files of the family real estate holdings, Tiger took a moment to catch his thoughts. He looked at the file and said, "I would like to sell some of these holdings."

Again Don Corso's brows shot up. "Why?"

"Because we can make better use of the money if we use it to finance new ideas and bright people."

He told his father of the world he would like to enter. The world of computers, communications, electronics, and energy. He saw the day when the family would have the capability to duplicate such conglomerate giants as IBM and Monsanto. He explained that those companies had started with nothing but an idea; so could the family.

Don Corso sat back as he weighed his son's words. "What makes you think you can do that without the government stepping in?"

"Because if the families go slow and remain low-key, they won't even know we're around. Not with the craziness in the world today. Between radical groups, street crime, and half the citizens dipping into the cookie jar, they'll have no time for us. By the time they wake up, it will be too late. The family will be so powerful, and so much a part of the structure, that government couldn't afford to allow us to go broke."

In the silence that followed, Don Corso's lips were tight. Then he asked many questions about his son's advanced ideas. When he finished, he sat there a long time in somber thought, as Tiger knew he had hit his target.

T IGER woke in a sweat from the nightmare of jumbled scenes of long-forgotten dead men, now alive as they reached out for him.

"It's all right, Joey, it's all right," said Jeanne gently as she put her arms around his shoulders and pulled him to her.

Tiger grabbed at her, holding tightly, burying his head deep in the folds of her embrace, clinging to her. He lay there in her warmth for a long time before her soothing words managed to penetrate.

Slowly he brought himself under control, lit a cigarette, and lay back on the wet pillow.

"It was a bad one, wasn't it?" she asked tenderly.

"They're all bad," he said in an exhausted tone.

Jeanne wished it were within her power to reach into his mind and remove his nightmares.

"I asked your mother once if your father ever had them, but she said no."

Tiger wasn't surprised. He knew his father had no conscience.

"Do you want to talk about it?" she asked.

Tiger shook his head. "It wouldn't help. It's a curse I have to live with."

"Try," she begged softly. "Maybe talking *will* help."

Tiger took a long drag on the cigarette, carefully watching the smoke dissipate upward.

"I was being chased by a man with a gun, but he had no face—it was blank. He was gaining on me when I tripped and went sprawling. When I looked up, a vulture hovered over me. It had cold dead eyes and a sharp open beak, wide enough to engulf me. As it swooped, everything went black and I was a kid again, maybe ten. I was sitting at a table opposite my father. His cold, cruel features measured me as he lectured me on the do's and don't's of manliness. Over and over he indoctrinated me in his philosophy. 'Learn the depths of your capabilities, practice self-denial, search out your enemies' weaknesses, and prepare to use them if necessary. If you have business partners, kill the one who opposes you. Understand the importance of being dependable, especially with your family and those you trust. Always keep your word or you will become a nothing.' It went on and on, until I needed to escape. Anywhere. Then I found myself running again and I was in Korea."

Jeanne remained silent, allowing the festering thoughts to expose themselves.

"Then I was back across the table from my father. 'Always do the unexpected. Be determined. Be one-directional when a job has to be done. Learn patience, aloofness. Learn that the secret of life is to live it to the fullest, but quietly. Practice the gun and knife.' I had to escape again from my father's madness. Then the faceless man was chasing me again. This time leading a small army of dead men, some I recognized, others I didn't. As I ran, I came to a cliff and in my fear I jumped into the blackness of space and into the open mouth of the vulture. That's when I woke up." The perspiration broke out again.

They remained silent for a long time before Jeanne spoke. "Do you think the faceless man chasing you was Don Corso?"

Tiger shook his head. "No, I think I was chasing myself."

Jeanne understood and her heart went out to him. Her husband was searching for his own identity. The who of *who he was,* rather than the person Don Corso had created.

She understood the torment of Sicilian training. The all-consuming need of the family structure. And once the

142

training was over, the contamination was there, a mold created forever in the image of Sicilian culture.

Jeanne also understood her Joey was a man trying to fight off that contamination, or if not succeeding, trying to understand it better. Her heart bled for his torment, and she knew it would be a long time before he learned to live with it.

W HAT offended Tiger the most was the smell of urine mixed with ammonia. He was sorry he had selected the men's room to meet with Bobby. He had been sitting in the center stall for over two hours, waiting and wondering if Mike the Cop had given the note to Bobby.

It had taken three days for Pete and Ralphie to organize a sham wedding reception. Pete had said his biggest problem was finding two hundred Italians who didn't look like Mafia. But he did it because it had to look real to fool the heavy tail on Bobby.

Footsteps approached, and Tiger grew tense as someone took the stall to Tiger's left. But from the sounds and smells, he knew it wasn't Bobby. God, thought Tiger, wanting to gag. Suddenly the room was filled with laughter.

"Hey, did you see the size of that broad's tits?" asked a loud voice.

He didn't answer, but he heard the rancorous laughter as someone tested Tiger's stall. He stiffened, but the man moved to the other end. Suddenly the cubicle to the right filled, and a package with a white covering envelope was passed under the divider. He grabbed at it as both stalls emptied, leaving him with the smells.

Since he couldn't leave before the end of the reception, Tiger decided to read what was in the white envelope:

Tiger
    I knew you would find a way to contact me. I am up to my eyeballs in wiretaps and surveillance teams. My investiga-

tion into the clerk's office cost me a good man, which seems to have stirred up a hornet's nest for me.

The clerk's office is riddled with rogue cops who have been replacing heroin with milk sugar as I suspected.

The detective Cahill you had me check on also works there as does Inspector Colby, who is head of the clerk's office.

The following documents will show a coverup is in force, but I still don't have sufficient evidence to take it upstairs. Tiger, before my man met with his "accident" he said the Feds knew what was going on, but that they were letting it happen.

I now know Malone was responsible for my transfer, but I still don't know where he fits into the picture. Also, I understand over a hundred million has been taken.

I believe I am still alive because they are ignorant of how much I know, but these documents could change that.

I don't know were this is going, but be careful.

Bobby

Tiger took a moment to put his thoughts together. He now knew it hadn't started with Turk's visit. It had been going on a long time, since moving that much narcotics required time, money, and organizing.

He picked up the first document. It was a letter from the Brooklyn district attorney's office to Inspector Colby of the clerk's office. It requested an investigation into tampering with evidence.

The second letter was a reply from Sergeant Phillip Defalco of the clerk's office. The sergeant found no evidence of dilution of the sample evidence but had found instead that much of the evidence had been mislabeled, due to overcrowding in the warehouse. The sergeant promised to correct the situation immediately.

Stapled to the letter was a newspaper clipping dealing with the murder of Sergeant Defalco of the property clerk's office. The sergeant was found in a parked police cruiser with his throat cut. Sergeant Defalco, thought Tiger, had one pair of balls to have signed his name to his own death warrant.

144

He picked up the third document. It was a report from Internal Affairs dealing with an investigation into two policemen attached to the Brooklyn property clerk's office. The two policemen in question were suspected of stealing heroin, but they were murdered before they could be indicted. Tiger realized these were the two policemen Patsy had killed.

Continuing the report, Tiger noticed that the two suspects had spent considerable time hanging out in Harlem. But nothing in the report indicated why two Brooklyn policemen traveled to Harlem to hang out. Were they into junk? Something about the letter bothered Tiger, until the name Doorknob hit him and he knew the shit was beginning to smell.

He sat back wondering what significance should be placed on the fact that all three policemen were Italian.

Hours later Tiger left the catering hall. He found the streets deserted and dark as he slipped into the first car parked at the curb. Pete pulled out into the traffic, as Ralphie fell in behind in another car.

Traveling along Linden Boulevard, they hit the Belt Parkway and headed east. Both men were silent, with Tiger's mind still reeling from the information in the documents.

The game being played at the clerk's office was a vicious one, and Tiger was tempted to send in a crew to blow up the place. Didn't they understand what they were doing? He guessed not, because of the greed that was getting to them. He now knew someone was using the family for distribution of the stolen narcotics, namely Sally Dell Delvechicco.

Suddenly Ralphie pulled alongside, wildly blasting his horn. Tiger quickly ran down the window.

145

"We got two cars following," he shouted.

Before Tiger could answer, Pete hit the accelerator, with Ralphie falling in behind. "Where to?" he asked, throwing a tight glance at Tiger.

"Stay on the parkway unless they start to move up. It's probably Malone looking to break balls."

"If it is Malone, then Bobby's cover could be blown."

Tiger couldn't worry about that now. Getting caught with the documents could get them all killed.

"They're coming up fast, Tiger," said Pete.

Tiger turned and looked out the rear window but only saw glaring headlights. Suddenly one set of lights zigzagged back and forth across the window, and Tiger knew Ralphie was playing cowboy to give him time to escape.

"Quick, get off this exit!"

Pete hit the pedal and pulled the car to the right and shot down the exit ramp. Suddenly there was a loud screech as Ralphie spun the wheel, blocking all the lanes. As they sped away, Tiger hoped Ralphie wasn't hurt.

Pete made a fast left, jumped two red lights, made another turn, and hit the gas pedal. At the Linden housing complex, Pete shot through the huge parking lot. There he cut the lights, pulled between two parked cars, and turned off the engine.

"When Bobby said he was blanketed, he meant he was blanketed," said Tiger.

"I guess your friend Malone isn't as stupid as you thought."

Tiger nodded agreement. "Let's find a phone."

They found one in the lobby of the first building. Tiger woke a sleepy Tony.

"You awake?"

"I am now. What's up?"

"Get out to Bobby's and tell him I think he's been blown."

"Shit. I'm on my way."

In the car Tiger felt sick thinking of Philomena and the kids. He hoped for their sakes Bobby was all right, although sweeping a police inspector under the rug wasn't that easy.

They headed up the Van Wyck where Tiger had Pete pull up at the last exit. Tiger handed Pete his pile of documents. "Make two copies and bury the originals."

"Where do you think you're going?" asked a nervous Pete.

"I'll grab a cab to the house."

"The hell you will. I'm going with you," said Pete.

But Tiger shook his head. "If someone is waiting for me, I want to be clean. These documents could get us both killed."

"I still don't like it," said Pete.

"Don't worry about it. Whoever it was took a shot and lost. Besides the dogs will give me plenty of warning," he said. "Oh, and have Rizzo get Ralphie out on bail."

"If he's not in the hospital," said Pete.

Tiger nodded, his lips tightening.

W ITHIN a half dozen blocks of his house, Tiger heard the dogs barking. He quickly ordered the taxi driver to turn around. But it was too late: He was boxed in, surrounded by a half-dozen unmarked cars. Drawn guns filled the windows as the driver shouted, "Don't shoot! Don't shoot!"

Strong hands pulled Tiger from the vehicle. Tiger tried to maintain his balance, but he was being jostled by too many hands at once. Suddenly he was hit from behind and he crumbled to the ground in a heap.

When he awoke, he found the ground cold. Foghorns sounded their eerie warnings, water slapped against the pilings, and Tiger knew he was on a pier. Still groggy, he attempted to turn over, but the handcuffs made it impossible and painful. His head throbbed, so he lay there waiting for the pain to pass.

Suddenly he was blinded by headlights, and shadowy figures seemed to float just beyond the edge of the light. One shadowy figure stepped into the light and stood in silhouette over Tiger's prone body. "Hi, guy, how's it going?"

147

Tiger recognized the voice: the computer, Smilin' Jack. But he couldn't focus on the face.

Jack squatted for a better look. "You've been a naughty, naughty boy. Now you know that's a no-no."

Painfully, Tiger tried to sit up but the effort was too much. He fell back.

"Take his cuffs off," snapped Jack from the shadows.

Tiger sat up, letting the blood flow into his limbs.

"That's better, friend. Here," purred Jack, "let me help you to your feet."

Tiger felt like rubber, but once standing he found himself eyeball to eyeball with Smilin' Jack. "What say, friend? You want to give me what you picked up tonight?"

Tiger's mind was so clouded he couldn't remember the question. "What did you say?"

The computer smiled and continued brightly, "I'm going to ask you one more time. What did you pick up tonight?"

Through the fog, the word "what" registered, which meant they didn't know what he picked up. For all they knew, it could have been a verbal meet. But he said nothing and hoped to stall for time.

But the computer's smile disappeared. He grabbed Tiger by the lapels and pulled him close. "You're not saying what I want to hear, friend."

Tiger just stood there, pretending to be totally out of it. The agent looked beyond Tiger to the shadows. "Did you search him good?"

"He's clean," shot back a voice.

The agent's grip tightened. "What did you do with it? Who did you slip it to?"

Tiger, his head clearing, found his anger returning. He started to brace himself for an onslaught, but before he could move, he was doubled up by an expert jab to his stomach. The top of his head exploded as he was jerked upright again.

"Where is it, bastard? Where is it?" he snarled.

But Tiger was beyond caring. The heat was making him sleepy and he just wanted to rest. He knew he had to hit the ground, but it didn't matter. Nothing mattered but sleep. Suddenly the pain surrounded him, enveloped him, smothered him. The body kicks came from every direction, his head, connecting with his groin, chest, back, legs, and ribs. Not knowing which pain to deal with first, he took refuge in blackness.

"For God's sake, you're killing him!" a shadow screamed.

Kick after kick, the hate poured out of Smilin' Jack, and Tiger knew he was slipping away.

"Leave the bastard lay there," the agent said, turning to a shadowy figure hidden behind the headlights. "You give me the information I want or I'll bury you."

"Hey, what the hell you yelling at me for? He outsmarted us all."

And Tiger recognized the voice he knew so well and could have cried if the pain hadn't been so great. Instead he slipped into blackness.

T HE row of rivets ran along the steel baseboard and Tiger knew he was in a cell. He attempted to turn his head toward the voices, but the pain put him back to sleep.

Tiger didn't know how long he had been out, but the voices were still there. Inch by inch, he turned his head, looked at the prisoners scattered about the cell. He recognized no one. He raised his head as two men approached. From their hard features, they looked like harness bulls, not Feds.

"Let's go, Corso."

Tiger steeled himself for another round of exercise. He really wasn't up to it, since his sore muscles were beginning to stiffen. As the cell door opened, he saw Lawyer Rizzo in the background. He was flooded with relief.

"We found him laying out in the street. He had no identification, so we put him in here," the detective said.

Rizzo rushed into the cell and knelt beside Tiger.

"How do you feel?"

"Lousy, the service stinks," he said, reaching for Rizzo.

Rizzo helped him to his feet, still groggy and sore. Shuffling out the door, Tiger brushed off any assistance other than Rizzo's. Together they made it down the stairs, past the rush of policemen in the main lobby, and to the street where Don Corso waited for him at the curb. With great effort he took a moment to settle into the back seat of the huge vehicle.

"Do you need a doctor?"

"No, nothing is broken."

Don Corso nodded and spoke to the hardface behind the wheel. Once in traffic, Don Corso looked at his son. "Who was responsible for this?" he hissed.

"The Feds," said Tiger simply, as he told the story. He said nothing about the informer, feeling that was a personal matter. As he told the story, he saw the strange smoldering hatred in his father's eyes.

"The bastards," exclaimed Lawyer Rizzo.

Tiger had difficulty taking his eyes from his father's face. He had never seen such a frightening expression in his life. The eyes narrowed to black dots. The skin was stiff and lifeless, and for the first time in his life he believed in the old wives' tale of the avenging angel.

"Give the driver Pete's address. I will have him picked up and brought to you. He is in great danger."

Tiger hesitated, wondering if this was another maneuver, but the cold look dissuaded him. At the first street phone, the driver stopped and got out. Tiger turned to Lawyer Rizzo.

"What shape is Ralphie in?" asked a worried Tiger.

"A couple of broken ribs and some bad bruises, but that's not the problem. The Feds are charging him with obstruction of justice. It's bullshit, but it may take something to get him out."

Tiger felt relieved, since Rizzo never spoke to impress. His father settled back, the wildness ebbing. "We are

150

after information. Revenge we can get later," he said, still smoldering.

But, thought Tiger, since Jack was making this personal, he wanted a shot at him. "Have you heard anything of Bobby Cassaro?"

But Don Corso waited until the driver returned to the car before speaking again. "I will send word to him, but I do not think he is in any danger. I don't even think our friend Malone knew a game was being played last night."

Tiger's brows shot up. "How do you figure that?"

"Because our Federal friends were running an interception on their own. I also believe they know the situation at the clerk's office and for some reason wanted to throw a monkey wrench into the machinery."

Tiger let out his breath.

T HE soreness was still there when he saw Jeanne sitting on the edge of the bed. Her smile was tinged with worry.

"How do you feel?"

"Not up to dancing. How about you?"

"A nervous wreck. It's been a crazy night," she said softly.

"You've been through it before," he said, carefully studying her features.

"I know, and I'll probably be through it again. But it never gets easy."

"Maybe I should go into another line of work," he said, trying to lighten her up.

She laughed. "Like a used car salesman?" She paused. "Pete and Ralphie are outside."

"What kind of shape is Ralphie in?"

"He has bandages too but in different places," she smiled.

He wanted to slap her on the rump, but she anticipated him and quickly moved out of his reach, rushing from the room giggling like a school girl. She left the door open for Pete and Ralphie.

Ralphie walked with a slight limp, and his arm was in a sling. Tiger could see he was hurting. "It looks like her husband caught up with her."

"It was the husband's boyfriend," quipped Ralphie as they shook hands. Neither wanted a bear hug.

"Who did this?" asked Pete questioningly.

Tiger told them to bring their chairs closer. "The Feds."

Both looked at Tiger in astonishment. "Did you recognize any of them?" asked Pete pointedly.

Tiger shrugged. "Smilin' Jack."

Pete half nodded, but Tiger didn't like the look in his eyes. "Don't get any ideas into that head of yours. He's mine," said Tiger. "Besides, I think he's a rogue who's involved in the clerk's office."

"Shit!" exclaimed Ralphie. "Now we got the Feds pushing junk."

"Looks like it," said Tiger, wondering why none of the narcotics had hit the street yet.

Pete examined Tiger carefully. "At what point do we go on the offensive against them. Or are you going to wait until they kill you?"

Tiger's eyes frosted over as he studied his friend. "I will decide when we move."

Pete shrugged and handed Tiger a pack of papers.

"What's this?" he asked, his brows knit.

"Before I gave your father's boys the documents, I made copies for you."

Tiger smiled.

Sixty minutes later, Big Che arrived from Pittsburgh. He was shocked at seeing Tiger wrapped in bandages. "Who did this?" he asked coldly.

"It was an accident," explained Tiger—not in the mood to explain.

152

The big man nodded his silence, but he knew well the signs of a good beating.

Tiger appreciated Che's concern, but it was a personal matter and there was other work to be done.

"What do you need me to do?" asked Big Che.

Tiger sent him up to Harlem to supervise a clock on Iggy and Weasel's haunts. He assigned ten men for his surveillance team.

After dinner Pete brought Momma Corso for a visit. She was vibrant and in a talkative mood and insisted on sitting on the edge of the bed. For forty years his mother had hardly ever spoken to him. But now she chattered incessantly, mostly about the old days, which gave Tiger the impression she was looking to bridge some confused gap between new and old.

She talked of growing up in a tiny world of six sun-scorched acres. The farm was ringed by tall hedges, and Momma often wondered whether the hedges were there to protect the insiders or the outsiders.

Working the farm required labor seven days a week, with two hours off every Sunday for mass. In the square where the church stood the neighbors met to renew and review the events of the past week. But Momma and Camille were forbidden to mingle with neighboring outsiders. Only one family, the Falzones, were allowed to visit the farm. They owned a piece of land in the vicinity, but Momma never knew where. Since the Falzones *padrino* and *madrino* — godparents—to Momma and Camille, it was assumed that Momma and Camille were betrothed to the Falzones' two sons. It was a prospect neither girl looked forward to, since each of the boys weighed over three hundred pounds. To leave the hedges to marry Angelo signified nothing to Momma, except someone eles's fields to work with the added burden of children.

His mother smiled suddenly. "Tony Corso was a bright light in a gloomy world. He had always been that to me," she said, wearing a far away expression. "He was like a wild animal turned loose in a world of sheep. He was big and he was hungry, with a look that froze most men," she said, pausing.

Tiger really wasn't interested in Momma's tale of his father's beginnings. He had enough bitter memories of his own, but Momma wanted to talk. So Tiger listened.

"I remember the first time I saw him. I was in the fields picking peppers with Camille. They appeared, as if from nowhere, well within the boundaries of the hedge. They stood there, the two of them, holding wicked lobos—shotguns—on their shoulders. They were dirty, dirty, with the wild look of wolves. I wanted to alarm my family, but I couldn't. I was fascinated and frightened at the same time. After a moment, both men turned and crawled through the hole they had cut in the hedge. I told my father what had happened, and my father and brothers took turns patroling the farm."

Momma took a sip of the wine Jeanne had set out for her.

"I found out later they lived in a cave high in the mountains. The man with Tony Corso was Pasquale Colombo, the only friend Tony Corso ever had. While Pasquale was a fire-eater, Tony Corso was a cunning, thinking man, always plotting and always suspicious of everyone around him."

Tiger got the impression there was a message in her story. Since all Sicilians were oblique people, Tiger waited and listened.

"That night we were asleep from an exhausting day's work. Suddenly I felt strong hands grab me so I could not scream. I was quickly gagged, tied up, and carried into the mountains. After long hours of travel, I was dumped on the ground like a sack of potatoes. The smell was that of a goat pen. I knew I was in a cave. It was dark and damp and the footsteps echoed. I was frightened and wanted to go home, but suddenly my clothes were ripped from me. I was pounced on by an animal."

Tiger saw the beads of perspiration on her forehead. He watched her, knowing she wanted to expunge the poison bottled up in her.

154

"At one point I heard Camille scream, but by then I was too numb to care. The madness seemed to go on forever, and then I heard my father shouting. I heard footsteps and I knew I was alone in the cave with Camille; but I was still gagged and tied and couldn't search for her. I tried to cut the ropes on a jagged rock, but they came back and I was dragged to the cave entrance. It was daylight and Pasquale dropped me at the entrance and hid behind a rock with his lobo pointed at my father and three brothers. Tony Corso also had a shotgun and stood outside the cave talking to my family."

Tiger had been watching her carefully. Her eyes were vacant, glassy. He wanted to stop her but he couldn't.

"They talked for a long time. My family was afraid of him, but I didn't care. I wanted him dead. This insult had to be avenged, either by my family, the Falzones, or me. But when I saw the priest hurrying up the mountain, I realized my father was saving himself.

"I didn't get married in a church with a white gown, surrounded by bridesmaids. I was married with my hands tied behind my back, lying on the ground like an animal.

"When the wedding was over, no one shook hands, kissed me, or said good-bye. We were now lepers, and without a backward glance my family walked down the mountain and out of our lives."

Tiger took a second to catch his breath as he looked into his mother's sad eyes.

"Then my new husband untied my hands and delivered me to another cave. Tony was always kind. We lived in the cave for three months. My husband and Pasquale would disappear for a day at a time and Camille would often think to escape. But to where? We had no money, no family, and no friends. So we stayed. Then one day Tony said we were going to America. I don't know why. I knew he wasn't afraid of the Falzones, who by tribal law had to avenge the insult to themselves. When I questioned him, all he would say was '*Lo avere a livarsi na petra di la scarpa.*' Which Tiger translated as 'I have to take the stone out of my shoe.'

"It was later when Camille came to America that I learned whose stone was in his shoe. The night before leaving the mountains, Pasquale and my husband sneaked down from the caves to take the stones out of their shoes. They killed all the male members of the Falzone family."

His mother's eyes hardened as she studied him. "You better remember. Don Corso outsmarts everyone."

Tiger smiled gently. "I have not forgotten. When do you want to visit Camille?"

"When you are well," she said, getting to her feet. "Now I will spend some time with my grandchildren." She leaned forward and planted a kiss on his forehead. "Until tomorrow, my son."

He lay there a long time after she left, sifting through her story, seeking some message. A few things jumped out at him. She still wanted revenge, unless something happened in the cave, or later in America, that changed her mind. His father, like all Sicilians, who never forgot or forgave, still had an eye on killing Camille. Finally, something that Tiger filed away in his brain: He noticed she never referred to him as "your father," but always called him Tony Corso or Don Corso. He also found disconcerting the impersonal way she spoke of him in the third person. To Tiger it seemed too distant for someone who had spent forty years with him.

T wo days later, Tiger was back in his new offices. He ordered breakfast from Lulu's for Pete and Ralphie. The buzzer rang.

"Yeah?" said Pete, looking at Tiger. "Big Che's outside."

Tiger was sure he showed his surprise. "Have him come in," he said, wondering what made Che leave his clock.

On entering the room, the big man smiled at the display of food. He shook hands all around and stood before Tiger, who remained sitting at the desk. "What's up?"

156

"It's slow as hell up there so I came to pay a visit. I miss the hell out of you guys."

Pete and Ralphie looked up sharply but remained silent.

Tiger's brows knitted as he asked, "What's happening in Harlem?"

"Not much. Iggy has been staying very close to his apartment."

"What about Weasel?" snapped Tiger.

"He seems to have stopped running, so I guess whatever he was setting up is over. He's been holed up for the past two days in his club," said Big Che, looking over the food. "That's why I sneaked down to say hello."

Tiger found Iggy and Weasel's actions strange. Since he knew Iggy only had ten men in his organization and Weasel had only five, both should have been hustling the streets for dealers if they intended to dump a hundred millon dollars' worth of junk on the streets. Tiger knew it would take at least two hundred dealers to set up a proper distribution, so why were they sitting around on their butts? He looked up at the big man. "I assigned you to that job because it was important to me and I wanted you on top of it every minute," he said coldly.

The big man accepted the rebuke and nodded. "I'll get right back on the job."

With Che gone, everyone seemed to have lost his appetite. Tiger wondered if his relationship with Che had changed. He had not seen disobedience before.

He sat alone for the rest of the afternoon. He took a moment to recall the hurry-up summons to Camille's the night before. He found her, as usual, in the foul-smelling cellar, and he guessed old habits were hard to break.

She sat there, her penetrating eyes measuring him, and Tiger was certain she was going to hit him with something heavy.

"Why did Don Corso take my sister from the hospital?" she asked quickly.

The question surprised him, since the answer was obvious.

157

"Because Momma was getting better, and I really believe my father missed her," he said sincerely.

"How do I know Don Corso won't try to use her to get at me?"

Shit, thought Tiger, here comes the paranoia. "Because now that my father knows where you are, he could have had you killed anytime he wanted to. But I don't think he is interested in revenge."

The intensity of her stare reminded him of the legend of *malòcchio,* the evil eye.

"I said nothing about revenge."

Tiger realized she was right. She had used the word in the traditional sense, while he had used it loosely. His father's attempted murder of Camille could have been spontaneous, the result of an argument that need not have resulted in an oath of vengeance. However, if Camille's paranoia was the result of some offense that Don Corso felt still had to be avenged, then the world was darker.

He chose his words carefully. "I don't know what's between you and my father. But I would forget it."

"Will Don Corso also forget it?" she prodded.

Tiger guessed living in a cage for thirty-five years would make anyone see shadows. "I told you, Camille. You are under my protection."

His assuring words seemed to mean little. "Even against Don Corso?"

He nodded. "Even against Don Corso," he said, suddenly aware of a strange glint creeping into her eyes. The look made him feel very uncomfortable as she probed the depths of him.

"Even if I killed Don Corso's baby?" she spat out at him.

The meaning of the words exploded all around him and he wondered what madness he had stepped into. Her words were a challenge, offering him a slight chance to back off from his promise of protection, for she had committed an unforgivable offense no Sicilian could overlook. But Tiger had given Momma his word. Reluctant as he was, he would still have to die if necessary to protect Camille.

Pete stuck his head in the door and all thoughts of Camille evaporated.

"You got a problem," Pete said softly.

"What is it?"

"Carlo Alessi is demanding an audience. He has a beef against some guy named Calamine."

Tiger couldn't remember the name Calamine. "Who is he?"

"An outsider."

Tiger knew the word "outsider" bothered Pete. "If the man's an outsider, tell Alessi to do what he wants with him," he said.

"I did, but Lorenzo Fortuno wants to defend the man before you."

Lorenzo was a likable, fair-minded man, while Alessi was a street-hardened animal. Both were made members, so he couldn't refuse to speak to them. "Bring them in."

After shaking hands, he invited them to sit and signaled Pete to leave.

"What can I do for you?"

Calamine was making a move against a trucking company Alessi wanted to control. He owned a small piece he used as a wedge to work his way in. The foreman of the trucking company was a street-smart Sicilian and a friend of the owner. It seemed every time Alessi made a move, Calamine thwarted it until it turned into open warfare.

"The bastard shot one of my men and blew up my fucking club," shouted Alessi. "And now I want the bastard dead."

Tiger felt the sting of Alessi's words but waved him to silence and looked at Lorenzo. "Your side?"

Lorenzo's side was quite different. He had grown up with Calamine, a wild kid from the streets, who later won a lot of medals in the the war. Calamine was totally loyal to his friends and not a man to be pushed around. Over the years, the owner of the trucking company had pulled Calamine out of several scrapes and Calamine felt he owed the man

159

something. He knew sooner or later Alessi was going to win, so he made a deal to let the takeover be friendly, to gently put the owner out to pasture, not hurt him, and give him a few dollars each year. That was agreed to by all parties in Lorenzo's presence.

"What went wrong?" asked Tiger.

"Carlo sent in some wise guy who caused all the trouble."

"Hey," shot back Alessi. "He knew that man was my representative. He shot the bastard anyway."

"Why?" shouted Lorenzo. "Because your man started pushing people around. We had a deal, a promise, but still your man beat the shit out of the owner to get him to sign away the company. Right away your man tried to treat Calamine like a floor sweeper. And every damn day Calamine was begging me to back off the Jew who was causing all the trouble."

"Jew?" asked Tiger in surprise.

"Yeah, a Jew. He sent a wise guy to treat a Sicilian like shit, but when Carlo refused to pull his man out, the wise guy raised his hands to Calamine. Calamine put him in the hospital."

Tiger had many Jews associated with his family. Of all the outsiders, Jews had an affinity for Sicilians, perhaps because of their own clannishness and the similarities of family lifestyles. But that's where the trouble began, their misguided loyalties. When they attacked a family member, they became Dobermans. Not understanding the subtlety of the Sicilian mind, they failed to understand how they were being manipulated.

"Why did Calamine shoot him?" asked Tiger.

"Because," said Lorenzo, "as soon as the wise guy recovered Carlo sent him back in. The first day back on the job the wise guy tried to run Calamine down with a forklift. So Calamine did what he had to do. He put two bullets in him."

"And why did he blow up the club?" asked Tiger.

"Because Carlo sent an army against him."

160

Tiger sat back deeper in the chair. "Where is Calamine now?"

"The bastard is out on the streets," shouted Alessi, "waiting to do more damage. He's crazy and I want to get that nut job off my back."

"And the takeover?" asked Tiger softly.

Carlo lowered his head. "The bastard owner called the cops when he got beat up, so I have to wait for the heat to cool."

Tiger realized there were no winners, only losers. He wondered how many good men would die before they brought down Calamine. What price would he have to pay for Alessi's pride?

Tiger looked from face to hardened face. "Is there no way we can resolve this?" he asked of the two.

"I demand my rights," said Alessi.

"Calamine has done nothing disrespectful. He protected himself as any honorable man would. His only crime was to refuse to lie in the gutter for a Jew."

It seemed to Tiger that Calamine was a victim of his own beliefs. A man of respect, a man Tiger could admire. A traditional man in a modern era. It was a rare person who would lay down his life to repay an obligation. A rare person indeed.

As to Carlo and his representative, both were fools, but as such he was protected by the Council. Once Calamine used violence, he was doomed; and blowing up the club only compounded the offense. In Tiger's mind, Calamine did nothing he wouldn't have done under the same conditions. But the Council's rules were omnipotent, and his hands were tied.

"Therefore," he said, looking at Alessi, "I must rule in your favor. However, if any more of my men get hurt because of this mess, you'll answer to me," he said, secretly hoping Calamine had the brains to get out of town, but doubting that he did.

161

A few moments after Alessi and Lorenzo left, Pete disturbed him again, this time handing Tiger a small, white envelope.

"It's marked 'personal,' " said Pete.

Tiger examined the bold writing on the face of the envelope: MISTER JOSEPH CORSO. Tiger wasn't used to such formal use of his name. He opened it and read the brief note:

IF YOU WANT TO KNOW WHO STOLE THE HEROIN FROM THE CLERK'S OFFICE, THEN MAYBE WE CAN MAKE A DEAL.

After reading the rest of the instructions, he handed the note to Pete.

"Where did it come from?" asked Tiger.

"Someone gave it to the outside man," said Pete. "You want me to stake out the area?"

But Tiger waved him off. "Let's follow the instructions. I don't want to scare him off," said Tiger.

Twenty minutes later Pete parked the car on the Rockaway pier alongside a pay phone. Pete and Ralphie stayed inside the car. At ten minutes to three the phone rang and Tiger picked it up.

"Yeah?" he asked.

"Is this Joseph Corso?" a strange voice asked.

"It is," answered Tiger.

"If you listen carefully, you might recognize my voice," said the stranger.

Tiger was alerted. "Where do I know you from?"

"I gave you a present once in front of your house."

Tiger knew he was close, but not close enough. "Keep talking."

"I said I was only a working man," the stranger said.

Tiger suddenly matched the voice with the face. "I got you," he said, remembering the detective who handed him the subpoena.

"Can we make a deal?" asked the detective.

162

"What kind of money are you asking?" inquired Tiger, wondering where the hell he was going to get ten percent of one hundred million. It would be cheaper, he thought, to burn the drugs and kill the ten percenter.

"I'll tell you when I see you," answered the detective.

"When will that be?"

"I'm watching you from the end of the pier."

Tiger saw the man's shadow in the phone booth at the end of the pier. "How do you want to handle this?" asked Tiger.

"You pick a place and I'll follow," the detective said.

Hanging up, Tiger made another call. A moment later he was driving off the pier with a black Oldsmobile following at a discreet distance. He headed across town and into the swamp to his cousin's incinerator. He drove through the huge doors, past the row of furnaces and the watchful eye of Frankie.

In the far corner he halted. Pete and Ralphie jumped out, keeping between Tiger and the cop. The tall detective stood silent as Pete took his gun before letting him enter the car with Tiger. Inside, the detective smiled.

Tiger didn't bother returning the smile. "What can I do for you?"

The detective shrugged. "I hope we can do something for each other."

The detective's well-tailored suit told Tiger this was no ordinary grafter, if he was one at all.

"My brother Phillip was the sergeant in charge of inventories at the clerk's office. He was killed by someone who worked there."

Tiger took a second to catch his breath. "What was your brother's name?"

"Phillip Defalco. I'm Alfred Defalco."

Tiger recognized the sergeant's name from the documents Bobby had given him. And he guessed the sergeant was fully involved. He also wondered if this detective had the merchandise in his possession. "What do you want from me?"

The detective took a long moment to measure Tiger. "The word on the street is that you're the new boss of the Bocci family. Is that true?"

Tiger remained silent.

"Okay, let me rephrase that. Since you are the new boss of the Bocci family, that means you have the drugs," said the detective coldly.

Tiger was taken aback. "How do you figure that?"

"Because the man who killed my brother and got the junk works for you," he snapped.

Tiger just looked at the man, wondering who was playing what game. "Are you saying your brother delivered drugs to one of my men?"

"That's what I'm saying," fumed the detective.

"Who's this guy?" demanded Tiger in anger.

"Your man Delvechicco, who owns the Doorknob."

Tiger sat back to collect his thoughts. "If you can prove that, you can have him after I finish with him," said Tiger coldly. He saw the doubt in the other man's face.

"How do you know this Delvechicco killed your brother?" asked Tiger in a softer tone.

"Because he had a meeting with him the day my brother was killed."

The detective avoided Tiger's eyes. "He was to deliver two kilos of heroin to him," he said, as he waved Tiger to silence. "It's not what you're thinking. My brother hated junk," he said softly.

"Then what the hell was he doing with two kilos?" Tiger asked coldly.

In frustration, Defalco blurted out, "Because the men in his squad threatened to kill him if he didn't get involved."

Tiger settled back, allowing each to gather themselves. Then he spoke softly, "How did your brother get involved?"

The detective took a moment to light a cigarette. "My brother was the inventory clerk in the property office. He found samples had been tampered with, so he went to his superior, Inspector Colby, who said he would look into it.

But instead, a half dozen patrolmen in his squad grabbed him and told him to take a piece of the cake or they would kill his kids."

"So he took a piece of the cake," said Tiger gently.

The detective nodded. "My brother said they were a crazy bunch of rogues who had already snuffed a couple of people."

"Why couldn't one of them have killed your brother?"

The detective's brows shot up. "What for? He already agreed to work for them."

Tiger told him of the documents Bobby had given him, omitting any mention of Bobby.

"I didn't know about the letter," said the detective, as his eyes cooled.

"I will have a talk with Delvechicco and if he's involved, he's yours. But I suggest you look around the clerk's office for answers."

The detective fell into a deep thought, and Tiger would have liked to read his mind.

"Can I see those papers?" asked Defalco.

Tiger nodded. "You'll get them tomorrow, but you better be careful."

The detective's eyes frosted over. "I intend to."

Tiger took a moment to catch his breath before asking, "What do you know of the men at the clerk's office?"

Defalco shrugged. "Not much. After my brother's death I did some checking but ran into a stone wall. That place is like Fort Knox. My brother said they were a sleazy lot and Colby was the worst of them."

"Do you know how they were taking the drugs out?"

Defalco shook his head. "He received the heroin outside the clerk's office."

"He say who gave him the stuff?"

"The first time it was two cops named Denato and Aielo, but both are dead now."

Tiger knew. They were the two Patsy killed.

"The second time it was two different men and the last time, when he was killed, I don't know who it was."

165

Tiger was alerted to the hesitation. "Did he say who the other two men were?"

"I checked both men out, and they're on night duty at the clerk's office."

"Their names," demanded Tiger, softly.

The detective reached into his jacket and pulled forth a packet of pictures and handed them to Tiger. "These are the only names my brother mentioned."

Tiger studied the pictures carefully. Tiger didn't like the photo of Inspector Colby, nor his beady snake eyes and ratty features. Three of the pictures jumped out at him. He recognized the gold shield detectives and his friend.

"You recognize any of them?" asked the detective.

Tiger shook his head. "No," he said simply.

PETE and Ralphie opened up a path for Tiger through the rush of screaming young people. The face of the Doorknob Club was nothing more than a brick wall with an awning leading to the curb. There were no windows, just a door in the center with an oversized brass-plated doorknob. Inside, dimly lit alcoves and arches allowed for privacy. The only two areas brightly lit were the bar area and the manager's office.

At the entrance to the manager's office, a big man, obviously the bouncer, blocked their path.

"Where you guys going?" he asked menacingly.

Pete stepped in, elbowed the man nicely aside, and stepped into Delvechicco's office. Tiger quickly recognized him from the video dossiers. He was a big man with ruddy, powerful features that looked as though they were carved from stone.

"This place is off limits," said Delvechicco, hunching his shoulders, preparatory to combat.

"You Sally Dell?" asked Tiger softly.

"Yeah, so what? Who are you?"

166

"I'm Joey Corso," he answered softly.

The change was instant, as Delvechicco broke into a grin and extended his hand. "Damn, I'm glad to meet you. You guys want some food or drinks?"

Tiger accepted the handshake but shook his head at the food and drinks. He sat at the desk and waved Delvechicco to the seat nearest him. "I just want to ask you a couple of questions."

"Sure, why not?" he said, looking askance at Pete and Ralphie. "Ask away."

"What is your business with the property clerk's office?"

Delvechicco shrugged. "Nothing, I didn't know it existed until a bunch of cops from there came in one night and tried to shake me down."

"What about?"

"They said Joe the Boss owed them fifty keys of H. I knew Joe Bocci never handled junk, so I told them to take a fucking walk."

"What happened then?"

"One of the asshole cops stuck his piece in my face and made a lot of threats. I told him he better use it or put it away before I stuck it up his ass. He put it away."

Looking at the man's face, Tiger believed he would do it. "Do you know a police sergeant named Defalco?"

Delvechicco shrugged. "Who's he?"

"He says he made deliveries of heroin here," Tiger said simply.

Delvechicco's face turned sour. "You're kidding. You sure he ain't got me mixed up with someone else?" he said in annoyance. "Call in all my workers and let them tell you if I even let someone in here with a joint."

"Why would he say that if it wasn't true?"

"I don't mean no disrespect to you, but I don't believe anything any cop tells me," he said, his anger rising. "But I'll tell you this. I don't let any junk in this place or any-where near me. You can ask anybody about me."

"But why would he say it?" persisted Tiger.

"It beats the shit out of me, Mister Corso, but I'm going

167

to tell you something. My kid brother was a junkie. For five years I threw away a fortune on that bastard, then he ups and dies of an overdose." A small tear filled the corner of each eye. "And if anyone came near me with a junk deal, I'd put a bullet in their brains."

Tiger gave the man a moment to get control of himself.

"Have you heard anything about thefts of drugs from the clerk's office?" asked Tiger.

Wiping away a tear, he shook his head. "When it comes to junk, I close my ears, but if you like I'll check around."

Tiger nodded and shook hands again. Another dead-end, he thought.

ΤONY Habu was a West Indian from Kingston, Jamaica. Drugs were a big part of his life, his culture, and his religion. He had come to America ten years before and settled in South Jamaica, Queens, where he was a high priest in the Rastapharian religion, a group that used marijuana as a part of their religious ritual.

A few years before, Tony had been stuffed into a car trunk by some street bankers. Tiger bailed him out, and Tony never forgot the favor he owed Tiger.

They sat in a sparsely furnished office in the rear of a small church. The odor of stale marijuana permeated the room.

"I had heard a big load of H was due to the dealers, but so far no one's received anything," said Tony, his long braids cascading down his neck.

"How about the Colombians?" asked Tiger.

"That's where I got my information. You know I don't let any of my people touch that shit."

"How long ago did you hear of it?"

"About a little over a month ago," said Tony.

"Any reason why nothing has hit the streets yet?"

Tony shrugged his slight shoulders. "Because it's probably smoke."

"Why do you say that?"

"Because any smart dealer waits until he has the material before he talks to anyone. By the time the street hears about it, the deal has usually already gone down and it's too late for the cops to get a lead."

Tiger knew Tony was right. So what was the game? He knew the heroin existed somewhere, yet it hadn't hit the streets.

That left one of two possibilities. Either the owner was dead and no one knew where the material was or someone was holding on to it. But why? Maybe, thought Tiger, it was smoke or smoke that was a diversion.

"Is it possible," asked Tiger, "that while the Weasel was priming the South Jamaicans, they were dumping the stuff somewhere else?"

The beads woven into Tony's braids sparkled as he shook his head. "Not in this city or state. For the amount they were talking about, New York is the marketplace. And if it was dumped here, I would know about it."

"But couldn't they make more money out of town?" asked Tiger.

"Sure you could, but if you're talking more than fifty kilos, and I get the sense you're talking a lot more than that, then you have a problem. Many things affect the potency of heroin. Age, temperature, moisture. The stuff won't last forever and to dispose of the amounts you're thinking about, it would take forever."

Tiger nodded his understanding and thanked Tony for his education.

"Oh, by the way," asked Tony offhandedly, "have you seen your brother Sonny lately?"

Tiger wondered where that was coming from. "Not for a couple of weeks. Why?"

"He's grouping with some bad dudes."

"Where is he?" asked Tiger, feeling the pain again.

"Harlem, with Sharky's boys. He's dealing and floating," said Tony, trying to be gentle.

Tiger felt the knot in the center of his stomach. He hadn't seen Sonny since he'd called in Dr. Epstein. He knew Sonny

169

was on the loose, but he didn't know where. Now he did—and Sharky was one of Iggy's dealers.

SHARKY's Place was on West 135th Street, deep in the heart of the black ghetto. Tiger knew the people there were hard criminals and revolutionaries.

In Sharky's domain, everyone knew each other and strangers were quickly challenged. The club was a whorehouse, a drug den, a drop for stolen goods, and a place where murder was cheap.

Tiger thought of Sonny and wondered what the hell he was doing with that crew. If he had some idea that Sharky was the route to Helen he was mistaken. Sharky and his pirates would leave him dead in an alley before he got near her.

Slowly Tiger cruised the area hoping to spot his brother, preferring not to use Sharky's Place as a starting point. The streets were full of pimps, hookers, dealers, and users. After two runs through the neighborhood he decided to head toward Sharky's.

Prior to entering Harlem, Tiger had Big Che and his men quietly infiltrate the area of the club.

Just a few doors down the street from the club he spotted Sonny, and what he saw made him sick. As usual, his brother was dressed in his leather Apache outfit. He was walking with glazed eyes, oblivious to everything and everyone on the street, headed in the direction of the club.

"Pull over, Pete," ordered Tiger. "He's heading for Sharky's."

Pete stopped the car just ahead of Sonny and opened the door for Tiger, who stepped out and took up a position blocking Sonny's path. As Tiger waited, he noticed his brother never missed a step, even though his eyes were now completely closed.

Suddenly a voice shouted, "Move away and let that man pass." It was a tall black man.

"I'm his brother," shot back Tiger.

"I don't give a damn who you are. That dude is strung out, and if you disturb him, he could become violent."

Tiger stepped aside, allowing Sonny to pass unmolested. He studied the tall black man uncertain if the man was a good Samaritan or a game player. The man was well dressed in sports clothes, looking neither like a pimp nor a dealer. "How long will he be like that?" asked Tiger.

"Who knows. Until the dream stuff wears off. Maybe an hour," the man said.

Tiger nodded his thanks and trailed slowly after Sonny. He was tempted to grab his brother and throw him in the car, but something held him back. What, he thought, if the man was right?

Ralphie, in the car, drove alongside the slow moving Sonny, while Pete hovered over Tiger as he followed his brother's slow progress.

Sonny entered to door to Sharky's Place, as people side-stepped him so as not to impede his movements.

The moment Tiger stepped into the club, he felt the hostile vibes. Many cold eyes turned toward him, but he decided to ignore them and concentrate on Sonny, who by some built-in radar avoided obstacles as he wended his way between the tables and the people.

Suddenly Tiger felt a thud and he went sprawling. He hit the floor and landed with his back against a wooden pillar. He quickly shook away the fog as a black man rolled over him. He knew Pete had decked the man. Instantly the room was filled with scraping chairs, screams, and flying ashtrays and glasses. He saw bodies charging to get at him.

He jumped to his feet. Fists pummeled him. Tiger kicked, chopped, and punched. He saw Ralphie swinging away. The throng was too thick for him to get through to his friends. Then he saw a raised ax about to descend on him. With little room to maneuver, he ducked under the blow, sending his shoulder into his assailant's midsection.

The force of his charge opened a swathe through the enemy, until the three of them linked up and fought with their backs to each other. Tiger swiftly kicked and a pistol went flying. He punched at faces to the right and the left and wondered how long he could keep up his strength. Suddenly he felt a kick in the balls. He tried to forestall the blackness. He fell to his knees, not noticing the blows that rained upon him. He remained conscious but immobile. He sensed a new tone to the pitch of the battle and knew something had happened. Through a fog he saw his troopers lashing out with baseball bats and lead pipes. He saw heads open and blood splatter as the main body broke and people scattered for the exits. When it was over, Tiger found himself drenched in sweat and needing assistance to stand. He took a moment to catch his breath before surveying the room. Sonny was still climbing the mountain against the rear wall. The few remaining blacks backed off as Tiger, gently but firmly, grabbed his brother's arm and nudged him forward. Sonny offered no resistance. He was still in a total fog. "Take him to the car," Tiger said to one of the troopers.

As his brother moved past him, he took a view of the carnage. He saw four men prostrate on the floor and another three trying to sit up as they held their hands to their bloody heads. None had the will to continue the battle. Tiger walked over to the terrified bartender and pulled him over the top of the bar. "Where's Sharky?" he shouted into the man's face.

"He ain't here," said the frightened man. "He don't come in till later."

Tiger pulled him closer. "You tell that black bastard, I'm coming after him," he screamed. "Do you understand that?"

At the man's nod he pushed him away. The man scampered out the door. He looked coldly at Big Che. "Smash this fucking place."

He watched as troopers used their bats and pipes to shatter bottles, mirrors, lamps, tables, chairs, everything that was breakable. Tiger's anger was still at battle pitch, but he knew it was time to move. "Let's go," he said to his troopers.

Black faces were everywhere as he stepped into the street and headed for the cars blocking the streets. Ralphie ran ahead to open the door for Tiger as the troopers mounted their vehicles and waited for Tiger's car to pull away. They fell in behind. In the distance could be heard the wail of sirens.

Pete was the first to speak. "Did you see those two cops standing in the hallway across the street?" he said in disbelief. "They didn't even have the balls to help us."

"Fucking cop bastards!" seethed Ralphie in reply.

Tiger paid no attention. Sonny had fallen asleep in the back seat.

AFTER Dr. Epstein left, Tiger walked up to the emergency apartments he maintained above his office. He nodded at the trooper stationed outside the door and entered. He found Sonny leaning on his side staring at the blank wall opposite him.

"How's it going?" asked Tiger softly.

Sonny jumped up from the bed and stood waiting for Tiger.

"Hey, man, what happened? How did I get here?"

Tiger hoped this wasn't another of his brother's cons. "You really don't remember my wrecking Sharky's Place?"

Sonny showed his surprise. "Why did you wreck Sharky's?"

"Because I thought you needed help," said Tiger softly.

Sonny just stared at him. "Was I that off the wall?"

Tiger nodded. "I would say so."

Sonny sat on the edge of the bed, staring at the floor. "I sampled some new stuff this morning and I guess I went over the edge. I'm sorry. I won't use that stuff again."

Tiger knew his brother was lying. "You don't sample heroin, you fill your system with it, purposely. What about going back for the cure and this time complete it?" he asked gently.

Sonny continued to study the floor. "I wish I could, Tiger, but I can't. I got a lot to do now," he said, beginning to fidget. "I need to keep on top of things for the next couple of weeks. Maybe I'll go then," he said, not looking at his brother.

"What do you have to do that you can't take a vacation?" asked Tiger. "Is it Helen?"

Sonny looked at him, his face turning sour. "Are you kidding? I don't need that broad anymore," he said haughtily. "I got heavy shit in my corner, and she don't fit into my future."

Tiger wondered why the turnaround. "What are you into that's so heavy?" he asked, wondering what lie was coming next.

Sonny rubbed his neck and exercised his shoulders before answering. "I can't tell you, but it's heavy."

"Why can't you tell me?" asked Tiger.

"I can't. Too many big people are involved."

Tiger changed the subject. "Have you been in touch with Helen?"

Sonny nodded. "Sure, a few times. But she don't interest me no more," he said casually.

"How the hell did you accomplish that?" asked Tiger with feigned admiration.

Sonny smiled slyly. "She sneaked out a couple of times to see me. Sharky set it up for me."

Tiger knew that last part slipped out involuntarily, but he decided to gloss over it. "I guess you and Sharky have become good friends, huh?"

Sonny smiled broadly and childishly. "He's been good to me. Because of him I'm a new man," he said, rotating his neck.

Tiger studied him. "Is that why you're still using the needle?" he asked coldly.

Sonny's nose screwed up. "You got that wrong, Tiger. It was stupid, but it won't happen again."

Tiger had seen the needle marks when he put Sonny to bed and he knew how much his brother was over it. "Who's your supplier? Sharky?"

Sonny registered genuine surprise. "Hell, no. I cop from a lot of places. I even sell Sharky some," he said smugly.

Tiger felt the pain in his stomach but stayed calm. He didn't bother to push the subject because he intended to deal with Sharky soon. "Since you're no longer interested in Helen, why are you hanging around in Harlem? Why with Sharky? You know he works for Iggy, who hates your guts. So why are you there?"

Sonny got to his feet and paced the floor before looking at his brother. "Hey, Tiger, I don't have to answer any more questions. You ain't my old man. So I'm leaving," he said, opening the closet to get at his clothes. But Tiger stepped in and blocked him. He looked coldly down at his brother. "I want to know what's going on in that head of yours, so you better tell me what I want to hear and if I like what I hear, then you may go. If not, I'll make you go cold turkey for the next week. Is that what you want?" said Tiger, as he watched the fear enter Sonny's eyes.

Sonny returned to his starting point at the edge of the bed. "What do you want to know?" he said with a sigh.

"I want to know why you refuse to go for the cure. This time a complete recovery. With Helen out of your life, you have a chance to rebuild yourself. You're young, you can start over. I'll even open a business for you. Any kind you want," he said, hoping he was getting through to him. "I want to help you in any way I can. Didn't I always do that for you as a kid? Fight for you?"

Sonny remained silent and still as Tiger spoke. Afterward he sat staring at the floor. Suddenly his eyes filled with tears.

Tiger saw the woebegone look and knew he was losing the battle.

"You don't understand," he said, continuing to study the floor near his feet, "it's all over."

Tiger just stood there, unable to move, either to recoil in horror at his brother's words or to move forward to comfort him. The abject misery of Sonny's words hit hard and left him numb.

"I know," continued Sonny gently, "you want to help me, Tiger. And I love you for it. But don't you see, nothing matters anymore. I'm dead inside. I don't feel nothing. I don't care for God, Momma, Papa, Carmine, you, people, or even for Sonny. If there was a drug to take to make me alive again, I would take it. If there was one person on this earth I could feel something for, I would drop on my knees and worship them, but I don't. I feel nothing and I know it's over. My mind and soul are burned out. All the love and medicine in the universe can't change me."

Tiger sat there trying to comprehend the incomprehensible. Perhaps Momma was right, the weak need all the love they can get and still it is not enough.

Tiger left the apartment door open, pulled away the trooper, and returned to his office.

THE following morning when Tiger returned to the office, he was surprised to find Sonny still up in the apartment. The night troopers said he never left the apartment nor used the phone. But he did order food twice during the night. Tiger found that odd, since Sonny had been in such a hurry to leave the night before. Well, he thought, if he wants to hang out that's fine with me, but I intend to watch the bastard.

He called Dr. Epstein to see to Sonny's needs. Then he checked in with the clocks in Harlem. Nothing. Weasel and Iggy were still dormant. And that was what was gnawing at him. If either of them had possession of the narcotics, wild horses couldn't keep either from trying to slip some on the market for a fast buck. Unless the stuff wasn't available. Unless it was lost, mislaid, or whoever hid it was dead. He thought of the family, but that failed to explain Weasel's setting up a network or the visit to Delvechicco by the off-duty cops.

But even so, reasoned Tiger, his inside man at the clerk's office was certain the drugs were getting out. So where was it disappearing to? Who was paying for it at the other end? And what were they doing with it if it wasn't hitting the streets?

He quickly calculated what a hundred million dollars in heroin weighed. His rough estimate came to about twelve hundred pounds, almost three-quarters of a ton. Damn, thought Tiger, that's a hell of a lot of dream stuff. He quickly divided and came up with an amount just short of five hundred kilos.

He remembered his one visit to look over the outside of the clerk's office. He had left with the impression that security was tight. If they managed to get it out, say in a briefcase, it could amount to no more than two kilos a day. It would take every day for almost a year to get it out. No, thought Tiger, they had to be moving it in bulk. Maybe a well-organized trip once a month. Which led to the conclusion Tiger didn't like. If they were taking it out in bulk, then the ring was bigger than he thought. If that was the case, the visit to Delvechicco was only the beginning.

Summing it all up, Tiger knew there was only one way to get the answers he needed to know. He didn't like it, but he had no other way. He had to snatch one of Colby's men.

He decided it was time to lay it all out for his father. So he made an appointment. After working his way through the milling hordes at his father's office, he entered the back room where he was waved to a seat. Everything seemed to be the same, but then everything always remained the same around his father. Only the absence of Toto was different.

"What did you need to talk about?" asked his father, looking up from counting his money.

Tiger told him about Weasel and Iggy setting up a network but failing to follow through.

"What bothers you about it?" asked Don Corso.

"Well, you don't open those kinds of doors and then slam them shut."

Don Corso nodded and Tiger continued.

He told his father of one night of being tailed by a gold shield and having to kill him.

When his father merely nodded, he continued. He spoke of Defalco's visit and the subsequent visit with Delvechicco. And last he told him of his intention of kidnapping one of Colby's men.

That snapped up his father's head. "What do you hope to accomplish by taking a policeman, when you could possibly get more information from Iggy or Uno Occhio?" he asked softly.

"Because I don't believe either man has the drugs in his possession. You know if they did they would be out hustling them."

His father nodded. "So my main problem is to find a new route to whoever is receiving the drugs."

"What will you do if the policeman you pick up doesn't have the answers you seek?" Don Corso asked enigmatically.

Tiger was prepared for that question. "I'll take the next policeman in line."

His father lit a cigar. "And if that policeman doesn't have the answers either?"

Tiger also expected that question. "I'll take them all out if I have to," he said emphatically. "I have a man inside the clerk's office; but because it's a closed club, he can't penetrate. I have no other direction to go in," said Tiger, knowing he was talking about a lot of killings. But there were more than the families at stake. If whoever had the narcot-

178

ics managed to use the drugs to put a wedge between the families, there would be wholesale slaughter.

The old man fell into deep thought before speaking. "There is another way," he said. "Do you remember the names of the policemen who are involved?"

Tiger nodded, remembering the rogues' gallery Defalco had shown him.

"Write down their names," he said, "and in a few days I shall select your target for you. One I am sure will have the needed information. Since a policeman is involved, we must walk carefully. When you get the information from the man, I want it to look like an accident. Do you understand that?"

Tiger nodded. "I understand, but why can't I just make him disappear?"

"Because the man you killed had a gold shield, and gold shields never go after a man unless he's sure he has something. He was either looking to nail you for something, or he was trying to scare you off. I believe he somehow tied you to what is going on in the clerk's office. The fact that he was willing to shoot first and ask questions later indicates his fear of you. That also means they will be coming at you again, so be very careful. As for Delvechicco, I will transfer him to my family for protection. I can place him out of their reach."

With the conversation ended, Tiger rose to leave, but his father waved him back to his chair. "There is another matter I wish to speak of," he said, almost beneath his breath.

Something in his tone alerted Tiger.

"I understand you did considerable damage to Sharky's Place. Is that true?"

Tiger was suddenly reminded of his father's long arm. Tiger nodded, "Yes."

"What did you expect to accomplish?" he continued softly.

The question surprised Tiger. "I don't understand," he said, wondering where his father was heading. To Sharky or Sonny?

"What I am asking is if it was personal or business?" Don Corso asked.

Tiger hesitated, then answered. "Both. I understood Sonny was dealing out of Sharky's Place. So I went up to check the rumor out. Also, if it gave me a shot at Iggy, through Sharky, I was going to take it."

"Then what happened?"

Tiger chose his words carefully. "I found Sonny, but he was in no condition to be questioned. Then the blacks around Sharky's resented our being there, and we had to hurt a few of them."

Don Corso's nod was barely perceptible. "And where is Sharky now?"

"I have men out searching for him."

"Why?" asked Don Corso.

Tiger sensed the trap and carefully weighed his words. "For two reasons. I wanted to talk and shake up anyone connected to Iggy or Weasel. And two, I wanted to find out why Sonny was hanging out around Sharky's, since Sharky hates Sonny's guts."

"And what did you learn?"

Tiger shook his head. "Nothing concrete yet."

His father sat back, puffed on his cigar, and studied his son. "Then I will tell you what you want to know," he said simply. "As for shaking up Sharky, you may continue, but I doubt if you will learn much from him. However, I have learned that your brother Sonny has been supplying Sharky with a considerable amount of heroin."

It suddenly made sense to Tiger. He remembered Sonny's saying he was copping from other dealers, which didn't surprise Tiger. Any street-smart addict could do that, but there is a sizable distance between copping and supplying.

"In the past month he sold Sharky alone two kilos of pure heroin." Tiger's eyebrows shot up. "Where the hell did he get his hands on pure heroin?" snapped Tiger.

"That's what I've been asking myself. How did he get his hands on it?" asked his father, pausing. "Did he rip someone off or is he involved with an importer?" Tiger didn't like either conclusion. If his brother had ripped off a heavy, then chances were they were looking for him now. And Sonny was hanging out in his place. On the other hand, if he was involved with an importer, then his brother had little chance of survival. Especially since he was an addict. Tiger knew importers fell into three ethnic groups: French, Corsicans, and mainland Italians. So who could Sonny be involved with? Damn, he thought, his brother was looking to commit suicide. Well, he was sure heading in the right direction.

"I want him out of the business," his father continued. "I don't care how you do it, but I want him stopped."

The tone of his father's voice warned Tiger that the line had been crossed and there was no turning back. "How far do you expect me to go?" he asked in alarm, knowing he had no intention of killing his brother.

Don Corso settled back in his seat, puffed on the cigar, and pointed his finger for emphasis. "You have a week," he said coldly. "If you wish to put him in the hospital with two broken legs, that's okay with me. If you wish to place him in a cure center, I'll show you that much respect. But if in one week he is still in the heroin business, then you step aside and I will handle the problem my own way."

For a moment Tiger was stunned by his father's words. Then he understood where his father was coming from. He also felt a sting of hate for his brother.

"I will deal with it," said Tiger with a heavy heart.

U PON returning to his office, Tiger found Sonny had left to take a walk.

"How long ago did he leave?" he asked.

"About two hours ago," shrugged Pete. "Is something wrong?"

He ran through the meeting with his father.

"Damn," said Pete, "now we have to find him again."

Ralphie looked toward the desk phone. "You want me to put out the word?"

Tiger wondered what the chances were that his brother had just gone for an innocent walk. "Don't put the word out, but send a crew out to find him and bring him back," he said with annoyance. Ralphie left immediately.

The phone rang and Pete quickly picked it up.

"You got an Inspector Colby outside."

Tiger showed his surprise and wondered what this was all about. "Have Goldberg handle him," he said.

Pete whispered into the phone and looked back at Tiger. "Goldberg says he doesn't have a warrant. He came to talk to you personally."

Tiger wondered what this new wrinkle meant as he walked behind the desk, turned on the desk lamp that activated a hidden recorder. "Have him come in," he said.

Ralphie held the door open for a tall, thin man. His white hair added a distinguished look—until Tiger saw the hooded snake eyes.

Tiger stood behind the desk to keep the man at a disadvantage. "Can I help you?" he asked softly.

"You can if you are Joseph Corso."

"I am," said Tiger, knowing he didn't like the man.

Colby studied Pete and Ralphie before turning his dead eyes on Tiger. "Can we talk privately?"

Tiger signaled them to leave and waved the inspector to the seat opposite him. But Colby selected the leather couch instead, and Tiger wondered why the inspector wanted to keep his distance.

"What can I do for you?" asked Tiger.

"I got some questions," he said.

"What about?"

"Let's start with Inspector Robert Cassaro," he said with watchful eyes. "I believe you know him."

"I know him."

"I also have reason to believe you are both involved in an enterprise in which I have a vested interest," he said.

182

Tiger heard the message loud and clear, but he decided to play out the game. He knitted his brows, hoping to convey an appropriate expression of confusion. "I can't imagine what Bobby and I could possibly be involved in that would be of interest to you. He is a childhood friend, but that's about the extent of our relationship," he said, gratified by the flick of anger in the cold eyes.

"Do you realize in one phone call I could have a hundred policemen down here to take this place apart?"

Tiger didn't care for the threat and decided to deal with it. "And in one phone call I could have a thousand lawyers here to straighten you out," said Tiger, knowing the gloves were off.

Colby took his time examining Tiger, then changed track. "Do you know a Salvatore Delvechicco?"

Again Tiger knitted his brows. "Am I supposed to?"

"Let's not bullshit, Mister Corso. I have enough police reports on my desk to show that you are the new boss of the old Bocci family and that Delvechicco works for you now."

Tiger returned the inspector's iciness. "If I was a boss as you say, you could hardly expect me to know everyone who works for me," he said, knowing Colby didn't like playing the game.

The inspector took a second to catch his thoughts. "This Delvechicco has something of mine and I want it back."

"And if you don't get it back?" Tiger asked softly, his anger rising.

Colby rose to his feet. "Then you're going to lose one worker," he said.

Tiger watched the tall, thin policeman open the door and walk out without closing the door after him. Fuck you, thought Tiger, you can chase Sally Dell until your heart stops. But he knew the inspector would be back. He had no other choice. With Sally Dell out of his reach, Colby would find himself in a dead-end. Then, his only visible target would be Tiger.

Like all grafters, the inspector believed himself due tribute from lesser people. Well, thought Tiger, I hope I'm ready for him.

As Tiger waited for word from Sonny, Sharky, or the selected policeman from the clerk's office, he found himself frustrated and unable to attack in any direction. So he decided to visit his troops in the field. Tiger had two dozen outposts spread around the five boroughs. Each was housed in a storefront social club and headed by a made member, whose job it was to oversee the operations in his territories. Tiger knew most troopers spent their entire lives living in remote outposts far from his headquarters in Brooklyn. They rarely, if ever, had the opportunity to see a boss in person. With that in mind, he set out to visit all the clubs to show his men he cared.

At each outpost Tiger met the made member and offered some suggestions for improving his operations, backed them in their decisions, and listened to his connected men report in or to receive orders. Then Tiger was off to the next club.

The next name on his list was Alessi's in Little Italy. Pete turned onto Mott Street, but as he approached Alessi's club, he spotted two police cars, and a small crowd outside.

"Drive past the club and park up the block," ordered Tiger.

Pete found a parking spot a few doors ahead as Tiger studied Alessi's through the rear window. He could see little.

"Go see what the problem is," he said to Ralphie.

Ten minutes later a harried Alessi followed Ralphie back to Tiger's car.

"Tiger," exploded Alessi, "that bastard is driving me crazy." He wiped his sweaty brow with a handkerchief.

"What the hell are you talking about?" asked Tiger.

But Alessi didn't seem to have heard. He continued,

"The son of a bitch just took a shot at me. Damn, if I didn't duck he would have blown my fucking head off," he said, his hate and nervousness apparent.

"What the fuck are you talking about?" asked Tiger in confusion.

"Calamine, that's who," he snapped back.

"How come he's still running around," Tiger demanded.

Alessi was sweating profusely. "Because the bastard is like a shadow, a fucking ghost."

Tiger wondered what kind of man this Calamine was. Or was it just that Alessi was incompetent? He spoke softly to get his words across. "I don't care how you do it, but you better put this situation right before you start to look bad," he said, noticing Alessi's hand trembling as he tried to light a cigarette.

"What the fuck do you think I'm trying to do?"

Pete saw the frost in Tiger's eyes and prepared for the explosion. But instead, Tiger said, "How many men do you have out looking for him?"

"About fifty, but they can't get close to him. The bastard is everywhere and nowhere at the same time. It's spooky."

"What about Lorenzo?"

"He hasn't seen Calamine since you gave me the decision."

Well, thought Tiger, Alessi better put Calamine in the ground fast because he couldn't allow all this at the expense of the family. By taking a shot at a made member, he became an outlaw. As such, all family members were obligated to shoot Calamine on sight.

"You have a week to straighten this out, or I will take care of the matter," he ordered coldly.

Alessi understood the warning. If he didn't get Calamine within the week, his troops would turn against him. "I'll get him," he said softly.

Tiger visited three more outposts before calling it a day.

On the way home he let his mind wander through a spectrum of odd thoughts. Why was Turk killed? Patsy? What was the bad blood between Camille and his father?

Where did Sonny get the pure heroin? Was Smilin' Jack a rogue? Where did Iggy and Weasel fit into the picture? Why did his father order his uncle to kill two policemen and hang them from a roof? He had to know how much of it all was tied into the clerk's office. That last thought disturbed him, and he would give a fortune to know the answer.

HAVING received no word on Sonny or Sharky, Tiger decided to relax at home for the day, but Jeanne had other ideas. She wanted him to take Momma, Camille, and Angelina shopping on Union Street.

With Pete and Ralphie hanging in the background, Tiger escorted the women through the many pushcarts filled with fresh fruits, vegetables, cheese, spices, nuts, and pastries.

The aromas were maddening as Tiger ate calzones, rice balls, stuffed sausages and peppers, and deep-fried eggplant. Meanwhile Momma and Angelina filled bag after bag with olive oil, cans of paste, spaghetti, provolone, mozzarella, anchovies, and whatever they could lay their hands on.

Later they spent an hour with Carmine at Saint Rocco's, where he quickly caught the women's festive mood.

When they returned home with their booty, Angelina quickly whipped up vermicella alla Siciliana and pasta'ncaiata. She topped it off with fresh cannoli and espresso. When the meal was over, Tiger thought he was going to die.

During the nuts and fruit, the old women talked the talk of days past. It seemed to Tiger the only thing the sisters had in common was recalling long forgotten dead people.

He often wondered what it was in the Sicilian personality that drove them into ancestor worship, to revere the past generations, even above their saints.

As a young man, his mother took him to Sicily to pay her respects to her father, who had recently died. They flew into Palermo and hired a driver to take them to the farm she was born on. Her three brothers refused to speak to her, so they made their own way to the Cappuccini Catacombs, where her father had been buried.

At the catacombs, he followed his mother down the narrow limestone steps and into a nightmarish hell he would never forget. Hundreds of cadavers lined the tunnels, with most of the bodies tied in an upright position. Tiger broke out in a cold sweat and could hardly keep from vomiting. There before his eyes were thousands of bodies decomposing, with flesh peeling, eye sockets empty, flesh peeled back from smiling teeth. The smell of death and rotted meat permeated the tunnels.

His mother stopped before the body of an old man who was dressed in his Sunday best. The suit of heavy fabric was old as were the tarnished shoes. A heavy nameplate hung from a cheap chain wrapped around his neck. Its handwritten inscription read, "MAI DIMENTICARE LA FAMIGLIA,"—Never forget the family—followed by the name Luigi Scapaci.

Tiger looked up into the sun-blackened features of his grandfather, feeling nothing, no ancestral obligation or sense of loss, just revulsion. He was thankful the eyes were closed as he studied the parchment skin covered with black spots at the tightest parts and starting to peel back, exposing the bone.

As his mother knelt in silent prayer, he examined the next skeleton in line. Bits and pieces of flesh still clung to the bones and the tattered remains of fabric told him it had been a woman. He turned over the nameplate to read it and was shocked at reading his mother's name. This was his grandmother.

He felt a strange identification with the bones that hung there and wondered what she had been like.

An hour later his mother rose, blessed herself, and kissed the lips of the dead man. Without another glance she ignored her mother's body and walked away, leaving Tiger to wonder.

187

Tiger had never forgotten that scene in the catacombs and thought it a hell of a way to show love and respect.

Years later, Tiger asked his mother about that day. He caught her in a moment of weakness, and she told him a strange story.

"When I was a young girl," said Momma, "I had a younger brother who died of malaria. He was six at the time. We were poor then and unable to afford a burial in the catacombs, so my father buried my baby brother on the side of a hill overlooking the house. From my window I would look up at the wooden cross that marked his grave. Years later, when the family could afford it, I asked my mother to buy a headstone since she held the purse strings. But I was slapped for my pains and told there were better things to do with money. So I took a vow that when I grew up, the first money I got I would buy a headstone, with angels and his name carved across it. But that day never came because one night there was a terrible storm, and the next morning I saw that the cross had been washed away. I searched the hill, hoping to find a sign or marker that would tell me where my brother was buried. But there was none. After that, I would often look out my window at the empty hill, knowing my brother was somewhere up there." Momma paused and looked at Tiger.

"It is a terrible feeling to lose something precious and never be able to find it again. That is why I never forgave my mother. She had forsaken her own blood."

RETURNING to his office, Tiger took something to settle his stomach. He sat there wondering why he hadn't heard anything regarding Sonny or Sharky. As to his brother, he had less than six days to get him out of the drug business before his father stepped in.

Tiger looked up sharply, as Pete stuck his head in the door.

"What is it?" he asked.

"Some woman outside says she knows you," said Pete.

"She say what her name was?"

"Helen. She says she's Sonny's girlfriend."

Tiger wondered why the fly was coming to visit the spider.

"Have her come in," said Tiger.

Street banking had taught Tiger that people were creatures of habit, rarely wandering far from their holes unless forced to travel by hunger. He wondered what Helen's hunger was.

He had seen her briefly about a year ago. He had been in Harlem attending a sitdown for his father when he saw Iggy's car pull up on the other side of the street, a skinny, wasted girl clung to his arm. It took Tiger a moment before recognizing Helen. She wasn't pretty anymore.

But even so, he wasn't ready for the creature Pete opened the door to. The elfin quality was long gone, the needle having taken its toll. Her once softly textured skin had collapsed into elliptical grooves. Her once elegant clothes hung from her body like rags on a wire coat hanger.

Helen stepped nervously into the room as Pete closed the door behind her. Under the desk, Tiger pressed the button that locked the door.

"How are you, Helen?" he asked. He smelled fear under her superficial smile. "Sit, tell me what I can do for you."

She sat gently on the edge of the chair, like a bird prepared for immediate flight. "It's important I speak to Sonny," she whispered, as she avoided his eyes.

"I'm afraid he's not here, Helen," he said, wondering what brought her here. "What can I do to help you?" he purred.

She fidgeted. "I just need to see him. He's the only one who can help me," she said nervously.

Tiger knew no way in hell was he letting her get near Sonny if he could help it. Looking across the desk at her emaciated features, he could understand his brother's being finished with her. "I'm afraid he's out of town for a couple of days," he lied sweetly, hoping not to spook her. But it was too late. In panic, she ran to the door, tried to open it, but the locks held.

"The door is locked, so why don't you sit down again?"

She pounded and kicked at the door in a frenzy, as Tiger wondered what desperation had driven her here. He knew Iggy wouldn't let her out of his sight without a damn good reason, since dealers were possessive, paranoid, selfish bastards.

During a lull in her pounding and kicking, he said, "You're not going anywhere, Helen, so you better sit down."

Instead she renewed her attack on the door. Tiger waited until she dissipated most of her energy and leaned back against the door exhausted.

"You better tell me why you're here, Helen," he said coldly.

"I just wanted to say hello to Sonny, that's all." She slowly sank to the floor, racked with sobs.

Tiger sat there waiting her out. When she was reduced to sniffles, he said, "You want to tell me why you're here, Helen?"

Terror filled her eyes as she trembled. "Please don't ask me, Tiger. I'll get killed."

Tiger expelled his breath, relieved at breaking the ice. He helped her to her feet and gently escorted her back to her seat. "No one is going to hurt you, Helen. Now tell me why Iggy sent you here."

His soothing words seemed to help, but the fires of indecision still raged. "Helen, you're under my protection, so don't be afraid," he said, waiting.

"Iggy didn't send me, he's been killed," she said.

Tiger was taken aback. "How? When?" he asked, still unable to believe her.

With trembling fingers, she lit a cigarette before answering.

"Early this morning."

"Tell me what happened," he asked softly, taking a second to catch his breath.

She filled her lungs again, which seemed to soothe her. "Some time around six this morning, the phone rang, waking us up. Iggy answered, dressed, and told me he was expecting company, and to stay in my room."

"Why?" asked Tiger.

The question didn't offend Helen. "I was never allowed out of my room when he had meetings."

Tiger nodded. "Go on."

"I could hear voices, but they were speaking too low for me to recognize any of them," she said, taking another drag on the cigarette. "After a half hour, I decided to go back to bed. Then the door burst open, and Weasel charged in like a crazy man. He held a bloody knife, grabbed me by the hair, and dragged me out into the living room where Iggy was." She began to tremble again.

"Go on," urged Tiger gently.

"It was awful. Blood everywhere. But I couldn't bring myself to look at Iggy. Weasel made me look. 'This is what is going to happen to you, bitch, if you don't do what I say.' He had a crazy look in his eyes," she said as the tears flowed.

"What did he want you to do?"

"He wanted me to find Sonny for him."

That surprised Tiger. "He say why?"

Helen shook her head. "All he said was Sonny owed him."

"What happened then?" Tiger asked.

"Then he let me go. He said I had twenty-four hours to find Sonny, or he would come looking for me."

"So you've been looking for him?" he asked carefully.

She shook her head. "Where's to look? After you busted up Sharky's Place I had nowhere to look except here."

Tiger nodded his understanding and pressed another button under his desk. He waited until Pete stuck his head in.

"Bring some food and coffee, and have the boys see if any of Weasel's people are in the neighborhood," he said and put in a hurry-up call to Big Che.

"What's happening up there?"

191

The big man grunted. "It's quiet."

"Where's Weasel now?" asked Tiger.

"At the club. He did go to Iggy's for a couple of hours. Maybe it was some kind of meeting."

"Who was with him when he went?"

"He was alone except for some big spade. But the guy left after a half hour."

"What did the eggplant look like?" he asked softly.

"Big gold earring in his left ear and a sharp dresser."

"Damn," exploded Tiger, "that's Sharky!"

"Who's Sharky?" asked Big Che.

Tiger was taken aback then remembered the big man had been out of town for many years. But still, the clocks were all from Harlem and one of them should have recognized him. What were Weasel and Sharky playing? Did they want to take over Iggy's operations or did they have bigger ambitions?

"Did you see Helen leave?"

"I don't know no Helen, but a skinny broad shot out of the place a half hour before Weasel did."

Tiger nodded absently. "Pull the clock on Iggy."

"Right," said the big man, but as an afterthought asked, "is there a problem?"

"Not anymore," he said, hanging up.

He didn't know what impact Iggy's death would have on all this, but he decided to get Helen tucked away in any case until he received word Iggy was really dead. It could all be a scam. But the terror in Helen's eyes made him doubt it.

Tony Orechicco sat in the chair Helen had vacated for the couch. Helen seemed more comfortable there, surrounded by all the hulking men.

"Pete will handle your transportation needs, and once you get to the island, keep away any nosy strangers."

The powerfully built youth nodded his understanding as he said, "Can I have Nino Penosi and Augello Pino? I'll vouch for both of them."

Tiger nodded his approval. He remembered back to the film of the Bocci shooting and how calmly Tony had taken out Johnson, dropped the pistol, and disappeared into the crowd.

When Penosi and Pino entered the office, Pete escorted them and Helen to a side door. She hesitated a moment and looked doubtfully at Tiger. "Where are we going?" she asked nervously.

Tiger smiled gently. "You're going on vacation, Helen, where none of Weasel's people will find you. When you get there, you'll have the run of the place. But don't try to contact anyone."

She nodded nervously. "Thank you, Tiger."

After she left, Tiger held Tony back. "When you get to Florida, let her have a few days to relax, then sweat the junk out of her," he said, feeling she had another shot at life, probably her last.

After Tony left, Tiger made a series of phone calls, then called Big Che. "Where's Weasel now?"

"Still in his club."

"If the big nigger comes back, have him picked up," he said, ending the connection.

Ralphie picked up the ringing phone and looked at Tiger.

"It's Marci, he's in Harlem."

"Ask him what's happening."

"He says the cops are crawling all over Iggy's place."

Tiger nodded. "Tell Marci to get lost," he said without further explanation. He could see the question on Ralphie's face as to why he sent someone to check on Big Che, but Tiger had other problems. Now that he knew Helen spoke the truth, he had to have some answers from Sonny.

"Send another ten men up to Harlem to look for Sonny," he said. What hole had his brother found to hide in?

T IGER was thankful all his operations were running smoothly, or at least, all but Alessi's. Some of Alessi's oper-

193

ations were faltering because so many of his men were looking for Calamine. Well, Tiger thought, he's got three days before my deadline and then I'll find him myself.

That Weasel and Sharky did away with Iggy meant little to him. It was the meaning of Iggy's death that mattered. The why of it? What was the game plan? What did Iggy have that Weasel needed? The heroin? True, that could be a tasty morsel, but worth killing his boss for? There had to be a larger reason. He knew One Eye knew little of bigtime dealing, and even if he knew all of Iggy's connections, he still wasn't smart enough to make a move. So Tiger wondered who was pulling Weasel's strings? Was it Colby? He didn't think so. Colby couldn't get out of his way. Was Weasel coming from a totally different direction? What was his desparate need for Sonny? Was he desperate enough to need Sonny's connection to the people with the pure?

Tiger picked up the annoying phone. "Yeah?"

"Lorenzo's on the line," said Pete.

"What the hell does he want?" Tiger snapped.

"He says Alessi's been shot."

"Put him on," Tiger said with annoyance.

Aт the hospital, Alessi's troops patrolled the corridors as Tiger was led to a private room where Lorenzo was waiting alone.

"What the hell happened?" asked Tiger in anger.

"Calamine called me yesterday wanting to meet to try to straighten out the problem. I told him if I could set it up he had to promise not to bring any weapons."

"And?" asked Tiger in anticipation.

"He agreed and Carlo also agreed," he said, with his usual deadpan expression.

"Where was the meet to be held?"

"At my club."

"Go on," said Tiger.

194

"Well, Carlo arrived with a dozen of his bozos and the moment he saw Calamine he started blasting."

Tiger was stunned. "He did that in your club?" he said in disbelief.

Lorenzo nodded. "That's right. The bastard didn't even offer to shake hands before he opened up."

Tiger was fuming, promising himself—if Alessi survived —he would bring him up before the round table. True, he had the right to shoot Calamine on sight, but not under the flag of truce, especially in another made member's territory. That's why the Council passed the law, to ensure territorial rights, to stop raiders from dumping unwanted bodies in another man's backyard.

"He also," continued Lorenzo, "missed two shots at Calamine and shot one of my boys."

Damn, thought Tiger. Alessi was in trouble now. This could mean a death sentence. "How bad is your boy?"

"He'll live."

"Then how did Alessi get shot?"

Lorenzo looked askance at Tiger. "When my boy was shot, Calamine headed for the door. Carlo smelled the kill and charged, but he tripped and his gun went off," said Lorenzo, looking away.

Tiger found himself unable to speak. "Then he shot himself?"

Lorenzo nodded with tight lips.

Tiger was livid. "This is turning into a fucking comedy," he said with bitterness. He glanced toward Pete and Ralphie, who were trying to hide their smirks. Tiger found little to be amused about. "Did anyone take out Calamine?" he asked in anger.

Lorenzo remained impassive as he shook his head.

"Christ!" was all Tiger was able to say.

"In the confusion of Carlo's being shot, he jumped out the window and escaped," he said, lowering his head in anticipation of the explosion.

But Tiger was too numb to move, dumbfounded. The anger broiled within him, hoping the bastard Alessi would die, saving himself the job of having him executed. "What kind of shape is Alessi in?"

"The doctor said he will be out tomorrow," he said quietly.

Tiger's brows shot up. "What the hell kind of wound did he get?"

"Alessi shot his balls off," Lorenzo said simply.

It started with a snicker, but soon Pete and Ralphie were rolling with laughter. Tiger glared at them in amazement, until he saw the insanity of the whole situation. He relaxed, getting caught up in the contagion of laughter.

Tiger knew there was no way he could call the Council together for a round table. They would have him committed. When the laughter subsided, Tiger got himself under control.

"Let's get down to business."

Tiger had met many men of Calamine's breed in Korea. Men for whom war had never ended. He was on the run and knew he faced a no-win situation. Tiger also knew the man would go broke to get Alessi.

"Keep four men in Alessi's room until he goes home. Tonight, hide a dozen men in Alessi's house. Sooner or later, Calamine will make his move and I want to be ready for him," he said, pausing and looking directly at Lorenzo. "As of this moment Calamine is declared outlaw and is to be shot by anyone who spots him."

"Yes, sir. I'll get the word on the street," said Lorenzo, a tightness to his lips.

At the door to the hall, Tiger pointed toward Alessi's room. "Do you think he's up to a visit?" he said, hoping the bastard was unconscious.

Lorenzo's features remained impassive as he said, "Sure, he'd love it."

AFTER leaving the hospital, Tiger wondered what new madness was lurking in the shadows. Then Pete informed him his father wanted to see him, so he headed over.

Inside, his father was, as usual, counting money; but he paused long enough to hand his son a slip of paper. "I have found the policeman," he said, returning to his piles of money. "He will have the information you seek."

Tiger read the name, surprised at not recognizing it from Defalco's list. "How can you be sure?" he asked carefully.

His father looked at him impassively. "Because I have reason to believe he was the originator of the heroin switching. Now he owns a home worth two hundred gees, two new cars, a boat, and an after-hours club. He didn't do all that on a policeman's salary," said Don Corso.

Tiger nodded, sure his father had hit the nail on the head. He put the slip of paper in his pocket and said, "Iggy is dead."

"I heard it on the radio. What details do you have?"

He told his father of Helen's visit, what his clocks had reported, and that he believed Sharky was in on the kill.

His father nodded. "Where is Helen now?" he asked.

"I have her in a closet," Tiger answered. Why had his father asked? He watched the old man lean back with a handful of money in one hand and a big black cigar clutched in the other, which he pointed at his son.

"If there is a possibility Weasel is connected in any way to the clerk's office, then we better know fast."

Tiger nodded, thankful to have something to sink his teeth into. He was also grateful there was no mention of Sonny.

As Tiger sat alone in the back of the big car, he wondered how best to pick up the target policeman.

Well, he thought, I'd better start with a clock.

Tiger made it a habit of personally handling any clock he himself was going to execute. Verbal reports from his troops were reliable, but not as reliable as doing it himself.

At four-thirty in the afternoon he picked up the trail of the policeman as he left the clerk's office. Pete drove Tiger and Ralphie drove another car, both stolen. They each had walkie-talkies.

They followed the policeman's car, a black Mark IV, to a bowling alley, three bars, and a storage garage. Tiger didn't know what these places were but he recorded the addresses.

At ten o'clock the policeman led them through the well-to-do section of Shore Road, then suddenly disappeared up a high angled driveway. Tiger had Pete park directly across the street from the entrance to the policeman's home. According to the information his father had given him, the policeman lived there with a wife, two kids, and a father-in-law. To Tiger that ruled out a pick-up at his house.

Pete nudged Tiger awake as the Mark IV moved slowly out the driveway, turned left, and headed for the Belt Parkway. In Sheepshead Bay, they ran along the waterfront, past the fishing boats, and ended up at an after-hours club called Jasper's. It was comfortably nestled between a yacht club and the water.

Tiger liked everything about the place, even the floating marina with the power boats tied up to it. Neon signs of cartoon characters ran the length of the soft-hued granite building. Tiger wondered how much the policeman had invested in it.

Pete parked between two cars, keeping constant observation on the Mark IV. The driver emerged, spoke to the doorman, and disappeared inside.

"The man has one hell of a piece of property there," observed Pete dryly.

Tiger noticed the almost-filled parking lot and wondered about making an offer to buy the place from the policeman's widow.

"Stay here," Tiger ordered. "I'm going to look around."

Inside he was impressed by the class of the customers, mostly businessmen and well-dressed women. Damn, thought Tiger, with this kind of business, that bastard didn't have to deal in junk.

Very slowly, he managed to work his way to the bar,

ordered a Seven and Seven. As he waited for his drink, he searched out his target. He spotted him sitting in a corner booth with a peroxide blond and two drinks.

After fifteen minutes, Tiger had seen enough. About to leave, his senses suddenly tingled and warning bells chimed. Fully alert, he looked around for the source of his disturbance. He found him at the end of the long bar. A pair of cold eyes were watching him. Detective Defalco.

Tiger was taken aback as the detective turned away, took a sip of his drink, and smiled at the pretty woman with him. Tiger guessed Defalco was clocking his target or someone else in the room. Either way, he didn't like his being there.

IT was still dark when Pete nudged Tiger awake. He found the parking lot empty except for the Mark IV. Tiger checked his watch. Four-thirty.

"Where's everybody?" he asked, shaking the sleep webs from his mind.

"Gone."

"Defalco?"

"Left about an hour ago," Pete said.

Tiger nodded, knowing the detective could still be in the area. "Who's left inside?"

"No one. Just the target."

Ten minutes later, his target emerged from the club, set the alarms on the building, entered his car, and drove out of the parking lot.

They followed at a discreet distance. Tiger radioed Ralphie to keep a sharp eye on Defalco, in case he was on to them.

An hour later, the target parked just outside the main gate of the clerk's office, walked two blocks to a diner, had breakfast, and returned to the clerk's office. He checked in with the guard and headed for his job in the administration building.

Tiger was sure the policeman was set until quitting time, but as a precaution he sent for a trooper, gave him the target's picture, and stationed him in a car across the street.

Back in the office, Tiger sent Pete and Ralphie to the apartments above for a few hours of sleep while he sat at his desk.

He thought of the policeman he had been clocking. He was certain he could put it all together, that is, if the policeman remained constant for another day or two.

Also, his worry over Sonny deepened. He found it troubling that his troopers couldn't get a lead on him.

The buzzer on the desk rang, and he snatched up the telephone. "Yeah?" he said in annoyance.

"Big Che is out here. He has to talk to you," said the trooper stationed outside the door.

"Send him in."

Damn, he thought, what the hell does he want here?

When the huge man entered, Che's face told Tiger something was wrong. "Weasel is outside in Lulu's restaurant."

He sat there as if he had been shot. The gall of him, thought Tiger, daring to show his face around here. He pressed the button under the lip of his desk, then picked up the phone and whispered into it.

"I was on the early watch when suddenly he shot out of his club, and we followed him here," continued Che.

Pete and Ralphie charged into the room from a side entrance. "What's up?" asked Pete, his gun out.

"Weasel's outside in the restaurant."

"Damn," said Ralphie, in shock and anger.

Tiger's knuckles were white as he gripped the arm of the chair. What kind of trap was One Eye trying to spring? "Go see what the bastard is up to," Tiger said to Ralphie, who rushed from the room.

"What do you want me to do?" asked Pete.

"Nothing. At least until we see what he's up to. I got enough guys outside so he won't be leaving alive."

Ralphie returned a moment later.

"Why's he here?"

Ralphie shrugged. "He didn't say. He just sat there eating his breakfast."

"Who's with him?"

"Two goons, but they're sitting at another table. Also, your boys are filling all the other tables."

Tiger sat for a moment wondering what this was all about. Something was wrong; he could feel it.

Pete picked up the buzzing phone, listened, grunted, hung up, and turned to Tiger. "The neighborhood is clean," he said.

Tiger rose to his feet and looked over at Big Che. "Have a car brought around to the rear entrance," he said, walking to the door. Tiger went into Lulu's.

Looking over the room, Tiger quickly spotted the two goons sitting opposite Weasel, who sat alone looking out of place in a white sharkskin blazer, tons of gold chains around his neck, earrings, and a small diamond in the center of his eye patch.

"What are you doing here, Weasel?" asked Tiger coldly as he balanced himself on the balls of his feet.

Weasel's smile fell short. "You have something of mine and I want it back," he said coldly.

Without a word, Tiger pulled Weasel to his feet. "Where you're going, you won't need Helen."

Guns quickly covered his goons as Weasel glared back at Tiger. "I got Sonny."

Tiger froze. "I don't believe you," he said, tightening his grip on Weasel's lapels.

"You better believe it. His life is in your hands. Do you think I would be crazy enough to step into the Tiger's cage otherwise?"

The madness continued to burn within Tiger, making it difficult for him to choose between his love for his brother and his hatred for the man before him. "Where's my brother?" he asked softly.

Relief flooded through Weasel, as he used his hand to press out the wrinkles from Tiger's grip. "Do we trade?" he asked coldly.

"We trade," said Tiger softly.

Weasel tried his smile again. "Good. Then give me Helen and you can have Sonny," he said, sitting down again.

"I don't have her here."

"Where is she?" he asked with a sour expression.

"I have her out of town," Tiger said, watching Weasel carefully, certain he saw a flicker of panic. So he said, "I'll have her here in the morning."

But Weasel shook his head. "No good, baby, I want her now."

Tiger shrugged, knowing something was out of kilter. "I still can't help you before morning," he said with finality.

"I don't trust you, Tiger, so I'm gonna tell you this once. You can fly Helen back from anywhere in the States in five hours. You got six hours. Then I kill Sonny."

Tiger knew the cards were stacked against him at this time, but after he had his brother back . . . "Where do we make the exchange? Here?"

Weasel's cold eye studied him. He shook his head. "No. We do it in Harlem. In my club."

Tiger hoped he didn't show his emotions. "I'll be there in six hours."

Weasel rose to his feet, pointing at his eye patch. "I still owe you for this," he said in cold hate.

Tiger was seething underneath, and a touch of color rose to the surface of his skin. "You're lucky I'm letting you walk out of here alive."

Weasel smiled hatefully. "I know."

TIGER paced the office while Pete and Ralphie burned up the telephones.

"I want all the troops out on the streets on this one, and

keep a blanket on Weasel until I get my brother back," he shouted to no one in particular.

Pete hung up the phone and looked at Tiger. "Helen's on her way," he said.

"And get those bastards back who are searching for my brother," he said, tasting his bitterness.

The anger was engulfing him. He found it difficult to keep from going to Harlem and burning the Kit Kat Klub to the ground. But Tiger held himself in check, knowing he would have to wait until after Sonny was free.

As he continued pacing, his mind raced, seeking and rejecting ideas, blueprints, schemes, and even very thin threads. Weasel had given the impression he was ready for a fast deal, yet he now knew he was outmaneuvered, outfoxed. Weasel knew he could never get out of Brooklyn alive with Helen. So he intended to have the exchange in Harlem all the time. Tiger wondered why.

"Get the car," he said to no one in particular. "We're going to Harlem."

O NCE in the car, Tiger felt less tense. He headed up the Harlem River Drive. With eight troopers about to move into the area, he wanted to see the exchange site firsthand. He wanted Harlem closed up so tight a cockroach couldn't escape.

He found West 116th Street to be a wide boulevard filled with armies of people. From across the wide street, he studied the Kit Kat Klub. Its windowless brick front and long awning gave the impression of many secrets hidden behind the façade.

"Take charge of this operation," he said to Ralphie, "and find out how many ways there are into the club. Talk to the super. Make it worth his while. I want troops on the roofs, in the cellars, and in the backyards. I want two dozen troops stationed in vans outside the club. They are to be used if we have to storm the place. I want people ready to hit the stores on either side," he said and then paused. "Also, thirty minutes before the exchange, I want your troops to occupy all the apartments above the club and stores."

Ralphie nodded his understanding, opened the car door, and hit the streets. Then Tiger and Pete sat in silence, each with his own thoughts.

Ten minutes later Ralphie returned. "Everything is covered. The troops will be in position in less than thirty minutes."

"Where is Weasel?"

"He's in the club. I have Rossi, Drago, and Sandy watching him. That should make him nervous," he said and returned to the street.

Tiger couldn't fathom Weasel's game. First he threw Helen to the wolves to obtain Sonny. Then when he somehow secured Sonny, he decided to trade for her. It just didn't jell.

Tiger was still positive Weasel was after his brother for his heroin connection. The question is, had he got it? If so, he would have no further use for Sonny. That was Weasel's normal thinking, but why the trade? What did he want from Helen? She had nothing left he wanted from her. Or did she? Then he was sure he had found the answer.

Tiger ran it through his mind again. After Iggy's murder, some overriding desperation compelled Weasel to send Helen after Sonny. Why? Because he now had whatever it was that Sonny possessed. That's when Weasel realized he had forgotten one little detail when he sent Helen out. He forgot Helen was a junkie and if given a little push would spill her guts.

As a witness to Iggy's killing, a jury just might believe her, and he would go away for life. He couldn't allow that to hang over his head, and he would have to kill her.

But there was a flaw in Weasel's thinking. Weasel had to know the moment Sonny was turned loose, he was dead. Which told Tiger that Weasel wasn't intending to turn his brother loose. How? An overdose?

That made sense, thought Tiger. But that still wouldn't stop Tiger from revenge. Weasel wasn't that stupid.

Tiger thought about it. What awaited him in the Kit Kat Klub?

He studied his watch, aware Helen would be landing in thirty minutes, two hours before the exchange.

As Tiger sat silently in the rear of the big car, his thoughts were heavy. The gnawing feeling that something was out of kilter, but he couldn't put his finger on it. He could smell it and then, like an exploding rocket, he was out of the car, dodging traffic, as he dashed across the wide boulevard and up to Ralphie's command vehicle.

"What's wrong, Tiger?" asked a concerned Ralphie as other troopers filled the street at the sight of him.

"Are you sure Weasel's inside the club?" he demanded.

The question surprised Ralphie. "Sure I'm sure. I got three men on him."

"I know, but make sure it's not a double," Tiger ordered.

Ralphie rushed off. Pete's eyes narrowed. "What do you smell?" he asked, alert to Tiger's instincts.

Tiger shook his head. "I don't know . . . I really don't know, but I have a funny feeling we're being had," he said, watching Ralphie run up to him.

"He's sitting in a booth with two goons and three broads."

"Are you sure it's Weasel?"

Ralphie nodded. "I'd know his 'Hi, baby' bullshit anywhere."

Tiger stood there, his mind probing, searching, but whatever it was, it was elusive. It wasn't connecting.

Pete's eyes narrowed. "What do you think it is?"

Tiger shook his head. "I don't know, but whatever it is, it's going to happen at the exchange."

Pete studied the stores and windows lining the wide street. "It could be a setup to get you out in the open," he said levelly.

But Tiger ignored the remark. Even Weasel, with his deranged mind, wouldn't have the balls to move against

205

him. If something happened to him, his father and the remaining three families would turn Harlem into a parking lot within two hours.

He was positive they didn't have his brother in the Kit Kat Klub or the surrounding area. That meant they would have to bring him into the neighborhood for the exchange.

For ten blocks around he had cars and spotters on every corner. He was doubtful any vehicle could escape their notice.

"Let's go see Weasel," he said, to everyone's surprise.

"Do you think that's wise?" asked Pete with narrowed eyes.

Tiger studied him. "I can't help it. I have to know what the bastard is up to before the exchange."

Ralphie nodded. "How many troops do we take in?" he asked softly.

"Just the three of us," Tiger answered, heading toward the Kit Kat Klub.

Inside, Tiger took a moment to adjust his eyes to the dim light. He noticed about thirty customers and goons and guessed Weasel liked crowds. He spotted the three troopers assigned to watching the man with the eye patch. Tiger moved in slowly on the booth, looking coldly from face to face, smelling the fear hidden behind the girls' weak smiles.

"Hi, baby, you're early," said Weasel with a broad smile.

Tiger studied the rest of the people in the booth and said, "Get rid of your friends."

The one eye flashed venom. "Hey, baby, the party don't begin for a while yet," he said with a laugh for the benefit of his guests.

But Tiger wasn't in the mood for his bullshit. He grabbed a handful of jacket, lifted Weasel to his feet, and pulled him close while Pete and Ralphie discouraged the goons from interfering.

"Now tell your friends to get lost," he said in a low but cold tone.

Weasel's smile wavered briefly. "Sure, baby, I understand. You want a private party," he said, as he signaled the goons to leave with the girls.

"That better, baby?" Weasel said, smoothing out his rumpled jacket.

Tiger sat at the end of the half circle booth. He had won an easy victory and that's what bothered him. Weasel was a king and the Kit Kat Klub was his castle. In his castle, his word was law. In the shadowy world they both lived in, power and strength were tools of authority. Without that authority, the jackals surrounding him would pull him to the ground. Yet he'd just dethroned the king in front of the jackals, and Weasel easily buckled under. Why? That bothered Tiger.

"Where is my brother?" Tiger asked pointedly, unsure whether he saw a flash of panic.

"He will be here," Weasel answered. "And Helen?" he asked with an edge to his voice that Tiger hadn't noticed before.

"I have her," he said, taking a shot in the dark. "But I will not make the exchange here," he said. This time he was certain of the flash of panic.

"Hold it, baby. I ain't going for that bullshit," Weasel said in alarm. "It's going to be here or nowhere."

But Tiger ignored him. "What's the difference? You put Sonny in a car. I put Helen in a car. Then we exchange. Simple, no?" he asked softly.

But he could see Weasel wasn't listening. Tiger noticed the fine beads of sweat just under the lip of the eye patch.

"No, no, no. We have the exchange here or nowhere," Weasel said with finality.

But Tiger was determined to push him to the wall. "In that case, there is no deal," he said, rising to his feet.

He could smell the panic as Weasel's hand shot out and stopped him. Tiger let out his breath.

"Hold it," Weasel said, looking at the two goons standing at the bar. "My boys have a stake in this, too. I'll have to talk to them," he said, rising at Tiger's nod.

Tiger watched Weasel huddle with the goons for a few

moments, knowing the huddle was a sham. But he had to let the game be played. The bartender placed the telephone on the bar for Weasel to make a call. Tiger hoped his bugman was on his toes.

Weasel returned to Tiger with a determined expression, not bothering to sit. "No deal," he said coldly. "You got fifty minutes left," he said with conviction.

Tiger just studied him and knew that someone was pulling Weasel's strings. He hoped the bugman could tell him who it was.

"We'll exchange in fifty minutes," said Tiger, noticing Pete's surprised look.

R ALPHIE sat in the rear seat with Tiger, who was looking out the car window at the Kit Kat Klub. "Pull all the troops out of the buildings and send them home," he said to their surprise. "Five minutes before the exchange, back off the spotters and clear the area." And as an afterthought, he said, "Also disarm the three troopers in the club. We're going in clean."

Tiger looked over at Ralphie. "Fifteen minutes before the exchange I want all those vehicles in motion, to make a pass of the club every three to five minutes. Keep one vehicle stationary. This one," he said, returning to his study of the Kit Kat Klub.

H E had ratty eyes, aquiline features, and he looked like the dog he had on a leash. "It's clean," the sniffer said.

Tiger thanked him and had a trooper drive the sniffer and his dog home. The sniffer had just solved one of two problems. He assured Tiger there were no explosives in the club or surrounding area. That left Tiger with the only answer possible, and now he understood why Weasel had selected the Kit Kat Klub for the exchange.

A trooper entered the car and whispered to Tiger, who waited for the trooper to leave before he spoke. "They're moving in."

Pete nodded and looked at his watch. "We got nine minutes."

Tiger nodded as Ralphie returned from issuing the orders he wanted executed. He noticed three cars pull up before the Kit Kit Klub.

"She's in the center vehicle," said Ralphie.

Tiger nodded and reached for the door handle. "Bring her into the club in exactly four minutes."

He crossed the wide boulevard with Pete in tow. Inside, he took a moment to let his eyes adjust to the dim light. Taking an open table in the center of the room, he sat. The club still held some customers, but the goons outnumbered them. From the corner booth, Weasel watched him as he coolly sipped his drink. After a moment, he put the glass down and half smiled. "Are you ready?"

Tiger ignored him, studied his wristwatch before looking up. "We still have five minutes," he said, lapsing into silence, knowing the die had been cast. Suddenly customers were drifting toward the exits. He wondered if it was by chance or by fear.

At four minutes to, the front door opened. Ralphie stepped in, looked over the situation, signaled, and four huge troopers stepped through the door followed by a small woman almost hidden by a circle of troopers.

Tiger looked over at Weasel. "I have Helen, now where is my brother?" he asked coldly, noticing the thin layer of perspiration covering Weasel's forehead.

"He'll be here. We still have three minutes," he said, with a slight nervousness in his voice. "Can I talk to Helen?" he asked, speaking to Tiger but trying to look past the four troopers.

"You can talk to her after I see my brother," he said, lapsing into silence again, as Weasel's single eye flashed out its hate.

At zero time, Tiger looked up from his watch as the rear door opened admitting three hardfaced men.

Tiger was quick to register Weasel's obvious relief. He heard a noise behind him, turned swiftly as three more men entered the front door, forcing Ralphie and the phalanx of troopers to slide over into the corner. The troopers created a solid wall against the intruders, protecting the defenseless woman behind them.

Tiger smiled inwardly, remembering the old days when exchanges were between honorable men.

"Hey, baby," smiled Weasel brightly. "The cavalry is here."

But Tiger ignored him as he saw Smilin' Jack emerge from the kitchen, his tight, false smile replaced by a real grin. Tiger watched as the determined agent strode purposefully up to him. He stepped up to Tiger, removed a white oblong slip of paper from inside his jacket pocket, and dropped it on the table before Tiger.

"This is a warrant for your arrest. You are charged with interstate transportation and aiding in the flight of a Federal material witness," he said, removing a pair of handcuffs from under his coat as one of Tiger's men stepped forward, scooped up the paper and began to read.

"Who the hell are you?" asked the agent coldly.

"I am Jonathan Witherspoon, attorney for Mister Corso, and this warrant appears to be illegal," he said, turning to face Tiger. "Do you know a Helen Stanowski?" he asked softly.

Tiger shrugged. "Who's she?" he said, measuring the agent carefully.

An angry Smilin' Jack brushed past Tiger and pointed in Ralphie's direction. "You have a woman hidden behind those men whom you freely brought into this club. That woman is Helen Stanowski, for whom I have an arrest warrant," he said, signaling one of his men to bring Helen over. But the woman ran past Smilin' Jack and threw her arms around Tiger's neck.

"Save me from these dastardly men," Naughty Lola cooed at a shocked Smilin' Jack.

Weasel's expression turned to stone and Smilin' Jack knew he'd been outfoxed. He glared hatefully at Weasel, who wished he had a hole to crawl into.

In the presence of Witherspoon, the lawyer, Jack could only rave about obstruction of justice.

Through it all, Weasel sat in the booth, stunned.

Tiger glared at him, knowing sooner or later he was going to kill him. But first he wanted to know where his brother was. He walked over, sat in the booth, and studied the glassy look in Weasel's eye. "Where's my brother?" he asked coolly.

"Your brother?" Weasel said, continuing his stunned stare. "I don't have your brother."

"I'm going to ask you one more time, Weasel. Now what did you do with my brother?"

The one eye came into focus. "I don't have him, Tiger, honest. I only said that to get Helen back."

The madness rose in Tiger. He reached out, pulled Weasel across the table and eyeballed him. "What did you do with my brother, you cocksucker?"

Jack and another agent moved in and forced Tiger to release his grip. "What the hell's going on here?" Jack demanded.

His anger at a fever pitch, Tiger turned his attention to Jack. He badly wanted to lash out at him for the beating he had received and for being involved in Weasel's dirty game, but it wasn't worth doing time for assaulting him. In Tiger's eyes, Jack was a degenerate rogue. But a powerful rogue, with the government behind him.

He turned a steady gaze toward Weasel, his hate obvious. "I'll see you around," he said, heading for the front door.

Outside, Tiger took pains to control his anger as he escorted Lola back to her car, letting her know he owed her a big one.

Witherspoon stood on the sidewalk until Tiger's car pulled out into traffic.

In the car, Tiger looked expectantly at Ralphie in the front seat. "Well?"

Ralphie broke into a wide grin. "We got him."

Tiger nodded his relief. "Where is he?"

"Waiting on 114th Street at Rocco's."

Tiger nodded, glad his brother was back safe and sound.

When he learned that the bugman traced Weasel's call to a phone booth on 148th Street, he blanketed the area.

A trooper found the booth, a black Caddie parked alongside it, three of Weasel's goons inside, and Sonny with them.

The trooper reported his findings to Ralphie, and in his opinion the goons were carrying guns. Storming the car could get Sonny killed.

But the trooper had noticed that every time someone attempted to use the booth, the goon behind the wheel got out, walked to the booth, and roughly chased the person away. He then outlined a plan to Ralphie he was sure would work. Ralphie liked it and reported it to Tiger, who gave him the go-ahead, but with one stipulation. The trooper was to wait until just before the deadline before putting the plan into action.

At five minutes before the deadline, the trooper punched in his hat, rolled up his collar, and staggered drunkenly toward the phone booth.

"Hey you, get away from there," yelled the driver, walking toward him.

But the trooper ignored him and reached for the receiver. But a hand shot out and grabbed his wrist. "Get the hell out of here," said the goon belligerently.

The trooper swayed. "Wassa matter? I only want the little woman," he said, reaching for the phone again.

"I told you to leave that fucking phone alone," he said lunging; but the trooper ducked under the blow, grabbed him, and wrestled him to the ground. As they rolled over on the sidewalk, the two goons guarding Sonny quickly left the car to aid their comrade. At that moment, a circle of troopers converged on the car, pulled out Sonny, and whisked him away. The other troopers moved in on the goons and left them bloody on the sidewalk.

BEFORE meeting Sonny, Tiger had Pete change vehicles twice, in case there was a tail.

At the social club, he found his brother, alone, sipping coffee in Rocco's private office. At the sight of Tiger, Sonny jumped to his feet, threw his arms around Tiger, and wept.

Tiger was taken aback, but only briefly, quickly realizing the strain his brother had been under. "Are you all right?" he asked Sonny softly.

Sonny shook his head.

"Did they hurt you?" he asked.

"No, but they were going to kill me," he said with a muffled sob.

Tiger eased his brother into the most comfortable chair, then sat opposite him. "Want to tell me about it?" he asked gently.

After a moment Sonny brought himself under control. "I don't know where to begin."

"Start with Weasel, when his goons caught you. How did they get you?"

Sonny's shock was apparent. "Weasel? What did Weasel have to do with the hoods who caught me?"

Tiger's annoyance showed. "Who the hell do you think had you picked up?"

Sonny shrugged. "I don't know, but why would he have me killed? What did I ever do to him?"

Damn, thought Tiger, he doesn't believe me. Was his mind that burned out? He sighed. "Where have you been for the past week?"

Sonny was surprised at the question. "I was at Sharky's house."

"You spent all week with him?" he said in doubt.

"Yes. He wasn't mad at me for what you did to his place. So I stayed with him until last night. I went out for some Chinese and they nabbed me and hustled me into a car."

Tiger saw the pattern, sure that Sharky had a part in the kidnapping. "Did they say why they wanted you?" he asked softly.

Sonny hesitated, but only for a moment. "They wanted to know who my supplier was."

"And?" Tiger asked carefully.

"So I told them. What else could I do? They would have chopped me up," he said, averting his eyes. "Besides I had the monkey on my back, and they wouldn't give me a fix unless I told them."

Tiger felt the bitterness of his brother's words and asked coldly, "What names did you give them?"

His brother hesitated, but something in Tiger's eyes warned him to be careful. So he gave the names.

Corsicans, thought Tiger, wondering how the hell Sonny managed to get hooked up with them.

It was obvious that after revealing his connection, Weasel had no further use for Sonny. He decided to use Sonny to get Helen back. It was now obvious that Weasel had had no intention of exchanging Sonny for Helen. Why? Was he intending to keep his brother hostage in order to ensure his own safety? Or was he going to kill him? Had Weasel gone over the edge?

Weasel's use of Smilin' Jack to secure Helen was pure genius, but stupid in the long run. Yet he wondered about this unholy alliance. He knew Weasel and Iggy had known each other over the years, but only lately did they begin running together. Where Smilin' Jack fit into the picture Tiger didn't know. He wondered what gave Weasel the idea he could fit into Iggy's shoes. Did Jack give him the go-ahead or did Weasel have some other power source? Did he have a direct line to the clerk's office? Or was Sonny's Corsican connection enough?

No, Tiger didn't think so. If Weasel had the clerk's office

and the missing narcotics, he would sell them. He was too greedy and ambitious not to.

Tiger studied his brother. "The truth of the matter is, your friend Sharky deliberately kept you in cold storage for a week before he threw you to the wolves. That's a fact, Sonny," he said, letting it soak in.

But his brother's expression remained blank. "I don't know who those hoods were, but I don't believe Sharky would have me hurt," he said simply.

Tiger wondered if Sonny was putting him down. Sonny was street wise, far from naïve, so he decided to attack from a new direction. "Iggy is dead," and saw the arrow hit.

"Weasel and Sharky killed him," he continued, handing his brother a newspaper clipping.

One look at the photograph of Iggy's bloody remains was enough for Sonny. He looked away. "Did they hurt Helen, too?" he asked.

Tiger shook his head. "I saved her."

Sonny accepted that, then asked, "Could I see her?"

"Not unless you think it's necessary. The fewer people who know where she is, the safer she'll be."

"I guess you really saved my ass this time. I was sure they were going to kill me."

Now came the unpleasant part for Tiger: Sonny's future. "Where do you go from here?" he asked Sonny.

From his pocket, Sonny removed a plastic bag filled with white powder and let it dangle. At the sight of it, Tiger's stomach twisted.

"That's all I have," said Sonny. "Just enough to get me to the Kentucky cure center. Will you help me get there?"

"I will help you," said Tiger, still unable to reach out for his brother. Perhaps, thought Tiger, Sonny had cried wolf too many times.

Sonny thanked him. "Will you at least let Helen know I'm taking the cure?"

Tiger nodded. "I'll see that she gets the message."

AFTER a few phone calls, Tiger put Sonny on the plane to Kentucky. He made sure the doctors would be waiting when the plane landed. He also sent along four troopers to keep his brother out of mischief.

An hour later he was back in his office, where Helen was waiting with Tony Orechicco and his boys. Helen sat nervously and Tiger couldn't blame her. Being thrown on a plane, flown to New York, and told to wait—for what, she didn't know.

He assured her everything was well and sent her back to Florida, where Weasel couldn't get near her.

After Helen and Tony and his boys had left, Tiger reviewed the whole situation. Neither Weasel nor Sharky could afford a live murder witness hanging over their heads. Tiger was sure of it. So long as they knew he had Helen, they would live in fear.

Smilin' Jack, on the other hand, was different. Rogue or not, he was still Federal and therefore untouchable. Tiger had no doubt the agent was using his badge and gun for personal gain, but so what? Even with proof of wrongdoing, the Feds were known to take care of their own. So Tiger knew he'd best watch his ass because he had stirred up a Federal hornet's nest.

Tiger turned his thoughts in a new direction, the target policeman.

While he was busy with the Weasel/Sonny problem, he had assigned two troopers to take his place on the clock. If the policeman stayed true to form, Tiger would take him tomorrow night. Now, after forty hours without sleep, he needed some.

TIGER knew the policeman and his staff were all that were left in the club. And according to the clock, the staff would be leaving within ten minutes.

After they pulled out of the parking lot, Ralphie slipped

from behind a bush, looked over the empty lot, and punctured the right front tire of the Mark IV, then slid behind the bush again.

Tiger watched the proceeding from across the street. He settled back and waited, apprehensive as usual at the upcoming hit.

Pete nudged him as the policeman emerged, locked the door, set the alarms, and walked to his car, stopping at the sight of the flat tire.

Tiger waited until the tire was almost changed before he nudged Pete to move out.

Pete pulled up before the club, perpendicular to the Mark IV and twenty feet away. Both men stepped out, ignored the policeman, as they admired the club. Tiger knew it was only a matter of time before the policeman became curious. He eased Pete closer to the Mark IV, gesticulating for the benefit of the policeman.

Tiger sensed the man walking toward him and turned, smiling in a friendly manner. "Hello, could you tell me who owns this place?"

The policeman's eyes narrowed and filled with suspicion. "Why?"

Tiger turned away, studying the club again. "Because I like it and want to know if it's for sale," he said, looking levelly at the man. "Do you know who owns it?"

The suspicion lessened, but the hardness remained. "It's not for sale," he said coldly.

"Then you're the owner?" said Tiger with surprise.

"That's right, and it's not for sale."

Tiger showed his disappointment. "That's a shame. It's certainly a beautiful place."

The policeman ignored the compliment, watching coldly as Tiger turned and headed for his car. That's when Ralphie hit him from behind.

Quickly, they trussed him up and tossed him into the rear floor of Tiger's car. Together they unjacked the policeman's car and tightened the lugs. Ralphie jumped into the Mark IV and followed Tiger out of the parking lot.

217

DEEP in the Canarsie swamp the huge incinerator doors closed behind the two cars as his cousin Frankie showed them where to park.

"Quick, take his clothes off," ordered Tiger.

Pete and Ralphie swiftly stripped the policeman as Tiger yelled to his cousin to bring a bucket of water.

It took a moment for the naked policeman to regain consciousness. He wore a bewildered expression as he stared dumbly at the others. Pete yanked him to his feet as Tiger donned a pair of leather gloves.

"What the fuck do you guys think you're doing? I'm a policeman!" he shouted in a commanding voice.

Frankie returned with the bucket. Tiger knelt and submerged his hands in the water.

"I told you guys I'm a cop!" he shouted indignantly.

Tiger just stared at him. Now that he knew his man was lucid, he drove his fist deep into the policeman's midsection. The blow took the man by surprise. He tried to double up, but Pete and Ralphie held him upright as Tiger drove in another blow, and another. He continued until the policeman was limp. Satisfied he was softened up, he asked, "What's your name?"

"I got no fucking name!" he spat back.

This was going to be a tough one, Tiger thought, knowing he had to break the man's will.

Tiger continued on the man's midsection, each blow precise, exact, designed to make the man beg for mercy. When he did, Tiger would beat him some more to let him know there would be none.

"My name is Mike Dunne!" he shouted.

But Tiger continued. "My name is Mike Dunne!" he screamed, trying to wiggle free. "For God's sake! Please!" Now we're getting somewhere, thought Tiger, lashing out at the man's midsection again, making sure the leather gloves were wet, ever mindful of not leaving any bruises for the police to find.

Before lapsing into unconsciousness, Dunne retched and they let him slip to the floor. Tiger studied him, waiting,

waiting for the man to regain consciousness. When he did, Tiger kicked him savagely in the groin.

The policeman rolled over and over as if shot from a cannon. He screamed in pain as Pete, Ralphie, and Frankie joined Tiger to make a circle around him.

Tiger waited for the spasms to diminish before signaling Pete and Ralphie to pick the man up.

"You ready now to tell me what I want to know?" Tiger asked coldly.

Tears of pain filled the man's eyes as he looked at Tiger liked a whipped pup. "What do you want to know?"

"I know you've been stealing heroin from the clerk's office, and I want to know how you get it out," he said, studying the man carefully, sure he was beaten.

"Can I have a cigarette?" he asked softly.

Tiger nodded, untied the man's hands as Frankie placed a cigarette between his lips. The policeman filled his lungs, exhaled, and looked at Tiger. "What do you want to know?"

Tiger had won. "How are you getting the narcotics out?"

"Through the D.A.'s office."

Tiger's brows shot up. "You better explain that."

"Before trial the district attorney's office always requests delivery of the evidence. A special courier squad signs for it, delivering it to the testing laboratory. After the trial, it is returned to the clerk's office for warehousing or ordered destroyed. On the return trip back to the clerk's office, the couriers switch the drugs for milk sugar."

Cute, thought Tiger, real cute. "How many men are assigned to the courier squad?"

"Ten."

"How many are in on the deal?"

"All of them," the policeman said simply.

Tiger was astounded. He hadn't realized the ring was so big. "What happens to the drugs?"

"We used to sell it and split the proceeds."

The words "used to" were not lost on Tiger. "Who bought it from you?"

"A guy named Delvechicco. He worked for Joe the Boss."

That threw Tiger. "You sold it directly?"

"Not directly. We had two policemen handle the connection for us."

Tiger didn't like Sally Dell's being in the picture. He was sure Sally was a smoke screen. "Who were the two policemen?"

"Denato and Aielo."

That made Tiger suspicious since they were the two Uncle Patsy had hung. Why was he throwing dead people at him?

"Those men have been dead for a while," he said coldly. "I want to know who's handling it now."

The policeman studied him. "Inspector Colby," he said.

Tiger was incredulous. "He handles it himself?" he asked.

The policeman shook his head. "No, the couriers still make the deliveries, but Colby runs everything."

Tiger wondered where the inspector fit into the picture. "Did Colby set up the original scam?"

"No," said the policeman, "we had the deal all to ourselves. Then one day the inspector hit us with enough evidence to put us away for life. We had no choice but to let him take over the operation. Now we work for him."

"You take the big risk and he gets the big money."

"That's about the size of it."

"Why were Denato and Aielo killed?"

The policeman shook his head. "I really don't know. I've heard different stories. That they had a deal on the side that went bad. That Internal Affairs was after them. I also heard they were about to blow the whistle to the grand jury on the Bocci family. You can take your pick. Since Colby took over, we only get the crumbs."

"Why?" asked Tiger.

The policeman shrugged. "Colby claims he has a lot of people to feed."

"Like who?"

"He didn't say."

220

Tiger let that soak in. "Why was Sergeant Phillip Defalco killed?"

The policeman looked askance at Tiger. "Colby and the guys around him didn't trust the sergeant. They said he was an honest cop who'd get everybody killed. He could have burned us all. We had no choice." He looked at Tiger for understanding.

Tiger took a shot in the dark. "Who was with you when you killed him?"

The policeman saw no understanding in Tiger's eyes. "Me, Sergeant O'Hara, and Sergeant Dubinski. We met him on the Belt Parkway. The four of us sat in the car with Dubinski and O'Hara sitting in the back. Dubinski shot Defalco in the back of the head."

So much for fair play in the drug world, thought Tiger. Defalco was killed because he was honest. Well, he at least got some satisfaction for Defalco. It was Dubinski that Tiger killed in Tony's scrapyard.

"Do you know who Colby sells the drugs to now?"

The policeman hesitated, but the look in Tiger's eyes prodded him. "The couriers say it's going to a Harlem dealer named Iggy Friedman."

For Tiger, another piece of the puzzle fell into place. But he still didn't understand it. Could this be another red herring? If Iggy had the stuff, the bastard would have sold it. Yet it wasn't on the streets. Why?

"Are you sure?" asked Tiger, still uncertain.

The policeman nodded his head. "Sure I'm sure. The couriers said they delivered each load to Iggy in a place called the Kit Kat Klub."

Now Tiger was sure he was going to come up smelling like a rose. He asked the sixty-four-dollar question: "Do you know a Federal agent nicknamed Smilin' Jack?"

Surprise showed on the man's face. "He's always hanging out in the inspector's office."

"What do you know about him?"

"Nothing," he answered. "But I think he's involved with Colby."

"In the narcotics?"

221

The policeman looked at Tiger. "What else would they have in common?"

Another piece of the puzzle fell into place. If Jack was involved in the drug scam, then he was doing the stockpiling. That takes a lot of money. And Tiger could only wonder where the money was coming from. That kind of money only comes from the government or the families. Which side was Jack on?

Tiger checked his watch, looked at Ralphie, and nodded. Without warning, Ralphie hit him from behind, sending the policeman sprawling.

"Dress him and throw him in the car," said Tiger. "We only have a half hour."

In front of Jasper's, Ralphie returned the Mark IV to its original parking spot in front of the club. Wearing gloves, Pete removed the flat tire, jack, and lug wrench from the trunk.

Ralphie jacked up the front end as Pete loosened the lugs and placed the tire on the ground next to the flat one.

With the stage set, Tiger studied the position of every item.

"Bring him out," he said.

They dragged out the unconscious policeman, positioning him on the ground facing the raised fender. Tiger pushed the man's head under the lip of the fender and his chest against the drum. He held the policeman in position as Pete and Ralphie pushed against the front bumper. The car slipped off the jack and fell on the head of the policeman.

Tiger took a moment mentally photographing his handiwork. It wasn't foolproof and perhaps a little sloppy, but it should work. The police might not be happy with the accident, but they would have to accept it.

A tired Tiger returned to his office. He sent Pete and Ralphie upstairs for forty winks. Ordering breakfast from Lulu's, he sat mulling over the past events. He thought about each aspect of the policeman's hit. Satisfied he'd made no mistakes, he relaxed. Even if the investigators called it murder, so what? They had no witnesses.

As for the hit on Dunne, he felt well rewarded by three new pieces of the puzzle. One, for what it was worth, he had learned who killed Sergeant Phillip Defalco. Two, he knew Smilin' Jack was a rogue. Three, Iggy and now Weasel were tied into the narcotics coming out of the clerk's office.

The new pieces helped flesh out the puzzle. The outside frame was complete. Now he had to find out what the center of the picture looked like.

He still needed to find a key piece to build on. He knew he couldn't move openly against Smilin' Jack and Inspector Colby because of their high positions. Although Tiger believed that any man who bleeds is touchable.

Tiger had little doubt that Smilin' Jack would be coming at him for the episode in the Kit Kat Klub. But how would he come? Tiger didn't know, but he would come. Not with a cheap shot, but with class. He didn't act like a Federal agent, more like an alley cat. Cold, vicious, no rules, and no pity.

With the untouchables put aside, he had to choose to move in one of two directions: Weasel or the courier squad.

He was positive Weasel was turning over the narcotics to Smilin' Jack, and interrogating Weasel would only lead to Jack and a dead-end.

The couriers, on the other hand, were more vulnerable but difficult to move against. He didn't intend to waste manpower and time clocking all ten of them. He had another way to go. Tiger remembered Shirley Jackson, the black chick he had interrogated. She was one of the three women sitting in the booth with Weasel and his goons at the exchange. For weeks she had been playing it cool, trying to cozy up to Weasel through her goon boyfriend. Now Tiger needed her.

He decided to call a friend at police headquarters for a favor. The policeman he had hit had given him a list of each member of the courier squad. If his friendly could match the names with the faces, then Shirley could keep an eye out for whoever showed.

Since he already had a clock on Weasel, he would need the bugman to rig up some kind of beeper system. Maybe in a belt buckle, or an earring, some decoration she could wear, but something she could press unnoticed to give his boys a warning a deal was going down. From that point on, he would play it by ear in trying to trail Weasel to the warehouse.

He let Pete and Ralphie sleep, took two troopers with him, and met with his police friendly.

Within the hour he was back in Lulu's to await the police photo. He was surprised to find Ralphie sitting at a table nursing a cup of coffee.

"What's up? Couldn't sleep?"

"I was hoping I could cut loose for a couple of hours."

Tiger nodded. "Sure," he said, but sensed something was wrong. "Is something wrong?"

His friend shrugged. "My brother just called. He thinks my old man had another stroke."

"Shit," exclaimed Tiger, feeling his friend's worry. "Do you know what hospital they took him to?"

"Saint Marie's."

Tiger nodded again. "A good place. Call me the moment you have word on him," he said, watching Ralphie rush out the door. He turned to Albee, the door guard.

"Have someone bring me a pot of black coffee."

Albee nodded, signaled a trooper, and opened the door for Tiger.

Tiger sat behind his desk mulling over what move he could make if he boxed Smilin' Jack into a compromising position. Short of killing the bastard outright, he knew the best he could expect would be the agent's dismissal and the drugs kept from the market.

Tiger smiled. If he managed to get Jack drummed out of the F.B.I., he would be waiting to extract revenge.

Tiger was suddenly shaken from his thoughts when Albee stuck his head in the door. "We got trouble in here."

"What is it?" asked Tiger.

"Cops."

Outside there was chaos. A dozen flack-jacketed detectives, led by Inspector Colby, were throwing troopers against the wall, frisking them, then herding them to one side of the dining room. Other detectives stood by, riot guns at the ready, while another group of policemen began dismantling walls, floors, and ceiling.

Tiger rushed across the room at Colby, but a detective stepped in front of him. Tiger shoved the man aside.

"What the fuck do you think you're doing?" shouted an inflamed Tiger.

Colby's dead eyes stared at him. "I have a warrant to search these premises," he said, holding out a document to Tiger.

Tiger snapped the paper from his hands and read it. "You know this warrant is bullshit."

"Maybe so," said Colby coldly, "but if you interfere, I'll have one of my men clamp you in irons."

The anger continued in Tiger, as one complete wall was ripped from its moorings. "Warrant or no warrant, you can't come in here and wreck my place."

Colby measured him. "I can and I will. So if you don't like it, sue me," he said with a dead, calculating look.

Tiger continued to fume, but he knew his hands were tied. He wondered where the fuck Goldberg was. The lawyer had standing orders to remain inside the club at all times.

Two policemen tried to open the door to Tiger's office, but the door, steel reinforced in a steel frame, held.

"Smash the fucking door down!" shouted Colby, as two policemen rushed forward with crowbars and axes.

Before Tiger could protest, Pete was brought in, arms handcuffed behind his back. One of the detectives escorting him was nursing the beginning of a large black eye. "What's this bullshit all about?" he asked Tiger.

"I think that bastard Colby is just breaking balls."

Pete looked askance at the wreckage. "Some ball busting," he said sourly.

Suddenly a triumphant Colby emerged from Tiger's office. He carried an armful of automatic weapons, fully silenced. His cold eyes glittered as he studied Tiger. "I got you now, you son of a bitch. You'll get fifty years for this."

Tiger recognized the weapons from his safe and knew the bastard had him.

The inspector stepped in closer and measured Tiger. "Want to make a deal?"

Tiger's eyes narrowed. "What kind of deal?"

Colby lowered his voice. "We can work this out. I won't make any charges against you in exchange for Delvechicco."

Tiger shrugged. "It's a good deal, except Delvechicco doesn't work for me anymore."

The inspector's expression turned sour. "Who does he work for?"

"My father, Don Corso."

Tiger heard the intake of Colby's breath. He knew Colby didn't want to tangle with his father in a showdown. After a moment, the inspector smiled. "Then why don't you call daddy. Let him know I have you in a box and if Delvechicco shows up here within the next hour, we'll forget this little incident," he said, pointing to the wall phone.

Tiger didn't believe what an asshole the inspector was. He was really going to let him call his father, to tip him to put Lawyer Rizzo into action. As to Delvechicco, his father would no more let Colby have one of his boys than he would turn himself into the police. But Tiger dialed, waited until he was connected with his father, then explained the situation. After a moment, he hung up and looked at the inspector.

"What did daddy say?"

"My daddy said to tell you to go fuck yourself," he said and was satisfied with Colby's discomfort.

The snake uncoiled, eyes dilated, as he spat at one of the detectives, "Book him. Book the whole fucking lot of them."

Iᴛ was late evening before Rizzo managed to get Tiger and Pete released. The rest of the troopers would be turned loose shortly.

As they sat in the back of the lawyer's limousine, Tiger looked over at Rizzo's chiseled features. "Where do we go from here?" he asked softly.

Rizzo smiled. "Relax. It's not as bad as it seems."

Three machine guns, two sawed-off shotguns, and six pistols, he thought, and the man said to relax. "How do you figure that?"

"Well," the lawyer said, "he made two mistakes. The warrant was for the public area of Lulu's restaurant. You were in the private dining room. Second, he broke open your safe and removed the weapons. He had no warrant for your safe. Either way, I can get the evidence of the weapons suppressed."

Tiger relaxed and returned the lawyer's smile.

"However," he said, letting the word hang in midair, "when you walk away from this one, next time he's coming at you a little smarter or a lot more vicious."

Tiger nodded his understanding.

Rizzo dropped them off at Lulu's. Tiger quickly called the hospital, happy to learn that Ralphie's father was out of danger.

Lulu sent a waiter with the photos his friendly had delivered while Tiger was in the lock-up. He dispatched a trooper to Harlem with a message to Big Che to slip the package, discreetly, to Shirley at the Kit Kat Klub.

Then he went home to sleep.

Aꜰᴛᴇʀ a good night's sleep, Tiger's thinking sharpened. He gave little thought to Colby and company, fairly sure they would give him a breather for a few days before they came at him again.

He narrowed his focus on the couriers, Weasel, and Shirley. She was now a key factor. If she could pull off the beeper signal, he could get in some good licks at Smilin' Jack.

He quickly picked up the buzzing phone. "Yeah?"

"Your brother Sonny's loose again," said Pete.

Damn, damn, damn, Tiger thought. "How the hell did he get past the troopers?"

"He tied bedsheets together and went out the window."

"Why the hell weren't they watching him closely?" he asked in anger.

"Because they thought they were supposed to protect him, not watch him."

Tiger hung up. He sat there wondering what the hell Sonny was trying to prove. What was driving him? What was the magnet that repeatedly drew him back to Harlem and possible destruction?

Did he only go to Kentucky to cool off? But from what? From whom? Sonny had to know that by leaving the sanctuary of the cure center, he was going to be a hunted man. Helen wasn't around to help him. Tiger certainly wasn't going on the hook for this one. Not against his father.

So why did he leave? He had to know all hands were against him. Well, Tiger thought, maybe there was no reversing the brain damage caused by the drugs.

Tiger thought of sending out some troopers to track him down but decided against it. He made his bed, so now let him lie in it.

He looked at his watch. Still early, he thought. He pressed the buzzer button.

Pete stuck his head in the door. "Yeah, Tiger?"

"Why don't we go pay our respects to Ralphie's old man?"

"Great idea, but Gaetano Abruzzi is out here. He'd like an audience."

Tiger found the request surprising, since Abruzzi was connected to Carlo Alessi. Although he was a made man, that didn't give him license to go over his boss's head.

He recalled Abruzzi's dossier. An impressive one. He had a long list of hits, many deemed impossible to com-

228

plete. But he did. Gaetano Abruzzi was a specialist of the first order. A survivor who always did the unexpected.

"Frisk him good before sending him in," Tiger said, promising himself to get a metal detector installed.

Abruzzi was lean and well dressed, the beau brummel type with the look of a man who spent a lot of time outdoors. A hunter. He stood attentively before Tiger's desk, waiting to be spoken to.

"What can I do for you?"

"I mean no disrespect, my don, and I told Carlo Alessi I was coming," he said, in a softly modulated voice.

"Did he give his permission?"

"No," said Abruzzi, simply. "I have heard you are a fair man, so I have come to speak a grievance. May I speak bluntly?"

"I prefer it," said Tiger, studying him, wondering what he had against Alessi to risk his enmity.

"I have been a man of honor for many years and always I follow the law of the family. I have been loyal and obedient, but never a fool or a flunky," he said, pausing to let that get across to Tiger. Which it did.

"Many times Carlo Alessi has ordered me to sweep floors, run errands, and otherwise flaunted his authority. I have never complained because he is of a little mind. A big man in the eyes of the family, but a little one in mine."

The words stung Tiger, because the man could be digging his own grave. But he remained silent.

"When I caught up with Calamine, my first thought was to put him under a manhole cover. But instead, like a good soldier, I reported to Alessi. He ordered me to take my prisoner out to his farm on Long Island. There he had a big grinding machine he uses for chopping up logs. I knew he wanted me to make Calamine disappear, which made sense. But he had other ideas. He wanted me to put the man alive into the grinder and a little at the time. After his legs came off and blood shot out everywhere, Calamine fainted so Carlo Alessi made me wake him up with smelling salts. He woke up and I lowered him further, but he fainted again.

I found no pleasure in the job, but it was obvious Carlo Alessi wanted to hear the man scream, he wanted to inflict pain, but he wasn't man enough to do the job himself. So I dropped him in the grinder and let it be finished," he said, his features deepening.

Tiger sat silent and attentive.

"I have done damage in New York, Chicago, Detroit, and a dozen other places. I've hit many men, many ways, but I never took a family hit and used it personally. If the contact was a problem, I made him disappear. If a message was to be sent, I mutilated the man in accordance with the rules of the message. But I never chopped up a man for personal fun," Abruzzi said, allowing a slight pause.

"So when I dropped Calamine in the grinder, Carlo Alessi took it personal and threw two shots at me."

"He what?" asked Tiger, in shock.

Abruzzi nodded. "That's what he did. When I saw what was coming, I lost my balance and fell. I was lucky not to have fallen into the machine."

"What happened then?"

"I ran like hell. What else?" he said. "Later, when he cooled off, I was able to reason with him."

"Why the fuck didn't you just blow him away when he tried to kill you?"

Gaetano Abruzzi lowered his eyes. "I couldn't do that. He's still my boss."

Tiger studied the man who was family through and through.

"Lately, Carlo Alessi has taken to having me park the car on street corners. With the windows open, he screams obscenities at every woman who passes. Regardless of who they are or who they are with. Now I say this with great respect, my don, but I cannot allow myself to be degraded for that man's pleasure anymore. And I have told him so."

"And what did he say to that?"

"He just laughed in his crazy way and told me to go fuck myself."

Tiger found Abruzzi's remarks disconcerting. "How long has this been going on?"

"Since he shot himself. He's not the same man. He's like a crazy man. Even the other troopers try to avoid him."

Tiger studied the man for a long time. "And what would you expect me to do with him?"

Abruzzi shrugged. "I don't know, my don, but when the cheese turns sour it has to be thrown away."

Agreed, thought Tiger. These were serious charges, punishable by death. That's what bothered Tiger. Alessi knew the law of one member attempting to hurt another without permission of the Council.

Could it be, wondered Tiger, the man had flipped? If so, he'd better see what the problem is.

"You will not return to Carlo Alessi, so hang your hat outside until I get to the bottom of this," he said, signaling that the audience was over.

Abruzzi's eyes smiled slightly. "Thank you, my don."

At the hospital, Tiger found Ralphie's father conscious but unable to speak. The stroke had affected his vocal cords.

Tiger hugged the old man. Over the years, he had grown fond of him. Ralphie, standing at the side of the bed, was misty-eyed, knowing his father realized he was being honored by Tiger's presence.

Before leaving the hospital, Tiger ordered Ralphie to relax and spend another day with his father.

In the lobby, Pete's beeper signaled an emergency call. Looking down at the personal display computer, he read the phone number and recognized it as belonging to one of the Harlem troopers.

He quickly returned the call. Sonny had been spotted strolling down 138th Street. The trooper was sure Sonny recognized him because he ducked into an alley and disappeared.

So, thought Tiger, his brother was home again, if one could call that hell-hole home.

"Your brother has balls hanging around that area," said Pete.

"It's not balls. He's just determined to get himself killed."

"You want me to send up a few troopers to look for him?"

Tiger sighed. "Don't bother."

The noisy social club hushed as Tiger and Pete entered. Most of the troopers stood or sat silent, others offered handshakes.

"Where's Carlo?" Tiger asked no one in particular.

A trooper pointed over his shoulder toward a rear door. Tiger nodded his thanks and headed for Carlo's office. He was disturbed at not finding a doorman on guard.

Inside Tiger had difficulty in recognizing the fat man sitting behind a feast of veal cutlets, spaghetti, roast chicken, pastries, and Manhattan Special coffee sodas.

Carlo Alessi had gained over thirty pounds since Tiger last saw him. He sat there, filling his mouth, almost oblivious of the visitors.

After a moment, Alessi looked up, filled his mouth again, and waved Tiger to sit. He washed down the food with soda.

"Sit, sit. Take off a load," he said, opening another bottle of soda. "You see I got that cocksucker Calamine. I got him good," he said with a bright smile, as he ripped off a chicken leg.

Tiger stood, looking at the obese creature. "I've been told you took a shot at a made member," he said coldly.

"Yeah. The fuck had it coming. He likes to do stupid things."

"So you shot at a member?" Tiger asked, seething.

"Yeah. So what? It's forgotten. It wasn't a big deal."

Tiger now had his confirmation. He stepped forward and swept the platters over the edge of the desk. The sound of shattering china thundered through the small room.

Alessi jumped to his feet, but Tiger's frosty eyes stayed him. "What the hell you do that for?"

Tiger stepped in close and glared at the man. Alessi nodded in subjection. But Tiger made note of the cold hate in the man's cruel eyes.

TIGER arrived at his father's office, and the hardface on the door quickly let him in.

As usual, he found his father counting his money. Tiger quickly recited the past events.

It took fifteen minutes for Tiger to complete his report concerning the interrogation of the targeted policeman and the information the cop had given him. He then laid out the plan he had in mind for following the Weasel to the rogue Fed and possibly to the warehouse.

"So what?" Don Corso said. "It means nothing unless you can find the drugs. Even if Smilin' Jack is a rogue, do you think his friends are going to desert him? Hell, no. They'll stick together and haunt you the rest of your life. But if you can put together a powerful case, one so strong that the Feds in Washington might dump the agent to hush up the matter, that's a different thing."

"I see what you mean," Tiger said.

"But don't let that discourage your investigation of the agent. You just might hit paydirt," his father said.

"I guess what bothers me the most is why the drugs haven't hit the street yet. What are they waiting for?"

"Perhaps his timetable isn't completed yet," Don Corso said.

As Tiger mulled that over, his father continued.

"I understand your brother's on the loose again. I have

a pick-up order out for him. So if he comes to you, put him in cold storage until he is fully cured."

Tiger felt his father was being more than fair.

"Also, I have another problem," Tiger said, outlining the charges against Carlo Alessi.

Don Corso remained silent, absorbing the news. Then he said, "These are most serious charges."

"I know, but I cannot overlook this man's actions."

Don Corso took a long time before answering, "I will notify the Council."

Outside, Tiger wondered who would speak for Alessi at the round table. The beeper rang. Pete answered the phone.

"Shirley came through for you. The guy from the clerk's office is there with a duffel bag."

"Who's in control?"

"Mike Amato until Big Che gets there."

"Where do we meet?"

"A block from the Kit Kat Klub."

Pete drove smoothy, cutting smartly but carefully through traffic, making it to Harlem in forty minutes. Big Che and Mike Amato were waiting on the street corner.

Lowering the rear window, Tiger looked up at the skull-like features. "Where's Weasel now?" he asked.

"Still in the club," grunted Big Che.

"What precautions have you taken so far?"

"I have all the exits covered, including the buildings on each side."

Tiger nodded. "Do the men have walkie-talkies?"

The big man nodded. "I also have one for you," he said, handing Tiger a small compact unit.

"I'll take over from here," he said, ordering Pete to a better vantage point.

"Notify me the moment anyone leaves the club with any kind of package," he said. He recognized the courier's vehicle by the Brooklyn license plate.

They kept the club under observation for two hours before a white Caddie pulled up in front. Tiger recognized it as Weasel's.

Ten minutes later, Weasel himself emerged loaded down with two heavy suitcases. He crossed the sidewalk, stepped into the rear seat of the Caddie, and closed the door. The Caddie headed into the traffic.

Tiger picked up the radio. "He's heading north. Pick him up at the corner."

A voice came over the radio. "He turned onto Broadway and is heading uptown."

Good, thought Tiger. "Let's go," he said to Pete.

As the reports came in, it was obvious Weasel was using an evasive zigzag pattern. He was jumping lights, doubling back, and circling the block, but Tiger's troopers were up to Weasel's tricks.

At 136th Street, Weasel's car suddenly pulled over to the curb. He got out and started walking with the two suitcases.

"Stay on him," said Tiger, "and keep an eye on the car in case it's some kind of trick."

After a long silence, Tiger grew impatient. "What the hell's going on?"

A voice reported in. "Nothing. He's covered three blocks so far. He just ducked into an alley!"

"Get someone at the other end of the alley!" shouted Tiger.

"I got it," said another voice.

Tiger looked at the back of Pete's head. "Get me there fast."

As Pete sped to the location, a voice jumped over the radio.

"He's gone. He just disappeared."

Tiger picked up the radio. "Close off the alley and wait for me." He wondered what the hell the trooper meant by disappeared.

Tiger walked slowly up and down the block-long alley. He looked up and down and sideways but saw no place Weasel could have escaped to. The fire escapes were out, not with two heavy suitcases. Besides, they were too high. As he viewed the alley, he saw that all the windows were barred or grated and the doors hadn't been opened in years. Yet he disappeared in this alley.

He looked at the trooper standing alongside him. "Tell me again what happened."

"Like I said, when he ducked into the alley, I moved in fast, looked around the corner, and he was gone. Vanished."

"Anything else?"

"That's it."

"You're sure?" Tiger asked desperately, "Think hard."

The trooper thought hard but still shook his head. Suddenly he was trying to remember something. "Wait," he said, knowing it was on the tip of his tongue. "I do remember the sound of clanking metal."

Tiger nodded, letting his eyes wander about the alley again.

He ordered the troopers to examine the brick walls against some possible secret entrance. Nothing. Then he had them move piles of rubbish. Still nothing.

But he knew Weasel disappeared near here, so there had to be an entrance to somewhere. "I found it!" shouted a trooper, as they all converged on a large steel garbage container. They pushed it aside, revealing a sewer opening in the ground.

"Get some flashlights and see what's down there," Tiger ordered.

Ten minutes later Mike Amato stuck his head out of the sewer.

"Where does it come out?" asked Tiger.

Mike shrugged. "I don't know. Fifty feet in it splits into four different directions."

Damn, Tiger thought, the bastard is blessed by angels.

He turned to Big Che. "Keep a clock on Weasel, his club, and his house. Report to me the moment someone spots him."

Walking away from the alley in disgust, Tiger ordered Pete to take him back to Brooklyn. As he settled in his seat, he looked over the alley once more, aware that Weasel was under there somewhere, like the sewer rat he was. As he dealt with the frustration, his one consolation was that he intended to get another shot at Weasel.

Suddenly Pete's beeper went off. He pulled over to a pay phone. After a short conversation, he jumped back into the car, looked over his shoulder at Tiger, and said, "Sonny was just spotted two blocks from here."

"Let's go," was all Tiger said.

On 138th Street, Rocky Crucci was waiting for Tiger. He nodded as Tiger lowered the window. "We chased him down those stairs to a cellar, and unless he has a secret way out, he's boxed in."

"Why did he run?"

"When he started down the steps, he turned and made us coming up on him. Then he bolted."

"Who else is with you?" asked Tiger.

"Snake and Blue Eyes. They're searching the cellar now."

Tiger nodded, knowing they were good men. He turned to Pete. "Get some men here and blanket the area. If Sonny is spotted, let him run, but clock him," he said, pausing. "And get Ralphie up here."

Was it possible that Sonny was tracking Weasel? Tiger didn't think so; Sonny wouldn't have the balls to tangle with Weasel again.

In the cellar Tiger recoiled at the putrid smell of stale urine, mildew, and dead animal flesh. There were piles of decayed mattresses, broken furniture, and rusted bed springs. Looking at all the filth, he remembered a time when Sonny and Helen made it a habit to live in these places.

As Snake moved some rubbish, rats scurried across the floor looking for a new hiding place.

It was a large room with many places for a man to hide, providing he was desperate enough to come down here. As the two troopers moved through the debris, hoping to flush Sonny, Tiger looked in other areas. The other end of the room was in total darkness. "Get some stronger flashlights down here."

Snake moved out fast as Tiger saw an old china closet in the corner. For an old piece, it was in pretty good shape. It stood out like a sore thumb. He opened the glass doors, thumbed through bits and pieces of abandoned books, pencils, papers, and other paraphernalia. He pulled hard on the lower drawer, freezing at the sight of cellophane bags filled with white powder.

Tiger was sure it was heroin. Pure. Blood rushed to his head.

"Cheez," said Blue Eyes, in awe. "Is that shit real?"

But Tiger didn't answer. His own thoughts were crowding in on him. If that stuff is pure, it is worth an easy million. So where the hell did Sonny get it? The Corsicans? Bullshit. They wouldn't trust Sonny out of their sight with a spoon-ful.

Tiger took a single packet and slipped it into his pocket for later testing. Snake returned with two large flashlights, spied the drawer full of white powder, and whistled. "Is that real?"

Tiger nodded. "Now destroy it."

Both troopers stared at Tiger. "How?"

Tiger shrugged. "I don't know. Piss on it."

Snake sliced open a packet and dumped it on the concrete floor. When they finished, they unzipped their flies, and urinated over the white powder. Then they scattered the mash over the floor with a stick of wood.

Satisfied, Tiger took one of the flashlights and headed into the dark recesses of the cellar.

This end of the cellar was an old storage area filled with piles of rusted washing machines, old refrigerators, bicycle parts, metal closets, a credenza, and a half dozen empty crates. Good hiding places.

Snake and Blue Eyes worked their way along the outer wall, examining every possible crevice.

As Tiger pushed aside a plywood panel, he saw the flashing knife, but it was too late. He heard the thud and felt the knife go deeper into his chest. For a brief second, he saw the madness in Sonny's eyes before he slid to the floor.

"Hey!" yelled Snake, moving swiftly after the fleeing Sonny, while Blue Eyes ran to aid Tiger, who lay where he had fallen, still shaken by the suddenness of the attack.

Tiger knew he was hurt bad but fought against going into shock.

"Cheez," said Blue Eyes, reaching for the knife handle.

"Leave it alone," Tiger said, slightly unnerved by the high pitch of his own voice. "Get me to my feet," he ordered.

Once on his feet, he felt a slight dizziness, but no pain. Not yet.

Suddenly Pete was beside him. "Christ, that looks bad," he said, putting his shoulder under Tiger's arm.

"Sonny?" asked Tiger.

"He got away, but he's hurt."

"Hurt? What do you mean, hurt?"

"I'll tell you about it later, but first I gotta get you to a hospital."

"No hospital," said Tiger weakly. "Get me to Doc Epstein. Also I have a packet of powder in my pocket. Have it checked."

Pete's expression turned sour. "Epstein's forty minutes from here. You'll never make it."

"Get me to Epstein and no one else," Tiger ordered.

Pete shrugged. "Then let's get you into the car."

On the sidewalk, Pete and Blue Eyes hurried Tiger to the waiting car, but not before he noticed the neighborhood onlookers staring at them in awe, particularly at the knife handle protruding from Tiger's chest.

Snake came running as Pete slipped behind the wheel.

"He got away!" he screamed, as Pete shot out into the traffic.

As the needle hit seventy-five on the East River Drive, Tiger lost consciousness.

TIGER grabbed at the hand reaching from the raging waters. He pulled a smiling Sonny onto dry land. A second hand emerged from the water. Tiger grabbed it, pulled,

239

and recoiled, quickly releasing the hand. He watched in horror as Iggy sank beneath the black water. Suddenly Helen, Iggy, Sonny, Turk, and all the other ghosts he ever knew emerged from the water, circled him, and began a slow rhythmic dance. They were covered in seaweed, with madness in their eyes, and they moved to the cadence of the tarantella, the dance of death. The dance of the tarantula.

They rotated, twirled, and twisted to the tune of their lunacy. Tiger was frozen, when suddenly the dancing stopped, and the group pointed off into the distance where a shadowy figure swayed back and forth.

Tiger was paralyzed as he recognized the convulsive hop of the tarantula. The death dancers swayed to the motion of the huge spider, and with each step they pressed little toy frog clickers. The silent clicks reverberated as the hairy creature closed in, antennae vibrating, jaws snapping. Closer and closer came the cold frosted eyes. As the mouth opened wider, Tiger could only see the blackness of the huge mouth, and then there was silence.

T HE white walls of the room burned Tiger's eyes. For a moment he thought Pete had disobeyed orders and put him in a hospital. But with his father sitting beside him, he knew he was in Epstein's private clinic.

"How long have I been out?"

"Twenty hours," his father said gently. "How do you feel?"

"Like shit and sore as hell," he said, feeling a slight spasm.

Don Corso smiled a rare smile. He patted his son's hand and said, "The doctor says you'll be fine."

Just then Dr. Epstein stepped through the door, his usual sardonic expression in place. "It's about time you woke up," he said, taking Tiger's pulse.

"When can I get out of here?" asked Tiger.

"Relax. You just got here. Besides, I'm a lonely old man. I'll need you to keep me company for a couple of days," he said, dropping Tiger's wrist. "Now, any more silly questions?"

Tiger accepted the sarcasm, knowing the doctor's bark was worse than his bite.

After the examination, Epstein walked to the door. "If you need me, I'll be just outside the door."

Don Corso was studying his son carefully. "Tell me what happened."

So Tiger told him, beginning with the signal from Shirley to Weasel's disappearance and the encounter with Sonny. Don Corso absorbed it all.

Tiger looked around the room for his clothes. "Where is my jacket?"

"Are you looking for the packet?"

Tiger nodded.

"Pete brought it to the doctor for examination. He said it was pure."

Tiger sighed. A profound sigh of disappointment. He had half hoped it would turn out to be milk sugar. But now he had to deal with the terrible thoughts about Sonny.

As if reading Tiger's mind, Don Corso said, "It's obvious your brother has gone over the edge. First he was a junkie, then a dealer, and now he's a degenerate supplier. Plus he tried to kill you. Now I will deal with him."

Tiger understood his father. He himself wasn't interested in Sonny. When he saw the piles of white powder, his brother was dead in his eyes.

"I told Jeanne I sent you out of town for a few days so she shouldn't worry."

Tiger nodded.

"And you get well yourself," he said, rising and planting a kiss on his son's forehead. "I'll be back tonight." He abruptly walked out.

Tiger lay there, his mind awhirl. Desperately trying to understand many elusive thoughts. Foremost was the incredible amount of pure in his brother's possession. Where

241

in God's name had he got it? He knew it wasn't from the Corsicans. A mongoloid idiot wouldn't trust Sonny with a million dollars' worth of pure.

And if Sonny was such a large supplier, what did he do with the money? If he had that kind of wealth, why wasn't he living better? He could let others do his dirty work, while he sat back and relaxed. But he didn't. Why? Could someone have a hold on him? Who could have such power? Helen? No. Maybe once, but not now. The pathetic creature he had holed up in Florida could hold no such power. So who?

And then the mist cleared. He remembered the night Smilin' Jack worked him over on the pier. He remembered the voice in the background. It was Sonny.

Along with his brother's other weaknesses, he was also a snitch, the most despised of men. It broke Tiger's heart that it had to be his own blood who betrayed him. As Momma said, Sonny was weak.

Now that the long dormant meeting came into focus, he saw the link. No, not a link, but a definite connection. The full import of the discovery shook him and he realized the genius of Smilin' Jack in using the son of Don Corso to peddle his junk. He wondered how many more people like Sonny Jack had at his disposal about the city.

He fitted the pieces into the puzzle, certain there was no other way Sonny could have come into possession of such a quantity of narcotics.

The anger boiled deep within Tiger. He saw a glimmer of why Sonny wouldn't stay put in the cure center. He couldn't; he was compelled to work the trade by Jack. The agent needed him as a street junkie for his own protection. Smilin' Jack knew no one would believe the word of a street junkie over the word of a Federal agent.

It also explained why the agent was so laid back with Colby. On one hand he held the club of incriminating evidence over Colby's head, while throwing pocket money to the inspector with the other. All the while, he was raking in the big bucks.

But where, wondered Tiger, did Sally Dell fit into the picture? Was that a private deal Colby made before Jack stepped into the picture? Had Colby dumped a load of horse to the two policemen Uncle Patsy killed and never collected for it? Did he want to collect the money without the agent knowing it?

Shit, thought Tiger, they're a worse bunch of snakes and spiders than we are.

Well, whatever club the agent was holding over Sonny's head, he intended to break it and set his brother free. Even if he had to kill Smilin' Jack.

Drowsiness suddenly overcame him and he fell asleep. During the night he awoke, finding himself under the watchful eyes of Pete and Ralphie.

IT was morning and he was hungry. With Dr. Epstein's permission Pete ordered steak and eggs for everyone. After breakfast, the doctor changed Tiger's dressing, checked the wound, and took his temperature. "Well, it looks like you're going to make it. An inch deeper and you'd be in your grave."

"Thanks, Doc," said Tiger.

Epstein's sour expression didn't change. "Don't thank me. I'll be glad to get rid of you."

Tiger smiled. "And when will that be?"

The doctor studied him. "Well, if you get some sleep today, in a couple of days," he said, stealing a slice of toast on his way out.

Tiger and his friends dug into the breakfast. "You guys get any sleep?"

"Enough. How do you feel?" asked Ralphie.

"Mostly numb, but weak."

"You want to tell me what happened in the cellar?"

But Tiger ignored the question. "You said Sonny was hurt. How did it happen?"

"I was on the corner making a call when I heard a car screech. Then I saw Sonny flip over the hood of the car, crash to the ground, jump to his feet, and shoot down the street. He was holding his side and limping, but he moved like the devil himself was after him."

Pete studied him. "Bad. If his adrenaline wasn't pumping and he wasn't in a panic, he never would have made the corner alive."

Tiger's lips tightened, then he told them what happened in the cellar and his belief that Smilin' Jack held a club over Sonny's head.

"Damn," burst out Ralphie, "this guy's really a degenerate."

Pete nodded his agreement, but said, "What now?"

Tiger looked from face to face. "Has Weasel returned to any of his haunts?"

Both shook their heads. "Nothing. And Sharky seems to have disappeared," Pete said.

"Since when?"

"Since the night of the exchange."

Well, thought Tiger, Sharky was either dead or in hiding. As for Sonny, he had a clock team out looking for him, but that held little hope for Tiger. He knew his brother would go to ground and being hurt, he would go deeper. Well, he thought, I can't do much until I get on my feet.

Two days later, Tiger was allowed to get out of bed and take a turn around the room. At first he felt a little dizzy, but after a moment he had himself under control.

By midday, Tiger wanted to go home, over Dr. Epstein's objections. Tiger felt he would mend faster under Jeanne's care.

He also refused to be transported by ambulance, preferring the back seat of his car. He did not want the neighbors to see an ambulance. Nor did he want to frighten Jeanne.

Before emerging from the car, Tiger removed the sling, waved to a couple of neighbors, and entered the house.

Inside, Jeanne took one look at his wan features and knew something was wrong. She gently opened his jacket and studied the large bandage. "What happened?" she asked, with tight lips.

Tiger shrugged it off. "An accident."

Jeanne looked at him for a long time before nodding with tightened lips, but she said nothing more about it. Tiger knew there were certain things his wife didn't want to know about.

That night Tiger slept fitfully, constantly awakened by the sight of a flashing blade and Sonny's maddened face.

In the early morning, the call came. Tiger rolled over toward the phone when the pain hit him. He snatched up the receiver. "Who is this?" he said in anger.

He heard a gasp and some gutteral sounds. "Who the hell is this?" he demanded.

"It's me, Sonny," the voice said with labored breathing.

For a brief moment, Tiger's mind suspended. His mind fought with two conflicting emotions. From one he recoiled, from the other he responded. "Where are you?" he blurted out, wondering if he hadn't made a mistake not slamming the door on his brother.

"I'm hurt . . . bad . . . Tiger," he said, with his voice fading in and out.

Tiger felt Sonny's pain and reached out to him. "For God's sake, tell me where you are," Tiger said, in desperation.

"I'm at the old country house," Sonny said, between gasps. "I need you, Tiger. I'm scared. Really scared."

His brother's plea encompassed him. "I'm on my way," he said, hanging up and calling Pete.

He thought of calling the Swan Lake Police Department to send an ambulance but decided against it. It had always been his experience that the Corso name always conjured up more questions than assistance.

Fifteen minutes later, Pete and Ralphie arrived. They

245

headed upstate to the country house. Tiger wondered how the hell Sonny had managed to make it that far in his condition.

As the miles ebbed, Tiger tried to put his mind in perspective. As usual, he was chasing after his brother again. Tiger to the rescue.

He thought back to the scene of the cellar, unable to forget the insanity in Sonny's eyes at the moment the knife flashed. Tiger knew had he not been in shock he might have reacted quicker. But in retrospect, he was thankful he took Sonny's blow rather than reacting instinctively and killing his brother. Tiger knew he wouldn't have been able to live with that.

Tiger wondered why he didn't hate Sonny. He had enough cause; perhaps he really did hate him. But if so, it was suppressed. Whatever the reason, he could no more hate his brother than he could hate any other sick person. Besides, his brother needed him.

All the way up the thruway, he had to believe his brother would be all right; that in the end, he would get Sonny repaired, both physically and mentally. Once he got Smilin' Jack off Sonny's back, Sonny would return to the cure center and get his life back together.

The pain of Sonny's wail told him he still unequivocally loved his brother, in spite of his faults, his weaknesses, and the offenses he had committed against himself and others.

Tiger believed that most of Sonny's flaws were the result of confusion. His brother was a sensitive human being, perhaps too sensitive to have been able to live under the hard thumb of his father.

Don Corso saw everything in black and white, while Sonny dwelled in a world of shades and shadows. He took his father's indifference personally, demanding love from someone incapable of giving it. Sonny needed love but received coldness instead. So his brother's resentment grew in proportion to the indifference. With nowhere else to turn, Sonny turned to Helen and drugs.

When Tiger arrived at the house, Sonny was not to be found.

Taking two steps at a time, Tiger ran to the upper level, shouting as he ran. Pete and Ralphie followed, pistols at the ready. Tiger ran from empty room to empty room as he called out Sonny's name, but he got no response.

At the last door on the left, Tiger hesitated. He didn't didn't want to enter that room. It was the only room in the house he refused to redecorate when he bought the house from his father. It was Sonny's old nursery.

Fighting against himself, he pushed open the door and found his brother. He was sitting at a child's desk, poised over a writing pad. He was dead.

Death was not a new experience to Tiger, but his brother's was. Sonny sat there, so still, so silent, so frozen, as if he was totally concentrating on what he was writing.

He couldn't accept the death. It was the wrong time to die.

Stepping forward, he looked into the glazed eyes. Drinking in the frozen features, the imperfect skin, the too wide brows, the aquiline nose, and the bitter lips.

Studying his brother's shallow features, a great anger filled Tiger. The bitterness rose from deep within. He found the resentment disturbing, uncertain from where it came.

For a moment, he was sure his subconscious was adding up the tab for the many offenses Sonny had committed against him. But no, he knew that wasn't the reason for the resentment. It was because, as usual, Sonny had taken the easy way out, leaving others to pick up the pieces.

But the anger in Tiger wasn't letting him off that easy, Sonny hadn't been some disadvantaged street kid who had to scramble to stay alive. He was the son of Don Corso, and he should have died a better death. Not like some cornered sewer rat, lurking in the shadows, then fleeing in panic from having tried to kill his own brother.

Sonny's circus was finally over, the entertainment he provided ended. The carousel has stopped, and Sonny's music has ended forever. But Tiger felt there was more. There had to be. His brother couldn't walk away like this, free, without paying his tab.

Suddenly Tiger lashed out, kicking the chair and sending the stiff body crashing to the floor. He pounced on the inert form, beating it on the face, arms, and legs, mindless it was once his brother. Tiger wanted to beat life back into Sonny to make him pay back for the pound of flesh he owed. But something, some force flagged his energy and he turned to his two cohorts. "Let's bury this bastard," he said, picking up the two sheets of paper on which Sonny had been writing.

As Pete and Ralphie carried out the body, Tiger began to read:

Tiger:
What can I say? I had it all. Tiger, I finally put it all together. A winner at last. But Tiger, life seems always to play its jokes. Now that I have won, I have lost.

I know you're rushing to me now. How do I know? Because you are the white knight charging to my rescue. You always did. You never let me down.

Do you remember the times we laughed about that? But this time, my brother, I don't think you're going to make it. I can feel the warmth closing in, but it don't feel so bad.

I have only three regrets about dying. Momma, you, and Helen. I still love Helen. Always did and now that she is free of Iggy, I intended to marry her. But even that no longer means anything.

You want to hear something funny. I don't care. I'm not scared. I feel warm all over and a little numb. Really, Tiger, for the first time in my life, I'm not afraid. I'm at peace.

Now that I know the end is near, I must hurry this letter to you. I have much to say. I'm sorry I stabbed you in the cellar, but I was scared. I knew you were also in the cellar, and if you caught me you would have sent me back to the cure center. I just couldn't let you do that to me, not now. I was too close.

I knew you wouldn't be able to understand the way things looked in the cellar, but I had finally put it all together and I was King of the Hill. Ask Helen. She will tell you. She knows the truth. She will tell you I am King of the Hill.

While everyone was chasing their tails, your baby brother, reached out and grabbed the brass ring. Me, the nobody, I did it all alone because I wanted you to be proud of me. To see me as a champion. To look up to me. To hear you say you loved me because I love you.

It is getting hard to write. If I can't finish this letter get to Helen. She can tell you everything.

The letter ended there. Tiger read it again, searching for more, but there was nothing else. He felt his brother was making a last-ditch effort to salvage something of himself. Something to take with him, to justify the waste he had been. And at the end, he sought to perpetuate his immortality, since a man survives his death only in the memories of the living.

Sonny was scared, thought Tiger, scared to the end. He slipped the letter into his pocket and rose to his feet. As he walked to the door, he felt his anger fade.

PETE and Ralphie had carried the body of Sonny off to the lake.

Looking down at his brother's lifeless form, he felt no more hate or anger, just regret.

He helped wrap the body in a tarpaulin, then picked up a shovel, and began to dig. Despite his recent injury, he dug with a vengeance, scooping up heavy shovelfuls and building up a rhythm of dig, scoop, and heave. Dig, scoop, and heave. Dig, scoop, and heave.

It wasn't long before he forgot why he was digging. Did he kill someone? Who? His mind was blank, blocked. He only knew he had to dig, scoop, and heave. Dig, scoop, and heave. Dig, scoop, and heave. Ours is not to question where or why, but just to do and die. Die? Who died? Sonny died.

Then he stopped digging, and the sweat ran down his body. He stood there, looking at the body of his brother as if for the first time.

Tiger dug in a frenzy, forcing Pete and Ralphie to stand by. Now they watched as Tiger dropped the shovel, walked

249

to Sonny's body, and dropped to the ground, panting for breath. He opened the canvas and exposed his brother's lifeless features. He kissed Sonny on the lips and cuddled his head gently on his shoulder.

"I'm sorry, Sonny," he whispered. "I don't want to bury you here like this, but I have to. I know you understand, because I can't let you hurt Momma anymore," he said, rocking back and forth with the body.

Don Corso sat as usual behind his stacks of money, but this time he stopped counting, settled back in his seat, and studied his son.

"How do you feel?"

"Much better," Tiger said, wondering why his father had sent for him.

His father's features softened. "You must be getting better, since you were able to go traveling in the middle of the night."

Damn, thought Tiger, his old man was having him clocked. Well, I'll take measures now. Did he also know his son was dead? Should he tell him anyway? He'd wait.

Don Corso lit one of his long black stogies while he studied his son over the flame of the match. He let out a puff of smoke and raised his eyes toward the ceiling.

"When a man is blessed with a son or sons it is a gift. One to be cherished because a son is the continuation of the father and all he holds of value. Every father has the dream that his children will perpetuate the family, take what the father offers that is good, his ideas, his beliefs, and his strength. It is the obligation he owes to those he brings into the world. On the other hand, the children owe nothing to the parents. A child is born free. Not into slavery," said Don Corso.

Tiger was at a loss to understand where his father was heading.

"A son is free to take the good of his father or choose his own good. But Sonny did neither. He listened to his junkie friends who filled his head with nonsense. Friends who wanted to burn down the old world and build a new one. But the new one was only in their heads," he said, looking sadly at Tiger.

"You may not believe me, but I loved Sonny. But since birth he was his own lord and master. All I could ever do was give him money, a place to live, a decent education, and the benefit of my experience. But when he rejected it all, I could still love him no less. Don't feel guilty about your brother's death. It was his choice, and we live or die by our choices. You did more for him than he deserved," he said, leaning forward.

"Well, he is gone now and I must thank you for your consideration of him and your sensitivity in hiding his death from his mother."

After a left-handed compliment like that, Tiger could only sit in silence.

"Now to another matter," Don Corso said, picking up a stack of bills. "The Council has given permission to terminate Carlo Alessi. But you are to handle it personally."

Tiger found the order strange. He wondered why it had to be a personal hit. Did the Council have doubts, was he being asked to make his bones in the name of the family?

T HE chest wound still bothered Tiger, but he had to go to the office. To put things in motion against Smilin' Jack and to seek vengeance for Sonny's memory.

According to the clocks, neither Weasel nor Sharky had been seen. If Sharky was running, he would be hard to find; but Weasel was a different matter. If in fact he was Jack's auxiliary, his second in command, then he was responsible for coordinating street operations and he would have to show sooner or later, since street distribution required it.

251

Big Che had his snitches but no one was talking.

Tiger glanced over at Pete. "Go outside, use a street phone, and call the bugman. Set up a meet in two hours."

As Pete left, Tiger settled back into his seat, deep in thought. The termination of Carlo Alessi would have to wait until he patched up his thinking on Jack and his warehouse where the narcotics were stored.

If he was on the right track, Jack was trickling the drugs into the street to keep the machinery well oiled, possibly at the rate of two million dollars' worth a month. At that rate, it would take him six years to dispose of what he had already acquired. That gave Tiger time to play with.

Ralphie picked up the ringing phone, listened, and looked at Tiger. "Detective Defalco is outside."

That surprised Tiger. Why was the detective exposing himself like this?

"Have him come in and let me speak to him alone."

Ralphie nodded and passed the detective coming in, closing the door behind him.

"This official?" Tiger asked with a slight smile.

The detective didn't return the smile. "Kinda."

Tiger nodded and settled back in his seat. "What's the problem?"

The detective didn't mince words. "My boss thinks you killed a policeman," he said simply.

Tiger was taken aback, although he was half expecting someone to come sniffing around. But he expected it from Colby's quarter.

Tiger turned on the left desk lamp, activating a jamming system in case the detective was wired. "And what do you think?" asked Tiger.

Defalco's features hardened. "If he was involved in killing my brother, I don't give a fuck," he said coldly.

Tiger inclined his head. "He was, but that's not for publication. That's for you personally."

Defalco smiled. "I'm not wired, so I didn't hear a thing. But my boss is still pissed. Not because you might have killed the policeman in question, but because you blew a

252

three-month investigation, and he didn't get the information you ended up with."

Tiger smiled broadly. "I can solve that problem. I learned a lot of things. I learned how the stuff gets out of the property clerk's office, who gets it, and who's behind it. I found out why your brother was killed and who did it."

Defalco sat with his mouth open. "You going to tell me?"

Tiger answered, "Not all of it. I'll give you enough information to satisfy your boss, but not enough to let him cheat me of my revenge," he said.

"You got a deal."

Tiger relaxed and told him about his brother's killers. He told of the couriers, naming two of them, keeping the rest of the list to himself. He explained it was Weasel who was receiving the drugs from the couriers, but not of Jack's part in the scam. Then he threw in Colby and company as a bonus.

Defalco nodded his approval. "Now I'll give you something. We've been on to Weasel since Iggy Friedman showed up dead. We believe he was involved in the hit but we can't prove it. We've been searching for his girlfriend, but she's probably dead already. My boss knows Weasel isn't smart enough to run such an operation, so we started looking behind the woodwork. We got a whiff of a rogue Federal agent hidden somewhere in the background."

"What makes you think that?" asked Tiger in surprise.

"Because we checked and believe his name is Tim McCoy, better known on the streets as Smilin' Jack. We had a friendly agent do some checking for us."

"What did he learn?" asked Tiger, holding his breath.

"Nothing. Not a damn thing. He heads up some secret department. Has his own private offices in the Federal Building, and the word is he has heavy connections in Washington."

Tiger was impressed.

"My agent tried to nose around but ran into a stone wall. No one was allowed near the place without a need-to-know pass."

"Could higher-ups be involved?"

Defalco shrugged. "We don't know. But if they are, we're at a dead-end. My boss isn't fucking with the Feds."

T HE bugman smiled his gentle smile. "I don't know, Tiger. It's heavy."

The bugman, with his slim build, fair hair, and peaches and cream complexion seemed out of place amid the oscilloscopes, feedback recorders, scanners, Dolbys, parabolic microphones, and dozens of the other bits and pieces that fill up the professional bugman's mysterious world.

"Is it possible?" asked Tiger.

"It's possible," he said, scratching the back of his head. "But improbable. The difficulties are enormous with all the if's: If the time factor is right; if your information is correct; if the subject isn't too paranoid. Then it's possible, Tiger."

"Want to try?"

The young man gave that a lot of thought. "It's going to cost you. Five thousand if I get him outside. Plus out-of-pocket expenses."

"And if you have to go inside?"

"Fifteen thousand. And if I get caught, you pay for the lawyers, judges, and whatever it takes to get me out."

Tiger nodded. "Anything else?"

"Yes. If I have to go to jail, it's going to cost you an extra two hundred dollars a day while I'm out of circulation."

"You got it," Tiger said and handed him three thousand dollars in cash, on account. Tiger felt the money was a good investment if the bugman managed to plant a bug on or near Smilin' Jack.

B ACK at his desk, Tiger's first order of business was to call in Gaetano Abruzzi, who now stood at attention before him. He handed Abruzzi a slip of paper. "Take a couple of the boys outside and pick up Carlo Alessi and take him to that address around one o'clock in the morning."

"What condition do you want him in?"

"Alive," said Tiger.

AFTER Abruzzi left on his errand, Tiger put in a call to Tony Orechicco at his island in Florida. Letting the phone ring ten times, Tiger assumed he had dialed the wrong number and dialed again. Still no answer. Odd, he thought, since he gave strict orders for Tony and the boys to stay put. He had the operator check the line, but nothing.

Annoyed, he decided to call again and give Tony a piece of his mind. Then the intercom buzzed.

Tiger picked it up. "Yeah?"

"Angelina Colombo is here."

"Send her in," Tiger said, surprised.

The first thing Tiger noticed was her pallid complexion, sure she was spending too much time in the house. The second thing he noticed was that the worry lines had grown more pronounced. He wondered why.

She stood nervously in his presence until he gave her a big bear hug.

"How are you?"

"I am fine, Don Corso," she said, smiling gently.

Tiger was embarrassed. "I thought my friends called me Tiger," he said, enjoying her slight blush. "How is Zi Camille?" He felt a slight pang of guilt at neglecting to visit her for a couple of weeks.

Angelina sighed. "She is as well as to be expected. She is slowly crawling within herself. She spends endless hours in her jail or moping around upstairs. But never will she leave the house. I guess she believes it's her sanctuary."

"Is she still on her kick about my father?" he asked.

Angelina smiled sadly. "She will always live in the shadows. That is her lot."

"Then why don't you look to yourself. You're not getting any younger."

Tiger wished he had bitten his tongue as the sadness entered her eyes. "Soon she will die and I will be free," she said, bravely smiling. "Enough of Camille and the tragedies. I have come to ask you for a favor."

Tiger's brows shot up. "Whatever it is, it is granted."

"Thank you . . . Tiger. I have outside a friend who has a problem."

Tiger didn't hesitate. "Bring her in."

A moment later Angelina entered with another woman in tow. A slightly older woman, wearing the traditional black of the widow. It was obvious that she had been doing a great deal of crying. Tiger gently escorted her to the chair before the desk.

"What can I do for you, signora?"

Nervously, she sat on the edge of her chair. "I need your help, my padrone. I have no one else to turn to," she said with a pleading half smile. "Angelina is my friend and she said you will help me." She ended in an involuntary sniffle.

"Tell me your problem," he said gently.

The distraught woman dabbed at her eyes. "It is my son Alfredo. Since his father Pepe died he is not the same. His look is wild, like a madness has come over him. He fights and gambles all the time. He is lost and alone and I cannot handle him, and . . . "

But Tiger gently waved her to silence. "What is the problem. Tell me so I may help you?" he said, wanting to get to the core.

"Two men came to my house looking for him. They say he owes them money and they say I have to pay. I gave them what I have saved, three hundred dollars. It is all I have. But they say I have to get them some more and they hit me," she said, raising her tear-filled eyes to him. "Where will I get more money for them?"

That's when Tiger noticed the blue welt she had been hiding with her handkerchief.

"I will wash floors," she said, in supplication. "I have no

256

money, but they say they will be back and hurt me and Alfredo. Please do not let them."

Again Tiger waved her to silence. "Where is your son now?"

She threw her hands into the air. "He run away when the men come."

"Who are the men he owes money to?"

"I don't know. Always I see them in the club on Union Street by my house. They sit and play cards," she said, her eyes filled with pleading.

Tiger knew the club. It was his. "How much does your son owe them?"

"Nine hundred dollars. It's so much money."

"You said they will be back. When?"

"Si, tonight."

Tiger sent her home with assurances he would take care of the matter. He resented kids like Alfredo, who walked around with a chip on the shoulder, and the moment someone knocks it off, they run to Momma for protection. He sighed. He knew out of respect to Angelina he would personally have to handle Union Street.

He called Florida again, again no answer, and his annoyance grew. He thought of calling a friend who lived in the area but decided against it, knowing if someone came near the place, Tony and his boys would put them away.

He buzzed Pete to have a trooper keep calling the Florida number.

He checked with the clocks. Nothing.

Two hours later the buzzer sounded. It was Tony, and Pete quickly connected him.

"What the hell's been going on down there?" Tiger demanded.

"We had a bad problem. Helen and Nino have been hit. I spent the last twenty hours at the police station."

"What the hell happened?"

"It happened late last night. Helen and Nino were watching T.V. when someone tossed two grenades through the living room window."

257

Damn, thought Tiger, as his anger and frustration rose.

"How the fuck could someone get so close without the alarms kicking off?" Tiger demanded, knowing Pete knew his business when he installed them.

"The cops said a rifle launcher was used. They found some shells on the other side of the bridge. They found an impression in the mud where the rifle butt was."

Tiger's mind whirled. He wondered how they found the island and how it was set up. "Has anybody been snooping around lately?"

"Only some hambone I chased away the other day."

"What was he doing there?" he asked.

"He said he was a snake hunter. He had a whole bag full of them. But I told him it was private property and he left."

"What did he look like?"

"Big guy, coveralls, flat nose, and black as the ace of spades."

Tiger ran that through his brain. "Did he wear an earring in his left ear?"

"Not that I noticed. No, wait, he did have one. A small one."

Sharky, exploded Tiger, so that's where the bastard has been.

He accelerated his brain, searching out any flaws that would alert him to a mistake. Then he saw a flaw and it hit him. Wanting to kick himself for being so stupid. He'd been set up like a Thanksgiving turkey.

He felt angry, knowing Smilin' Jack was laughing at him. He also understood why the agent was so laid back. Why shouldn't he be? He had Helen in his pocket from the moment she returned to New York.

Whatever cock and bull story Weasel told Jack to lure Tiger to his club, the name of the game was to get Helen spotted. Even switching Lola for Helen wasn't enough. Jack must have had his agents at all the airports. Jack knew Tiger wouldn't dare bring Helen back to New York.

But Tiger couldn't quite grasp the reason for the whole thing. If Jack wanted Helen out of the way, he could have just arrested her. Or was he playing two games? One to nail Tiger for himself and another to get Helen for Weasel. The first he could accept, but why the hell would he care what happened to Weasel?

The deeper Tiger probed, the more confused he became. He only knew he had lost a good man, had been outfoxed, and he didn't like the feeling.

"How soon will you be coming back?"

"This is a jerkwater town. The killings are a big excitement, so I guess they'll hang on to us a while longer," he said bitterly. "What do you want me to do about the bodies?"

"Helen doesn't have any family so see that she gets a decent burial. As for Nino, I'll call his family and arrange to have the body flown back," he said, hanging up. He sat there deep in thought. With Helen dead, perhaps now Weasel and Sharky will show themselves.

R ENALDO Baldicuccio was the made member in charge of Union Street. After a warm handshake, Tiger asked to see the loan book, checking the name Alfredo Lanza against the charts. The collector of record was Nick Bocci.

"Tell me what you know of this Nick Bocci?" Tiger asked.

"He's a good hustler," nodded Renaldo.

"Is he rough?"

"Very. He's third generation Bocci," he said, keeping his gaze level. "I've had to put him in his place a few times because sometimes he don't listen."

"Why not?" Tiger asked.

"Because he's a Bocci." His meaning was clear. "His old man did twenty, and by the time he got out of the can, the kid was already contaminated by the rest of the Boccis. You got a problem with him?"

259

"He has a collection against Alfredo Lanza. Tell him to leave it alone. They are friends of mine."

Renaldo nodded. "It shall be done," he said. "Now may I ask you a question?"

Tiger nodded.

"Do you know a man named Lici Parasi?"

Again Tiger nodded. Remembering the skinny kid who hung around the porno stores looking for a hustle. "What about him?"

"There's a large printing plant on First Avenue and Ninth Street. He's running a book there, taking all the action from the workers."

"So?" asked Tiger, showing his impatience.

"So he says he has your permission to operate the book. That he's a friend of yours."

Tiger studied Renaldo, understanding his meaning. No outsider may use the power of the family without proper permission.

"See that he gets a good beating, then chase him out of town," he said simply.

"May I have the factory?"

"You may," said Tiger, getting to his feet.

At that moment the door opened and a young man entered. Tiger wondered who gave this buck the license to walk in unannounced.

Tiger looked questioningly at Renaldo. "Who is this?"

"Nick Bocci," he said, embarrassed.

Tiger looked coolly at the powerfully built, streetwise youth, whose sneer seemed built-in. "You have a loan on the books against Alfredo Lanza?"

The youth nodded. "Yeah, but his debt's been paid."

Tiger's eyebrows shot up. "Paid? Paid by who?" he asked, remembering Mrs. Lanza's battered face.

"By me," he said, not even trying to hide his cockiness.

Tiger took a moment to control his anger. "Why?"

"For two reasons. Even you cannot interfere with a collection. No one can. It's a Council rule."

"And the second reason?" Tiger asked. His eyes began to frost over.

"When I lose a client I always pay his debts."

That's when the wildness filled Tiger. He moved swiftly. Weeks of frustration and tension erupted. Suddenly Nick Bocci was yanked upward and over Tiger's head. Tiger began to bang Bocci's head against the wall, then threw him against the doorjamb, where he crumbled in a heap. With a vengeance, Tiger rained kicks on the unconscious body until his strength faded.

Renaldo watched in awe at the fury of the attack; Pete and Ralphie stood by stoically.

"I think you killed him, Tiger," Pete said, staring at the quiet form.

Tiger looked at no one in particular. "If he's still alive, see that he's put in a room with Alfredo Lanza," he said, walking out the door.

T HE black Cadillac drove through the huge doors, which closed behind it. It drove past the rows of furnaces, stopping just short of where Tiger stood. Gaetano Abruzzi was the first to emerge, followed by two troopers. Tiger was confused when Alessi wasn't dragged from the vehicle. Could he have had a heart attack on the way? He looked over at Abruzzi. "Is he dead?"

Abruzzi's cold eyes remained lifeless. "He's still alive."

Tiger walked up to the vehicle and peered in the window. Carlo Alessi sat there, rocking back and forth, saying his prayers.

Tiger removed his pistol, cocked it, and shouted, "Come out, Alessi! It's all over."

But the rocking continued. Tiger jerked open the door and leaned in. Carlo Alessi was totally out of it, mumbling, "I don't want to die. I don't want to die."

Tiger looked down at the animal who would stuff his mother into a furnace for kicks. Now as he stared at the hulk of flesh, this pile of shit that had once swore to uphold the laws of honor, who pledged no quarter to his enemies. Who provoked Calamine to his death. Who personally killed a baker's dozen men, all victims of his cruelty, arrogance, and misguided pride.

Look at the bastard, thought Tiger, the fat slob is scared shitless and singing himself a death lullaby.

A wildness gripped Tiger as he grabbed a handful of his jacket, yanking the man from the car.

He was mindless of Alessi's piglike squeal or the fresh smell of shit.

"Please, Tiger. Don't kill me . . . please."

Tiger found the pleading unnerving. He punched Alessi in the mouth to shut him up, but the squeals grew louder. Tiger emptied his pistol into Alessi's body. He grabbed Abruzzi's gun and blew away most of Alessi's head.

Taking a moment to get himself under control, he scanned the silent faces of Pete, Ralphie, and the other troopers. He knew he had made a bloody mess of the killing.

"Bring over the hopper," he shouted at Frankie.

Frankie activated the hanging cable, guiding it to one of the furnaces.

Two of the troopers tossed Alessi's bulk into the hopper. Frankie moved forward and locked it into the furnace. He pressed the button and Alessi's body was ground into pieces, which slid into the furnace. Sparks flew as the liquid of the body hit the hot coals.

When it was over, Frankie poured absorbent powder on the blood on the tile floor.

Tiger glanced over at Pete, who was using the wall phone. When he hung up, he rushed to Tiger. "The clock has spotted Sharky."

"Where?" Tiger asked, his adrenaline still warm.

"Spanish Harlem. They'll call as soon as they nail him."

"When they do, have him brought here," Tiger spat, looking at the hopper.

Tiger sat in the car, waiting. They waited for over an hour before the phone shook them out of their lethargy. Pete rushed over and grabbed it. "Yeah," he said, listening.

"They're on the way," he shouted, to Tiger's relief.

TIGER noticed the blood-soaked handkerchief wrapped around the trooper's hand as he helped drag Sharky from the car.

"What happened?" asked Tiger, pointing to the hand.

"The black bastard stabbed me," he said, fuming. "I hope I get a piece of him when you're finished."

Tiger just stared at the trooper. Then he looked at Sharky, who was being held by two troopers. His hands were cuffed behind his back. He knew Sharky wasn't afraid, recognizing the hate in the man.

Tiger stepped forward and kicked Sharky between the legs and heard him groan as the troopers held him upright.

Tiger stood there, waiting for Sharky to recover from the pain and get himself under control.

His hate-filled eyes stared at Tiger. "Is that the best you can do?" he sneered.

"I'm just warming up, so you'd better start talking," Tiger said. He whispered something to Frankie, who quickly rushed away.

"Motherfucker!" Sharky spat back.

Tiger smiled inwardly. We'll see, Mister Sharky, we'll see.

Frankie returned, carrying a portable propane torch. Tiger lit it, carefully studying Sharky's features. As he adjusted the flame, he saw a flicker of fear.

"You gonna tell me what I want to know, or do I burn that earring off your ear?" Tiger said, moving the blue white flame toward Sharky's face.

Sharky's eyes were glued to the flame, but he slowly nodded.

That was easy, thought Tiger. He knew any man who adorns himself with flashy jewelry had to be vain, and he knew vain people can't stand being disfigured.

"Now we'll start with your friendship with my brother, and don't start with the lying. I know you set him up for Weasel's goons. I know you were present when Iggy was killed, and everything else. Now, were you buying junk from my brother or were you selling it?"

In desperation, Sharky looked at the hardfaces surrounding him. He saw no mercy there. "Buying. He had some of the best stuff around. It was good and it was cheap so I bought it."

He was seeking understanding in Tiger's eyes.

"How many buys did you make?" he asked.

"Six. It was pure."

"How do you know it was pure?"

"Because I tested it and the dude overdosed . . . "

Tiger felt a pang of guilt at the death his brother had caused.

"It was good shit. I tried to get Sonny to lead me to his connection, but he wasn't buying that."

"Where did Weasel fit in?"

"When I couldn't get your brother's connection, I told One Eye. And together we set up a meeting with Sonny and Helen.

"But Sonny wasn't buying that either. The day you wrecked my place, we were supposed to have another meeting later that night. What happened?"

"One Eye was going to snatch Sonny, but you took him away after the fight."

Tiger was grateful for that. "What brought on Iggy's death?"

"I saw One Eye the next day, on his way to visit Iggy. When we got there he started ranting and raving about the drugs Iggy had hidden somewhere. One Eye wanted to dump some of the stuff for fast cash. One thing led to another and One Eye put a shiv between Iggy's ribs. I couldn't stop him; he was too fast. Then he told me to take off, so I went to a pad I keep on the side. That's where your brother tracked me to. One Eye told me to keep him overnight and turn him loose in the morning, when his boys would pick him up. And that's the last I ever saw of him. I heard later he was still in action. So if something happened to Sonny, don't blame me. I had nothing to do with it," he said, in all innocence.

Now Tiger was ready for the big questions. "When did

Weasel send you to Florida?" he asked, carefully watching for Sharky's reaction.

That took Sharky aback.

"I know you hit Helen yesterday and I want to know how you knew where she was."

Sharky shrugged. "When Iggy was killed, I told One Eye I didn't like leaving Helen alive, but he was so greedy for Sonny's connection he was blind. When he realized what he had done in turning her loose, he became worried. When Sonny found me in Spanish Harlem, I called One Eye and he told me he had an idea how to get Sonny's connection and Helen at the same time. All I had to do was turn Sonny loose the next morning and stay around the house and wait for his call. I don't know what happened after that, but two days later he called and sent me to Florida, with Helen's address."

"Where did you get the grenade launcher from?"

Sharky's gaze was level. "I have friends."

Tiger nodded. "Do you know a Fed named Smilin' Jack?"

"I know his name from the streets but I never met him."

Tiger continued the interrogation until he was satisfied, then turned to the wounded trooper. "He's yours."

The impact of the words stopped Sharky cold. He had been sure through all the questioning that Tiger would have him beaten up and put in the hospital. But Tiger's coldness left him frightened.

"Hey, Tiger, I never did anything to hurt your brother, nothing."

But Tiger had a closed mind.

"And Helen was just a pig broad who meant nothing to you. So what do you have against me? I never hurt you," he said, sweat running down his features.

But still Tiger said nothing, as the troopers dragged Sharky toward the hopper.

"I never hurt you, Tiger. I swear I never hurt you," he screamed, as Frankie pushed the button, activating the

265

loud machinery that drowned out Sharky's screams as he was lifted and thrown into the hopper alive.

That's for Nino, thought Tiger. With Sharky gone, he had one down and two to go: Weasel and Smilin' Jack.

In the car, Tiger realized Weasel had used Smilin' Jack to get the information of Helen's whereabouts. Then he used Sharky for the coup de grace.

Well, thought Tiger, two can play at that game. He turned to Pete and Ralphie. "I think it's time for a Mattanza against Weasel and Smilin' Jack," he said, gauging them.

Pete looked up sharply, expelling his breath. "It's about time," he said, fingering the pistol under his jacket.

Ralphie looked perplexed as he looked from face to face. "What's a Mattanza?" he asked.

"In Korea we used it against the Gooks," Pete said.

"But what is it?" Ralphie asked again.

Tiger smiled. "It's an old Sicilian custom. Once a year, or whenever they feel threatened, Sicilian men let go in the ritual of Mattanza. The word comes from *mattana*, which means 'madness.' The coastal fishermen lay out a row of nets and boats and close off the lagoon. Slowly the tuna are driven toward the shore. If allowed to, they could easily drive the fish onto the dry beach and catch them there. But that's not in the rule book. After the fish are bunched together in a wild thrashing madness, the fishermen enter the water with a razor sharp knife in each hand, and the blood-letting begins. A contest of vicious tuna against the viciousness of the fishermen," said Tiger, pausing.

Ralphie was fascinated. "Who wins?"

Tiger shrugged. "Sometimes it's the tuna, and sometimes it's the fishermen. But in most cases, half of each gets killed."

Ralphie was wide-eyed. "What the fuck kind of fishing is that?"

"To the Sicilians, it's letting off a little steam. After the bloodletting, they return to their placid ways until they are forced into another Mattanza by either hunger or revenge. Everyone has the Mattanza in them."

Ralphie smiled. "Then let's start herding."

When they returned to the office, Tiger called in a lot of markers that were owed to him. He also made a note to check the computer for a friendly Federal agent, trying to get a line on Smilin' Jack.

He himself sat there jotting down every bit of information he could remember against the rogue. He also wondered if Jack fell into the clerks' scam or if he designed it.

To Tiger, Smilin' Jack was like a hovering hawk. The sky was his playground. And he was too high up to touch, unless heavy artillery was brought in.

Well, thought Tiger, even hawks are creatures of habit and leave tracks of themselves somewhere. Tiger had to find those tracks. He had to know if the man was married. Did he have children? Parents? Where does he live? Where does he hang out? Does he have emotions? Or, in general, what makes him tick?

Tiger knew this was not a man who roamed by night and hid by day. This was a man able to function in the highest and lowest circles. A smart man who enjoyed the game. He carefully picked his prey, watching, waiting, then swooping down for the kill. He knew how to hunt, how to plan a strategy, how to herd his prey into the pens. Tiger knew he was a Mattanza man. Someone very special. A person so special that Tiger wanted personally to trap him.

Pete and Ralphie dropped Tiger off at his home, then continued on their way. Tiger was tired. It had been a long day and a night of relaxing was in order.

But at home with Jeanne and the children, Tiger found himself still thinking about Smilin' Jack and Weasel.

TIGER was in his office early the next morning. He had been awake half the night searching for some weakness in

Weasel's and Smilin' Jack's defenses. He found one possibility. He was waiting for Cat to arrive.

Tiger knew Cat's father, an old-time box man who had apprenticed with the famous safecracker Jimmy Valentine. Now the younger man was following in his father's footsteps. He was a specialist, an expert in sonic, vibrator, ultrasonic, and every other type of alarm system ever invented.

Young Cat was a contract burglar for hire only to those who could afford him. His fee was high, but he did considerable business with the families and large corporations.

Tiger's father had once hired him to break into the Italian Embassy, crack the safe, and photograph the contents. The burglary went well: The alarms were disconnected, the safe opened, and the contents photographed. He closed the safe, connected the alarms, and sneaked out of the building. A block away, Federal agents nabbed him—because they had the place staked out trying to find their own way in. At F.B.I. headquarters on East 69th Street, they developed the negatives, then whooped for joy. They were so happy at the information they let Cat go free, paid his fee, and hired him as a consultant. For a bonus they gave him a copy of the information for his clients.

When Cat arrived, he was wearing designer jeans, a tailored polo shirt, and sneakers. He walked with the softness of a stalking cat. His eyes flickered over everything, the desk, chairs, pictures, Pete, and Ralphie. Even the recorder hidden in the base of the lamp. Tiger smiled and turned off the lamp.

Cat sat gently on the edge of the chair, smiling across the desk at Tiger. "How are you, Tiger?" he asked, in a soft melodious tone.

They shook hands warmly.

"What do you have for me?" he asked.

Tiger spread out a roll of blueprints for his examination.

"Study these," he said, nodding at Pete, who quickly took the side entrance to the upper floors.

Cat studied the prints as Pete returned and placed a briefcase on the desk, withdrawing to the couch.

"Tricky. Tricky as hell," Cat said, scratching his head.

"Can it be done?" Tiger asked with intensity.

Cat took a long contemplative pause. "I think so. I just happen to have a friend who helped install the system in this very building," he said, tapping the blueprints.

"You're kidding," said Tiger.

"It's an old system. The best there was when it was installed, but it's junk today, outmoded. It's my experience that they think because it's never been hit, it's foolproof. Hell, it just means they've been lucky. And this building is no exception. That's what I'm depending on. When someone feels secure, that's when they are vulnerable."

"Can you handle it?"

Cat nodded. "But it will take me a few days. I need some information."

Tiger nodded and indicated the briefcase. "There's twenty-five gees in there. With another seventy-five upon completion."

Cat took a moment before speaking. "The usual arrangements if I get caught?"

"I'll pay the lawyers, judges, and whatever it takes to get you out," Tiger agreed, smiling.

Putting the briefcase under his arm, the money uncounted, Cat shook hands with Tiger, nodded to Pete and Ralphie, and walked out.

Well, thought Tiger, now we wait and see if Cat can get into Jack's private files.

Pete picked up the buzzing phone and looked at Tiger. "It sounds like your Aunt Camille."

Tiger was surprised, since Zi Camille was not given to social calls. "Hello?"

"You come," Camille demanded.

"Is something wrong?" Tiger asked, hoping Angelina was all right.

"You come," she repeated and hung up.

Damn, Tiger thought, his heart skipping a beat. "Let's go."

And he headed for the door.

Pete moved swiftly through traffic, crossed Linden Boulevard, and drove into the old Italian section of small houses. At the bungalow, Tiger rushed up the path and banged on the door.

"Angelina, it's me, Tiger."

Suddenly the door was flung open, and Angelina stood with a pistol in her hand. "What is wrong?" she asked nervously.

"Is everything all right?" he asked, his concern lessening.

"All is fine. I was just nervous at someone banging at the door."

Tiger relaxed. "Camille called at my office, which made me nervous. That's why I rushed over here."

Angelina had a knowing look in her eyes. "That figures. She's getting more paranoid by the day."

Tiger half smiled. "I think she was born that way."

She smiled. "Now that you are here, come in for a cup of coffee and see what your old aunt is fired up about."

Tiger told his boys to wait in the car, then followed Angelina into the small but neat kitchen. Camille sat at the table, an espresso pot next to her. Tiger noticed the three cups.

"How are you, Don Corso?" she said, pouring a cup of coffee for him.

"Fine, Zi Camille, and you?"

She nodded, but her eyes said otherwise. "Your face smiles, but your eyes say other things," she said, measuring him.

Surprisingly, he looked deep in her probing eyes and wondered what was coming at him. She was being a little too nice.

"Are things going well with you?" she asked softly. Almost gentle.

Now he felt like a mouse being played with by a Sicilian cat. "As well as can be expected," he said, deciding to bring her game to a head. "If you have some questions to ask me, Zi Camille, why don't you ask?"

Her lips cracked slightly. "I see," she said, "you also have the gift."

Tiger wasn't an Angel of Death. Shit, he thought, between her mysterious phone call and her cat and mouse games, it wasn't hard to figure. Remaining silent, he allowed the quietness to thicken.

"Pasquale Colombo," she finally blurted out.

"What about him?" he asked, keeping a tight grip on his thoughts.

"Why was he killed?"

Well, thought Tiger, it's finally out in the open. He wondered if she were asking or telling him.

"I know who killed him," she said, looking from Angelina to Tiger. "I must know why."

Tiger circled the question. "You tell me why you think he was killed. You must have some idea."

But she only shook her head. "I want you to tell me."

Tiger was taken aback. "How the hell would I know?" he blurted out, wondering if the old witch wasn't the Angel of Death herself.

Her long penetrating gaze made Tiger nervous, but he held his silence.

"You are a don. You have the power to find out," she said simply.

Tiger wanted to relax at her words, but knowing the trickiness of the Sicilian mind, he couldn't. "Why must you know?"

"Then I will know if it was business or revenge?"

Tiger was slow to answer. "And if it was revenge?"

"Then I will tell you a secret," she said, her eyes focused on him.

"Stop it, Camille!" demanded Angelina. "I know where you are heading. You don't want an answer. You just want to say something you have no right to say."

The old woman studied Angelina. "He has to know the truth," she said with ferocity. "He must know the obligation of the secret."

For the first time ever, he saw anger in Angelina's eyes and he didn't like it.

"Why?" she shouted her demand. "So you may get even with Don Corso?"

The old eyes burned with vehemence. "Why not? He killed me," she snapped back with a wildness, as the memory of that night flooded back. "He came back to steal my baby."

"Basta, basta!" Angelina shouted.

But Camille was beyond stopping. The madness burned brightly. "He stood there in my home, right there in the doorway. See that spot," she said pointing.

The insanity in her eyes forced Tiger to look where she was pointing.

"He stood there demanding to know where the baby was, but I would not tell him. He threatened me, but I laughed in his face. Then he hit me, but I didn't care. I didn't care because I hated him. Hated him for the filth that once he put in my body. I hated him for the terrible thing he did to me and I wouldn't give him the satisfaction of knowing," she said, her energy seeming to dissipate. Terror entered her eyes. "Then I knew he was going to hurt me, but even then I didn't care. I hated him that much. So I told him where the baby was and I laughed as I told him," she said, suddenly silent and staring at the floor.

Tiger looked at Angelina as the silence engulfed them in a cloak of numbness.

Tiger was the first to speak. "Where is the baby?" he asked, wondering if it was he, Sonny, or Carmine.

Her dead eyes raised to him, the loathing returning. "I killed him. I bashed his head against a tree," she said simply.

So that was the secret that had kicked out the pillars of her mind. What a waste of a life, for both the mother and child. Tiger resented his father's actions but understood. He was Sicilian and when pushed was beyond control.

"For that," said Tiger, "you wasted a lifetime."

Slowly the old woman raised her eyes to Tiger. "That is only half the secret," she said coldly.

But Angelina was on her feet. "You will say no more."

"I must do what I must do," she retorted.

But Angelina would have no more. "If you do, old woman, I will leave. I shall go away and who will take care of you then, old woman?"

Camille sat back as if slapped. She looked up at Angelina with pleading eyes and spoke in a strange Sicilian dialect, "But there is an obligation . . ." Tiger was surprised he understood it.

Angelina glared at her. "It is not yours to speak of."

Suddenly Camille turned ashen and clutched at Angelina's waist.

"What is it, Zi Camille?" she said, concerning her face.

The old woman pulled her down, whispered in her ear, then rested her head against the chair back.

With a frightened expression, she looked to Tiger for help.

"Help me to get her to bed."

Gently he picked up the frail old woman, carried her down into the cellar, and placed her on the bed. He started to loosen her collar, but the look on Camille's face told him she was dead.

Christ Almighty! he thought, images jarring in his head. Won't this madness ever end? For a moment he could only think of his mother and Sonny and now Zi Camille. How was he going to live with that?

Angelina closed Camille's eyes before putting her arm around Tiger's waist and forcing him up the stairs to the tiny kitchen. There she poured him a large glass of brandy.

"Drink it now," she ordered.

In a stupor, Tiger sipped, his mind unable to grasp at the kaleidoscope of thoughts filling his brain.

"She is gone, Tiger," Angelina said gently. "It has been a long difficult journey, but I am glad it's over. Now she can rest."

Tiger understood she was trying to reach him, but all he could think of was, "What will Momma say?"

"She wanted to die. I think that's why she called you. She

273

knew her time was near, but like all frightened people, they say things they don't mean. It is the hate talking."

She poured a glass of brandy for herself.

"For thirty years I have been shut up in this house with her. Listening to her pain, her lamentations, and her hate.

"I know you are wondering why I gave up my life for Camille. I can only say because Pasquale asked me to. I came to see a brother I loved with an added bonus to coming to America. When I arrived at this small house, it was like a mansion to me. I could be more than comfortable here. I knew Camille needed me and that made me feel wanted, needed. You may find it difficult to accept, but over the thirty-five years I have been here, I grew to love Camille, with all her craziness."

Tiger studied her a long time. "May I ask you a question?"

"Of course."

"What drove you here from Sicily?"

"I was born into a family of seven brothers. A girl didn't matter in a Sicilian family. I was always an outsider in my own home. My father and brothers were a quarrelsome bunch, spending their lives fighting. I spent my youth patching them up. After a while, blood and death held little meaning for them and I became conditioned to their way of thinking. I thought everyone everywhere lived the same way," she said.

"Men will always fight," said Tiger in defense. "Some will fight for causes, some for glory, some for a woman, some for greed, and some because they are stupid. But that is the way of the world," Tiger said matter-of-factly.

She nodded, "That is true, but it is always the women who are left to pick up the pieces. It is the women who come away with warped minds from the meaningless of men's games, of their tempting death." She paused, embarrassed at saying so much.

Tiger felt her embarrassment and changed the subject to get away from thoughts of death. "Don't you miss your family?"

She shrugged and with a deeper embarrassment, said, "I have no family. The vendetta took them. All except Pasquale. I was alone when he called me."

"Why didn't you marry?"

"Why? So I could spend my life waiting for the neighbors to bring my husband home in a box?" she said bitterly. "That's why when my brother sent for me I was not offended by the lonely years with Camille. In one way we were tranquil. But now that she is gone, I do not want to see the world outside. I don't think I want to see men's games being played again," she said sadly.

Tiger felt embarrassed. "I didn't mean to stir up your pain," he said softly.

She smiled gently. "My bitterness is not directed at you. You do not play the games other men play."

"Thank you," he said, accepting the compliment.

"Like my brothers, you were raised as a weed to live the hard life, but you're really a flower that was forced to be something else. You are a feeling man in an unfeeling line of work," she said, waving his protests aside. "And I see the look of death about you; that is not normal. A smell of finality, like the youth in a war who starts out innocent and then his character is twisted by what he has seen and done. But that is not the real you."

"What makes you think you know me so well?" he asked defensively.

She smiled. "I had seven brothers who lived the hard life. They lived it well because they enjoyed the blood and death. Hating seemed to be everything. They hated the Church, the priests, the people, their neighbors, and even themselves. But Tiger, you are certainly not of their breed. You are above them. For the first time since I know you, I see death in your eyes and soon hate will become your master. Please don't let them do this to you," she pleaded, looking away.

Tiger understood what she was saying and he loved her for it. But he had no intention of becoming like her brothers or Don Corso.

Getting up, they walked to the door together. "What is the obligation, the other half of the secret?" he asked bluntly.

She smiled sadly, carefully choosing her words. "You will have to ask your mother. It is her secret," she said, closing the door behind him.

F OR three nights, lines of quiet mourners filed past the mother-of-pearl casket. Most of the mourners wondered who Camille was.

As expected, Don Corso never showed up.

Each night, Tiger had Pete pick up Momma and Jeanne and take them to the funeral chapel to pray before the coffin.

Tiger found it surprising that the weeping widows were not in evidence. Who was responsible for their absence?

During the three days, Tiger tried to find a few moments alone with his mother to tell her how he felt about Camille and possibly to talk of Sonny, if he had the courage. But Momma was never alone, and when the night ended she looked so weary he didn't have the heart to burden her with his guilt feelings.

On the morning of the fourth day, the mourners said their final good-byes and the coffin was closed forever. It was transported to Saint Rocco's, where Father Carmine Corso conducted a requiem mass. Later at the cemetery, Carmine said a farewell mass and led the mourners in placing a rose on the coffin before it was lowered into the grave.

The dignity of the proceeding impressed Tiger. It was unlike those other funerals where someone was always trying to throw himself into the grave.

After the funeral, mourners surrounded Momma to say good-bye—until the next funeral, to promise to call and say hello, but who never would. After the crowd thinned out, he found himself alone with Momma.

"Try to find time for us to be alone," she said.

"Yes, Momma," he said, as she disappeared into another group.

As was customary, the mourners gathered after the funeral for food and companionship, to blunt the edge of death.

At the bungalow, Angelina was the perfect host. The table was filled with heaping platters of spaghetti, veal and pepper omelettes, and numerous other delicacies.

Five hours later the feast was over, and the women washed the dishes while the men retired to the living room to smoke.

Later, Tiger said a gentle goodnight to Angelina, promising to look in on her. Her eyes reminded him of a lost puppy. What the hell was she going to do with the rest of her life? He had offered to set her up in a business in Sicily, but after thirty-five years in America, she had no one there.

Well, thought Tiger, let her get her head together, then he would see what she wanted to do.

He dropped Jeanne off at the house, spent a few minutes with his children, then took Momma home. Pete and Ralphie followed in another car.

Tiger was tense, almost afraid to be alone with his mother.

She removed her veil and looked with a steady gaze at her son. "Sonny is no more?" she asked, a gentle accusation.

Tiger was sure his mother was working on intuition, but for most Sicilians that was enough. He lowered his eyes before answering, "He is no more, Momma."

She took a long time before answering. "Do you know where he is?"

He wanted so badly to lie to her, but he couldn't. "Yes, Momma."

"Then you will take me to him. Now," she demanded.

"It's a long trip, Momma." He was concerned for her health.

"We go," she said with finality.

They reached the country house in less than two hours.

277

Once there, he escorted his mother to the brush-covered grave, while his two friends stood discreetly off to the side.

Momma stood looking down at the mound, as Tiger knelt and tried to tidy it up.

"Do not disturb the grave. Let it be our secret," she said, looking for a place to sit.

Tiger offered to get her a chair from the house, but instead she preferred to sit on a fallen tree trunk.

"Did you do this?" she asked, pointing to the mound under which Sonny rotted.

Tiger felt the pangs of guilt and found it difficult to answer. "In a way, Momma."

Studying the tormented features of her son, she said, "Tell me what happened."

And for the next twenty minutes he spoke of Sonny. He left out little in the telling. When it was over, Tiger stared at the mound, not knowing what else to say. He knew Sonny was beyond pain, sorrow, or prayer, but the living weren't.

Tiger stood there waiting for Momma to speak, to say something, anything. To rip into him. But instead she just sat there staring at the untidy mound of dirt.

Slowly she raised her eyes and looked through the woods to the lake beyond. "It's peaceful here. It's strange how God weaves his webs and always comes up with the right answers. I could not have chosen a better resting place for my son. Perhaps now Sonny will find happiness."

She raised her moist eyes to her living son. "You have no guilt in this. You have done more for my son than he deserved," she said, gently patting his hand.

Tiger wanted to cry in gratitude for this gift she was bestowing, but then he thought of Camille in her cellar and the pain returned.

"Come, we will walk."

Silently, Tiger followed her to the edge of the water, stopping near the boat shed.

"Angelina told me what happened to Camille that night. Do not blame yourself for that. We all knew her time was short." She fell into silence again and looked over the blue and green tones of the lake.

"I always loved this place. It was our sanctuary, a home, nothing more. No business was ever spoken here, no visitors were allowed, only us. The family, Camille and Pasquale," she said, with a wistful sigh.

"It was always so peaceful then, as it is now. A different time and place. Even Carmine and Sonny's laughter was soft and peaceful."

"Not mine?" Tiger asked.

A sad film covered her eyes. "No. You never laughed. How could you? You were the son of Don Corso. Raised, trained, and guided for the hard life."

Tiger realized his mother was right. He was much too frightened of his father to think of fun and games.

He felt comfortable at that moment. Dare he speak of the secret Camille spoke of? Yes, he must. "Camille spoke of a secret, an obligation, but Angelina said only you could explain it," he said softly, prepared to back off at the slightest resistance.

It was a long time before she spoke, only after putting her hand on his. For comfort? For assurance?

"It is difficult to talk of it, but even after forty years, I still wake up screaming from the nightmare of being raped. My honor was taken from me by force."

"What do you want, Momma?"

"What you cannot give me, my son. Revenge."

Tiger was taken aback. "If it is revenge you want, Momma, I will get it for you," he said, prepared to do what was necessary to rid her of the cancer that had festered in her so long.

She half smiled, a haunting smile. "Do you have the power, my son, to clean my soul? To remove my dishonor? To return my innocence, my virginity? To remove my pain? Can you, my son? Can you bring life back to the dead?" She asked all these questions softly, but with bitterness.

For a moment Tiger was confused, not quite understanding the full meaning of her words. "I don't understand."

Taking both of Tiger's hands in hers, she smiled sorrowfully. "Of course you don't. The man who raped me is dead."

It took a considerable length of time for his mother's statement to sink in. Suddenly the bomb exploded, shattering his thoughts, suspending him in a void. His mind floated in a world of nothing. Zero.

Suddenly, a word drifted by, and the word became a thought. Then the thought became Patsy Colombo, then his father.

"Year after year, my hate for Pasquale grew," she said with a bittersweet sigh. "But so long as my sister Camille lived, I could not carry out the obligation. The madness of it drove me to a breakdown. Endless times I begged my husband to end my misery by killing him, but Don Corso always said it was not time. These things take time; they must not be done emotionally," she said, a small tear in each eye.

"If you knew how many times I wished Camille would die and free me from my burden. But year after year she hung on with no end in sight. I could not tell my husband Camille was still alive, so I became confused, divided in my loyalties. In the end, Pasquale was killed for other reasons," she said, lowering her head and wiping away the tears.

Welcome, Tiger, to the Corso/Colombo world of madness, he thought. He was numb, unable to feel the depths of his emotions. It was a hell of a way to find out that the man who created his bitterest memories wasn't his father. He felt no hate, love, or resentment. Just numbness.

T HE following morning, Tiger sat behind his desk trying to relax, but the thoughts kept crowding in on him.

Patsy was dead and buried and all that remained of his existence was his son. A son who never knew him.

On the other hand, how does one shut off a lingering habit? Good or bad, he was linked to Don Corso by forty years of living together. Even though it was a lie. No longer were they blood of blood.

He didn't love Don Corso, nor did he hate him. At least, not in the normal sense. Resent him? Yes. But true hate? No. He also realized he was questioning traditional law, that the son avenge the father, but Tiger reasoned that the circumstances were different. True, had he known his mother's problems stemmed from her hatred of Patsy, he would have killed him. Father or no father. But now he didn't feel the hate necessary to hunt down and kill Don Corso.

Pete's entry into the office scattered his thoughts. "Bugman's here."

Tiger looked up sharply. So soon? he thought. "Send him in."

Halfway across the room he could feel the bugman's excitement and quickly waved him to a chair. "I think we got him," he said, handing Tiger a list of phone numbers, some circled in red.

Tiger studied them. "What are these numbers?" he asked, indicating those circled in red.

"They were the ones most frequently called, so I ran a special check and put the address alongside."

Tiger nodded his approval.

"The first one is a private office in Washington, D.C. I couldn't pin down whose it was because the address is the Justice Department," he said, with a slight smile.

"The second was the Brooklyn police property clerk's office."

"Do you know who Jack spoke to there?" Tiger asked.

Bugman shook his head. "The pen register picks up numbers, not voices."

Tiger nodded his understanding.

"The third was to a warehouse on 138th Street in Harlem."

That sent a tingle through Tiger. I'll look into that, for sure, he thought. "And this last circle? Weasel?"

Bugman nodded. "I think so because your target only calls it late at night. But there's something strange about the calls. He made ten calls in three days. The first two calls went through a switchboard. The next eight went direct."

"What do you make of it?" Tiger asked.

"All the direct calls were at three-ten in the morning. It sounds like a signal."

Tiger studied the Harlem address. Two blocks from the Kit Kat Klub. The bastard has balls, he thought. Tiger thanked Bugman and gave him another briefcase with the promised payment in it.

He sent two troopers to check on Weasel. Troopers he knew would recognize Weasel but wouldn't be recognized by him.

Then he decided to check out the warehouse himself.

O<small>N</small> Jerome Avenue, two vehicles loaded with troopers cruised the black neighborhood, slowly passing the warehouse in question. It was a rundown loft building with most of the paint peeling from the sign splashed across the front of it. But enough was left to read the name: SPEEDY MOVING AND STORAGE.

Tiger took another turn about the area, scanning for possible trouble but saw nothing out of line. He certainly expected little problems from the winos, junkies, and dealers who filled the doorways.

Stopping at the alley where Weasel had disappeared, he studied the rear of the warehouse. Many of the windows were broken, and the fire escape was so rotted it was unusable.

Tiger walked through the alley to the next street and examined the stores located there: a shoe repair shop, a mom-and-pop grocery store, and a barber shop. Looking at the warehouse, Tiger didn't think anyone in his right mind would store two tons of heroin in it.

Tiger had both cars brought around and parked directly in front of the warehouse. Troopers stood leaning against the vehicles as Tiger, followed by Pete, Ralphie, and two troopers entered the building.

Inside, the grubby little office wasn't much cleaner than the outside. Empty and half-empty coffee containers were scattered everywhere, among the files, in the stacks of old newspapers, even on the chairs.

Behind a makeshift counter, a pot-bellied man looked up from his girlie magazine long enough to throw Tiger and his entourage an uninterested look. "We're closed," he said, returning to his reading.

Tiger took a moment to measure the shabbily dressed man. "Can you help me, mister?" he asked in his gentlest voice.

Without lowering the magazine, he snapped back, "Do you have an account here?"

"No, but . . ."

"Sorry, we're closed."

Tiger nodded to the trooper standing alongside Ralphie.

The trooper stepped forward, threw the magazine across the room, and hauled the warehouseman to his feet.

"What the hell is this?" shouted the startled man.

"Can you help me now?" asked Tiger.

The shifty eyes took in the scene and nodded, "Sure, sure. What can I do for you?" he said, trying to regain his composure. "I didn't mean to get snotty, but I get a lot of creeps in here."

Tiger nodded his understanding. "I know what you mean. I have the same problem."

But looking over the unfriendly group, the man was not about to ask what line of work Tiger was in. "What can I do for you?" he asked, with new understanding.

"I was wondering how you go about renting storage space here."

"How big a space?"

"Average. What's the procedure?"

The man shrugged. "You just rent it. Cash in advance. An average-sized space runs twenty-two a month. For that you come and go as you please within working hours. Also you supply your own lock, but I get a key in case you skip out." He had reverted to his normal insolence.

Tiger ignored the man's tone. "Do you have any long-term renters that go back, say, two years?" he asked carefully.

The man's eyes narrowed. "Sure. Why?"

Tiger let the unanswered question linger while he removed a roll of money from his pocket. Slowly he peeled off five new one hundred dollar bills, spread them on the counter for the man's inspection. "Because I want you to let me take a look. We're not here to steal anything, but we are looking for something."

"What are you looking for?" the man asked, his suspicion lessening as he studied the bills on the table.

"I'll tell you if we find it," Tiger answered.

The man thought about it, studied the cold expression on the faces around him, and picked up the five bills.

He removed a ledger book from the file cabinet, picked up a ring of keys, and said, "Follow me."

They took the elevator to the fourth floor. The corridors were lined with doors, each with a padlock.

Checking the ledger book, they stopped at the first door. The man opened the door. The room contained mostly cardboard boxes, bits of furniture, mostly personal belongings.

At the tenth door, a bell sounded. The warehouseman rushed to the wall phone, spoke into it, then swore, and looked at Tiger. "I got a guy looking to move out without paying me," he said, handing the ring of keys to him. "When you finish, I'll be in my office," he said, rushing off.

Tiger continued, checking off the list after examining the room. Nothing.

They hit pay dirt on the eleventh try. Tiger could see the white powder through the plastic. For a moment, he held his breath, unable to believe his eyes. He was ecstatic about snatching the brass ring from Smilin' Jack.

"This shit is pure milk sugar," said a trooper.

Tiger was taken aback. "You sure?"

284

"Sure I'm sure. I know the difference between milk sugar and heroin or coke. One's a powder, the other's a crystal."

Tiger marked the trooper for future examination and a check on his dossier. He wanted to know why the man knew so much about narcotics. He might have a pit viper in the family.

Looking over the mountain of plastic bags, Tiger wondered what the hell was going on. Was it possible this was a cover for the real stash somewhere else? In another room?

"Open every door on the list," he ordered.

When the task was completed, they came up zero.

Tiger returned the keys to the warehouseman and asked a question. "What's the name registered to Room 314?"

Pot-belly checked another ledger. "John Smith."

Not very original, thought Tiger.

Bᴀᴄᴋ in his Brooklyn office, Tiger received a call from one of the troopers he had sent to check on Weasel.

"Is it him?" Tiger asked.

"I don't know. I haven't spotted him yet. Did you know this address turned out to be a hotel?"

That surprised Tiger. "What kind of a hotel?"

The trooper grunted. "I've been in better jails. It's a junkie and dealer paradise."

That should make Weasel feel right at home, thought Tiger. But he'd better be careful because Weasel wouldn't go anywhere without being surrounded by his friends.

"Buy some clothes that reflect the locals, then check into two different rooms, one above the other," Tiger said. "Then take turns sitting in the lobby, and sooner or later he will show up, if he's there."

"I have it," the trooper said, breaking the connection.

Now, thought Tiger, if it is Weasel, it would be time to continue the Mattanza, the herding.

285

If Weasel is knocked out of the box, Colby and company would be next. Once they are eliminated, Smilin' Jack would be cut off from the herd and apt to make a mistake. One mistake might be enough for a clear shot at him.

Tiger knew he was walking around the agent on egg-shells. The man was as cunning as a wolverine, but for the moment Tiger felt he had the upper hand. He was now the hunter running his prey to ground. But Tiger was not about to become overconfident. As the Sicilian lore goes, "If you dig two graves, one for you and one for your enemy, then you will be sure of your revenge. But if you dig only one grave, your body might fill it while your enemy walks away."

T HREE hours later the call came. Weasel was there, on the second floor, in Room 212. "I'm in Room 213," said the trooper with a chuckle.

"Bring in a couple of extra men to keep on standby, but make sure you don't spook him. Have Scaffo make a detail drawing of the building and get it back here right away."

Now, Tiger thought, we wait.

He thought of Weasel, wondering if he owed the man anything. There were certain rules of tradition. A loose code that tied them together, but in Tiger's mind, Weasel never followed any codes of honor or respect. No, thought Tiger, I don't owe him anything.

Thirty minutes later, when Scaffo arrived, Tiger, Pete, and Ralphie studied the layout of the building. The exits, hallway, cellar, and the location of Weasel's room in relation to everything. They took a long time examining the plans before speaking.

"Was Weasel alone?" Tiger asked Scaffo.

"He had two goons," Scaffo said. "He seemed to know everyone in the place."

Tiger expected that. It was Weasel's kind of place.

The two goons had Tiger worried.

He continued studying the plans, knowing he didn't like the looks of things. There were too many things that could go wrong.

"What chance of getting friendly with a worker? Maybe the bellboy? A porter? Even the desk clerk?"

"Zilch. They're all headhunters, suspicious as hell, and we stand out like sore thumbs. They don't appreciate Whitey in their hotel."

Tiger understood.

Well, he thought, that left him only one answer. He could either blow up Weasel with a bomb or go in like gangbusters. Since he needed answers, it would have to be an assault. Taking out anyone who got in the way.

Silencers, of course, would have to be used. That advantage he needed. Also a van, extra vehicles, and possibly a diversion. Maybe a fire on the top floor?

His mind ran through the details, working out the flaws, and weighing the risks. Then he explained it to the others.

TIGER cut through the lock with the boltcutters, carefully snaking the chain through the iron-grilled door, hoping the damned thing wouldn't creak as he gently pushed it open. It creaked, but not enough to disturb anyone.

Scaffo led the way across the cellar to the stairwell, followed by Pete, Ralphie, and six troopers, and by Shirley Jackson of the Kit Kat Klub.

On the second floor, Shirley checked the corridor. Clean. Then Scaffo, Shirley, and the troopers rushed across the hall and into Room 213 while Tiger stayed in the stairwell with his friends.

Ralphie stood guard, watching through the small window of the exit door, while Tiger and Pete settled down to wait.

Tiger knew Weasel received his call at 3:10 A.M. Then,

allowing ten minutes for talking and ten for certainty, his plan would kick off at 3:30.

The waiting reminded him of Korea. It was always the same. The last few minutes before an attack were endless. Instead of time flowing, it seemed to pause between each second.

Three-thirty and it was time. Tiger tensed. Suddenly voices could be heard shouting in Room 213. Suddenly Shirley was in the hall facing Scaffo.

"You bullshitted me. You promised me forty bucks and that's what I want to be paid!" she shouted at him.

Scaffo looked annoyed. "Hey, I told you, I must have lost some money," he said, holding out a twenty dollar bill. "Here, take this twenty, and let's go back inside."

"Screw you!" she shouted. "I ain't no nickel and dime hooker!"

Ralphie intently watched Weasel's door, but it remained closed.

"Look, bitch," shouted Scaffo, trying to pull Shirley into the room, "I'm going to kick your ass!"

Shirley screamed and struggled to free herself, as Ralphie noticed Weasel's door open slightly. He nodded at Tiger.

As they struggled, Scaffo fell against Weasel's door and it gave. The troopers filled the corridor as Tiger charged across the hall and flew past Shirley, over Scaffo, and hit Weasel with his shoulder. As Tiger rolled over Weasel, he came up on his feet with his pistol waving. But Weasel was alone.

"Get him out of here!" he shouted as Scaffo and Ralphie picked up the stunned Weasel and dragged him out the door. Troopers lined the hall with drawn guns, herding the curious back into their rooms.

"This is a police matter, so go on back to your rooms!" a trooper shouted, as Weasel was carried to the stairwell.

As they hurried down the stairs to the cellar, no one followed, and they hit the narrow alley leading to the street. There a van and three cars waited.

Throwing Weasel into the open van, Ralphie and two troopers followed. The driver quickly threw the van into gear and pulled out into the traffic.

As Tiger entered his vehicle, he saw the cowboy car with its hood up blocking traffic and pursuit.

Staying within the speed limit, the caravan took over two hours to reach Tiger's country house.

After throwing off the alarm system, Tiger stepped aside for Weasel to be dragged in and dumped in the cellar. A trooper was left to guard him.

"Make a pot of coffee," Tiger said to no one in particular, as he rummaged through the freezer. Coming off the kidnapping, Tiger found himself starving. He also made it a point to block out all thoughts of Sonny and the nursery room upstairs.

Finding a dozen steaks, Tiger had a trooper thaw and cook them while he thought about the night's work. He was worried about Shirley. She was a spur-of-the-moment decision. Although he thought she was a stand-up chick, she could still tie him to the kidnapping. He sighed, making a mental note to check on her from time to time, looking for any deviation in her behavior. He wouldn't want to terminate her if he didn't need to.

After the dishes were washed, Tiger looked at Pete. "Have our friend brought up here."

From a small case, he removed the hypodermic syringe Dr. Epstein had given him. It was filled with sodium pentothal.

A wide-awake but terrified Weasel was dragged into the room and lashed into a wooden chair. Tiger knew this cocky bastard wasn't going to give him any "Hi, baby" tonight. He was disgusted by the fear in Weasel's eyes. It was always the same. The wise guys spent their lives trampling on others, but when it's their time to pay the piper, they quiver.

At the sight of the syringe, Weasel's eyes widened and the terror mounted.

The doctor had warned Tiger that the serum could be dangerous to an agitated person, so Tiger needed to calm Weasel.

"I'm not going to hurt you, my friend. You are too valuable to me alive. But I need to have some answers, truthful ones."

Weasel had difficulty forming the words. "I'll . . . I'll tell you anything you want to know. I . . . swear to God I will, Tiger. I won't lie to you," he pleaded.

"You've lied to me before," Tiger said coldly.

"Honest, Tiger. I give you my word."

"Your word?" said Tiger in surprise.

"Yes, on my honor. I take an oath on my mother, anything," he pleaded, with tears running down his cheeks. "I know you're going to kill me, but I never did you any personal harm."

"I'm not going to kill you," Tiger said gently.

"I don't believe you, but I never hurt you."

Tiger studied him. "I give you my word I'm not going to kill you," he said gently.

Weasel just stared at him, eyes narrowed in suspicion. "On your honor?"

"On my honor. I just need the truth to certain answers and it's nothing personal, my friend. But I must find my own answers. The ones you can't hide from me," he said, picking up the needle.

Weasel squirmed. "You're going to needle me like I did to Sonny . . . "

But Tiger assured him the drug in the syringe was truth serum. "Here, look at the color."

After that Weasel, still frightened but calmer, let the needle slip home.

Tiger waited a moment for the serum to take effect before speaking.

He asked gently, "Tell me why you killed Iggy."

"Because I knew he had a big stash of heroin hidden, and I wanted to start moving it. But he said he wanted to keep stockpiling it."

"How did you know he had a stash?" asked Tiger.

"Because I had delivered over forty kilos to him two weeks before. So we got into an argument and I guess I just blew my top," he said, the sweat running down his face. "It was stupid because I never found the stash."

"How did your friend Smilin' Jack feel about that?"

"I didn't tell him," Weasel said simply. "With Iggy dead, he had no choice but to give me Iggy's job."

"Then tell me, how did you find Helen in Florida?"

"Helen called me from your island and told me she wanted me to help her come back to New York."

Tiger was taken aback. "Why would she do that?"

"She was a junkie. You can't account for what goes through their heads. Maybe she was homesick."

"Then why did you have Sharky kill her?"

"Because she was a witness, and so long as she lived, we both were in jeopardy."

Tiger took a shot in the dark. "Did you kill my father's banker Turk?"

"Yes."

"Why?"

"Because Iggy ordered me to. He said he was asking too many questions."

Well, that cleared up Turk's death, Tiger thought. Nothing else made any sense. "Do you know a Salvatore Delvechicco?"

"No."

"Were you in any way involved in the Bocci killing?"

"No."

"Who is your connection in the Brooklyn property clerk's office?"

"I don't know anyone there. I don't even know where it is," he said simply.

"How did you get the drugs?"

"What drugs?"

"The ones Iggy was stockpiling."

"From the D.A.'s office. How, I don't know. I just know I got a delivery every month."

"What do you do with the drugs now? Do you turn it over to Smilin' Jack?"

"No. But he has me deliver it to a warehouse on 138th Street."

"To Room 314?" Tiger asked.

"Yes."

Now Tiger was confused. "You delivered the heroin to Room 314 yourself? Was it ever out of your sight or opened by you?" The latter seemed more likely to Tiger.

"It never left my sight and I never opened it."

"You mean you never snipped a few samples."

"No, never."

That surprised Tiger. "Why not?"

"Because Jack scares me," Weasel said simply.

Tiger took a moment to reflect. If Weasel and Iggy were storing drugs in Room 314, then what the hell happened to the heroin? "Who tested the drugs after you received them?" Tiger asked.

"I did."

"But you said you never opened the packages."

"Just to test them."

Tiger raised Weasel's eyelids suspiciously, but the eyes were in the right position. Raised skyward. Now he knew someone was switching the plastic bags. Probably Jack.

Now Tiger took a new tack.

"Why did you bring my brother Sonny to this house?"

"Because he came whimpering to me he wanted Helen back. Since he had nothing to trade with, he said his father and brother had money hidden there. So I went to have a look."

"Why was my home wrecked?"

"Because Sonny is a crazy bastard. When we didn't find any money, he started breaking things. He kept screaming how much he hated his father. He went crazy and took a

292

sledgehammer to everything. Then I saw the money. It was in the chimney. That's when he calmed down and laughed about getting married to Helen."

"Did you intend to give Helen to Sonny?"

"Not in a million years."

Though Tiger's anger rose, he let the remark slide. "What did you do with the money?"

"Kept it."

"What did Sonny say to that?"

"What was he going to say? I had it," he said simply.

Hatred filled Tiger. He fought to keep his hands from Weasel's throat.

For the next two hours the questioning continued, but that seemed to be all that Weasel knew. He nodded for a trooper to put the prisoner back in the cellar.

He sat for a moment sipping his coffee and pondering his confusion. Nothing seemed to matter but where Jack had the drugs hidden.

Should he bury Weasel in the woods or in the lake? The lake won because Tiger didn't want him in the same ground as Sonny.

Pete followed him to the garage, making certain he had enough bags of cement. He sent a trooper to look around for some kind of container to stuff the body in.

When everything was ready, he sent for Weasel.

He was sorry it was still daylight. He preferred darkness for this kind of work.

"Can I have him, Tiger?" Ralphie asked. "I haven't made my bones for you yet," he pleaded.

Tiger's head snapped up. "What the hell are you talking about?" he said, remembering back twenty years, to the time they were in state prison together. Folkenhandler was a convict who snitched to the warden because Tiger was running a gambling operation. As a result, Tiger was placed in solitary confinement, then transferred to the maximum security prison at Attica. Left alone, Ralphie threw the snitch down a flight of steel stairs and killed him.

"But," Ralphie countered, "not since you became boss."

Tiger was unable to resist the childlike pleading. "He's yours."

The two troopers held Weasel firmly. He was still groggy from the drug. It annoyed him that the one-eyed bastard was not wide-awake for a final "Hi, baby."

They dragged Weasel into the garage in the presence of the steel drum and the pile of freshly mixed concrete. At the sight of it, Weasel's eyes widened. "You promised, Tiger. You gave me your word."

Tiger studied him. "And I intend to keep my word. I'm not going to kill you. He is," pointing at Ralphie.

Weasel was stupified as Ralphie blew away his face. The two troopers quickly dropped the body and stepped away. Tiger and Ralphie kneeled down to examine the kill.

"Sloppy," whispered Tiger. "Turn him over and put two shots behind the left ear."

The flat crack of the silencer ended the job, and Tiger thought to himself, two down and one to go.

He had the two troopers dump the body into the steel drum, fill it with wet cement, and level it to the top.

Tiger's only regret was not giving Weasel a good beating first.

Four hours later, when the cement had hardened, they threw a chain around the steel drum and dragged it to the edge of the lake. Then they let it go and watched as it rolled down the hill, hit a rock, and then sail off into the air before splashing into the water. It bubbled to the bottom.

Inside the house Tiger felt a cup of coffee was in order. Pete had the garage floor cleaned and scrubbed. As they sipped their coffee, Ralphie sidled up to Tiger and whispered, "Why the two bullets behind the left ear?"

Tiger took a moment to sip his scotch, then poured the rest into his coffee before answering. "One is to cut the vocal cords. The other is for the brain. If he survives, he cannot speak, write, think, or mumble in delirium."

Ralphie nodded in awe. "Oh," he said.

BOOK THREE

With Weasel's termination, Tiger felt he was on a roll. A slow, cautious, downhill roll. With Smilin' Jack at the bottom of the hill. He knew Jack's immediate problem would be to replace Weasel with someone he could trust to receive the courier's drugs. A difficult task at best. He envisioned no replacement on the immediate horizon.

If Jack was forced to take the drugs directly from the courier, that would make him extremely vulnerable.

Tiger sat behind his desk fighting off all thoughts of Don Corso. His former father. But it wasn't working, and the thoughts crowded in on him.

In one swoop, his mother took away one father, replacing him with another. A stranger. A dead stranger. A father who bequeathed him millions . . . and nothing else.

He dreaded the thought of his next meeting with his father. He couldn't escape that. He had to report on the warehouse and Weasel's termination.

Yes he dreaded it, knowing he would have to keep his emotions bridled. Like all Sicilians, Tiger was practical. He still needed the power of Don Corso until after the ritual of acceptability. Once made, he would at least be on a par with the heads of the other families. Ordering coffee from Lulu's, he decided to put off reporting to his father until the evening.

Pete stuck his head in the door. "Cat's here."

The youthful Cat stalked across the room, smiled gently at Tiger, and settled on the edge of the chair.

"What do you have for me?" Tiger asked impatiently.

Cat handed him a packet of typed sheets of paper. "First, before you read them, let me explain some things," he said, leaning forward and waiting for the restless Tiger to subside. "Getting into the building was no problem. The floor he's on is tight, lots of fancy alarm stuff. But I got in."

Tiger became excited. "What did you find? These papers?"

"No. Nothing," Cat replied simply.

Tiger was taken aback. "Nothing?"

"Not a damn thing. It's just an empty room. With an empty desk, a phone, no files in the filing cabinet," he said, pausing. "I did find a dozen changes of clothing in the closet, and that was it."

Confused, Tiger asked, "How do you figure this?"

Cat shrugged. "Either he has another office hidden away somewhere, or he's only using the office for changing," he said.

Seeing Tiger's troubled expression, Cat smiled. "While I was there I managed to hide a mike in each jacket."

Tiger looked at him in awe, then returned Cat's smile.

"Those are the transcripts," Cat said.

Tiger laughed. "You did good," he said, staring at the sheets of paper.

"I'm glad because those mikes cost eleven hundred dollars each. I'll send you a bill," he said.

Tiger nodded his approval as his excited eyes scanned the transcripts. "Your money will be delivered to you tomorrow."

Cat nodded, stood, and shook hands. "I'll send over the transcripts daily. At least until Jack decides to have one of his suits cleaned."

After Cat left Tiger ordered another pot of coffee and settled back to read the transcripts.

Two hours later, he stopped reading, rubbed his eyes, and felt the tightness in his shoulders.

The transcripts gave a better picture of his enemy. Smilin' Jack was very adroit in dealing with other agents, his superiors, and the mystery voices from Washington. He seemed always to know what they wanted to hear, and he delivered his reports expertly. He walked a tightrope in those conversations that impressed Tiger.

Slowly Tiger analyzed each typed conversation, seeking some clue as to whom Jack was talking and what importance each conversation had for both parties. He found nothing that related to his immediate problem.

Finally, on the last transcript, he connected. It was a conversation between Jack and two men, possibly couriers (Cat's note: possibly in a vehicle).

JACK: I'll be receiving the goods myself from now on.
\# 1: That's good enough for me.
\# 2: Do we get paid in the usual manner?
JACK: Yes, but a new man will handle the payroll.
\# 1: Same location?
JACK: Yes. He'll be wearing a white denim jacket with a gold pin in the left lapel.
\# 2. Good. We can handle that.
JACK: What about delivery?
\# 2: Well, this one is expected to be a biggie. A heavy haul.
JACK: That's no problem.
\# 2: After this we intend to let things cool down for a while.
JACK: How come?
\# 2: We think someone is on to us. Colby thinks so too.
JACK: He say why?
\# 2: Something to do with one of the families.
JACK: Probably the Corso bunch. Fuck them. I can handle them. Now when will I receive the goods?

299

1: We'll deliver on the second.
JACK: Same place?
2: You got it.

The transcript ended and Tiger settled back in his seat. So many complications came to mind. The possibility of putting a clock on Jack seemed almost impossible. He was too slick not to spot a tail. On the other hand, covering ten police couriers also seemed dangerous. And it would require so many men. They'd have to stop doing anything else.

But what, he thought, if they moved up the timetable? He could lose out and have to wait for the next delivery. That might be weeks away, and Tiger didn't want to wait that long for a shot at Jack.

He decided to compromise and start his clocking on the twenty-ninth. Five days before delivery. Again doubt was setting in. He wondered if, perhaps, he shouldn't be seeking an easier solution.

Tiger finally decided to stay with the clock at three days before delivery. But, thought Tiger, he had a new problem. The second of November was All Souls' Day, a sacred, frightening day for Sicilians.

If Tiger mounted an operation on that day, he would be forced to complete it an hour before sundown. And Jack's meet might very well be after that time.

He wondered what to do, knowing that Don Corso would spend the day of the second securing the doors and windows, against the werewolves, sorcerers, and witches, and awaiting the arrival of his soothsayers. They all would sit in attendance during the long fearful night of *la notte dei morti* —the night of the dead.

For forty years, Tiger had attended those dreadful nights, filled with mumbo jumbo, waiting for the dead to return to visit their loved ones and to torment their living enemies.

At sundown, after all the families were secure behind locked doors, a candle was placed in each window of the house so the dead might find their way to their living loved ones, trailed in the cloak of darkness, by the demons and aggrieved enemies who meant to do harm to the living.

The night of the dead was split betwen those who sat at windows studying each person who passed on the street, hoping for a glimpse of a loved one returning, and the other half cowering, away from the windows and doors, surrounded by amulets, religious pictures, crude drawings of fishes as a symbol of Christ, and the werewolves, whose purpose was to ward off the *occhio morte*—the eye of death.

To Tiger, every year was the same. A long night of praying, incantations, potions, magical rites, and trances—each group in constant conflict. One calling forth the dead while the other was chanting for them to stay away.

At dawn the climax always peaked in a frenzy of madness, with werewolves, witches, and sorcerers all screaming imprecations in hysterical voices to come, to go, to come, to go. Until even Tiger, like all the others present, was caught up in the insanity of the moment. They listened to the eerie wailing of the dead resenting their return to the grave.

No, thought Tiger, shifting his thoughts back to Smilin' Jack, All Souls' Day was not a good time to go on an operation. But what choice did he have?

Pete stuck his head in the door. "Rizzo on line zero."

"Yeah, Mike?"

"I'm going to need you in court tomorrow."

He didn't like the sound of that. "How come?"

"Our friend Malone has thrown a monkey wrench in the works. I think it's bullshit, but he'll try to raise your bail and hold onto you."

"Do you have any idea what he's got?"

"Who knows? I'll deal with it in court. But, like I said, it's probably bullshit."

Tiger hoped so.

The rest of the day Tiger spent checking on his outposts. He ended the day at Don Corso's office.

Trudging up the path, he felt queasy in the pit of his stomach. He was sure Don Corso didn't know he knew

301

Camille's secret. So he had better keep his emotions under control.

Entering the small office, he saw Don Corso sitting in his usual position. But he sensed a shadowy form sitting behind his father. Toto?

His heart skipped a beat. No, the shape was wrong. The outline was shorter and stockier. Whoever or whatever it was, it exuded evil and it spooked Tiger.

Don Corso was aware that Tiger was nervous in the presence of his new shadow. But he chose to act as if nothing unusual was hidden in the room's darkness.

"What has happened?" he asked.

Tiger found it difficult to concentrate on his report with that thing in the background. He wished the interview was over, so he could get the hell away.

He quickly completed the report dealing with the warehouse, Room 314, and Weasel's termination.

Hesitating slightly, Don Corso looked at Tiger. "Have you considered that perhaps the narcotics weren't shipped but switched to another room in the warehouse?"

Yes, Tiger had thought of that, but he doubted it. There would be little difficulty moving in and out of the warehouse. For a hundred bucks, the warehouseman would let you take home the whole building. "I'll look over the building again, just to be sure," he said, anxious to leave.

And Don Corso allowed Tiger to leave. Tiger could not help but believe that the old man was not so anxious to hear the report as he was to let Tiger know of his new shadow.

Was it a warning? wondered Tiger.

T HERE were no spectators in the courtroom, only participants. Tiger sat alone on one side with Lawyer Rizzo while Malone sat with Colby, a battery of lawyers, and an array of uniformed police officials.

Tiger guessed the display of brass was meant to impress

the judge. He also noticed that Malone and Colby seemed to be arguing, with Colby taking the offensive. Well, whatever it was, Tiger knew it was not going to be to his advantage.

"Are you prepared to put forward any new information?" asked the judge, looking directly at Malone.

It took a moment for one of Malone's lawyers to force his bulk into a standing position. "May I approach the bench?" he asked.

Tiger looked at Rizzo, expecting an objection. There was none, and the judged waved the lawyer to approach him.

Tiger was not sure he liked what was going on, but the awareness in Rizzo's eyes told him he was alert for anything.

The lawyer and the judge's whispering made him nervous, and he looked at Mike Rizzo. "What the fuck are they talking about?"

"Relax, Tiger," Rizzo said. "As soon as I know, I'll deal with it."

That was small comfort to Tiger.

After a moment, the lawyer went back to his seat and stared at the judge, who shook his head and looked at Rizzo.

"Will the defendant please stand?"

Tiger didn't like the feel of the whole thing and felt he was about to be sentenced to life.

"Case dismissed," said the judge, gathering up his papers and leaving the courtroom abruptly.

Tiger was bewildered. Mike Rizzo smiled and shook Tiger's hand. "I told you it was all bullshit," he said. "Let's get the hell out of here."

"That's it?" Tiger asked. "It's all over?"

"For this case, it is," Rizzo said, smiling as he escorted Tiger out of the empty courtroom.

When Tiger settled into the back seat of his car, he was elated at being able to torment Malone and Colby.

"Where to?" Pete asked.

"Let's go back to the office."

Pete drove parallel to the river along the long stretch of Furman Street. Tiger remembered the two detectives who had hidden in his car after his last court appearance.

Was it Malone or Colby who decided on the dismissal? Well, whoever it was, it was good to see the two of them at each other's throats.

Tiger knew when he finished wrapping up Mister Smilin' Jack, he would turn loose Detective Defalco and Bobby Cassaro against Colby and company. He had enough on the clerk's office for Alfred and Bobby to collect a chest full of medals.

Pete slowed up as Tiger looked up at a flashing police car parked up ahead. The uniformed policeman at the side of the road waved them to pull in behind the police vehicle.

"Want me to take him out?" asked Pete. "I could always claim the accelerator jammed."

"What for? We're clean."

Pete pulled up and lowered his window. "What's the problem, officer?" he asked.

"May I see your license and registration?"

Pete tried to lighten things up as he reached for his wallet. "Was I speeding?"

But the face under the dark glasses remained stony as he waited for identification. After receiving the papers, he studied them carefully and looked into the rear seat at Tiger.

"Your name?" he asked.

"Joseph Corso," Tiger answered.

After a long stare, he nodded and looked at Ralphie. "Your name?"

But before Ralphie could answer, they found themselves covered by a .38 Police Special. "Put your hands over your heads and get out," he commanded. And as if by signal, two unmarked vehicles pulled into line behind Tiger. The cars spilled out half a dozen men with drawn guns.

Before stepping out onto the pavement, Tiger looked at the policeman, hoping to see a possibility of discussion, but the coldness of his features told him he didn't have any.

304

Slowly he stepped into the street to the group waiting to handcuff him and hustle him into the first vehicle. The last glimpse he got was Pete and Ralphie being relieved of their weapons. And then they were moving swiftly down the street.

Stuffed between two detectives, Tiger couldn't turn to see what was happening to his friends.

The car sped along the river, turned and continued along Van Brunt toward the old Coast Guard Station in Red Hook.

Ten minutes later, deep within the factory zone running along the deserted Todd shipyards, they turned into an alley, pulled into a closed garage, and closed the overhead door down after them.

As the car pulled to a stop at the other end of the empty garage, Tiger guessed Colby and company meant business this time. He knew the only chance he had at all was to keep a powerful check on his emotions.

Taken from the car, he was escorted to a small partitioned office and cuffed to a high-backed chair.

One detective, whom Tiger recognized as one of the two who had surprised him in his car, sat by the door on guard. The others quickly left.

Tiger could not tell from his manner of sitting whether he was waiting for some higher-up—perhaps Colby or the interrogator or an executioner.

"Do you mind if I smoke?" Tiger asked, glad to hear that his voice was strong.

"No smoking, no talking. Just listen," he snapped. "Your old boss Joe Bocci owes us six hundred grand. Now you owe it to us."

Tiger tried not to laugh, but he couldn't help himself. "I'd like to help you, but I left my wallet at home."

But the man was devoid of humor. "You won't be so cute after I finish with you," he said coldly. "When my partners return, you are going to make some phone calls and raise the money or you'll never see the light of day again."

The door opened. Two detectives carrying a long coil of

hemp entered. Quickly one fashioned a noose and threw it over Tiger's neck.

The other end of the line was thrown over a ceiling rafter and secured to a radiator. There was barely enough slack for Tiger to breathe. Tiger had to sit upright to keep the pressure off his adam's apple. He watched as one of the detectives used a Magic Marker to draw a series of lines on the rope, one inch apart.

A table was drawn up to Tiger, a phone placed on it, while another detective set up a tape recorder and fitted earphones to his head.

"Now let me educate you," said one of the detectives icily. "Every hour that the money is not here, we tighten the rope one inch. You understand?"

Tiger nodded.

"Now give me the first number you want called."

Looking at the determined faces surrounding him, Tiger knew there was no way he wasn't going to have to pay. He also knew that the moment he paid, he was a goner. The money was no problem. He had ten times that entrusted to him by the family. The problem was only three people could use the key. Don Corso, Mister D, and himself. If he called Mister D and somehow managed to convey the urgency of the request, Mr. D would follow instructions and deliver the money without question. But that wouldn't help Tiger. They would kill him immediately. So he had to swallow his pride and call Don Corso.

"Call 555-3636," he said, giving Don Corso's private number.

The detective dialed, looked at the detective wearing the earphones, who nodded when Don Corso came on the line. He placed the receiver to Tiger's ear.

"Yeah?"

"It's me. Tiger."

"Yes, Tiger," he said cautiously.

"I need you to pick up six hundred thousand dollars in cash."

Don Corso's hesitation was slight. "From what safe deposit box do you want it from?" he asked softly.

"From box number twenty-four. I have enough in it," Tiger said, knowing that twenty-four was the code for trouble.

"I'll get it for you. Can you give me a few hours?"

"No!" snapped Tiger, letting him know of the urgency.

"Can you give me three hours?"

Tiger looked over at the marked rope. "Just about."

After another brief hesitation, Don Corso said, "I'll take care of it. Oh, by the way, Rizzo told me you ran into our old friends. What did they have to say?"

Tiger saw one of the detectives' eyes narrow. "The usual bullshit. I told them they'll get their money," he said, now knowing Don Corso had pinned his problem down to Colby.

"Where do you want the money delivered?"

The detective with the earphones held up a slip of paper for Tiger to read.

"To the bartender at J. P. Clarkson's."

"I will get right on it, and if you need more, call again," he said, disconnecting the line.

As the detectives settled back, Tiger knew the hardfaces would be scurrying in many directions in search of him. But would they be in time?

For the next hour all four men sat in silence, Tiger supposing they were waiting for some signal that the money had been received. But after an hour passed, the knot was tightened another notch.

He wasn't in pain, but the dead weight of his body made his neck muscles numb, which prompted him to wonder what condition Pete and Ralphie were in. Were they dead or alive?

Time passed slowly, with Tiger keeping his body rigid.

At the end of the second hour, the rope was tightened again. This time he felt the pain of slow strangulation. He knew Don Corso would not deliver the money until the last moment. Not if there was the slightest chance of saving him. At least he hoped that was Don Corso's plan.

Tiger's breathing became labored, and with his neck twisted he found it difficult to fill his lungs.

Twenty minutes into the hour, the lightheadedness started, and the fog closed in on his mind. Slowly the mist cleared, and a circle of vultures filled his view. Suddenly their expressions reflected both love and hate. The sharpened beaks and dead eyes slowly superimposed a new form. The faces became recognizable: Camille, Sonny, Turk, Iggy, Weasel, and the other walking dead. They were all waiting. Waiting for what? For him to die or to live?

"We got the money," shouted a detective gleefully after hanging up the phone.

But Tiger had not heard; he was out of it.

"What are we going to do with him?" the detective asked, indicating the hanging Tiger.

"Let him hang," said the one who had hidden in Tiger's car.

Suddenly a knife flashed, and the taut rope was severed.

"We got orders to make him disappear," the older detective said in annoyance. "So let's do it."

One detective shrugged, but the other one suddenly slapped Tiger across the face. "I owe this bastard, and I want him awake when he gets it," he said, lashing out at Tiger again.

The other detectives shrugged, slipped into their jackets, and took a moment to watch the floor show.

The vibrations in Tiger's brain grew in intensity until he was close to the edge of consciousness. He knew where he was. But some instinct warned him against opening his eyes. He steeled himself against the sting of the slaps, as he sucked in gulps of life-giving air.

"He's coming around, so let's get the hell out of here," said the older detective.

"But I told you he owes me."

"So finish waking him up in the car," he snapped back.

Tiger felt the pressure on his wrist as the cuffs were removed and he was lifted to his feet. That is when Tiger opened his eyes and pulled the string attached to his belt. In the close quarters, the gun shot was muffled, as Tiger quickly turned slightly to the detective facing him and fired again with his buckle gun.

The remaining detective was clutching for his pistol when Tiger pulled the last string. The bullet slammed into the detective as Tiger moved and snatched the pistol from the astounded detective.

Tiger saw a movement to his left, turned, and fired again, as he backed against the wall in preparation for a new attack. But there was no further movement except for the groaning of the older detective.

Tiger took a moment to catch up to himself. He looked around at the slaughter and wondered at the futility of the whole thing.

What now? he wondered. Three detectives dead. Shit.

He knew he dare not leave the bodies to be found. The resulting outrage would haunt him into his grave. He expected no surprise visitors, since they were intending to take him somewhere else to dump him. That meant he had a little time to decide what he had to do.

In the garage, he found their vehicle. He took the keys from one of the bodies and siphoned off a gallon of gas and returned to the small office. Dragging the bodies out to the garage, he piled all three in the deep trunk of the car. Tiger hoped no blood dripped into the street before he reached his destination.

Back in the small office, he picked up the pistols and handcuffs, doused the room with gasoline, and spilled a trail leading out to the garage.

He cranked open the overhead garage door, letting the late afternoon sun in. He ignited the trail of gasoline, watched it speed toward the office, then drove out with his damning cargo.

Sticking mostly to side streets, he made his way to Tony's scrapyard.

One look at Tiger's face told Tony there would be no friendliness today. "Trouble?" he asked, with narrowed eyes.

Tiger nodded. "I got three stiffs in there to get rid of. And the car too."

Tony looked at him in awe. "Cheez, you don't fuck around. Who are they?"

"Cops," was all Tiger offered as explanation.

Tony scratched his head and looked around the yard. "Well, it's almost dark. We'll use the big press."

He shouted to Nicola, his crane operator, indicating for him to pick up the vehicle. Tony supervised the operation by loosening the lugs and letting the wheels drop off. Then he watched the car arc overhead, poise over the gaping cavern of the press, and drop into place. A fifty-ton lid slammed down with a crunch. It compressed the whole vehicle into a four-by-six bale.

As the huge press unscrewed, Tony stood by waiting for the bale to emerge.

"What are we waiting for?" Tiger asked.

"I want to check the bale to make sure there are no arms or legs sticking out. We don't need any problems."

When the bale of crumpled steel arrived, Tony checked it out. "It's clean," he said. "Let's get a cup of coffee."

In the office, Tiger sipped his coffee. He wasn't into explaining the three bodies, and Tony wasn't into asking about them.

"Bobby's still in Siberia and feels they're going to keep him in cold storage forever."

"I'm sorry I ever got him involved."

Tony shrugged. "Why? He's a big boy. He knew what he was getting into."

Tiger agreed, thankful his head was beginning to clear. He wanted to call Pete on the beeper, but how could he use Tony's phone for a call back, especially if the beeper had fallen into the wrong hands.

Damn, he had to get to a phone and check.

Borrowing one of Tony's cars, he drove until he was clear of the area. Then he stopped at a street phone, quickly dialed Pete's number, and left the phone booth number. When five minutes passed, he was certain there would be no return call. He felt sick and angry, wondering what condition his friends were in.

Tiger was too wound up to pay attention to the scarcity of hardfaces in Don Corso's outer office. As he moved

310

across the room, the rear guard didn't bother to announce him and just opened the door.

At the sight of Tiger, Don Corso jumped to his feet, wearing an expression of disbelief, awe, and relief.

Tiger instinctively felt Don Corso was about to embrace him. Feeling self-conscious about it, he crossed the room and sagged into a chair against the wall.

Concern flooded Don Corso's features. "Are you all right? Have you been hurt?"

Tiger took a second before answering. "I'm fine. It's just that I'm still a bit shaky."

"Can I get you something? Brandy?"

"No. No. I just need to catch my breath," he said, looking over at the older man. "Do you know what has happened to my two friends?"

Don Corso pulled his chair closer. "I have everyone out looking for them. And for you, too," he said with a sad sigh. "Tell me what happened."

He told Don Corso of the courtroom, the kidnapping, the hanging, the killings, and the destruction of the bodies in Tony's scrapyard.

When he finished, Don Corso remained silent and deep in thought. After a moment, he slowly rubbed his chin. "I wonder exactly what Malone's whole involvement was. Is he part of the deal or just a dupe?"

"Does it matter?" asked Tiger.

"It could," said Don Corso.

As Tiger shifted in his seat, he found the older man staring at him with frosted eyes. "They did this to you?" he asked, indicating the rope burns.

With his finger tips, Tiger softly touched the raw burns. He hoped he didn't have to live with the scars the rest of his life. Colby will pay for this, thought Tiger.

As if reading Tiger's mind, Don Corso said, "You will have your chance. My men captured Inspector Colby an hour ago."

Tiger was taken aback, speechless, unable to do anything but stare at the older man.

"He claims he had nothing to do with the kidnappings. He said they took matters into their own hands because they couldn't find Delvechicco."

"What else would he say? What are you going to do with him?"

"When I thought you were dead, I intended personally to terminate him. But now you may have the pleasure."

Tiger sighed, having had enough killing for one day. "It's been a tough day. I'll pass."

Don Corso nodded his understanding. "I will deal with it," he said as his desk phone rang. While he talked in hushed tones, Tiger glanced into the shadows behind the desk, but he could discern no movement or outline.

Don Corso returned the receiver to its cradle and Tiger didn't like the look on his face.

"What is it?" he asked, his heart pumping faster.

Don Corso filled his lungs before speaking. "Your friend Pete has just been rescued. But they had already killed your other friend."

"Ralphie?" Tiger uttered.

Don Corso nodded. "My men were closing in on a warehouse in Long Island City when they heard a shot inside. Thinking you were inside, they stormed the place. It was barely in time to save Pete, but not in time to save Ralphie. I'm sorry."

Tiger wanted to cry, and he would have except for Don Corso's presence. Tiger knew how the older man felt about a man crying. First-born Sicilian males are weaned on the credo that a man never cries, no matter what. But were it not so ingrained in his upbringing, Tiger would have let loose with a flood of tears.

But he didn't cry. Instead he squared his shoulders and said, "What did you do with the men you captured?"

"Both men were terminated," he said simply.

"Christ," said Tiger, "five dead policemen and Colby yet to go."

"Seven," corrected Don Corso.

Tiger's head shot up. "Who is the seventh?"

312

"The bartender who received the money. He also works for the clerk's office."

Damn, damn, damn. In his mind, he saw the storm clouds gathering and all hell breaking loose. "There is no way seven policemen who worked together and disappeared together isn't going to create an explosion. So how in God's name can you put a lid on this?"

Don Corso sat a long time measuring Tiger. Maybe he thinks I'm panicking. Or maybe the strange look in the older man's face was his way of searching for quick answers.

"There is nothing we can do," said Don Corso. "I know it will be a hurricane, but it won't be a tidal wave. So we will weather it. We always do," he reassured Tiger. "The eye of the storm will pass over us in about ten days. They will close down a lot of our operations and round up everyone for a media circus. That's when our friends on the newspapers will begin dropping little bits of information of a private gang war going on behind the scenes of the clerk's office. Especially when Colby is found dead with a load of heroin in the trunk of his car. Our friendly reporters will also discover that our dear inspector and several of the missing policemen were living well beyond their means."

Tiger's tenseness eased somewhat. It could work, he thought. Yes, it could work. Damn it, it has to work.

"Now," said Don Corso, "we have to get to this rogue Fed and tie him into the drugs and the clerk's office. Even if we don't recover the drugs, his exposure will cool the heat quickly and give our friends on the newspapers a field day," he said, showing one of his rare grins.

Tiger searched for flaws, but Don Corso's logic prevailed. He took a moment to relax and change tack. "I want to give my friend Ralphie a decent funeral."

Don Corso's eyebrows shot up. "With a policeman's bullet in him?"

But in Tiger's mind, he saw a wooded area where Sonny was buried in a lonely unmarked grave. As he pictured the brush-covered mound he felt the pain, injustices, and dis-

313

honor he showed a brother who died without mourners or a gravestone.

No, Ralphie would get better than that. He was the real brother Tiger never had. As he looked at the older man, he knew in his heart that there was no way in hell he intended to sweep his friend under a rug and deny their friendship ever existed.

He carefully measured Don Corso. "My friend will have his funeral. He will have mourners, friends, flowers, and whatever it takes to put a friend to rest in peace."

Don Corso sighed a heavy sigh, recognizing the determined look in Tiger's eyes. "I will have the bullet removed, and I will have a friendly doctor issue a death certificate," he said. "But beyond that, I can do no more."

Tiger nodded. "Thank you."

THE following morning they placed Ralphie's remains in the cellar of a friend's mortuary while the doctor completed a long medical history of heart disease.

Tiger spent the rest of the morning making funeral arrangements. Then he had to take care of the unpleasant task of notifying Ralphie's family of his death and the circumstances of his murder.

Tiger was most worried about Ralphie's father, fearing he might suffer another stroke. But the old man was made of strong stuff. He accepted the news in a normal Sicilian manner, which belied the pain he was feeling underneath.

Yolanda, Ralphie's older sister, went off the deep end. She ran screaming from the room, refusing to believe her baby brother was dead.

When she returned, she had a different look in her eyes. She swore she would have revenge on the cops who did the killing. But the father, who was carefully studying Tiger, cautioned her to be silent. He was sure Don Corso had more to say.

Painfully Tiger explained that a large number of dead policemen were involved, and why the truth must never be revealed.

"It was the only way we could have the funeral."

Both father and daughter understood that. There would be no peace for Ralphie until he was laid to rest properly. They promised to spread the word on the street that Ralphie had died of a heart attack.

Tiger was embarrassed when the old man kissed his hand, thanking him for the respect he showed the family in telling them the truth.

Pete drove back to the office. He and Tiger had spoken little since they were reunited, but their smoldering hate was jointly fueled by silent thoughts of vengeance. They had only one major enemy left: Smilin' Jack.

Arriving at the office, Tiger found a new packet of transcripts from Cat. He quickly read them but they contained little of importance.

Sitting alone in his small office, Tiger felt empty without Ralphie. Like a cripple without the use of his limbs.

He found it difficult to believe it was only yesterday morning that he had sat in court alongside Mike Rizzo. It seemed like a lifetime ago.

He was now sure it was Colby who had set him up. Sharp as Malone was, he wasn't that bold.

He picked up the phone and buzzed Pete.

"Yeah?"

"Have someone listen to the news and get back to me."

"Anything special?" Pete asked.

"You'll know when you hear it," he said, breaking the connection.

He wondered what Malone would do when he heard about Colby's body being found surrounded by a stash of heroin. Would he panic, run around huffing and puffing, narrow it down to the Corso family, specifically to Tiger? Or would he keep his distance, not wanting to get near the Colby scandal.

If Don Corso figured right, the storm would hit within

the week. Then it would take another week for the tide to turn in their favor with the friendly media. That, thought Tiger, should have them out of the woods within the month.

That sounded good to Tiger, but for only one thing: November the second was eight days away. Smack in the middle of the planted stories. Right in the middle of the newspaper stories of a silent drug war, with policemen fighting policemen at the property clerk's office. Would Smilin' Jack have the balls to continue his operation in the middle of such publicity? Tiger doubted it.

Pete stepped into Tiger's office, looking questioningly at Tiger. "I heard the news. You knew this was coming?" he asked softly.

Tiger nodded. "Don Corso made it personal."

Pete half nodded. The lethargic depression he had fallen into lifted slightly. "I never thought I would say this, but I owe your father one."

At the word "father," Tiger winced.

I⊤ was a small chapel, decorated with soft colors and dim lights. Pete stood off by himself, alone in his private thoughts, but ever watchful of Tiger.

Yolanda sat beside her father in front of the coffin, as representatives of the Canzanna family.

Tiger had earlier chased out the weeping widows, those dreaded vultures of death. He glanced over at Ralphie's still form, forever asleep in the casket of mother-of-pearl lined with white silk. He was surrounded by a mountain of floral pieces and still they were coming, crowding the space for mourners.

A long line of mourners filed past Ralphie, said their silent prayers, paid condolences, and returned to lounge around the hall or leave.

316

Occasionally a friend, a relative, or a special trooper broke away to offer condolences to Tiger.

Angelina came with Jeanne and Momma. They wore faces strained with sadness for Tiger's loss. He was glad Jeanne hadn't brought the children. This was no place for them. They had plenty of time before they need to be assaulted by the face of death.

Tiger was lost in his own thoughts, when suddenly Momma was sitting opposite him. Looking at her sad expression, he knew she wished she could transfer Tiger's hurt to herself.

"He's gone, my son. We know you have lost a dear friend. Someone you loved very much. I can see it in your eyes. But always remember that a man is dead only when he is forgotten."

Since coming into the chapel and seeing Ralphie laid out, Tiger had fought against the emotions that engulfed him. But now Momma's words penetrated and his heart broke. He fought to stem the flow of hot tears resting in the corners of his eyes, hoping they wouldn't overflow their banks. But he lost, and Momma took him gently in her arms as he sobbed.

Jeanne and Angelina quickly stood, blocking any onlooker from seeing Tiger crying.

Jeanne understood the price her husband was paying with his tears, that he was breaking the unwritten law that a Sicilian male never cries. Tiger felt comfortable in Momma's warm embrace, and he stayed a moment longer to get himself under control.

She wiped away his tears. "Are you all right, my son?"

He nodded, sniffed once, and knew he would be all right. "I'm fine, Momma," he said, hoping his smile wasn't a death grin. "Thank you."

She touched his cheek as Jeanne and Angelina resumed sitting. Tiger wanted to ask Momma if Don Corso was going to make an appearance, but he knew the old man would not. He knew it wasn't disrespect to him or to Ralphie, but that he attended funerals only in utmost privacy

317

—or openly to flaunt his presence at the funeral of a dead enemy.

Suddenly Tiger was stupified to see Inspector Robert Cassaro enter the chapel, wearing his full dress uniform, replete with brass buttons and white gloves. His walk was stiff and military as he moved through the watchful mourners, knelt in silent prayer, then stood and smartly saluted Ralphie. After a few gentle words with the father and Yolanda, Bobby headed toward Tiger, who met him halfway.

"You shouldn't be seen here, Bobby."

"Why not? I owe Ralphie one for Colby and his friends."

"You got balls," Tiger said, shaking hands.

"Fuck them all," Bobby said, as he walked out.

Tiger watched in admiration, knowing Bobby's gesture of respect was going to cost him.

The night dragged on with Tiger waiting for the eleven o'clock curfew, so he could spend a few moments alone with his friend.

As he sat there amid the buzzing of many whispered voices, he found the odor of fresh-cut flowers overpowering. He glanced over at the coffin. He wanted badly for Ralphie to know what their years together meant to him. He remembered Ralphie's lazy smile, the slightly mad eyes, and the uncompromising loyalty in his heart.

Yes, Momma was right, a man is never dead so long as someone remembers. And Tiger knew there would be no forgetting.

Tiger was brought out of his reverie as a trooper rushed up to Pete. The look on the trooper's face warned Tiger that he had trouble.

He jumped to his feet and met Pete halfway across the room.

"Malone's got an army of cops outside."

"Don't let anyone in for five minutes," he said, waving to Carmine. He could see by Momma's and Jeanne's expressions that they too smelled trouble.

"What's the problem, Tiger?" Carmine asked.

318

"I got cops outside, so take the women to the director's office until it's over."

"What will happen to you?" he asked, surprising Tiger with his obvious concern.

"I'll probably have to spend a few hours at the police station," he lied to his brother. "Now move before this gets out of hand."

No one spoke until the women left the room. Then Tony Orechicco broke the ice. "You say the word, Tiger, and we'll hold the bastards off until the lawyers show."

But Tiger knew the storm simply had broken sooner than expected. He wondered how Malone had narrowed it down to him so quickly. Was it possible the fat slob had tied Ralphie's death into the disappearances?

Tiger glanced over to four pallbearers who entered, closed Ralphie's coffin lid, pushed the flowers aside, and began to push the coffin from the room.

"Keep everybody out for five minutes," shouted Tiger, as troopers rushed toward the front lobby.

The coffin disappeared into a waiting elevator, and suddenly his troopers broke against the weight of many flack-vested policemen. Troopers were shoved against the walls as other heavily armed policemen ran up the stairs alongside the elevator.

Tiger and the rest of his troopers were herded toward the front door, where paddy wagons, flash bulbs, and a battalion of police waited.

At police headquarters they were herded into the main lobby. Their identification was checked, and troopers were sent to various parts of the huge building.

As Tiger waited to be processed, he estimated that there were about two hundred cops and robbers crammed into the main hall. As they shuffled slowly forward, I.D.'s were examined. When it was Tiger and Pete's turn, a squad of detectives surrounded them and hustled them down the hall to a waiting elevator.

Malone sat behind his desk, tapping his fingers as Tiger and Pete were shoved into wooden chairs facing him. Ma-

319

lone surveyed Tiger. "Now you don't have your friends here to protect you, so you better give me the answers I want to hear."

Tiger remained silent.

"You've been playing a lot of games lately, but I know everything you've done. I just want to hear it from you," he said, pausing to let it all sink in.

Tiger still maintained his silence.

"So start talking," Malone said, raising his voice an octave and slamming his beefy hand down on the desk.

Tiger took a moment before speaking. "May I ask why I have been brought here?"

Malone's eyes sparkled. "Murder, obstruction of justice, and a million other charges I can bring against you."

Again, Tiger did not speak.

"Where were you on the morning of the twenty-fourth?" Malone demanded.

"In court," Tiger answered simply.

Malone smiled a mirthless smile. "And where did you go after you were dismissed from the courtroom?"

"I had a cup of coffee with my lawyer and then returned to my office," Tiger said, not liking the sneaky, knowing look in Malone's eyes.

"Do you remember being stopped by a traffic officer on Furman Street?" he asked softly.

Tiger's stare was level. "I don't remember such an incident."

Malone nodded in the direction of a group of detectives. One stepped forward, taking a position directly in front of Tiger. Tiger recognized the street-hardened face, but he didn't know who the man was.

"Do you know this man?" Malone asked softly.

Tiger studied the face, shrugged, and shook his head. "No."

"You don't remember me, fella?" he asked, in a menacing voice.

Tiger recognized the voice, but the last time he saw this face it was covered with a helmet and dark glasses.

"I don't know you, fella."

"On the morning of the twenty-fourth, at eleven fifteen, Officer Polk stopped you for a violation. When you refused to show your identification, he called for backup and you and your partners were arrested. But somehow on the way to the police station, they disappeared. Now I want to know what you did with those policemen."

Tiger hoped he wore the proper expression of shock. "Are you fucking crazy?" he asked, half getting out of his chair.

But Officer Polk grabbed Tiger's shirt front and pulled him forward. Tiger saw the hatred in the man's eyes and knew the moment of truth had come. "You lying bastard. You killed them!" he screamed. "You killed them, you bastard!"

When Tiger was certain no one in the room intended to intervene, he straight-armed the man, sending him sprawling into Malone's desk.

Then it hit the fan, as a roomful of bodies rushed forward to get at him.

The first time Tiger was ever arrested, he was young and inexperienced. He learned the hard way how never to allow a policeman to handcuff him during an interrogation. For the first lesson, he was cuffed to a steel-barred door and asked a lot of questions while they cut into his upper teeth with a hacksaw. God, did Tiger beg for mercy! But there was no mercy. Especially when he wouldn't tell them what they wanted to hear. So they cut through eight teeth before he passed out.

In the mad throng closing in, he saw the handcuffs in the hands of one of the detectives and the old fears returned. He lashed out at the nearest man. Tiger knew as long as he remained on his feet, kicking, biting, and punching, the madder they would get. And the madder they got, the more likely they were to beat him into unconsciousness. They did.

WHEN Tiger opened his eyes, the first thing he saw was the whiteness of the walls, and he knew he was in a hospital. He looked over at the glass-fronted door, where a uniformed policeman stood guard.

Turning, he saw Pete in the bed next to him, his left arm in traction and his head swathed in bandages. Tiger wanted to reach out and touch his friend, but the movement sent a sharp pain into his chest and he passed back into oblivion.

When he awoke the second time, a white-jacketed man was taking his pulse.

"How do you feel?" he asked.

"Like my chest was caved in."

"It is. They broke four of your ribs. It must have been one hell of a party."

"How is my friend?"

"All things considered, he's not bad. A slight fracture of the skull, a broken femur, but only one broken rib," he smiled. "But you'll both live," he said, writing on the chart.

"You and your partner must have interesting occupations. You're both a mass of scar tissue," he said, looking up at the uniformed policeman, who was letting two well-dressed men into the room.

Harness bulls, thought Tiger, guessing it was time for round two.

"Can I help you, gentlemen?" asked the white-jacketed man.

They flashed their badges, flipping a thumb toward Tiger. "We got some questions to ask our friend here," said the shorter one, whom Tiger recognized from his confrontation in front of Saint Rocco's with Malone and Carmine.

"This man is in no shape to answer any questions."

The short squat detective didn't like what he was hearing. "I could come back with a court order," he said, coolly.

The attendant's jaw tightened. "Then I suggest you do that. And when you come back, you're still not going to talk to my patient until I say he's well enough."

After an exchange of glares, the detective nodded. "I'll be back." They left.

"Thanks, fella," said an exhausted Tiger.

The anger was still in the man's eyes as he turned on Tiger. "Don't thank me. I'm a doctor, not a fucking policeman."

F OR three days, Tiger and Pete remained in their hospital cell. During that time, Tiger heard nothing from Lawyer Rizzo, Jeanne, Momma, or even the policemen who were so anxious to question him the first day.

He asked the doctor for a radio or a newspaper, but the doctor said no. Since Tiger was still listed as a prisoner, no privileges were to be granted.

Tiger knew the law. He had to be booked within twenty-four hours or turned loose. But it was now over seventy-two hours, so why was he still here? Was it possible they had booked him without his presence? Wasn't that illegal? And what about the hearing? So why the hell was he still being held?

Tiger felt the anger and frustration building, especially with the second of November only two days away. He knew one thing for certain, if Malone grabbed Ralphie's body with the bullet hole, Tiger was never going to see daylight. Even the mighty Don Corso couldn't help him.

Late in the evening, the policeman on the door permitted Rizzo to enter with Tiger and Pete's release papers. The lawyer's cold, stern look warned Tiger and Pete to keep their mouths shut until they were well clear of the building.

A private ambulance waited with two of his troopers wearing attendants' uniforms.

Rizzo quickly filled in Tiger and Pete. The cops had booked them without their presence. Then they tried to bypass arraignment and head straight for the grand jury for an indictment, with no bail for Tiger. But Rizzo headed them off, called a few judges, and managed to have bail set. One million dollars each.

"Where do we stand now?" Tiger asked, hungry for answers.

"They have ninety days in which to bring in an indictment against the both of you. So that gives us some time for maneuvering. In the meantime, all hell has broken loose and everything has become a circus," said the harried lawyer. "As soon as I get your boys out, they lock up your father's group. Then they run around the circle again."

"It's that bad, huh?" asked Tiger, studying the lawyer's worried features.

"I would suggest you and your troops get the hell out of town until this begins to cool."

Tiger nodded his understanding, then changed the subject. "How do we look on the murder raps?"

Rizzo shrugged. "I really don't know. I haven't had a moment to breathe since this started. But I know one thing, Malone and the district attorney wouldn't try to hold you over for the grand jury with only that cop as a witness."

Tiger's eyes narrowed. "I don't understand."

"Malone is too scared a rabbit to go up against me with only one loaded pistol. I'm sure he has some gimmick in the background."

"What should I do?" Tiger asked.

He saw the panic in Rizzo's eyes. "Don't do a damn thing. I want you to cool out until I get a handle on things. If something comes up in regards to Malone, I'll handle it," he said, staring at Tiger. "Do you understand?"

Tiger nodded. "You're the boss," he said, thinking only how he could help Rizzo beat the murder raps against him.

"Where will you go to cool out?" Rizzo asked.

"Upstate."

"Your father's place at Swan Lake?"

Tiger didn't bother reminding the lawyer the place was now his. "Yeah, my father's place."

"Is the phone number still the same?" Rizzo asked. When Tiger nodded, Rizzo said, "Good. I'll call you there if I need you." The ambulance let Rizzo out at the corner, where he hailed a cab. Tiger turned to the ambulance driver and gave him an address.

The funeral parlor was dark and deserted as the ambu-

324

lance pulled into the side entrance. Tiger emerged, pressed the bell, and waited. The door opened and he was hurried in by the funeral director.

In the dim light, the man's sharp, ascetic features took on an even dourer expression.

"Did we lose the package?" Tiger asked anxiously.

Tiger saw what passed for a smile. "We were faster than they were."

He was sure the director heard his sigh of relief. "Thank you, my friend."

The director bowed at the compliment and indicated that Tiger follow him to a small, neat office. The director unlocked a metal cabinet and carefully removed a clay urn.

"These are your friend's remains," he said, handing Tiger the urn.

Tiger held the urn gently. "Thank you, my friend."

The older man bowed in the style of the Old World. "I was happy to serve you, Don Corso."

Tiger leaned forward and kissed the man on the cheek, not knowing how else to express his gratitude.

As Tiger left the flustered man and walked out with Ralphie's urn under his arm, he wondered who the hell Malone had in the background to hang him with.

Leaving the funeral parlor, Tiger tracked down Trooper Abruzzi, putting him in charge of finding and clocking the eyewitness policeman.

Abruzzi nodded his gratitude at the assignment. "When I have the target in sight, what shall I do with him?" he purred menacingly.

"Just clock him until I tell you to hit him," Tiger said, not looking forward to another cop killing. But he knew he might have to go through with it if he wanted to survive.

WHEN Tiger arrived at his country house, two troopers were waiting to help him settle in.

One trooper quickly prepared a late dinner of steak and eggs, the other rewired extra phones into the master bedroom, Tiger's new command post.

Thirty minutes later, Big Che arrived with a new contingent of troops. He also brought up from the city all the newspapers Tiger had requested. Also his Uncle Lulu had sent up a packet of transcripts from Cat. He was thankful he had the foresight to order Tony Orechicco to start the clock of the couriers on schedule.

Now that he was back in his element, Tiger's mind began to clear. He found nothing new in Jack's transcripts, so he was sure he was going to complete his operation.

That was a fact Tiger could deal with. It was what Malone had hidden that gnawed at him. It could only be an eyewitness. Someone who could corroborate the policeman's statement. But who? Where was he stationed to have seen the kidnapping?

The questions ate at him and he wondered if perhaps he had a traitor in his organization. Well, thought Tiger, at this point it was all speculation. For survival, he needed facts.

After dinner, Tiger and Pete scanned the pile of newspapers in search of information. He hated seeing his face plastered on the front page, although he received a little comfort in noting the picture was an old and not very good one. Like most people in his profession, careless photography was to be discouraged. The last thing he needed was to be a target for every asshole who wanted a trophy to hang on the wall.

As he read the papers, the stories grew wilder and wilder with each edition. They went from policemen disappearing to mysterious societies, to dons who push buttons, sending men to their doom, to ritualistic murders, attributing dozens of murders to Tiger personally. They ended always with prophecies of the end of organized crime.

To Tiger, it was all bullshit, but it sold papers.

T HAT night, Tiger found it difficult to sleep. The bandages around his chest twisted, tightened, and itched. He poured water on the bandages to relieve the itching. He sat on the edge of the bed because it seemed to be the most comfortable position.

He thought of Jeanne and the children, wondering whether they were asleep or watching the Late Show. Most likely the children were doing fine. Rosario, in particular, would be losing sleep with his new computer. That would keep him busy while Tiger was away. But Jeanne was a different matter. Secretly, she was a nail biter, a worrier. Not that Tiger minded. It was a warm feeling to know he was loved. He had little of that.

He glanced at Ralphie's ashes resting on the night table, feeling the pang of the loss of his friend.

His mind returned to the first time they had met. It was through a street banker who worked for his father. Tiger had heard of the young buck who ran the breakwater docks with an iron fist. Tiger had also heard Ralphie was looking to get into better things. Since Tiger was recruiting for his new gang of thieves, he wanted to meet this new thug. When he did, he liked what he saw.

It was strange, Tiger thought, you can know a man for forty years and never get to know him. Or you can know a man for five minutes and be friends for life.

He stared at the urn, feeling emptiness for the part of him that had died. Tomorrow he would send a trooper back to Brooklyn with his friend's ashes. Tiger knew the Canzanna family would want Ralphie's remains.

O N the morning of the thirty-first, Tiger received word from Abruzzi that he had the target in sight.

Thirty minutes later a trooper arrived with a sealed envelope from Rizzo. Tiger closeted himself in his command post. Tiger quickly ripped it open to find a black piece of

327

paper with the name GUIDO CASTALDI typed in the center.

Tiger couldn't link up the name. He handed the note to Pete. "Do you know who this guy is?"

Pete read the name, nodded, and said, "Sure, he's one of our troopers. Why?"

"Mike Rizzo says Malone has him hidden to use against us later."

Pete was stunned. Forgetting for a moment his injured arm as he snatched up the phone, whispered into it, hung up, and looked at Tiger. "If that fucking bastard is walking the streets, we'll find him."

"I doubt if you find him. It's most likely we'll find him hidden in one of Malone's protection programs," he said. Who would tell him where Castaldi was hidden?

After lunch, Tiger and Pete retired to the command post to plan out the upcoming operation against Smilin' Jack and the couriers. Carefully they examined every newly arrived report sent up by Cat and Tony Orechicco.

Neither Tiger nor Pete deluded themselves this was going to be anything but hairy.

From interrogating Weasel, Tiger learned that ten teams of couriers were working out of the district attorney's office. Tiger assumed only three or four would be assigned to move evidence between the clerk's office and the court. The other six would be used for pickups and deliveries of evidence at city morgues, police laboratories, precincts, and so forth. That, thought Tiger, helped cut down on his manpower problems, providing the drugs hadn't been switched on the previous day. That would return him to zero and one hell of an operation would go down the drain.

Tiger was certain it would be one of the court couriers who would deliver the narcotics to Jack.

"We are using five cars to clock each courier," said Pete. "Should we add more?"

"No. If we can't do it with five, we can't do it."

Pete hesitated, looking perplexed.

"What's your problem?" Tiger asked.

"It's Jack I'm worried about. I'm wondering what kind of location he had in mind for the exchange. A parking lot, some deserted street, or in an enclosed building where we won't be able to see the turnover."

Tiger nodded slightly. "That had me worried for a while, but I have arranged for us to spend the day at Cat's place. From there, we can monitor Jack."

Again Pete looked perplexed, warning Tiger that he had another problem. "Now what's your problem?"

Pete shrugged. "What happens if Jack wears a jacket that doesn't have a transmitter in it?"

Tiger just stared at him.

T IGER was tired from the long night before and an early morning rising. They had left Swan Lake before daylight, accompanied by two troopers, one driving.

In Brooklyn, they settled into Cat's laboratory, amid the monitors, scanners, oscilloscopes, and all the other paraphernalia of his trade.

Cat sat quietly at his console adjusting and fine tuning his equipment. He threw a switch, filling the room with the smooth resonance of Smilin' Jack's voice.

Pete's sigh was audible.

Jack was talking to someone in an office. Then the sounds of traffic, a car starting, and radio music. For the next three hours, Tiger got the impression the agent was constantly in motion. Flittering from one thing to another. Calling secretaries, dealing with other agents, making and returning phone calls.

Jack gave the impression he enjoyed using other people to do his bidding.

Tiger grew bored listening to Jack's voice, thankful when the first clock moved in.

"My target has left the building and heading east on the Belt," said Tony Orechicco, team leader of the first unit.

Tiger placed a red pin on the large map indicating the location of the courier.

To Tiger, it seemed to be one hell of a long way around to get to Harlem.

"Stay on him," said Tiger.

"This is leader two," broke in Ferdi Gazzo. "He's heading up Flatbush Avenue."

Another possible strike-out, thought Tiger, because the second courier was heading into heavy rush-hour traffic.

"Stay on him," Tiger said, knowing Jack just might have changed the location for the exchange.

From Weasel, Tiger had learned that the couriers always delivered the material to him in Harlem so he assumed Jack would do the same, but with Jack one could never be sure.

Tiger sat impatiently waiting for the other two unit leaders to check in. After thirty minutes his patience snapped.

"Come in units three and four."

Both answered in unison.

"What the hell's happening?" he demanded.

"They haven't come out yet," each answered.

Tiger wondered what the tie-up was.

"This is leader one."

"Go ahead, Tony," answered Tiger.

"We're heading across the Verrazano Bridge toward Staten Island."

Tiger moved Tony's pin forward on the map.

Staten Island was in the opposite direction so he was sure leader one was out of the ballgame.

"Stay on him," Tiger answered, not wanting to take any chances.

Ferdi Gazzo's target was stuck in Brooklyn traffic so Tiger scratched leader two.

"My man just came out," said leader three, Mike Amato. A moment later he said, "Heading across the Brooklyn Bridge."

This might be it, thought Tiger.

"But he has three uniforms in the car with him."

Tiger was taken aback. What was he doing with three uniformed policemen in the car and where was his partner? Tiger knew something was wrong; he could smell it.

He quickly radioed the last leader, stationed outside the courthouse.

"Yeah, Tiger?" answered Big Che.

"Keep on the lookout for a solo courier."

"Got you."

Tiger knew it could be nothing. Or something.

"Leader three."

"Yeah, Mike?" answered Tiger.

"We're in Lower Manhattan."

"Where?"

"Across from police headquarters. The targets are having a cup of coffee in a restaurant."

"Out," said Tiger, wondering if he should scratch number three.

A few minutes later Tony reported in. "We're heading for the Richmond Avenue exit."

Ferdi's target was still tied up in traffic.

And Mike Amato's group was having coffee.

At six o'clock twilight was setting in as Tiger looked out the window. He knew Don Corso and the rest of the family were safely behind locked doors, waiting for the Night of the Dead.

Ferdi Gazzo called in that his target had pulled into a driveway on Ocean Parkway and seemed to have settled in for the night.

Mike Amato's courier left the three uniforms in the restaurant and proceeded to an open air garage in midtown. He then went into a coffee shop.

Tiger found that strange. The man had just left one restaurant to have coffee in another. That needed watching, decided Tiger.

"He's out," cracked Big Che's voice over the radio.

"How many men does he have in the car?"

"Two," answered Che.

That still left the missing courier. "Have one of your

331

vehicles remain behind until I know what happened to the one that disappeared."

"How will he spot him?"

Tiger made a quick calculation, estimating the courier should be carrying at least thirty pounds of narcotics. "He'll be carrying a large package," he said.

"Got you," signed off the big man.

In a moment Che was back on the radio. "My target's heading up the Brooklyn-Queens Expressway."

Tiger felt the excitement. The target was heading in the right direction.

"Stay on him."

A new voice came over the radio. "This is Vito."

"Yeah, Vito?" said Tiger, speaking to the man left behind.

"Nothing happening."

Damn, thought Tiger. "Give it another half hour, then disappear until I call you."

Now Tiger was forced to pin all his hopes on Big Che's courier.

On the map, Tiger followed Che's progress up the expressway. After passing over the Kosciusko Bridge, the courier had one of three directions to go in. Long Island to the right, straight ahead to Queens, or left to Harlem.

Suddenly, Smilin' Jack's voice boomed over the speaker. "I'm glad you got here."

Tiger was stunned, as were Cat, Pete, and the two troopers.

"The fucking jury took all morning to convict the bastard," said a voice Tiger recognized as one of the couriers.

"It's going down," said a shocked Pete.

Anger and frustration were building up within Tiger. "Do you know where the voices are coming from?" he asked in desperation.

Cat pushed back one earphone and looked at Tiger. "He could be anywhere," he said, returning to the dials.

"Where's your partner?" asked Jack, with no whisper of suspicion.

"He had to stay behind to finish the paperwork. He'll meet me later when we pick up the money," said the courier.

Cat looked over at Tiger. "It sounds like it's in a bar or coffee shop."

Tiger nodded. "I know," he said, reaching for the walkie-talkie. "Leader three, leader three."

"Yeah, Tiger?" answered Mike Amato.

"It's going down. They're in the coffee shop together."

"I'm ready," he said. "That means they have to come back for the goodies."

"Okay, let's go get the cookies," said Jack. "How much did you bring?"

"Forty-three keys."

Tiger heard Jack's delighted whistle. "It's Rolls-Royce and Riviera time," he laughed.

The courier let out a chuckle.

On the radio, Mike Amato kept up a running commentary of the target's movements.

"The courier is standing by his car and waiting for Jack's car to be brought down by the attendant."

Tiger shook hands with Cat and headed for the door when Mike's voice broke in again.

"I don't believe it."

"What's the matter?" asked an anxious Tiger.

"These two bastards have the balls to carry out the exchange right in front of hundreds of people," he said, in disbelief.

As Tiger's car pulled into traffic, he guessed Jack was getting cocky. A dangerous attitude.

"They're heading in the direction of the Westside Highway," said Mike.

So Tiger ordered the trooper driving to take the Brooklyn-Battery Tunnel, which led to the Westside Highway. Tiger guessed he was about ten minutes away from catching up with Mike.

"He's turning south on the parkway," shouted Mike.

Something was wrong. "What did you say?"

"He's heading south and running parallel to the river."

Damn, thought Tiger, he should be heading north.

Once in the cavernous tunnel, Tiger ordered the trooper to speed up, knowing radios would not transmit under the river.

Emerging from the tunnel, they headed north up Twelfth Avenue toward the oncoming Jack.

"We are crossing West 10th Street on Twelfth Avenue."

Tiger calculated the distance between him and the oncoming caravan. "Make a U-turn here and wait for them."

The trooper pulled over to the side of the road and parked.

"What's your position, Mike?"

"Two blocks short of Canal Street."

Tiger knew Jack was only three blocks back. He tensed as he studied each passing headlight. "What is the color of his car?"

"A Porsche, color red," answered Mike.

Tiger spotted the car as it zoomed by. He ordered his trooper to fall in line behind Jack's vehicle.

"I'm on him, Mike," said Tiger.

Now Tiger had time to wonder where the hell the bastard was heading? Some instinct warned Tiger that Jack was not heading toward his stash of drugs. Neither was he in the mood to play a cat-and-mouse game of tracking the agent all over the map. Not with Malone and his forces on the prowl.

He didn't know why, but he told himself he had to take Jack now. But this section of Manhattan was a bad place for rough stuff.

Tiger knew Jack had only two directions to go in. To take the upcoming Brooklyn-Battery Tunnel or beyond to the Staten Island Ferry. If Jack made the mistake of selecting the ferry, he would have him in a box, but the tunnel would be another matter. For one thing, thought Tiger, the traffic moving through it is too swift for any cowboy kidnappings. Besides there were at least twelve armed toll takers on the Brooklyn end.

As they moved along, Tiger was surprised to see the Porsche pass up the tunnel entrance, also the ferry terminal. That left the agent only the trip around the horn, the southernmost part of Manhattan.

By this time, Tiger had lost all sense of Jack's reasoning.

"Mike," he shouted into the radio, "we have to box him in within the next four blocks."

"Okay, Tiger."

Tiger knew the horn around the Wall Street area teemed with people during the day, but after five o'clock, the area quickly became deserted.

As the caravan moved forward, the traffic light ahead blinked amber. Tiger wondered if Jack would jump the light. He didn't.

In a flash, Tiger pulled alongside Jack's car on the left at a slight angle. Mike did the same on the right, thereby effectively blocking in Jack. Tiger and the trooper were the first out of the car, and a startled Smilin' Jack looked into the barrels of two pistols. Yet as Tiger looked into the limpid eyes, he knew the rogue was going to try for it and there was no way to stop him short of killing him. But Mike slid into the Porsche passenger seat, pointing his pistol at Jack's head and removing the agent's gun from its holster.

Tiger and the trooper pulled Jack out of the car. Pete hit him from behind, dumping him in a heap on the rear floor of Tiger's vehicle.

As they drove back to Swan Lake, Tiger and Pete kept Jack pinned to the floor with their feet and Pete's gun pointed downward.

Back in the safety of his country house, Tiger let out a sigh of relief. After coffee and sandwiches, Tiger had the rogue agent brought up from the cellar.

Tiger noticed the man's arrogance had returned as he was strapped to a chair in the living room. But the man's smugness vanished at the sight of the hypodermic syringe in Tiger's hand.

"Don't you have the guts to shoot me?" he said, in an attempt at bravado.

But Tiger was not in the mood for the man's overbearing manner, keeping in mind that this was the degenerate who kept his brother in drugs, the same man who intended to flood the streets with junkies, play one family against the other, while building a kingdom for himself on the misery of others. What was worse, this man had sold out his gun and his badge.

He filled the syringe with sodium pentothal. He nodded for the troopers to hold Jack. While he watched the agent struggle to avoid the needle, Tiger plunged it home.

As the drug took effect, Tiger pulled his chair closer and spoke softly.

"What is your name?"

"I am Special Agent Joseph Magaddino."

That took Tiger aback. "I thought your name was Tim McCoy."

"That is my cover name."

"The name Magaddino, is it Italian?"

"No, my parents were from Sicily."

That explained many things to Tiger. A bell also rang in Tiger's head, and he took a shot in the dark. "Are you related in any way to Gennaro Magaddino?"

"My grandfather."

Tiger let out a low whistle. Don Gennaro Magaddino was an old-time war lord who had ruled Brooklyn in the twenties.

Tiger changed the subject. "Who do you work for?"

"The Department of Justice."

"How long have you been with them?"

"Eleven years, three months, two weeks, and three days."

That figured, thought Tiger. Computer smile was also a computer brain.

Now Tiger felt Jack was ready. "What is your involvement with the Brooklyn property clerk's office?"

Slowly the story unfolded. "It started over two years ago with the arrest of a low-level drug dealer. The man made a statement that his drug connection was a policeman who was stealing drugs from the clerk's office. My investigation found out that a number of policemen were stealing. The investigation went clear up to Inspector Colby, the director of the clerk's office."

Tiger listened quietly.

"Since the whole operation was pilfering only a small amount of the narcotics stored there, I knew it was time to put a stop to it before it got out of hand. I knew that more and more drugs would be on the street."

Tiger wondered when the agent turned rogue, but he wasn't ready for those questions yet.

"So I broached my superiors in the department with an idea I had kicking around in my head. I believed so long as the clerk's office continued to hold a gold mine in drugs, greedy policemen were going to try to beat the system. On my recommendation, the department placed me in charge of a sting operation to control the flow of narcotics from the clerk's office and into Federal possession. At the same time, I set in motion a series of red herrings designed to hold everyone in abeyance until sufficient narcotics had been removed from the clerk's office. At that point, my agents would leak to the Sicilian families that one of the families was in the process of stockpiling vast amounts of drugs in order to corner the market."

Tiger listened in silence as he searched for flaws, but so far he found none.

"I was certain we could kill two birds with one stone. Get the families at each others' throats and acquire over a hundred million dollars' worth of drugs that weren't going to hit the streets again."

Pete and the other troopers in the room were enthralled, but Tiger felt a flood of emotions run through him, ranging from admiration to anger. Admiration for a brilliantly designed plan.

"That's when I made it a point to pay my respects to Inspector Colby, a sneaky, slimy creature. I told him I had enough to put him and his flunkies away for a thousand years if they didn't accept my offer to take over the operation and run it like a proper business. Especially when I promised to make them all rich. I warned him and his men that should they be tempted to move against me, I had copies of all the documents in a friend's possession. At first Colby and his boys objected when I told them I was paying twelve percent of the wholesale street price; but since they had no choice, they accepted. I also informed them that the twelve percent was only a token payment, to tide them over until all the narcotics were milked from the clerk's office. At that point, we would dry up the market, wait a suitable time, and then flood the market and make a killing." The agent paused.

"Did they accept the deal?" Tiger asked.

"Not at the first meeting. They thought I was crazy to try to milk the whole bundle. But in the end their greed got the best of them."

"Where did Sonny Corso fit into your plans?" asked Tiger.

"He didn't. I never met him."

That shook Tiger, so he checked the agent's eyes to make sure he was still under. "Then how come you used him to set me up in the Kit Kat Klub," Tiger asked, a slight edge to his voice.

"Who are you?" asked Jack.

"I am Joey Corso."

Jack hesitated, seemingly to absorb that information.

"I still never met your brother."

Tiger curbed his anger. "But you were at the exchange."

"I don't know what you mean by exchange. I went to the Kit Kat Klub because I was informed you were holding a woman against her will. I came away from that fiasco with egg on my face and the impression I had been used by Mister One Eye."

"And you never gave my brother any heroin?"

"No, never."

Tiger was thrown off base and wondered where Sonny got the pure. He made a mental note to open a dialogue with the Brooklyn Corsicans.

338

He changed the subject. "What was your relationship with Iggy Friedman?"

"After straightening out Colby I needed a flunky. Someone who was known in the business but not connected to any organization. I needed someone greedy but controllable. So I picked Iggy Friedman. Then I had a snitch who owed me set up Iggy for a drug buy. When I arrested him, he offered me a considerable bribe but I refused. When he raised the ante, I wavered. I knew he was desperate because I had him with two ounces of pure, a life sentence. I put Iggy in my car, handcuffed him, and then we talked. I gave him the impression I was after a lot of money. More than he could make in ten years. When I had him begging, I made him an offer. I promised to let him go in return for his setting up a network of street dealers for me."

Tiger signaled a trooper to bring him a cup of coffee.

"Iggy was suspicious at first, but I convinced him that my gun and badge would protect him. I saw that the temptation to deal with a Federal license appealed to him. So he accepted the deal.

"My deal was simple enough. My new partner was to use a warehouse he owned to store the drugs as they were received. He was to test the quality first, then seal it in plastic bags and place them in storage. In a room he was to select," said Jack pausing.

"Why did you go through all this nonsense, when you could have dropped off the drugs at F.B.I. headquarters?"

"For a number of reasons. I had no intention of ever letting those drugs back on the street. But for appearance sake, I wanted the streets to know I was in action with Iggy. But I had two main problems. One, I needed to convince my new partner he was in control of the operation. Like all street dealers, his ego would get in the way and soon he would have to let it slip that he was a big man. Before long, it would filter to the streets, knowing Colby would have an ear to the sidewalk. I needed that credibility with Colby. I had also convinced Iggy we were going to stockpile the drugs for two years before making one big score. And in that time Colby would wonder where the hell the drugs were going. I let Iggy sell some but I withheld the bulk of it. From time to time, I gave him samples to enhance his credibility on the street. I also had a terror session with Iggy. I put a pistol to his head, informed him that if just one grain of the white stuff turned up missing when it came time to tally, I would blow his fucking head off.''

Tiger believed he would have.

"My second problem was Inspector Colby. I knew it wouldn't take him long to pick up the whispers coming from Iggy and Harlem. I had no fear the inspector would move against my partner. I knew he would accept the information he was receiving.''

"And he did," said Jack.

"Then the drugs are still in the warehouse," said Tiger, holding his breath.

"No. They are in the cellar of the Federal Building in Brooklyn.''

That surprised Tiger. "How the hell did they get there?''

"It took about a month for my agents to find what room Iggy had the narcotics in. With a duplicate key they sneaked in once a month and replaced the drugs with milk sugar.''

Slick, thought Tiger. "What room was it?''

"Three fourteen," answered Jack.

"Where did Salvatore Delvechicco fit into the picture?''

"He didn't. I just needed a patsy to point the finger at.''

"Why?" asked Tiger.

"Everybody knew the Boccis were the greediest of the families. I knew when this scam was over, we would need a target to blame. Delvechicco was it.''

"But why him?''

"Why not him? He was a known Bocci henchman. We knew any rumor we started would be believed by the other families.''

Tiger found the deviousness of the agent annoying. Very Sicilian.

"Were you involved in the Bocci killing?" Tiger asked, taking a shot.

"Yes, in a way. I put a bug in Colby's ear that after the scam went down, and since Bocci was the intended target, it would be wise to set up a series of little disturbances to help point the finger at the Bocci family. Colby came up with the idea of throwing a scare into Joe Bocci himself by having someone take a shot at him. Somehow on the drawing board, Colby liked the idea so well he expanded it to a full-blown embarrassment of the Bocci family."

"How did Johnson fit in?"

"Colby recruited him. Johnson was facing a heavy fall on a drug rap. The inspector promised him just two years if he cooperated. He cooperated. I let Colby do it his way because I had already reached the halfway mark in stockpiling, and a little media exposure of a junkie trying to kill Joe the Boss wouldn't hurt."

"So what went wrong?" Tiger asked.

"We don't know. The bastard was only supposed to wave the gun around until someone knocked him to the ground. Instead, the crazy bastard started shooting . . . "

"What would explain his actions?"

"Nothing. But I had always felt someone was hidden in the background pulling strings."

"Why do you say that?"

"I don't know. Just a feeling."

Tiger was sure Don Corso could tell him who pulled the strings.

"Who was the black chick with Johnson?" asked Tiger.

"I don't know. I thought she was a loner."

Tiger decided to move on to another subject. "Why did you have taps placed in my old office?"

"I didn't."

"Could any of your staff have?"

"Not without my okay."

Tiger found the answer annoying, mostly because that left only two possibilities. Malone or Don Corso. From the chief inspector he would expect it. But from Don Corso? Against his own son?

Mulling over the information, he accepted Don Corso as

the culprit, especially if he planted the bugs after he killed Toto.

"What part of the puzzle is Malone?"

"Just a two-bit grafter with good connections. He owed Colby something from the old days. I never knew what, but whenever Colby needed something, Malone did it."

That would explain Bobby's transfer to Staten Island.

"How did you learn of my meet at the caterer's?" Tiger asked.

"Colby's men had found a snitch at the clerk's office and Malone transferred him. When the snitch showed up dead, I decided to take a closer look at Inspector Cassaro. From the Corso files, I found a connection between Don Corso and Cassaro. Your father paid for his education."

"That still doesn't explain how you knew of the meet."

"Mike the Cop let me read the note before slipping it to the inspector," Jack said simply.

"How did you turn my brother Sonny?"

"I myself didn't. He came to me, or I should say, to the department."

"I don't believe you," said Tiger, in shock.

"It's true. He came to the department and stated that he was the son of Don Corso and wanted to work for us."

Tiger felt the anger rising. "Why? What did you have on him?"

"Nothing. He came on his own."

That shook Tiger. He felt a sting of anger toward his dead brother. He could not conceive of Sonny betraying his own father. Perhaps Sonny had lost all sense of reason, but Tiger didn't think so. So he looked elsewhere for his brother's motives.

"I don't believe you," said Tiger, taking a shot in the dark.

"It's true. He came on his own."

That bothered Tiger. He knew his brother had been a lot of things, but an out-and-out snitch? No way.

"What information did he give you?"

"Just little tidbits, insights, good only for filling in on

your family's profiles. It was obvious your brother wasn't privy to the inner circle. Or even the outer circle."

Tiger continued searching for his brother's motives. "What did you mean when you said my brother wanted to work for you? Work against the Corso family, or in general?"

"He just seemed to want to get even with the dealers."

"So he went to work for you?" asked Tiger.

"On family matters I had no use for him. He was small fry, but he often visited the other agents at the office with bits and pieces of information. Nothing special."

Tiger still was not satisfied, something was missing. "How often did he visit the Federal Building?"

"Quite a bit. He was always having coffee with the other agents."

"Anyone in particular?" asked Tiger.

Jack's hesitation was brief. "Not really. No one special."

Tiger pounced. "You seemed to hesitate. Why?"

"Because in the beginning he tried hard to get close to Johnny Aloe."

"He's an agent?"

"No, a lab technician."

"A chemist?"

"Yes."

Now Tiger knew he was walking on egghells. "They were friendly?"

"In the beginning, they seemed to like each other. Your brother was always bringing coffee and porno films. Then suddenly Johnny turned off on Sonny."

Tiger's heart beat faster. "What did the Johnny Aloe look like?"

"He's Japanese."

Bingo, rang the bell in Tiger's head. Johnny the Jap, thought Tiger, Sonny's old college chum who used to deal on campus. He was always pushing homemade qualudes he manufactured in the chemistry lab.

Was Sonny trying to rekindle an old friendship and got rebuffed? Well, whatever it was, Tiger was sure his brother was up to something. People like Sonny didn't get friendly with cops without a good reason.

Tiger checked the agent's pupils and continued the questioning, wanting to fill in all the facts. When he finished, he sent the agent under guard to the cellar until he decided what to do with him.

Now that Tiger had the final truth, he turned inward, angry at himself for having been so wrong in his thinking. At the end of his mental flagellation, Tiger was convinced the agent was a smart Sicilian.

"You sure the serum works?" asked a dubious Pete.

"It works," said Tiger, disappointed.

Tiger sat in the room alone, assessing and reassessing the situation.

Then he returned to the living room where Pete and the other troopers were still sitting quietly, waiting for Tiger's next move. He sat at the table with Pete, poured himself a mug of coffee, sipped before speaking. "What do you think?"

"I think he was telling the truth," said Pete.

Tiger agreed. He felt the agent had not been preindoctrinated or whatever they do to spies in the movies. But that didn't solve his immediate problem. He was already swimming in an ocean of hot water. One more disappearance could blow the lid off this town. Even the family couldn't stay in the kitchen then.

Although Tiger was certain the agent's death could not be traced to him, the Feds would still ask a lot of unnecessary questions. And the press, too.

Leaving the table, Tiger headed to the cellar with a heavy heart. He saw no way but to let the agent go.

Downstairs he waved away the guard, looked over at the agent sitting with his back against the pool table, his knees drawn up. Jack's eyes followed Tiger's every move, as Tiger sat on the floor facing him.

"Do you want a cigarette?" Tiger asked, extending the pack.

Jack's cool gaze studied the pack. "Is this my last one?"

"It could be," said Tiger, keeping his gaze level.

Jack studied the look in Tiger's eyes. "No thanks, I just gave up smoking," he said, regaining some of his old cockiness.

They studied each other for a long silent time. "You know, I still owe you for a beating," said Tiger coldly.

The agent smiled. "So sue me."

Tiger was tempted to take a pipe and clobber the man. Instead he said, "What would you do if I were to let you go?"

The smile left Jack's face, and his eyes narrowed suspiciously. "I'd put you away for a thousand years," he answered simply.

"I was afraid you would say that. But why? I only invited you to my home for a little friendly conversation."

The agent's eyes softened slightly. "I figure it's a hundred years for kidnapping, another hundred for imprisonment of a Federal officer, not to mention obstruction of justice, car theft, and a dozen other charges."

Tiger ignored the agent's answer and studied the man's hard features. He noticed Jack's skin was lighter than most Sicilians, but the eyes and nose were right. It was the blond hair that bothered him. Sicilians don't have blond hair.

"Do you dye your hair?" he asked, out of curiosity.

"Sure do," said the agent, his smile returning.

"Why?"

"To give me a WASP look," he said simply.

Tiger wanted to smack Jack across his smug face. "You ashamed of your heritage, Mister Magaddino?"

Jack didn't turn a hair at the name. "I've never been ashamed of my background, only of my relatives," he said.

"They probably paid for your fine education," shot back Tiger.

Anger filled the agent's eyes as he glared at Tiger. "Let me tell you something, Mafia man. My family never gave me spit. I worked my butt off to get through school," he said, staring coldly at Tiger. "No one ever bought me off with blood money."

Tiger suddenly didn't know what to make of the man. But he knew one thing. No man who was a man would turn against his own people. He changed the subject.

"I found forty-three keys of heroin in the trunk of your car. What were you going to do with it?"

"I was taking it back to my office before lowering the boom on everyone. Especially what's left of the clerk's office."

Tiger's brows shot up. "What's that supposed to mean?"

Jack's sneer returned. "Don't you read the papers? You're a celebrity. A famous cop killer," he said with contempt.

Tiger studied the computer man. "That bothers you?"

"Not me. Whatever happened to Colby and his friends they deserved."

"So what's your problem?"

"It's your cold-blooded methods I don't like. Like my relatives, you solve all your problems with murder."

"Sometimes it's forced on us," said Tiger, softly.

"That's bullshit," Jack said viciously. "My grandfather always said, if a man gets in your way, knock him down."

"And don't you agree?"

"I don't. It's easier to go around him."

"And if he won't let you go around him?" Tiger asked.

"Then I'll knock him down."

Tiger studied that for a moment. "Then you're talking about a one-step difference. We knock down the moment they get in the way. You allow an extra shot," he said with cold contempt. "You are not noble. You're stupid."

Anger flushed Jack's eyes. "Because I live by a rule of decency you don't understand."

Tiger laughed. "That's horseshit and you know it. There's only one rule. Like the keeper of the rules would say: We exist in a world without rules, except one, the rule of survival. Strike first and fast. But somewhere along the way your values were twisted and now you live by the rules outsiders tell you to live by."

Jack balled his fists, and Tiger hoped he would let one loose.

Suddenly the agent's features softened. "I have to agree with you there. I sometimes wish I could forget the rules they taught us. Then I could wipe out hoods like you and your father with impunity. It would solve a lot of problems."

"Now you're talking like a wise guy," said an annoyed Tiger.

A pall of silence fell between them.

"Where do we go from here?" asked Jack carefully. Tiger was sorry Jack's words brought him back to reality.

"I don't know yet."

Jack's features turned soft. "What's there to know? You have me and a fortune in junk, so what's left to know?"

A sudden flash of anger filled Tiger as he coldly looked at the agent. "You have some idea in your head I did this all for the junk?"

"Is there something else you bastards care for?" snapped back Jack sharply.

A coldness filled Tiger. He rose to his feet slowly, walked to the corner of the room, picked up an ax handle resting there, and walked back to face the agent. "You calling me a fucking dope dealer?" he said, stepping closer, as he raised the club over his head. He was tired of the righteous bastard's smugness.

Although he knew he was facing sudden death, Jack held his ground. "Then what the fuck were you after? Why did you go through so much trouble to kidnap me?" he asked defiantly.

Tiger's anger held at fever pitch, but something within him fought to allow the condemned man his last smug speech.

"Because I thought you were a rogue agent about to dump your shit on the street."

They glared at each other. One about to lash out with the club and the other prepared to spring. Even in his blind anger, Tiger was able to see the change in the agent's eyes. There was doubt, suspicion, and bewilderment.

347

"Maybe we are on the same side in this," he said, still suspicious.

"We are, in a way," said Tiger, as he lowered the club carefully. "I've been tracking you for almost six months and knew you were behind the stealing from the clerk's office."

"I was, but not to put it back on the street."

"I know that now, but the only reason you're not dead is because I thought your stash was still out there."

The agent stared at Tiger with new respect. "So you also took out Sharky and One Eye," he said in wonderment. "I knew Colby was spooked by you, but I didn't know why. Now I do. He caught one of your men and was about to use him against you. Now Malone has him hidden away."

Tiger studied him. "If it's true, what's your position?"

Jack showed his surprise. "Me? I'm Federal. I deal with degenerate cops all over the country. Unless I know the man personally, I wouldn't trust the lot of them. My department takes a similar view."

Tiger felt the man was telling the truth. He knew the agent was not afraid to die, but he wasn't suicidal either. He thought hard and long before asking the next question.

"If I were to let you go, where would that leave me?"

"Since this was the end of my scam, I would force the state to institute a new security system. Then I would crucify the cops and the D.A.'s office."

"And the families . . . ? Tiger asked, leaving the question hanging.

"Obviously with the scam at an end, I can't get them to kill each other, can I? But that won't stop me from coming up with a better scheme for putting you out of business. Oh, and while I'm getting a medal, the publicity should cool things for a while. At least long enough to rebuild my fires . . ."

"You hate us that much?"

"Don't take it personal. I'm Sicilian, I need to hate something," Jack answered, with a slight smile.

They talked for another hour over coffee and cigarettes

before Tiger led him to the Porsche parked in the driveway, the package intact in the trunk.

Neither bothered to shake hands, but they understood each other a little better.

As Jack turned the key and the engine sprang to life, Tiger stuck his head into the window. "Remember, I still owe you a beating."

Jack laughed as he put the car in gear and headed down the driveway.

Over dinner, Tiger told Pete of the conversation in the cellar.

"Think he'll come at you again?" asked Pete with narrowed eyes.

"I don't think so, at least not on this deal. But he's a Sicilian. He'll never forget and he'll be back with a better scheme."

Pete's expression turned sour. "I think we should have just shot the bastard."

Tiger stared at him. "One day I may be sorry I didn't."

Tracking down Jack's narcotics scam had been a long painful road for Tiger. Looking back on the casualty list, it came to fourteen on the scoreboard for the visitors and one for the good guys. In Tiger's mind he was the loser, because he had lost Ralphie.

Well, at least it was over and it was time to pick up the pieces of his life. He badly needed some time with Jeanne and the kids, but mostly with Jeanne.

For now, he intended to cool out for a couple of days to get his health back.

349

T HE call from Don Corso came on the second day. He assumed the old man wanted a report since the media, with planted stories, were now swarming around the clerk's office. The circus was keeping Malone busy defending his relationship with Colby.

That evening, Tiger made a run into the city. For the flunkies in Don Corso's outer office, it was business as usual.

When Tiger stepped into the old man's office, he made it a point to try to catch a glimpse of the new playmate, but he was hidden in the darkness.

Tiger was anxious to get home to Jeanne, so he rattled off his report. Only once did Don Corso react and then only long enough to raise an eyebrow. That was when he told him that Sonny was a snitch.

When the report was completed, Don Corso asked only two questions. "Are you satisfied the Feds got all the drugs?"

"Yes, I am."

"Then where did your brother get his supply?"

"I don't know, but I intend to have a meet with the Corsicans."

Don Corso nodded his approval. "Good. I would like that cleared up." And then with what Tiger took to be a smile, "You did good. The Council will be happy."

Tiger remained silent. More interested in Jeanne than in glory.

"Guido Castaldi is somewhere in Brooklyn. We're trying to track him now," said Don Corso.

Tiger nodded, knowing he intended to do some tracking of his own.

"How involved in your affairs was Castaldi?"

Tiger was sure he showed his surprise. "He wasn't. I only used him just once, at the warehouse. Other than that he floated from outpost to outpost as he was needed," he said.

"Then what the hell does Malone want with him?"

Tiger shrugged. "I think if Castaldi was in enough hot water, he would say anything Malone wanted to hear."

Don Corso's nod was imperceptible, and Tiger knew he had hit the target.

"This thing might get a little out of hand, so I want you well protected. Tomorrow you take the ritual."

Tiger was filled with warmth and surprise. "When?" he asked, hoping his voice was level.

"Tomorrow night," Don Corso said, handing Tiger a slip of paper. "At this address."

T IGER made love to Jeanne twice that night. Each time she matched his need. Later she lay warmly in his arms as he smoked and looked contentedly at the ceiling.

"Joey?" she asked softly, almost in a whisper.

"Yes?"

"While you were away, they were saying a lot of bad things about you in the papers and on T.V. and the radio."

"So?"

"They say you killed a lot of policemen."

He felt a chill at the way she had said it. "They say a lot of things. Don't pay any attention."

"Momma said this time they are going to try to put you away for good."

Tiger wished this line of questions would cease. "Momma shouldn't say things like that."

But Jeanne was not letting go. "Is it true? Is it bad this time?"

Tiger blew a cloud of smoke skyward. Thinking hard how best to calm her fears. "Ever since I was a kid they've been trying to put me away. It's the same old game. You know that. You've been through it before. So forget it. If it gets serious, I'll tell you to start packing."

"You promise?" she begged gently.

"I promise."

She nodded and snuggled deeper into his embrace. "Everytime you come home, another piece of you is dam-

351

aged," she said, indicating his bandaged chest. "Soon there will be nothing left to make love to."

Tiger laughed and they fell into a soothing silence. "Joey?" she asked. Tiger tensed.

"Yeah?"

"I've never asked you what you do or even if what they say about you is true, but will you do me one favor, Joey?"

He looked gently down at her. Tears were filling the corners of her eyes. "What is it, Jeanne?" he asked softly.

"Don't let them take you away from me."

He smiled warmly at her, planting a warm kiss on her forehead. "I'm not going anywhere, Jeanne."

She smiled and snuggled in, but Tiger could feel the fear emanating from her.

T IGER decided to visit his office to see if Malone was going to let his fruit store open again. He was pleasantly surprised at finding Sergeant Alfred Defalco waiting for him in Lulu's.

"Now that Malone's busy elsewhere, I thought you'd show here," said Defalco as they shook hands.

Tiger smiled warmly. "Let's have some breakfast in my office," he said, indicating for a waiter to bring food.

"What brings you down here?" Tiger asked, waving Defalco to a seat opposite him.

"Official business and to say thank you for my brother."

Tiger shrugged off the thanks, more interested in the official business. "What's your problem?" he asked, noticing the sergeant fidget slightly.

"Four cops and Colby?" he asked, lowering his eyes.

Tiger's eyes narrowed. "What about them?"

"I'm assigned to investigate five homicides."

That could be helpful, thought Tiger. "Congratulations."

Just then two waiters entered, set up a table and two

chairs, and filled the table with platters of food and coffee. Then they withdrew as Tiger poured out two cups of coffee and waved Defalco to dig in. But instead the sergeant lit a cigarette.

Tiger's eyes narrowed. He deliberately filled two plates with ham and eggs, placing one in front of Defalco. He sat back, sipped his coffee, waiting for him to sample his food.

When the sergeant leaned away from the plate of food and instead took a long deep drag on his cigarette, Tiger asked, "You're not hungry?"

Defalco shook his head. "I ate a half hour ago."

Tiger nodded his understanding. "Have some coffee. It will wake you up."

But again Defalco waved him off.

Tiger remembered the old Sicilian saying, "Only Italians break bread with their enemies." It was a saying Tiger had heard often. Italians always lulled their enemies with a fine meal, then killed them. In Sicilian culture, they must warn the enemy he is an enemy. By refusing to break bread with Tiger, Defalco was sending the warning that he was an enemy.

"You were saying?" asked Tiger coolly.

"I said that's a lot of cops to bite the dust."

"I'm sure it was," said Tiger, digging into his food.

Defalco studied Tiger. "It doesn't bother you that they were policemen?"

Tiger felt no more for Colby and his men than he would have for a rattlesnake attacking him. "I feel sorry for their families. If they had families. But what's that got to do with me?"

"That's all you feel?"

Tiger studied the detective. "They were degenerates who killed your brother and would have contributed directly to thousands of deaths. What do you feel about that?" asked Tiger, his eyes boring into Defalco's.

"I know you are right, Tiger, but you should have handled them differently."

Tiger stared at him over the rim of his cup. "I don't

353

believe I'm hearing this conversation. And what would you have had me do differently?" he asked coolly.

"Damn it, Tiger, you didn't have to kill them," exploded Defalco.

Tiger took a moment to dab at his mouth with a napkin, then he settled back in his seat, carefully gauging the detective. "What makes you think I killed them? They could have run away?"

Defalco looked up sharply. He waved his hand as if to erase what he had said. "Okay, I said it wrong. But five cops are dead and it's not right."

Tiger stared long and hard. "Why?"

"Because they wore badges," exploded Defalco.

Tiger was taken aback. More surprised by the outburst than annoyed. "So do fraternities, so do department store cops, firemen, and garbage collectors. What makes your degenerates and murderers so special?"

"You know what I mean. The law is not always perfect, but it's all we have."

"Maybe it's all you and your friends have. Me, I'm a thief and I've never pretended to be anything else. My line of work don't approve of cops. I never promised anyone not to be a thief; but cops, that's different. Cops make promises, cops take oaths to uphold the dignity of the white knight club. But they're not white, they're gray, tarnished by the badge they wear. Yet I've never met a cop who didn't sooner or later believe that he was the law."

"Damn it, Tiger, I know a lot of cops are crooked. But it's our job to root them out."

"That's bullshit and you know it. Cops become cops because they want to be above people. And after a while on the job, they expect some tribute, like the Roman legions. And when they don't get their tribute, they take it and fuck what's right or wrong."

"You are wrong. There are a lot of good men in the department."

But Tiger waved him off. "Maybe there are, but they are swamped by the degenerates. Colby and his friends sold their low-life souls to the highest bidder. Yet you have the balls to tell me those cocksuckers should have been judged by the fraternal rules of Roman mercenaries," said Tiger, taking a moment to pause in the dead silence.

"Sergeant, I don't know if those cops are dead or alive, but if they are dead, then I hope they rot in hell."

The detective stared a long time at Tiger before shaking his head. "You're a hard man, Tiger."

Tiger laughed. "Do you know what your problem is? You see yourself as a white knight, but you're really Don Quixote fighting the windmills. And when the windmill finishes with you, you'll be chopped meat. And a martyr to the badge. A cheap nickel-plated one at that." He softened his voice. "Why don't you come in with me. I'll show you how to beat the windmills."

The detective laughed. "I appreciate that, but I have to do things my way. I came here out of respect because I still owe you. And I promise I will forget everything I know about you to this date. But starting tomorrow, I will begin from scratch to find out what happened to those cops."

"And if you do?"

Defalco took a long time to answer. "I will turn in my report."

Well, thought Tiger, there is nothing more to say. He guessed it was his lucky month because the whole fucking world was out to get him.

T IGER spent the next hour at the bank. As usual, Mister D escorted him to the computer room, pressed his buttons, and left him alone. He found six names above the rank of captain. Carefully he memorized each file, seeking the best one to approach with his offer. Then, as an afterthought, he decided to contact all six.

By three o'clock he was sitting in the rear room of a sleazy bar off King's Highway. He sat at the table with six strangers. A den of snakes and spiders, he thought.

The leader of the Corsican group was a man named Randli Nati, dark-skinned, with cold watchful eyes. He was a man not normally given to answering questions. But because Tiger was who he was, he showed great respect. After many questions, he told Tiger honestly that he'd never met or known his brother Sonny. Even if he had, he still would not have done any business with him without checking first with the Corso family.

After the meal, Tiger was still nowhere. Except to wonder where Sonny had got the pure.

AT seven, Tiger pulled into the long driveway of the huge mansion. He was alone. Tiger looked up at the shadow-splashed structure with its Gothic spires, arched stained glass windows, parapets, and granite block walls. The only things missing, thought Tiger, were the moat and drawbridge. The house exuded desolation and evil.

Were it not for the many limousines parked in the wrap-around driveway, Tiger would have assumed the place was deserted. No lights showed anywhere.

As he emerged from the car, two hardfaces stepped from the shadows. "May I help you?" said one. Neither face was visible.

"I am Joseph Corso."

"You are expected," said the same voice, indicating with the wave of an arm that Tiger was to follow him. The other man melted back into the darkness.

Tiger was led to a rear entrance, which opened onto a huge salon. The room was resplendent with a pink marble spiral staircase topped with balustrades of alabaster marble. The walls were paneled in fine oak and enhanced by classic, museum-quality paintings.

Tiger was waved into a large but dimly lit study where

four cold-eyed men sat around an oversized circular table. Tiger matched the hard faces with their names. Don Trevicanno, Don Ciampa, Don Degorio, and Don Vici.

Tiger noticed they were all old, thin, and small of stature. The skin was stretched over their faces, giving them a skull-like appearance.

Glancing beyond them into the shadows, he spied his father-in-law Tommy The Lip Ippolito and another man he remembered from Bocci's funeral. But Tiger could not remember his name.

This, Tiger knew, was the seat of power. From this room the Council ruled the five families. Quiet, shadowy men, recluses who shut out the world with its prying eyes. Each man at that table was the real boss of a family, and people like himself, Tiger, were only figureheads. These were the warlords, gods unto themselves.

Tiger had no idea which Council member controlled which family. He only knew his father-in-law and the other man were the judges. The final deciders in Council disputes.

Tiger looked from face to face, wondering to which one he would report once he was made. Was it to be to Don Trevicanno opposite him, staring coldly his way? Or was it Don Ciampa, whose gnomelike appearance made Don Corso apprehensive? Was it to be the vacant-eyed Don Degorio? Or the creature: the malevolent hunchback sitting to his right, the one with the dancing eyes that so frightened Tiger? Tiger glanced over at the empty chair at the table and wondered who was missing. And why wasn't he here? Each family had to be represented.

Tiger realized the answer. Although it was not unexpected, he was nevertheless stunned. It was the numbers game as usual. He who commands the most troops is the boss. Tiger knew Don Corso personally controlled six thousand troops and his father-in-law controlled two thousand. They controlled the marble factory. The few thousand troops left didn't matter. They were the bosses by virtue of their power. Tiger knew one man did not have to sit in attendance. The *padrone di tutti padrone*—the boss of all bosses—Don Corso.

Tiger was elated. Nothing could stop him from being made, because in their eyes his father was the supreme ruler of all the families. Tiger was giddy at the power he was being handed. It made his head whirl. Then he quickly sobered, feeling a pang of fear, from a direction he did not quite understand. That's when the fear set in and he knew he could lose it all by the flick of Don Corso's finger.

Tiger's attention was brought up sharply by a stiletto and a revolver being placed on the table before him. Also a small polished stone was placed before each man at the table, and in front of the empty chair. Two extra stones remained on the table and Tiger assumed they belonged to his father-in-law and the other man.

Then a slip of paper, a glass of water, and box of matches were placed on the table by Don Trevicanno, who looked coldly up at Tiger.

"Joseph Corso," he said, as if from a distance, "are you prepared to be judged?" He spoke in the bastardized Latin that is latter-day Sicilian.

"I am ready," said Tiger, expecting a row of black-hooded men to chant their way into the room.

Looking stern and watchful, Don Trevicanno placed the revolver crosswise on the stiletto. "These are the weapons you will live by. They will be your protection and your comfort against all enemies of the family. Use them swiftly and in honor. Your enemies shall become our enemies, and our enemies shall become your enemies. Do you agree?"

Tiger did not hesitate. "I agree."

In unison the others in the room chanted, "He agrees."

Tiger felt the desire to laugh, but the coldness of the eyes surrounding him stopped him. Fuck them, he thought, if they want to believe all this bullshit, who am I to say otherwise?

Don Trevicanno picked up the slip of paper, crumbled it into a ball, placed it in Tiger's cupped palms, and lit it with a wooden match.

As the ball of paper burst into flames, Tiger almost pulled back, but Don Trevicanno's riveting gaze held him in check.

"As this fire burns, so will your soul if betrayal is in your heart. If your thoughts are not pure, the gods of vengeance will be visited upon you. Do you agree?"

"I agree," said Tiger, fascinated by the fire that threw no heat, just a pungent garlic smell.

"He agrees," chanted the others.

Reaching across the table, Don Trevicanno took the stone from before Don Ciampa and placed it to the left of the revolver. A second stone was taken from Don Degorio and placed a slight distance from the other, on the right side of the gun and knife. Two more stones were placed above the others. These stones belonged to Don Vici and Don Trevicanno, making a perfect square around the weapons.

"These were the stones of virtue, integrity, justice, and honor. They are the sentinels of our family life. Do you agree?"

"I agree," said Tiger.

"He agrees," chanted the others.

Taking the two stones from the center of the table, Don Trevicanno placed them above justice and honor, then looked passively over the flame at Tiger. He picked up a glass of water and doused the flame. Tiger felt the cool water run through his fingers, as Don Trevicanno picked up the remaining stone from before the empty chair and placed it in Tiger's palms.

"We the guardians of the house of seven points bid you enter our home and our family," he said tonelessly, indicating the two stones above the square. "This is the stone of the moon and the stone of the earth. In your hand you hold the sun stone. With it you shall complete the pyramid of life. When you place the stone, you will become a man of honor, of respect, wealth, and power." Don Trevicanno watched Tiger's eyes closely. "Do you, of you own volition, wish to enter the house of the seven points?"

Tiger wished to hell they wouldn't drag this thing out so, but with all eyes upon him he quickly said, "I do."

"He does," chanted the men around him.

Don Trevicanno guided Tiger's hand to the apex of the pyramid. After placing the stone in position, Tiger settled back and noticed the seven stones made a perfect house.

Don Trevicanno reached for Tiger's hand, quickly slashed it on the third digit and let the blood run through Tiger's fingers and into the don's palm. The stiletto blade was swiftly bathed in the hot blood. Don Trevicanno handed it to Tiger.

"Use this well. You are now brother to the house of one, the family. Also the fire that singed your hands will identify you forever. Wherever you go in the world, men of honor will do your bidding." He kissed Tiger on the right cheek. Tiger stood at attention as the others filed by, gave him their kiss, and left the room. Then Tiger was alone with Don Trevicanno.

"You will continue making your reports to your father," he said, dismissing Tiger.

Outside, Tiger noticed the emptiness of the driveway. Only his car and one limousine remained, telling him who owned the huge mansion.

Don Trevicanno was high in the family structure, but according to the placement of the stones, he was only of the square, while Don Corso was the apex of the pyramid. Yet Don Trevicanno lived in splendor while the old man lived a threadbare existence.

So Tiger reported on the meeting with Randli Nati, the Corsican leader. Don Corso showed little interest in the report, which surprised Tiger. As to the meeting with the Council, he seemed even less interested.

With the report over, Don Corso stopped counting his money long enough to settle back, light a cigar, and study his son.

"With the narcotics business behind us, I think it's time for us to look to the future. To where the family will be in ten to fifteen years. The growth of the family will depend on how times change and on how we control our own changes. You talked one day of the future family, of the time when we begin to hide the past. Well, that time is upon us. We cannot continue to be protected by the knife and the gun. We need stronger weapons, more power in the proper places. *Our* power," he said, pausing.

Tiger wondered why the hell the old man was talking to him like this when if he didn't kill the eyewitness cop, he wouldn't have a future.

"But," continued Don Corso, "before we can think of the future, we must deal with the present. Namely Guido Castaldi."

Tiger felt better, knowing the old man was onto his problem.

"We have located the traitor."

Tiger's heart skipped a beat. "Where?"

"It doesn't matter. He won't be there long. He is being transferred to a permanent location, where he will be terminated. As delicately as possible."

That still didn't solve Tiger's problem. "Wouldn't it be simpler just to hit the eyewitness cop? Especially since I already have him targeted?"

Don Corso's head shot up, his eyes a thin coat of frost. "You are forbidden to make any moves in that direction without my permission. Do you understand that?"

Tiger understood.

Don Corso continued, cunning now showing in his eyes. "Together the two witnesses are enough to convict you, but if we eliminate the traitor, Malone might drop the case for lack of evidence."

"And if he doesn't?" asked Tiger carefully.

"Then Malone's case will collapse when we hit the policeman," said the older man dispassionately. "I would hesitate hitting the policeman until all avenues are exhausted."

Tiger understood. "Otherwise this town will be unlivable for me."

"Yes. They wouldn't let you function. Malone would plant a small army on your doorstep, not to mention the possibility of an overzealous cop setting you up for a hit."

That prospect didn't excite Tiger.

"So we must make every effort to cripple Malone's investigation."

As usual, Don Corso's reasoning was sound, so Tiger said, "Where do I go from here?" wondering what his being made would mean to his position as a boss.

"Everything is back to normal. Why don't you try to relax a little, and take your family to Swan Lake for a few days?"

But for Tiger, Swan Lake held too many ghosts. "I think I'd rather take the kids to Disney World."

Don Corso half smiled. "That's good. That's good." He returned to his stacks of money. "Oh, if you find time, try to find out where your brother got the pure."

Tiger tensed. "Is it important?"

"No, not at all. It's just one of those loose ends that bother me."

S TEPPING from the private plane, Tiger and his family were met by Pete and Tony Orechicco with two rented station wagons. One was for Tiger, Jeanne, and the kids, the other for the luggage. Tiger looked at the mountain of suitcases and wondered what the hell they left in New York.

Tiger's thinking in coming to the island was to acquaint his family with the place in the event New York became uninhabitable. He liked the place and it would be a good base to operate out of. He knew with enough money, he could turn the swamps into lush lawns and make the place a paradise.

Driving through the marshlands, Tiger noticed that Jeanne did not look too pleased. But the moment they crossed the drawbridge, she brightened. "It's lovely, Tiger," she said.

Cathy and Rosario were even more excited at the two ponies tethered in front of the house.

"Dad, who owns the ponies?" asked Rosario in awe.

"You and Cathy do," he said, greatly enjoying the wonderment in their eyes.

Cathy smiled up at Tiger. "Which one is mine, Dad?"

"Well," said Tiger, "since you are the smallest, you get the little one."

They galloped off to meet their new friends.

Turning to a smiling Jeanne, he said, "Do you think we can make cowboys out of them?"

She hugged his arm. "I think it could be fun to try."

As they walked to the house, Tiger glanced at his son and daughter sitting on their ponies while two troopers led them around the island.

Inside, Jeanne found the house breathtaking. After Helen was killed, Tiger hired a decorator to redo the ranch house. Tiger knew his wife would like the blend of Italian Provincial and the rough texture of cedar, exposed beams, and granite.

Tiger was delighted as Jeanne's eyes danced everywhere. From the large ultramodern kitchen to the all-brick dining room to the sunken living room. She ran from room to room, delighted by each new surprise. There was a bedroom for each of the children, replete with shelves and closets.

Returning to the living room, she kissed Tiger and looked knowingly at him. "I could be happy here, Joey," she said simply.

Tiger knew she had received the message: "It might come to that."

Her features turned reflective as she nodded her understanding.

Suddenly there was a cacophony of barks and shouts.

Rushing outside, Tiger found his Dobermans Devil and Satan tormenting the ponies in preparation for attack.

Tiger shouted and the dogs settled down.

Jeanne smiled. "I think you better introduce Devil and Satan to our new friends."

Tiger nodded and commanded the dogs to sit. He had the children bring their ponies for a thorough sniffing by the dogs. When it was over, the dogs decided to investigate the rest of the island.

As the attendants buckled him and the children in, Tiger looked over the frail, twisting monorail structure of the ride called Suicide Twist. He didn't especially appreciate the idea that the operator of the ride was controlling the ride from the ground while he was in the air. If he was to die, he wanted the pilot with him.

After his children's attempt to kill him, Tiger suggested saner forms of entertainment, like cars crashing into walls or walking through fire.

Jeanne impishly took delight in his misery by pointing out the really daring rides.

That night, back on the island, they built a campfire on the front lawn and roasted marshmallows while the troopers sat and watched.

Later Tiger took Jeanne for a tour of the island, pinpointing certain landmarks—the places where 3.6 million dollars was buried in glass jars.

"Why are you telling me this? Are you expecting trouble?" she asked, her eyes alert.

"No. Let's say it's a bribe."

"What kind of bribe?"

"You can have all this money in return for one promise."

Her eyes turned serious. "I don't need your money to make you a promise."

"You will when you hear this one," he said, passively.

"I promise, Joey."

"That you will never take me to that fucking Disney World again."

Jeanne burst into laughter and threw her arms around Tiger. "I promise, and now I'm going out and spend all that money on a new wardrobe."

TIGER found himself unloading suitcases long after the children fell asleep. All through the long flight home, Rosario and Cathy had talked only of the island and their ponies.

It had been a long day, and Tiger was exhausted. So he decided to leave all the extra luggage in the garage overnight.

Tomorrow would be soon enough to unpack.

He cleared away a few things to make room on the closet shelf for suitcases, when he spotted the large bag he had half forgotten. It contained Sonny's personal belongings.

He hesitated opening it because of an eerie sense of intrusion. But Tiger felt there were greater considerations than respect for his brother's memory.

Sonny seemed to have an endless supply of leather vests. He searched each, including the linings, hoping to find something. He found nothing. He was not even sure what he was looking for or if there was anything to look for.

He found many photographs of Sonny and Helen. Both were thinner and younger in the pictures, and in every picture Helen's elfin quality surfaced.

Looking under an sweatband, he spied a small-caliber Derringer and wondered how long his brother had been packing it.

Continuing to search, he found a dozen sets of different credentials, including matching credit cards and birth certificates. He checked off the names, but none rang a bell. He slipped them into his pocket, sure that he would find a use for them sometime or other.

A packet of letters from Helen to Sonny were next in line for examination. Most were sent to him when he was in prison and later in the cure center. They were crammed with promises of a bright, beautiful future. Some future, thought Tiger.

Suddenly Tiger straightened. He found one letter only three months old. It was addressed to Sonny at a number on Atlantic Avenue. He made himself a mental note to check out the address.

Again the letter was filled with promises of love, and he

found it annoying that Sonny was in contact with her throughout all his bullshit games. Suddenly, one line stuck out. "When this is over," she wrote, "we will be free of everyone."

The words bothered Tiger. What was it that would make them free? Drugs? Money? Both? Could they have expected to have run away on the forty thousand dollars stolen from his house? No. Weasel had grabbed that.

Could it have been the pure he found the night his brother had stabbed him? There were enough drugs there to have retired on. Why hadn't they?

The questions plagued Tiger and the answers eluded him.

Was it possible Helen stole the pure from Iggy? No. He couldn't buy that. Helen might have been in a position to pass some information to Sonny, but she certainly was not in any position to do more. Iggy kept too tight a rein on his property.

For a moment he put aside the packet of letters and continued searching.

In Sonny's wallet he found the name and address of SPEEDY MOVING & STORAGE.

Again, he thought of the letter, rejecting the very idea that his brother could have pulled off a deal against Iggy. It wasn't feasible. Even had he stretched his imagination and given Sonny more credit than he deserved, he was still stuck with the overwhelming odds against it. For one thing, where would he have got a key to the warehouse. How did he learn what room the drugs were in, secure a key to that room, and know that the material would be there at that moment?

No, there were too many variables.

Finding nothing further in the wallet, Tiger felt a sense of disappointment.

He searched it again. Nothing. He turned it over in his hand, not wanting to discard it. He was drawn to the long trucker's billfold decorated with peace symbols and flowers. Something in the design bothered him.

Taking a moment to study it under a magnifying glass, he again found nothing.

He turned it over and over, upside down and right side up, and then it hit him. Raising the wallet to the light, he tilted it slightly and saw the printed impression of an overlay design. Its sheen overrode the original dull symbols.

He realized the overlay had been made with a thin ballpoint pen.

Leaning on the hood of the car, Tiger traced over the lines of the design. After completing it, he looked at it through the light, sure that it was some sort of map.

Tiger rotated the abstract design, hoping to strike some note of recognition. What looked like water and a wharf line were on the bottom, while two parallel lines ran perpendicular to the water. At the right end of the parallel lines, four square boxes of two each flanked the double lines. This was topped by what looked like railroad tracks. The boxes ran counterclockwise with the numbers 241 through 246 within. Only the box numbered 246 had a circled X. At the other end of the parallel lines was another circled X.

Tiger was sure the parallel lines were a street, bordered on one end by water and by a railroad at the other end. The boxes could be houses with the street numbers on it. But what the circled X's stood for, Tiger could only guess. But he didn't think Sonny drew a map on his wallet for his amusement.

Tiger made another tracing and hid it in his wallet. Finished, he returned to the car and searched the glove compartment for street maps. Nothing, but he promised to get maps in the morning.

In the office, Pete sent a trooper to buy a selection of street maps, especially of the Harlem area. Then they laid them all out on the floor, hoping to match the landmarks. They batted zero.

Tiger felt he had nothing to lose by a visit to Speedy Moving and Storage, where he showed Johnson, the warehouseman, Sonny's picture.

Johnson studied the photograph, but he was doubtful. "Is this an old picture?" he asked.

Tiger nodded. "About three or four years old."

The man studied the picture again. "This could be Mister LaCasta in Room 844," he said finally.

"Is he a long-term renter?"

Johnson checked his files. "Yes. Almost two years."

Tiger was excited. Just about the time Sonny went to work for him. "Is it possible I could look at the room?" he asked softly. He was surprised at how quickly the warehouseman handed him the key.

"You know the way," he said, like an old friend.

On the eighth floor they stopped at Room 844. Tiger nervously inserted the key, unlocked it, and pushed against the door. It was dark in the cubicle and as Tiger flipped the light switch, he found the room filled with what he hoped he wouldn't find.

He stood there assaulted by the sickly smell of milk sugar and old plastic glue. After searching, they found no heroin, but enough paraphernalia to tell him this was the factory for the repackaging.

His mind swirled and he was filled with doubts, suspicion, and disappointment in realizing both Sonny and Helen had set up this operation right after Iggy and Jack had formed their partnership.

It was now obvious to Tiger that Sonny used the money he skimmed from his stores to finance the warehouse, transportation, and the hiding of the narcotics. It was incredible. Absolute madness in concept and execution. He now realized Sonny had worked long hours before replacing the stolen drugs with milk sugar. Then he returned the false packages to Room 314.

To Tiger it didn't make much sense because it was full of holes. True, neither Jack nor his agents would have reason to suspect the packages were switched, that was the lab people's responsibility. So why, wondered Tiger, didn't they catch the switch and test it?

Was it possible Sonny had someone on the inside? In the lab? An old college chum named Johnny Aloe, alias Johnny the Jap? Was that the reason he was hanging around the Federal Building? Did they make a deal and decide to cool their friendship in public? Tiger thought so, but were the Feds that incompetent? Or was Sonny that cunning? After all, he was a Sicilian. The overall plan was brilliant and the operation flawless, so why he would leave a detail like that hanging around loose? No. Sonny and Johnny the Jap were in it together.

Tiger leaned against the wall to steady himself. Stunned by the realization that the Elf and the Dreamer had caught the brass ring. Believing it held the key to their own private heaven. A Utopia of love created by a mountain of white powder.

Now Tiger understood Sonny's death note. "I am King of the Mountain." He meant a mountain of heroin. He felt sick.

He had to admire their ingenuity. The Feds, the police, and even the family were outsmarted by a couple of street junkies. But his admiration did not last long. He remembered his brother's slow decay.

Tiger could forgive Helen because she was a loser from the day she was born to a hooker mother and an alcohol-soaked father. But his brother Sonny was a different matter. He had choices. Many. Yet he chose this.

Tiger found it a paradox that Sonny needed heroin in order to build his Utopia. So he set out to steal enough drugs to keep himself in oblivion forever. Then he was prepared to sell enough, just enough, to kill a thousand miserable faceless people like himself. Those poor creatures he most identified with, his friends, junkies.

O N the way back to Brooklyn, Tiger decided to check out the address on Atlantic Avenue. It turned out to be in a rundown section with a pawnshop, shabby Arab restaurants, and a Gypsy fortune teller. Number 246 Atlantic Avenue was boarded up.

Tiger studied the area and looked beyond the subway kiosk on the center island, across a wide avenue, to the sign LONG ISLAND RAILROAD in fading paint across the front of an old dirt-mired building.

Tiger had Pete head the car down Atlantic to see if it ended at the water. It did.

To the right of the water was a row of neighborhood stores, topped by an apartment. There was no opposite street. It was all parkway.

Tiger studied the roadway where the map indicated an X and saw nothing. Not even a manhole cover. Certainly nothing to indicate a secure place to hide a fortune in narcotics.

Back at the railroad, Tiger examined the boarded-up house. He found it inconceivable that someone would hide a hundred million dollars' worth of heroin in a neighborhood teeming with derelicts, junkies, and thieves. But he checked the lock anyway, assuming it hadn't been opened in years. But the lock on the boarded-up store was new.

"Let's check the neighborhood for real estate agents. I want to know who owns this building," he said to Pete and the two troopers.

An hour later they found the place and thirty minutes after that, they had a set of keys and a lease.

Picking up a couple of flashlights, they returned to the building. Pushing open the door, they were greeted by the rank odor of mildew. With creaking steps, they ascended to the first level, opened an apartment door, and found it empty. Not even a broken piece of furniture. The rest of the apartments were the same.

They smashed the lock to the cellar. As they descended the slippery steps, Tiger brushed away the spider webs. In the cellar, they walked slowly through slushy mud, pushed aside pieces of old furniture, stepped around an old boiler, and watched rats scurrying away from them. Running the flashlight beams over the cellar, they found nothing.

"Shit!" exclaimed Pete in disappointment.

Tiger felt off balance. He was unnerved, wondering if he weren't getting too old to chase shadows. Perhaps, he thought, in his anxiety for quick answers, he was overlooking the obvious. He knew paranoia had a way of using blinders on its mad dash toward obsession.

In his mind, he examined the tracings. Racking his brain, knowing if Sonny wasn't a total fucking idiot, then those circled X's had to have meaning. He ran the flashlight beam over the empty room, hoping against hope he had missed something. He hadn't.

In frustration, Tiger grabbed the iron bar resting against the wall and began jabbing at the walls, gouging out large holes in the plaster. All he succeeded in doing was to cover themselves with debris and dust. Undaunted, Tiger pounded the steel bar against the concrete floor. In spite of the heavy mud, sparks flew.

Slowly, Tiger crossed the room, pounding the floor as he went. Finally he was rewarded with a hollow sound. He continued tapping until he outlined a large square eight feet by six feet.

"Get a couple of shovels down here," he said to no one in particular.

As he waited, he fought to control his impatience and studied Pete in silence.

Ten minutes later, two troopers skimmed away the muddy surface, revealing two steel doors.

Tiger noticed Pete and the troopers were apprehensive about entering the unknown. What made Tiger hesitate was the muddy slime. It had not been disturbed in years. Then how the hell did his brother know so much about the place?

Tiger now wondered if indeed Sonny had ever seen those doors before?

Well, decided Tiger, it was the moment of truth. He reached for the recessed handles and yanked the door open only to let it quickly fall back into place. One whiff of the putrid smell coming out was enough to send them scurrying up the stairs.

Outside, they took a moment to get themselves under control.

"That shit is poison," said Pete, taking a deep breath.

Tiger nodded. "We'll need gas masks before we go into that hell hole," said Tiger, noticing their expressions of agreement.

On the way back to the office, Tiger gave Pete a list of equipment he would need by morning, when he intended to enter the subcellar.

At the office a message waited for him.

He sped across town and arrived within the hour at his father's office.

"Guido Castaldi is no more," was all Don Corso had said.

Instead of going home, Tiger decided to return to his office. On the way back he called Lawyer Rizzo to stand by, knowing Malone would be coming for him.

Tiger was picked up two hours later and interrogated by Malone for over six hours. He pounded and pounded at Tiger, but Rizzo fielded the difficult questions. Reluctantly Malone let him go, but with promises of vengeance.

Now that Tiger was back in the media spotlight, he was forced to cancel his expedition into the subcellar. At least until he knew which way Malone was going to jump. But Tiger had no illusions: Tin gods always lived in fear when they lost control of a situation.

Tiger was most surprised by the media. He thought as usual they would be nailing his hide to the barn door, but they were fairly subdued. He guessed they were like all New Yorkers: They didn't like snitches.

On the third, he was summoned to a meeting with Don Corso. "I have just received word that Malone is getting an indictment and will go ahead with the trial eight weeks from now."

Since the news was not unexpected, Tiger said, "I guess he likes his publicity. What does Rizzo say?"

"He thinks Malone and the rest of the police department intend to nail you. Any way they can. A little lying or terrorism won't stop them."

Tiger nodded his understanding. "Then I have to go for the hit," he said bitterly.

And they might come for you, he thought, not caring if the old man read his mind or not.

"Then I'll set up the hit," he said, knowing he had time. With eight weeks before the trial, anything could happen. Malone could have a heart attack, the policeman could die of natural causes, or the tooth fairy could steal the D.A.'s records.

T HE gas masks helped as Tiger opened the steel door. He pointed the flashlight beam, picked up a set of stairs that ended in total blackness. It was a long flight of steps. Suddenly, he became confused. What was it that threw him off balance? The mud. There was no mud on the steps, just layers of dust. Tiger ran his beam beneath him. There were no footprints in the dust either. How the hell did Sonny know about this place if he had never been here?

Continuing, Tiger moved to the right as everyone ran lights over the chamber. It reminded Tiger of the bunkers in Korea. Looking ahead, he saw no footprints in the dust and knew this tunnel had not seen a human in thirty or forty years.

So he reversed his course until he spotted another flight of stairs. The steps there were covered with footprints. Tiger took a moment to calculate and realized the flights of stairs were ten feet apart. His flight led up to the boarded building, but the second flight led to the cellar of the Gypsy fortune teller. He guessed the Gypsies must have moved in after Sonny's death.

With that problem solved, Tiger's beam followed the footprints that headed down the long tunnel. From the map tracing, Tiger knew the tunnel ran straight for over a mile.

"This place gives me the creeps," said one of the troopers.

"Yeah, it reminds me of my apartment," said another.

Tiger remained silent, not wanting their fears to get to him. Along the dreary route, they passed broken crates, broken whiskey bottles, and other debris, which indicated to Tiger that this tunnel had once been used as a bootleggers' drop.

As the rats scampered by, they raised trails of dust. Tiger wondered where the hell rats found food down here. A dozen feet ahead, they found a partial answer. A skeleton lay against a wall with two bullet holes on the left side of the skull.

"Shit!" said Pete.

Tiger smiled as Pete continued looking over his shoulder at the skeleton.

"You're making me nervous," said Tiger softly.

"I wonder who it was," Pete said, letting the eeriness and the shadows get through to him.

"Probably one of the broads who were to meet us at the cemetery," Tiger said, with a slight chuckle.

"Shit."

Tiger assumed they had passed the halfway mark. A little further along, they found two more skeletons. One was without a head. Tiger wondered what happened to it.

"Maybe the rats used it as a bowling ball," said Pete, laughing at his own joke.

But Tiger didn't find it amusing. They continued to pass scattered debris, and from the amount of dust on the cardboard containers, he guessed the place hadn't been used since the Second World War. How, he wondered, did his brother ever stumble onto it? Let alone have the balls to come down here alone?

Suddenly the tunnel widened into a room, a wide chamber filled with decayed wooden frames. Tiger spied the remnants of paper target sheets. This tunnel had been used as a shooting range.

Then he saw it, the two large wooden crates resting against the rear wall. The sight of the six-foot crates convinced Tiger that he had completed his quest.

Slowly Tiger approached them, carefully checking for booby traps. He found none.

A large band of steel was wrapped around both crates and secured by a heavy padlock. He looked around for a metal bar with which to break the lock. Finding nothing, he ordered Pete to blow it away. When the echo of the gunshot faded away, Tiger ordered two troopers to open the crates. Then he knew what a hundred million dollars worth of heroin looked like. He didn't like the look.

The plastic-wrapped packages were stacked to the top of the crate. Tiger assumed the second one held the same.

Tiger understood the dealers and suppliers who were only after a fast buck. People, Tiger knew, the government could put out of business in six months. But he also knew they wouldn't because it was a matter of method. The government was shoveling millions into cure programs that would never work and millions more into trying to stop the smugglers who were continuing to beat the government because the smugglers knew how to play the numbers game. They knew enough heroin would always filter through to make the game worthwhile.

Tiger knew the street value of heroin was about three to five thousand dollars an ounce. Yet the government was capable of producing the drug for less than twenty-five dollars an ounce. One hell of a discrepancy, Tiger thought.

Tiger had no illusions. He knew the two crates were not going to change the world. Not when every ship and plane was bringing in new supplies each day for the needle-hungry addicts.

It was the future of the families he was most concerned with. The future of Jeanne and the kids and the greater future he was now a part of.

Like it or not, the new family had to be part of this society and as such, they would have to deal with these problems. It could no longer allow contamination by drug degenerates. This was what disturbed Tiger the most. He was aware the new family could not grow in a decaying society. Where the energies needed to combat its enemies would be dissipated by the internecine war for drug profit.

375

He remembered his youth, remembered when the old-time dons first imported the dream stuff into this country. They used the excuse that the drugs were only going to be used by blacks. Now the children of the dream merchants were the new breed of addict.

This, Tiger knew, was what the family had to guard against, the sins of the father being visited upon the sons.

Looking at the crates, Tiger thought of Smilin' Jack and knew he was going to call about the drugs. Slowly, they made their way back to the boarded cellar, slammed the steel door shut, and removed their gas masks.

"Shit, I need a drink," said Pete with a nervous chuckle.

Suddenly, Tiger looked up to find Big Che standing in the shadows. His long, drawn expression told Tiger there was trouble.

"What is it?" Tiger asked, curious how the big man knew about the cellar.

"Your father's upstairs."

Tiger's eyebrows shot up. "Here?" he asked, in surprise, as a funny feeling began to tighten in the pit of his stomach.

"How did you know I was here?" asked Tiger, suspiciously.

Big Che shrugged. "Your old man called me and told me to meet him here. When he showed up, he sent me down here to look for you."

"How long have you been waiting?"

"Over an hour."

Tiger was too keyed up to ask more questions. Instead, he said to Pete, "Before you come up, seal this place good."

Out on the sidewalk, Don Corso's black car was parked at the curb, sandwiched between two other cars filled with hardfaces.

As Tiger opened the rear door, he spotted other cars up and down the street. He wondered what was happening to warrant so much security.

Tiger settled in the seat next to the old man.

"What's going down?" he asked.

Don Corso's enigmatic features measured Tiger. "You

tell me," he said, pointing to the boarded-up building. "What's going on in there?"

Tiger thought it was a hell of a time to make a report, but he gave a brief one. He explained about Sonny's wallet and the subsequent finding of the drug cache. When it was over, Tiger saw the pleased gleam in Don Corso's eyes.

"I was just about to call the Feds to haul it away."

"Are these the drugs the Feds believe are in their vault?"

Tiger smiled coyly. "Yes, but I don't think they'll be too embarrassed at getting them back," he said, pleased with himself. But suddenly, for some reason, he did not like the cold calculating look the old man was giving him.

"Will they give you a reward? A medal? A commendation or a handshake?" Don Corso's voice was heavy with sarcasm.

"So what am I to do with the stuff? Give it back to the clerk's office?" he asked, knowing the old man did not like the question.

"No, but there are other uses for it," Don Corso said.

The old man's tone was a little too soft, so Tiger quickly elevated his mental defenses. "Such as?" he asked.

Don Corso shrugged. "Since no one knows the drugs exist, why should I give them back."

The words hit Tiger like a bombshell. It was not so much what the old man had said that disturbed him as what he was not saying. It was a turnabout, totally against all he had been taught. Drug-dealing was the supreme crime that made you a degenerate.

He had known Don Corso for forty years, knew the man could not abide narcotics. Yet here he was suggesting that the right or wrong of it was not to be considered because he found a way to make a fast buck. A one hundred million fast buck. Tiger's mind swirled, and he knew he wasn't going to be able to deal with it.

"You can't do that, Pa," he said, a little nervously.

Don Corso's eyebrows shot up. "And why not?"

"Because it is dishonorable."

The old man studied him, letting out a soft sigh. "You

are right. Honor is our most precious possession. But I'm afraid you throw that word around a little too loosely. You seem to have some idea that honor is some white knight defending against every justice in the world. Well, in Sicily the word has a different meaning. You may be as noble as you please, but only within the family structure. Blood to blood. Not to outsiders. But where the family's welfare is concerned, then survival overrides honor. Without such rules, we would have been destroyed long ago. That's why the family always needs money, if only to protect our survival. Our wealth is what keeps the cops at bay."

"But that makes us no better than the degenerates we've been executing," Tiger said, studying the old man. "It was you who often told me it was the Italians with their damned drugs that almost destroyed the family years ago. Are you telling me it's now the Sicilians' turn? Do you know what everlasting scars it would create? Scars we would never be able to erase," said Tiger, expecting a thunderbolt to explode.

But instead Don Corso said, gently, "And what would you have me do with the drugs? Destroy them?"

Tiger was suddenly alert, smelling the cat playing with him. "Yes," he said softly.

"So you could get your medal?"

The words stung coldly and viciously, and Tiger felt anger rising within him. "No, because the families could not survive as junkies. The law would never forget or forgive. This time the scars would be permanent."

Tiger watched Don Corso's eyes frost slightly. "We are *not* going into the drug trade."

Tiger pulled up short. "What does that mean?" he asked suspiciously. "It's only a one-shot deal. A fast score, then we're out of the business."

Tiger's mind tripped as he shouted, "That's bullshit and you know it. You're talking about blood money. The same kind of blood money that killed your son."

The frost turned to ice. "You dare to say that to me?" Don Corso said, a terrible madness in his eyes.

Suddenly Tiger's life flashed before him. Knowing his death was close, but it didn't seem to matter, all he had worked for, everything he believed in was turning to ashes. With Ralphie dead and a list of dead men haunting him because no one was safe from the cancer of drugs, not his children, and certainly not the future families. Was this the reason he took the oath of justice and honor? So he could become a fucking dealer? He didn't think so, and he knew he couldn't deal with it.

"I dare because if it weren't for drugs, we might have saved Sonny," he said bitterly.

"What for? Your brother was a nothing. A gutless, spineless creature who had dreams of being a big shot. Another Caesar, but he was only an asshole with big dreams and little balls. Were it not for the drugs he would have found some other form of suicide."

"That's not true. You never gave him a chance," Tiger snapped.

"He had his chances. Even Father Carmine had more balls than Sonny did. So I don't want to hear no more of my sexual mistakes," he said, regarding Tiger coldly. "As for you, you will in no way interfere with the removal of the drugs."

Tiger knew he was faced with his moment of truth, and the flames of rebellion still burned within him. "I can't let it happen," he said simply.

Don Corso showed his surprise. Almost as if he hadn't heard. "Have you forgotten who you are talking to?"

Tiger carefully regarded the old man. "What will you do? Kill me like you had my father murdered?" he asked bitterly, knowing he had stunned the don.

The older man sighed. "So it comes down to that," he said, taking a moment to study Tiger. The ice in his eyes defrosted, replaced by sadness. "I did not murder your father. I killed an animal who was coming at me with fangs bared."

The words filled Tiger with loathing. "Damn you," he said bitterly. "You have known for years I wasn't your son," remembering the bitterness and indifference. "You kept me a prisoner with your damn lies. What were you afraid of? That I would get to know him? Or even worse, get to like him? Then where would you be?" Tiger was shouting, and he wanted to cry, to release the bitterness and hate. He wanted to kill this man before him.

Don Corso spoke gently. "To Pasquale Colombo, your mother meant nothing. She was only a woman he found convenient at times. Nothing more or nothing less. Like an eagle, he was a loner, incapable of love. He was a bird of prey, a hunter, always keeping himself at a distance. Caring for nothing or for no one."

"He must have loved Camille for the hate she bore you," snapped Tiger.

Don Corso ignored the outburst. "He felt nothing. She was his mate. She tended his cave. She was an object, nothing more."

Tiger felt the car closing in on him. Don Corso was partially right, yet it was Tiger's right to have known. Even to have been rejected by his father.

"I make no apologies, not to you and not to anyone else. It was your mother's secret, so I had no right to speak of it."

Tiger understood that. Still, he had the right.

"But I will tell you this. You are my son. My only son, and when I am no more you will inherit all I own. Do you think that was decided lightly? Your star was cast the day you were born, no matter whose son you were. That's why I trained and groomed you in the ways of the old world, preparing you for the hard and bitter life of the family. The family one day I hoped you would head. It was not a whim, a game of chess, a toss of the coin. Before you were ten years old, I knew what you were made of, because I knew the stuff your mother was made of. Of her whole family, she was the only one with balls," he said, pausing to shift to a more comfortable position. "You should ask yourself a question. In all the years Pasquale Colombo knew you existed, did he ever look you up? Did he ever think enough of you to show he cared, to walk the floor with you, to cry inside when you hurt and not be able to comfort you or even . . . to offer to give you his name?"

Tiger was hurting, his mind twisted and torn. "I don't believe you anymore!" he shouted, realizing he had almost stepped into a trap. He thought, now he is offering me the love I never had. Now he is offering me medicine after the body is already mortally diseased.

The sadness remained in the old man's eyes. "Now I will tell you why your father was terminated."

Tiger flinched at the word Don Corso used to describe his father's murder. Now he knew he hated this enigmatic man with a passion.

"Pasquale Colombo was a trusted friend for over sixty years. But for the past few years a strange transformation came over him. It wasn't until after his death that I learned that Camille was still alive. Then I understood the depth of his hatred. It wasn't because I tried to kill her that he hated me. It was because I didn't kill her. He was the Eagle and he could not abide my failure. Well, that's academic now," he said waving Tiger to silence.

"I started to see signs of his treachery. There were two attempts on my life, and some of my key personnel disappeared. The moves were sheer genius, and it took me a while before I narrowed it down to your father. So I set a trap. I had been aware that some policemen were stealing drugs from the police property clerk's office. So I sent your father to interrogate one of them. I wanted to know who was buying the drugs from the policemen. One week later he reported back that it was the Bocci family," he said pausing.

"Is that why you had Bocci killed?" Tiger asked, taking a shot in the dark.

Don Corso shook his head. "No. I knew Joe the Boss was not into drugs. He was terminated for his past crimes. Your father lied when he made the report fingering the Boccis. I ordered an interrogation of one policeman, yet two were killed. Why those two? There were ten policemen stealing

381

from the clerk's office. That's when I knew the depth of Pasquale Colombo's treachery. He killed them because he knew who really was buying the drugs and selling them secretly in California."

Tiger held his breath, certain something important was coming.

"It wasn't one of the families. It wasn't the Feds; they weren't in the picture yet. It was your father."

Tiger had been expecting a cheap shot like this, but this was lower than he expected, and he shouted, "You're a fucking liar!"

Surprisingly Don Corso remained calm. "Am I?"

"You're damn right you are. You're trying to sell this bull-shit because of the fast buck you found in a tunnel."

"What about the money you found in the graveyard? Where did you think it came from? Or didn't you think I knew about it?" he said, carefully watching Tiger.

Tiger's mind split down the center as one side rebelled against believing what the old man had said, while the other half thought of the money, the island, and the millions still buried. Junk money. Blood money.

"I treated Pasquale good. Gave him bits and pieces of the action. A percentage here, a percentage there, but not enough to account for that bundle he left you, not to mention what he probably stashed away for Camille and Angelina."

Tiger was stunned. "Why didn't you say something? Let on you knew?"

"For the same reason I said nothing when I knew it was you who killed my man Toto. I wanted to see where you were heading."

Tiger just stared at him, unable to answer.

"I knew, with over five million dollars in your pocket, you could buy what you believed was your freedom. So I offered you a larger carrot, being the boss of your own family. If you were willing to throw that away, then I would take serious your wanting to leave. But I was betting you wouldn't. I was betting you would come to your senses and return to the family because, like me, you loved it. Your desire to run away was an emotional decision, but your decision to return was logical, laced with ambition. I waited, wondering which way you would jump. When you killed Toto, I knew I had won. That's when I pulled out all the stops to pave the way for you. I went to visit Momma, telling her I knew that Camille was still alive, but I would forgive her so long as she stayed out of my home. Then I spoke to the Council.

"Of course, you are wondering why I bothered in the first place, and I will tell you the truth. There are two reasons. One, I need you because I can't handle it all myself. The second reason is even simpler. It is time for you to prepare to take over from me."

Tiger was alert, uncertain what game the old man was playing.

"There is not much time. There is much to be done," Don Corso said, lighting a cigar. Tiger sensed something wrong. Was it the slight shake of the old man's hand or was it just the flame flickering?

"It is important that you fully understand what it will mean when I am gone. With my death, you will become one of the most powerful men alive. You will no longer have the luxury of making mistakes. Your decisions must be precise, logical, and exact. Without preparation, my death would send shock waves throughout our family, and the other families will start to play games. That must be guarded against. The Corsos and the Ippolitos control most of the loyal soldiers, so you will have to deal swiftly with any rebels. Demand their loyalty and allegiance quickly. If they hesitate, even slightly, you must kill them immediately."

Tiger wondered why the old man was talking in this manner. Was he sick? Why hadn't Momma said something? No, Tiger was sure, it was some kind of a ruse.

"I know what you're thinking, but the situation is too serious for games."

Tiger was surprised the old man had got past his mental

guards. "Why do I get the impression you are talking in the past tense?"

Don Corso's enigmatic features remained somber as he stared at the floor. "Because I believe my time is near."

Tiger was taken aback, but suspicious. "Are you sick?"

"No," said the old man, looking up, "there is nothing wrong with me."

Tiger found the conversation confusing. "Then what is the problem? Are one of the families going to make a move? A hit?"

Don Corso shook his head as his eyes filled with sadness. "*Stregoneria,* the death of the old ways," he said simply.

For a moment, Tiger was not sure he had heard correctly. Or was the old man just pulling his leg? "Witchcraft?"

"It is *maledetio.* Someone has put a curse on me. A *morte augurio,* a death wish, by someone who knows the old ways and has a powerful hate."

Except for the tightness of the man's features, Tiger would have laughed. "Do you really believe this?"

Don Corso seemed ashamed. "If I didn't, they wouldn't be able to cast a spell."

Tiger's mind was light. He found it difficult to understand the fear he thought he saw in his father's eyes.

"What are you going to do? I mean if you believe it, then what's to be done?" he asked, wondering if his brother Carmine understood these things.

"Nothing," answered Don Corso, with a long sigh. "My *gòbbo stregone* is fighting to lift the veil, but it takes time."

That woke Tiger up, as he remembered the strange shadowy figure sitting behind his father in the office. Now he understood who it was. It was the deformed, malignant Don Vici, the hunchback, Don Corso's private witch doctor.

"What now?" Tiger asked.

Don Corso shrugged, "I shall carry on as long as I can, but should I falter, you are to take control of the families. The Council will approve. If, on the other hand, I should win, you will forget this conversation."

Tiger nodded. "How much time do you have?"

Again Don Corso shrugged his heavy shoulders. "Who knows? These things take time. Maybe a week, maybe a month, or maybe a year. It all depends on whose magic is strongest."

Tiger didn't bother speculating on who was lowering the veil on Don Corso. He had too many enemies. It could be someone in the old guard. There were still two of the five families still based in Brooklyn. Both Italian. One was made up of mostly Calabrians, members of the ancient order of the *Fratellanza*—the Brotherhood. They were mostly thieves and smugglers. And the other was the bloodthirsty Camorra from Naples, terrorists, poisoners, arsonists, murderers, and mutilators. Tiger knew neither dared take on the powerful Sicilians in open warfare. But they might resort to any other method to get even with Don Corso.

From his years of training, Tiger knew Don Corso could trace his origins back to his grandfather's membership in the original *LiberaleLéga, Piccolo Itàlia*—the Liberal League, Young Italy Society—and later, after Garibaldi's expedition in 1860 to free the Sicilians from the hated Spanish Bourbons, to the *Società degli Amici*—Society of Friends, or *Mafióso*.

It was Giuseppe Mazzine, the revolutionary, the man who refused a pardon from death from the Italian government because he said he loved Sicily beyond all earthly things. He was the man who formed the organization called *Mazzini Autorizza Furtivo Incèndio Avvlenaménti,* which is shortened to Mafia. Mazzini authorized robbery, arson, and poisoning; the purpose of the new organization was to rid Sicily by any means of the dreaded Spanish Bourbons. Later, after their defeat, the society turned against the brutal landowners, who were bleeding the life from the peasants.

The code of honor in such membership was manliness, politeness, boldness, audacity, firmness, self-reliance, recklessness, and defiance to any enemy.

To the peasants, what was good was mafiusu. What was

honorable was mafiusu. The sun, the moon, flowers, cats, dogs, all animals, things of good quality were called mafiusu.

Not so with the Italian Camorra of Naples. It was a secret society whose members for over a thousand years swore oaths to take lives, to leave mutilated corpses on the side of the road for purposes of striking fear into the inhabitants. Who slashed faces, rubbing in garlic so the wound would never heal. In truth, they were animals.

Since a child, Tiger had heard frightening stories of the Camorra in America and their hatred for everything Sicilian. The bodies they buried in the Brooklyn swamps and the mutilated bodies they left on Brooklyn streets. And for this, one day they were repaid tenfold. In a six-month war, most members of the Camorra were destroyed. Those left licked their wounds and stayed in line, killing only when threatened and then cleanly.

No, Tiger knew he wasn't in a pretty business. He knew the other two families would like to return to the old ways, but that must never be allowed. Tiger knew there would be many attempts of the Camorra to rear its ugly head again. Thugs and other low life would always seek ways to make a fast buck, even in his own family. They might try to bring in drugs in an organized way, and they would have to be dealt with brutally.

That is why what Don Corso was doing was wrong. To Tiger, gambling, pornography, street banking, and unionizing weren't crimes. He could live with them, but drugs, gratuitous murder, and terrorism were.

Don Corso pointed to the boarded-up building. "I am taking that problem out of your hands, so I will permit no interference or I will forget you are my son."

Tiger kept his lip buttoned though the anger quickly returned.

"When you are in my seat you will understand what the families have to defend against. The law is impotent to beat us legally so they use economics against us, knowing every arrest and harassment is costly. The law enforcement people understand our problem of purchasing high-priced lawyers, crooked politicians, and the other bloodsuckers with their hands out. That is why the families need reserve money, if only to protect our own interests. Take your present predicament. Though it was instigated by those greedy bastard policemen, every law enforcement group in the state will use whatever dirty tricks they can to convict you of those murders. That's why the only way to stop their madness is to hit the eyewitness policeman, then use their own law to free you. But even then they will make us pay a heavy price in time and money to keep you mobile and elusive."

Tiger was sure this speech was leading somewhere, so he remained silent.

"That's why I'm changing the timetable on the policeman's hit. I want you free and clear of all this in ten days."

Tiger was taken aback. "Why so soon?"

"You have your man targeted, don't you?"

"Yes, but . . ."

Don Corso waved him to silence. "Then let's get it out of the way. Let's get it settled so you can leave for the island as soon as possible. I want you to pick fifty soldiers as your private entourage, because I intend to punch in all the families' computer files. D'Elessandro is ready to install a new computer terminal on your island," he said, relighting his cigar. "Until my problem is solved, I want you to do nothing but familiarize yourself with the whole operation. When you find extra time, prepare plans to open new avenues of business. Begin selecting new personnel for recruitment and for the think tank."

Tiger had the wind knocked out of him. He was being handed the brass ring, the boss of all bosses, and he found it scary.

"Also, when and if you take over, the Council will select someone to pose as my successor for the media's benefit. That will keep the heat off you and leave you mobile."

Tiger guessed the old man had all the angles figured.

As Tiger left the vehicle, he pushed all thoughts of the drugs aside. Perhaps because he was weak and bribable. Maybe it was because he had heard his father's words and understood a new dimension of responsibility. Whatever it was, he didn't know, but he knew the anger was gone.

T IGER ordered a trooper to drive him home while he brought Pete up to date on Don Corso's conversation. When Tiger finished, Pete remained silent for a long time.

"Before you do what you're thinking, Tiger, I suggest you look at things from a different perspective. If you disobey your old man, everyone will turn against you. They will have no choice. How could you expect them to overlook such a slap in the face? You push them and you'll lose everything. It's not worth it. For what? Outsiders who don't give a shit about you? Tiger, we are Sicilians. We're a culture, a breed of people who took the bullshit of all those outsiders for three thousand years. Now it's our turn, and we owe them nothing. You have an obligation to the family now. You swore to protect it and it's not wrong. Outsiders are a breed of legal mercenaries, made up of people who believe in nothing, just the money they get to hurt us. I'm with you, Tiger, any way you call it, but for my part I wouldn't give an outsider the sweat off my balls."

T HEY rode the rest of the way in silence. Tiger withdrew, wrapping his thoughts around him. He knew Pete was right. Don Corso was right, yet he had trouble dealing with it. Circumstances had molded steel around his brain and he couldn't break through. He was aware that if he disobeyed Don Corso and the Council, it was his death sentence; but even if the old man overlooked that, what would his life be like? Would Don Corso, Don Ippolito, or the Council ever trust him again? Would anyone?

What would Smilin' Jack do? Get him a job as a porter?

Give him a medal for meritorious service? A handshake for a job well done? Chalk it up to the fortunes of war?

On top of that, he still had the upcoming trial. Where would that leave him? Should he go it alone with just him and Pete? How? Even if they killed the policeman, he still needed Don Corso and the Council to survive the aftermath.

By the time Tiger reached his house, he had half made up his mind. He didn't like it. Not one little bit, but he could live with it. But still he had that feeling of betrayal. A self-inflicted betrayal created by some unfathomable signals. Was it created by the years of bitter indifference, loneliness, and distrust? What was it that caused him to reach out for something to believe in? The rightness of something bigger than himself, Don Corso, the Council, or the family?

Well, thought Tiger, he had to find out the other half of his decision.

He ordered Pete to pull over to a pay phone so he could call the special number Smilin' Jack had given him. Tiger had no intention of betraying the family, but he needed an answer to a gnawing question.

It took a few minutes for the agent to answer, "Magaddino."

"This is Joey Corso," said Tiger, sensing a slight hesitation.

"What can I do for you?" Jack said, a distance in his voice.

Tiger decided not to mince words. "That stuff you confiscated from the moving warehouse?"

"What about it?"

"Was it ever tested?"

Again he sensed the hesitation. "Twice. Once when it went into the laboratory and just before it was destroyed."

"Any chance of a foul-up, a switch?"

This time the pause was obvious. "Are you referring to the switch your brother made with his girlfriend?"

Tiger was dumbfounded. "How did you know?"

"I owe you my life, so I'm going to wipe the slate. I knew

your brother's game. He tried to get around some of the agents and to the chemists, but your brother was a junkie, you know. So we let him knock himself out with his little game."

Tiger wondered if Jack's game was cruel or poetic justice. He also found himself back at square one. Where did Sonny get the drugs? "When did you tumble onto my brother?"

"Almost a year ago. We wondered why a Corso would be so helpful to us and why he was hanging around the office. Then one batch of narcotics came in milk sugar, and we suspected your brother. We tightened security. Although we played the game, we never let him get another batch of narcotics."

After hanging up, Tiger took a moment to get his thinking into line. He guessed Sonny lived on his drugs for a long time until Tiger found it in the cellar. Now he understood why his brother was so insane. He had lost his stash. But had he gone to the packages in the tunnel and tested one, he would have really blown his mind.

Now he wished he could be there when Don Corso tested his prize winnings.

Well, thought Tiger, the dream of a hundred million dollars' worth of nobility went up in smoke.

H E arrived home late in the afternoon, thankful Jeanne was home alone. Something in his face warned her, because she merely looked closely at him. "It's time to run," he said, simply.

She stiffened slightly. "When do we leave?"

"I want you and the children in Florida by the end of the week."

"And you?" she asked, a slight worry in her eyes.

"I'll be down next week."

"Can't you come with us?" she asked.

"I can't yet. I have some fireworks first."

"Can they hurt you?"

Gently he took her into his arms and smiled gently. "I'm in no danger. They are."

She hugged him tightly. "Are you sure you'll be all right?"

"I'm sure. I just don't want you here for the circus."

"And the house?" she asked.

"It will remain as it is. Someday we'll be back."

Suddenly she was in tears and her body started to rack with sobs. Tiger held onto her tightly. "What is it, Jeanne? What's wrong?" he asked softly, shocked at her breakdown.

As she nestled her head in his shoulder, she cried. "When will it all end, Joey? Please tell me when the pain will stop? Why can't we be normal, be ourselves? Enjoy each other?" she said, raising her tear-stained face to him. "Momma says it will end soon, but I don't believe her. I don't believe anyone anymore, Joey. Is this what you want for your son? To raise him as a warrior? To fight in the wars of the hard life, for glory and for family? So I can grow old waiting for the day they bring you or Rosario home in a box like they did my brother Dominick?" By now, she was practically screaming and hung to him even tighter.

Tiger had never seen Jeanne like this before. "Please, Jeanne, listen to me," he begged, as her sobs slackened. "It's almost over. There will be no hard life for Rosario. I never raised him for that. I swear to you. Do you think for a minute I filled my body with scars so my son should go through the same thing? Do you think I would expose our son to the life that killed your brother? No, Jeanne. I'm surprised you thought so little of me."

Lowering her head, she clung to him, refusing to raise her head. "I know you love him, Joey, but he's trapped into who you are, what you are, what my father is, and what Don Corso is. Tell me, Joey, how will he escape that?"

Placing his hand gently under her chin, he raised her head and studied her, but she continued to avert her eyes. "He's going to have to live with it. That same way every celebrity's kid does. He'll travel in circles that make him comfortable. He will use his wealth to protect himself like all the rich do. Rosario is not just any kid. He's the son of a don and nothing will change that. Life is life and there are no guarantees except death, so he will have to take his chances like every other ordinary person. I want Rosario to enter the world of corporations, surrounded by legitimate people of his choosing. He will never need bodyguards to protect him from the people of my world, but he might need them in the whore corporate world. But no matter what, he must never be afraid to live, and he will have to accept who he is and not be ashamed of where he came from. Otherwise, he'd best change his name," he said, softly, as she raised her eyes and nodded her acceptance.

"I will explain to the children that we are leaving. Although I doubt they'll find it difficult going back to the island," she said, with a wisp of a smile.

LATER in the afternoon Tiger met with Trooper Abruzzi in his Uncle Lulu's private dining room. Tiger decided to get right to the point. "Is your target still lined up?"

"Yes, my don."

"Good. Then is there any reason why he can't be hit on Friday night between six and seven?"

The hard-featured hit man thought for a moment. "None, but it would be easier between eight-thirty and ten."

"Why?" asked Tiger.

"Because between six and seven he has dinner with his wife and three kids. I'd rather not hit him anywhere near his family. However, he always goes to visit his girlfriend around eight-thirty. It would be no trouble to bang him when he arrives."

Tiger nodded. "Do it then."

When Abruzzi left, Tiger called in Lulu to make arrangements for an elaborate birthday party on Friday night.

FRIDAY morning, Tiger took Jeanne, the children, Satan and Devil, and two mountains of luggage to a small private airport on Long Island. They had a plane warmed up for their trip to Florida. He had already sent Pete ahead with a contingent of troopers to be waiting when they arrived. Rosario and Cathy were enjoying the adventure and couldn't wait for the plane to be airborne, but Jeanne seemed a little apprehensive.

"Will everything be all right, Joey?" she asked.

Tiger smiled warmly. "I promise I will be in Florida no later than Tuesday."

She continued to study his face. "Honest Injun?" she asked, almost in a whisper.

"Honest Injun. I have to attend a birthday party at Uncle Lulu's then I'll spend the weekend with Mike Rizzo's family."

Jeanne read much more into his assurances, but she smiled bravely and clung to him.

ON Friday night, hundreds attended the party given for Mike Amato. At 9:45 Tiger received word the policeman was terminated. Ten minutes later, Tiger quietly left the restaurant accompanied by Mike Rizzo, three lawyers, and a contingent of troopers.

Mike Rizzo's house on Long Island was a magnificent two-story English Tudor structure. It was replete with electrified fences, guard dogs, and uniformed patrols.

Tiger had always found Luna Rizzo a delightful woman, full of life, always bubbly. She was a beautiful, elegant woman who wore her heart on her sleeve for Mike. Tiger was surprised to hear the three children were to be away for the weekend and he wondered if it was by design.

After a delightful late-night dinner, the three enjoyed two hours of enjoyable small talk, then Mike carted Tiger down to the den for coffee. All through the evening, Tiger wondered where the lawyers had disappeared to.

"The shit is hitting the fan in Brooklyn because our friend Malone is all over the place."

Tiger half smiled. "Any chances he will come here?"

Mike showed his surprise. "Here? It's out of his jurisdiction. Even if he had a warrant he still couldn't get in."

Tiger nodded his understanding and said, "Where do we go from here?"

"On Monday I'm moving for a dismissal of your case. And unless they can show good cause, the district attorney's office will have to do it."

"And if they don't?" Tiger asked in his quiet voice.

Rizzo smiled. "You will have to understand the business I'm in. Assistant D.A.'s only take appointments because they have political ambitions. They can't win votes in the future if they lose cases and this is now a losing case."

Tiger allowed himself the pleasure of a smile.

But Mike's eyes hardened. "We're not out of the woods yet," he said carefully.

Tiger pulled up short. "What do you mean?"

"I have my associates fighting to get us into court on Monday morning. I want you to realize once in the courtroom, you'll be surrounded by one hell of a lot of hostility. There won't be a cop in that room who won't want to shoot you." Mike stopped to let the thought sink in.

And it sank in. Not deep enough to frighten Tiger, but enough for him to be careful. "Can I take some of my boys with me?" he asked, immediately wishing he had bitten his tongue.

"Hell, no. I want a dismissal, not a massacre."

Tiger didn't like the idea of being so exposed, but he guessed that's the way it had to be. Nevertheless, Tiger intended to wear his gun buckle. "Whatever you say, Mike."

Mike understood the look in Tiger's eyes. "Don't worry. You're not going in alone. I ain't that crazy yet. I've hired a private security outfit to surround you in court. You'll be in good hands. It's made up of ex-special-forces men. Each is highly trained and licensed to carry firearms. They will be more than a match for whatever comes their way. I just want to get you in and out of court as fast as possible and have you on your way to Florida before they even know what's happening."

Tiger smiled. Mike had it all together. He hoped.

Tiger sat in the rear of the limousine alongside Mike Rizzo. On the car seat opposite Tiger sat a short bull-necked man with yellow, brittle skin that reflected years spent in hot scorching climates and jungles. Although the man was soft spoken, Tiger sensed the man's hidden power.

"My name is Colonel Izzo, Mister Corso, and my men are all highly experienced. With your cooperation we'll have no problems."

The colonel spoke with a tone of assurance that Tiger found comforting. He knew he was in the hands of a professional.

"When my men are ready, we'll move out," said the colonel.

Tiger glanced out the window at the parking lot where small groups of men were concealing weapons under their business suits. He noted they all wore the same-colored suits, and by the fine tailoring, he was sure it was bullet-proof fabric. They knew their business.

"Now this is where I'll need your help, Mister Corso. No matter what happens, you stick on my ass. If in the court-room, I should squeeze your elbow, you are to immediately follow me wherever I go. That's important. I already have men in the courtroom and surrounding area. So if anything goes down, just ignore it. Follow me, and I'll get you out free," he said softly.

The area outside the courthouse was a circus of police-men, T.V. crews, and curious spectators. As Tiger emerged from the limousine everyone surged forward, but Colonel

Izzo's men pushed everyone aside and bulled their way into the building.

The corridors were equally filled with people, and Tiger stayed on the colonel's tail as his men formed a wedge and forced their way into the courtroom, down a long side aisle. The colonel placed Tiger in the first seat of the second row amid four full rows of brown-suited men. Alert and hard-eyed.

Looking over the room, Tiger caught the cold, hostile stares. Policemen of every rank openly glared at him, making no effort to disguise their hatred.

At that moment the judge entered and everyone rose to pay respect. Sitting, the black-robed man shuffled papers until the murmuring crowd quieted down.

Tiger took a second to search the room for Malone, but he was not to be seen, and he wondered why.

The tall bespectacled judge cleared his throat as he glanced toward Mike Rizzo. "I have carefully examined your brief. Do you have anything to add?"

"No, your honor," answered Mike Rizzo.

Tiger felt the tension in the room, and he knew he was sitting on a powder keg.

The judge nodded and looked over at the clean-cut man sitting at the prosecutor's desk. "What is the position of the district attorney's office?"

The young man stood slowly, pressed down his pin-striped suit and brushed back his hair, knowing he was the center of attention. "Your honor, I wish to make it perfectly clear that the district attorney's office finds this a despicable act of obstruction of justice. I also wish to make it clear that such lawlessness will not be condoned," he said as the crowd murmured its approval. "I say again this was a cowardly insult to the people of this community, and we will not take this lying down," he added.

Tiger knew Mr. Pinstripe was openly playing to the spectators. He could tell by their serious expressions that the colonel's men didn't enjoy the speech. Tiger looked over at Mike to see how he was taking this game. He was surprised by the bright smile Mike returned.

In anger, the judge banged his gavel, determined to quell the beehive of murmurs. Mike Rizzo rose to his feet, a plastic smile frozen on his face as he looked from the young prosecutor to the judge.

"Your honor, it would seem to me our learned colleague Mister Rudolph has come here to make political speeches rather than addressing the charges in my motion," he said, continuing his bright smile.

The judge nodded and turned to the assistant D.A. "I am asking you again. What is your office's position on this matter before us?"

The young man fidgeted, shuffled papers, seemingly uncertain what he wanted to say. "It is obvious to me, your honor, that the murder of Police Officer Jonathan T. Dodge was an outright attempt to frustrate the purpose of this court. My office's position is that we intend to pursue this investigation so that this community will know that we are not remiss in our duty to the good people . . ."

Tiger knew the bastard was racking up points for the newspapers and was thankful when the judge banged his gavel madly. When it was quiet again, Tiger noticed some of the colonel's men had their hands under their jackets. Tiger felt the tension in the room when Colonel Izzo placed a hand of caution on his shoulder, pressing him to remain seated.

The judge stood and glared at the young prosecutor. "Mister Rudolph, please approach the bench," he ordered.

A blanket of silence descended over the courtroom and the young man looked as if he was walking his last mile. At the bench, they spoke in whispers. But by the cold, angry look in the judge's eyes, it was obvious he was dressing the man down. After a moment he waved Mr. Pinstripe away.

The district attorney's man was obviously embarrassed and showed signs of apprehensiveness. Regaining his composure, he cleared his throat, looked over the spectators, Tiger, Mike Rizzo, and finally the judge.

Tiger knew the fuse was lit and everyone in the room was expectant.

"Police Officer Jonathan T. Dodge's testimony was the

foundation of my case. His death has made prosecution impossible. The people move to dismiss the indictment."

Like a mad explosion, pandemonium broke out as Colonel Izzo squeezed Tiger's elbow. "Let's go and keep low," he said, as he charged through his men and headed for a side exit. A shot rang out but Tiger barreled after the colonel's backside as they sped down a flight of stairs. For a moment Tiger wondered about the shot, but wondered for only a moment as they cleared another flight.

He was surprised at how easily the colonel's men cleared the way.

As they emerged outside the courthouse, few people were in evidence. Tiger's limousine was pulled up on the grass as the wedge split and Tiger was shoved into the rear seat with Rizzo.

"Get the hell out of here," shouted the colonel as the big car shot forward with a trooper behind the wheel. Tiger looked out the rear window, half expecting to see the police department in hot pursuit. But instead he saw all the colonel's men blocking the streets with their vehicles.

MIKE Rizzo remained in the car as Tiger walked up the familiar walkway. The hardface stationed just inside the door nodded and passed him in. Salvatore DeVito, a family retainer, quickly informed him Momma was in the kitchen.

That's where Tiger found her. She was having her usual late breakfast of olives, cheese, and espresso.

After a hug and kiss, she poured him a cup of coffee while watching him intently. "Is it over?" she asked softly.

"Yes, Momma, it's over."

Her lips tightened. "It is always over," she said and spoke as if to herself. "It is always over. Everything ends, then begins again, but always turning in a new direction," she said, raising her eyes to him again. "So now my son, you have come to say good-bye."

"Not good-bye, Momma. You know I'll be back."

But she waved him off. "At my age all good-byes are final."

"So why don't you come with us? We have lots of room and would love to have you."

She smiled one of her rare smiles. "I would enjoy such a visit, but not now. I have much to do."

Tiger laughed gently. "Like what? Sitting around the house all day?"

For a brief moment, her eyes flared in anger and Tiger knew he had hit a nerve. Why?

She quickly changed the subject. "Did you say good-bye to Don Corso yet?"

"No. Should I have?"

She was slow to answer. "No, I guess not. When did you last see him?"

"A week ago," he said, remembering back to the meeting in the car.

"And how did he look?"

The question was a little too casual for Tiger, who wondered what she was seeking in this cat-and-mouse game? He found the question odd since she sees him every day. He shrugged. "He looked as usual. Why?"

She ignored the question and threw another one at him. "What did you talk about?"

Now Tiger knew she was on the hunt. "The usual business problems and my going away."

She pounced upon that. "Was it his idea for you to go away?"

"It wasn't anyone's idea. We both knew it was something that had to be done."

Whatever it was she was seeking, the determined look in her eyes told him she was not letting go.

"Did you talk about Angelina?"

"No," said Tiger.

"Did you talk about Camille?" she asked with equal intensity.

Tiger didn't like the question, but he didn't want to lie to her. "We touched on it."

"And did you talk of Pasquale?"

He sighed, knowing she wasn't letting go her hate for him. Even though he was dead. "Yes, Momma, we talked of Pasquale."

A bright gleam sparkled in her eyes. "What did you speak of? Tell me?"

So he told her Patsy was killed because he had turned bad.

Her gaze was sharp and penetrating. "What do you mean turned bad?"

So Tiger explained.

Momma was in shock. "That's why he killed Pasquale? Because he caught him in a lie?"

"It was a lot more than that, Momma," he replied defensively.

But Momma waved him off. "I know Pasquale needed killing, but he said he had him killed because he lied?" she said, seemingly stunned. "He kills my enemy for a lie, but he does not kill to protect my honor," she said, raising her eyes to him. "What Don Corso has done was bad. It is not to be forgiven," she said, her eyes burning into his.

Tiger didn't like the look in her eyes. There was a touch of madness in them.

"If I ask you to kill Don Corso, will you do it?"

Damn, thought Tiger, here we go again. He really was not ready to deal with this. But her blazing eyes told him he was going to have to. He didn't know how he was going to do it, but he was going to hit Don Corso because Momma wanted it. "I will take care of it, Momma."

Her weary eyes measured him a long, long time. "And why will you do it, my son? Will you do it because I ask you to or because you want to do it?"

Tiger searched for an answer that would satisfy her. One that would finally set to rest her unrelenting hate. Having never lied to Momma before, he was not about to start. "Because I love you, Momma. If killing Don Corso will bring you peace and help to bury the pain, then I will do it."

Momma's brows shot up. "My pain? What about your

pain? Your real father is rotting in his grave, unavenged. Does that not cause you pain?"

Tiger sighed, "I know you're not going to like this, Momma, but Pasquale Colombo meant little to me. He was only a shadow. What do you expect me to feel for a man I never knew. A man who never loved me or even cared if I lived or died. No, Momma, I can't hate him with your hate. I never knew enough about him to hate him," he said, as the pain entered her eyes. "You wanted him dead, he's dead. And if you also want me to kill Don Corso, fine, I'll do it. I'll do it only because you asked me to. Not because Don Corso killed the right person for the wrong reason."

Momma sat there staring at her son, realizing he had lost an important part of himself. Something vital to his well being, his heritage. She pushed aside her plate of food and smiled brightly. "Then let us forget it. It would not make me happy to have you kill him," she said, gently, almost wistfully.

Tiger was thrown off guard by this sudden reversal, but then he always had trouble understanding Momma.

She rose, walked around the table and gently placed her hands on his shoulders. "You have a long life ahead of you, so always remember to be good to yourself. Now I want you to go to your family and tell them that soon I will come for a visit."

Tiger felt impotent and knew he had hurt her. "Momma?" he asked softly.

But she put her fingers to his lips. "Hush, my son. Give me a big hug and a kiss and have yourself a safe trip."

For the first time in his life, he felt the pain of being shut out of her thoughts. He sadly walked out without another word.

Long after Tiger was gone, Momma continued to stare after him, feeling no anger at what he had said, just disappointment. The son she had given up to the hard life was everything Don Corso wanted. A duplicate of himself, with but one flaw: He was no longer a pure Sicilian, but half American.

She returned to the table, poured herself a cup of coffee, and stared long and hard at the food.

She wanted to cry, not in self-pity, but in frustration. Tears seemed to be the only release she had. Her mind was in turmoil between what was, what is, and what will be. Her past life had been cold and brutal, dominated by men who never cried, who found life a never-ending battle. Men who increased their wealth and power as the way to allay their fears of starvation and depredation.

But in the present, Momma found the fears unfounded. Momma knew there was not hard life in this rich America, yet the men continue to carry the scars long after the memory had faded into habit. But for Momma the memories still burned deep within her. She could remember sixty-two years of men's brutality, indifference, and subjugation.

In Sicily, when her father and brothers deserted her at the mouth of Tony Corso's cave, she seemingly accepted her fate with pure Sicilian stoicism. Inside, however, her guts were ripped out of her. She saw her body abused, degraded, and turned into a cesspool for the whim of an unfeeling man. Even her marriage was a sham—an event arranged by men for each other's convenience, while her soul and honor were disregarded.

Well, thought Momma, for forty-seven years she had lived with the scars of that day, and now it was time for her to teach the men the meaning of cunning.

Momma knew Sicilian men hunted only by experience. Years of mistakes and hunger taught them to get the jump on their prey by always attacking from the high ground. They hunted by rote, using only limited amounts of guile and cunning. To Momma, it required little ability to hide in ambush, then attack, and slay an enemy. What took cunning was to convince the victim one was harmless. Of no account. Too unimportant to be considered. Soon the prey would be lured into a false sense of security and killed. That to Momma was cunning. Women's cunning.

For over a thousand years Sicilian women fought alongside their men, labored alongside their men, had their children, shared their hardships, their pain, but never the good times, their joys.

Sicilian men used the word "honor" as a badge to fight over, to kill over, or to die over. Women saw the men's so-called honor as self-centered. It was always *their* honor, *their* integrity, *their* justice. When women did good, the men took the credit for their ability to select a fine woman. But if the woman did bad, they were jeered and scorned. It was the *man's* honor and integrity at stake. But still, Momma understood all of this and accepted it because the hard life made hard rules. Since the man was the stronger, he shouldered the greater responsibility. After all, the unwritten rules were devised by the powerful men of the tribe of which she was still part.

Now it was Momma's turn to use the unwritten rules to her advantage. In all her years in America she was untouched by it. Her heart, her thoughts, and her fears were still Sicilian; and one of the great truths of the ancient unwritten code was that her man defend her honor.

She also knew the years in America had not rubbed off on Don Corso. His culture and beliefs remained intact. Not so her son Joseph, who tempered his judgments with fairness. But her husband was still the cold, cruel, self-centered man of honor he had always been. Then why, wondered Momma, did he not avenge her honor? Because, thought Momma, in this world of men, it was not to his advantage. Since men made the rules, they could ignore them at their whim.

That's what left Momma so frustrated. If Tony Corso had not intended to avenge her honor, he should have stepped aside allowing her to deal with her hated enemy. However, since her husband took it upon himself to close out any chance she had to avenge her soul and doomed her to eternal perdition. To Momma, this was the ultimate pain. One she could no longer endure.

In her mind, after Don Corso eliminated her chance to be avenged, he condemned himself to death by ancient law.

The shuffling footfall startled Momma and her thoughts

were shattered. Standing in the doorway was a wizened old woman. Tiny, bent and twisted by the weight of the huge hump on her back.

"It is time, madonna," she said softly.

Momma studied the grotesque, spidery figure of Amelia Vici, wife of Don Vici, the *stregone*—witch doctor—now fighting to lift the veil for Don Corso.

Momma remembered when Carmine was ordained. It had a great effect upon her. She no longer knew fear because she had her own angel, a passport to heaven. She found it a warm feeling being so close to God, especially with her own priest to guide her.

Momma wanted to save the world, to sprinkle joy upon everyone. And she would have saved the world, had her world not come tumbling down upon her.

It happened one night, very late. Her husband spoke in his sleep about the death of Camille. Now she knew her sister was dead. She tried to shut it out, to deny it to herself. Not because Camille was dead, but because it was blood of her blood that was shed. She sought solace in church, in all the saints, in God, but little helped as the knowledge gnawed at her. She started to lose her balance. Her mind split, with each part beginning to hate the other. In the end, she was left with choosing between her family's welfare and God. She could not decide, so her mind shattered.

It was a year later when she awoke in the hospital and learned that her hated enemy Pasquale Colombo was dead and a woman claiming to be her sister was alive and in America.

After Momma and Camille were finally reunited, she learned the truth of what had happened over thirty years before. The truth she had learned did not lessen her hatred for Pasquale Colombo, and it magnified the new one she felt for her husband, Don Corso.

Momma knew at last that there was little chance of discovering the real reason for Pasquale Colombo's death. But it no longer mattered. Camille was blood of her blood, and her husband's violence against her sister was grounds for the vendetta.

She knew in the Sicilian code of vengeance there were three acceptable methods of killing an enemy: by the stiletto, by the gun, or by *magìa.*

Since the knife and gun were male weapons, Momma chose magic. But magic was not something easily available. She needed help. The right kind of help.

Over the years, she had on occasion met Vito Scopo, the oracle, the man who sees the future. Vito Scopo was a man wise in the ways of sorcery. He was also an *affascinatóre*—spellbinder, a man well schooled in the ways of the *maledizióne*—curse.

Momma knew Sicilians never accepted the black arts of witches or satanism. Instead they believed that saints, warlocks, wizards, ghosts, enchantresses, hags, and crones were all servants of the Lord. As such, they were masters over the Devil and his demons. Sicilians also believed that if they were morally right in their fight against their enemies, then the forces of good would marshal around the offended party and allow *il malocchi*—the spell of the evil eye—to be invoked.

Vito Scopo informed Momma that the strongest force she could secure to achieve the curse of the evil eye was to enlist the aid of Fata Diu Madrinna, who was beloved by the heavens. Such fairygodmothers were smiled upon by God because of their infirmities. Their twisted bodies and hunchbacks were filled with special love and benevolence. Not so with male hunchbacks, who were filled with malignancy and evil.

Momma knew only one female *gibbósa,* Amelia Vici, wife of Don Vici, a close associate of Don Corso. Dare she approach such a person? If her husband should hear of it, she would have little ability to defend herself or achieve her revenge. But Momma was desperate. With nowhere else to turn, she made the approach fearfully and most respectfully. She told Amelia Vici of her most terrible problem. The wizened old woman smiled brightly and took Momma

405

under her wing. She spoke of many things, understanding Momma's torment. She, like Momma, resented the arrogance of Sicilian men.

Momma followed the crablike movements of the old woman as she went up the stairs to Momma's bedroom, which was filled with the paraphernalia of Amelia's craft. The walls were covered with paintings of the Blessed Virgin, the Madonna, saints, and replicas of amulets of fish, the symbol of Christ, hanging by their mouths, birds, eyes, human limbs, human and animal skeletons, teeth, horns, claws, cloves of garlic, and miniature icons. Shears to cut through the evil, sharpened stilettos to impale the spirits.

All the statues in the room were swaddled in layers of cloth. Bandages were also wrapped around and around until completely covered, then wrapped again in chains to frighten the statues not to interfere or reveal what Amelia and Momma were doing.

Amelia worked her way to the dressing table, which was decorated as an altar. It was filled with unlit votive candles, statues wrapped in black cloth and chains, sketches of fish, and centered by a large sheet of clean white writing paper.

Amelia instructed Momma to stand alongside her, placed a crown of rosemary leaves on Momma's head, then wrote in the center of the white paper, the nine digits, arranged in a square. They were the core of mathematical magic.

$$276$$
$$951$$
$$438$$

In every direction, those numbers equalled fifteen, an odd number, a number all Sicilians knew to be magical and lucky.

On the number "5" Amelia sprinkled a handful of consecrated seeds (grown before a statue of the Blessed Mother). She then placed a small piece of iron in Momma's left palm and a handful of earth in the right palm. Then she spoke softly:

"Daughter of the earth and daughter of Janus, protector of the January month I was born in, and Blessed Mother, hear me in this moment of need and lower the veil over our offender . . ."

The chant became a singsong, monotonous of tone, but a lullaby to the gods until Momma was caught up in the power of the thought connection. Chanting for their souls until the thought became fact.

In his office, Don Corso sat, slowly counting his piles of money, keeping cadence with Don Vici's chant as he sat in the background, hidden by the shadows. One by one, the spidery creature's hand passed over the knots of the rope as he fought to raise the veil.

THE END